THE ARCHBISHOPRIC
OF CANTERBURY

By the same author:

SAINT WULSTAN : PRELATE AND PATRIOT

published (S.P.C.K.) 1933

THE ARCHBISHOPRIC OF LICHFIELD (787–803)

published 1964

THE ARCHBISHOPRIC OF YORK : THE EARLY YEARS

published 1967

The Archbishopric of Canterbury:

FROM ITS FOUNDATION TO THE NORMAN CONQUEST

BY

JOHN W. LAMB, Ph.D.

(Canon of York)

WITH A FOREWORD BY

THE ARCHBISHOP OF CANTERBURY

THE FAITH PRESS LTD.

7 TUFTON STREET · LONDON · SW1P 3QD

FIRST PUBLISHED IN 1971

© *John W. Lamb, 1971*

283. 4223
∠197

181821

PRINTED IN GREAT BRITAIN
in 11pt. Baskerville type
BY THE FAITH PRESS LTD.
LEIGHTON BUZZARD LU7 7NQ

SBN 7164 0205 X

CONTENTS

FOREWORD

I am sure that there will be a widespread welcome for this story of the early centuries of the See of Canterbury. The author is a parish priest who in the midst of his pastoral ministry has pursued his scholarly studies with the use of first-hand sources and now presents the third, and most valuable, instalment of them to the public. There exist already admirable works on the history of the pre-Conquest Church, and admirable monographs on its important figures. The distinctive character of this book lies in the presentation of the main stream of history from the standpoint of the story of the Primatial See.

If our Church today is, after centuries of Christian civilization, conscious that it works in a missionary situation, with the task of going where the people are and converting many from a quasi-pagan apathy, then the atmosphere and the lessons of the days of Augustine or Theodore or Dunstan are nearer to us than might be supposed. This book therefore will help us both in our study of the past and in our reflections on the present. It will reinforce once again the dictum of a Huguenot divine, whom Bishop Hensley Henson used to love to quote, that 'the Christian Church is an anvil which has broken many hammers.'

MICHAEL CANTUAR :

June 1970

PREFACE

This volume completes the trilogy on the English Archbishoprics of the Anglo-Saxon Church. The two former studies of the archbishoprics of Lichfield and York cannot be separated from the history of the archbishopric of Canterbury. Although the existence of the archbishopric of Lichfield may be regarded as an interlude which impeded the development of the Church in England, the continuance to the present day of the primatial sees of Canterbury and York sufficiently testify to the fulfilment of the plan which Pope Gregory I sent to Augustine for the constitution of the Church.

More than thirteen and a half centuries have elapsed since then, but the archbishopric of Canterbury still remains the living link in the long chain of history which binds together inseparably for ever the Church of England with the Church of the English people which St. Augustine founded.

When the administration of the Church to-day is compared with that of the Anglo-Saxon Church the problems which emerge appear to be essentially the same. In recent years the question has arisen concerning the advisability of sub-dividing large dioceses in both provinces. Local commissions, appointed to examine this problem, have made recommendations for the creation of new dioceses and the consequent increase of the episcopate. Archbishop Theodore in the seventh century was confronted with the same problem, and acted on the principle, as Bede records, 'Let more bishops be added as the number of the faithful shall be increased.' To-day the increase of the episcopate may be needed not as in Theodore's day, because of the growth in the number of the faithful, but because of the movement of population and its concentration in new towns and developing areas.

Apart from the lessons which may be drawn from the history of the Archbishopric of Canterbury in Pre-Conquest times, inspiration is to be found in the knowledge that, with few exceptions, men of sanctity of life, learning and wisdom have held the highest ecclesiastical office in the land, and have guided the Church, as indeed to-day, to fulfil the divine commission in an ever-changing world.

JOHN W. LAMB

June 1970

THE MISSION OF ST. AUGUSTINE

To the ancient dictum of Cicero 'History indeed is the witness of the times, the light of truth'[1] may well be added in this twentieth century the observation of an anonymous writer that 'History is a succession of stories the substance of which varies according to their truth.' There are innumerable stories, some of them having survived through many ages, which seem to possess a perennial attractiveness even if the grain of truth within is wrapped in the husk of legend.

Typical of such stories is that recorded by the Venerable Bede, in his *Ecclesiastical History of the English Nation*, concerning Gregory the abbot of St. Andrew's Monastery, Rome, who, while walking accompanied by some of his monks through the market-place of Rome, between the years 586 and 588, saw English boys, white of body, fair of countenance and beautiful hair, for sale. On inquiring of what nation they were, Gregory was told they were called Angles. Giving a punning reply, he said, 'They have angelic faces, and as such are meet to be co-heirs with the angels in heaven.'[2] Some credibility may be lent to the story from the letter which in 595 Pope Gregory I addressed to the priest Candidus in which he directed him to spend a part of the revenues of the Gallican Patrimony on the purchase of English slave boys and then to send them accompanied by a priest to monasteries in Rome.[3]

It is significant that it was at this time that he resolved to lead a mission himself to Britain there to convert the natives to the Christian Faith.

Although compelled by papal authority to set aside his personal wishes in this matter his missionary zeal was never quenched and was destined in later years to inspire some of the greatest missionary enterprises of the Church. Within a few years the whole situation was changed for Gregory when Pope Pelagius II died and he was elected to the Apostolic See and duly consecrated to the Pontifical Office in September 590.

The most outstanding characteristic of Gregory's pontificate was undoubtedly the missionary enterprises which he initiated for the recovery of heretics and the conversion of the heathen. Of all his extensive missionary activities, including the conversion of the pagans of the islands of Italy and of the fierce Barbaricini, his greatest achievement was the evangelization of Britain which he began when he commissioned and sent Augustine with his band of forty monks from Rome.

From his knowledge of the fathers such as Tertullian, Origen, Eusebius, Chrysostom, Jerome and Theodoret [4]; the attendance of British bishops at the councils of Arles, Nicea and Rimini [5]; the acceptance in 455 of Pope Leo's direction concerning the date for the observance of Easter [6]; the missions of Bishops Germanus and Lupus; and the missionary activities of Palladius, Ninian, Patrick and Columba,[7] Gregory would have been well aware of the existence of an indigenous Church in Britain.

But over and against all this knowledge of Britain it seems probable there had reached him the lament of the historian Gildas in his *De Excidio* that the Britons 'never preached the Faith to the Saxons, or English, who dwelt amongst them.' [8] Evidence of how well-informed he was of the religious situation in the northernmost parts of his patriarchate may be found in the marriage between the Christian princess Bertha, a daughter of Charibert, king of Paris (which Gregory of Tours says took place as early as 560 [9]) and Aethelbert of Kent, who later became Bretwalda, when it was stipulated that she should have the freedom to practise her Christian religion. In order to facilitate this she was accompanied by her chaplain Bishop Liudhard of Senlis. So detailed was this information concerning Bertha's practice of her religious faith that Pope Gregory I later wrote to her and reminded her that it was her Christian duty to bring her husband to an acceptance of the Christian Faith.[10] In writing to the Frankish queen mother, Brunhild, a kinswoman of Bertha, Gregory wrote 'We inform you that it has reached us that the English nation, by God's grace, desires to become Christian but that the bishops who are in the neighbourhood have no pastoral solicitude for them.' [11] Similarly he wrote to the two young Frankish kings, Theodoric and Theodebert, 'It has reached us that the English nation, by the mercy of God, desires earnestly to be converted to the Christian Faith, but the priests in the neighbourhood take no notice and delay kindling the desires of the English by their exhortation.' [12] It is evident that the urgency of the missionary opportunity came to Gregory with cumulative force. Queen Bertha had for some years practised her Christian religion but it had aroused little more than the curiosity of the English people among whom she lived. Bishop Liuhard, her chaplain, lacked missionary zeal and in consequence his ministrations were ineffective in their influence to bring Aethelbert to an acceptance of the Christian Faith. Gregory therefore decided not to delay his projected mission to Britain. He would not wait until the English slave boys, whom Candidus had purchased on his directive, had been fully trained in Rome to carry back the Faith to their own people but would send a band of monks under the leadership of Augustine.

Whatever were the high hopes with which the mission set forth from Rome they were destined to be shattered on journeying through Gaul where they heard from the inhabitants stories of the horrors perpetrated by the invading Saxons and the ferocity of the natives of Britain. Yielding to the fears and desires of his monks Augustine led them back to Rome.[13]

Pope Gregory I was determined that his missionary enterprise should not be abandoned. He addressed a letter to Augustine and his monks in which he wrote : 'It is better not to begin a good work at all than to begin and turn back. My beloved sons, you have begun this work by the Lord's help, you must therefore bring it to completion.' [14] He also announced in his letter that he had appointed Augustine to be their abbot, by this means giving full authority to Augustine over his band of monks. Gregory also turned his attention to practical problems and advised that they should take with them Franks to be interpreters since they were ignorant of the language of the English. As they left Rome for the second time the pope, in July 596, sent letters of commendation to eminent and influential persons whom they might meet on their journey across Europe, including the more important bishops in Gaul.[15]

Among these was Virgilius of Arles whom Gregory later appointed his Vicar in Gaul and conferred upon him the dignity of the *pallium*, informing him that his Vicariate extended throughout the kingdom of Austrasia, Burgundy and Aquitaine. It is clear, therefore, in view of the relationship later established between Virgilius and Augustine, that as Vicar of Gaul and metropolitan of Arles Virgilius possessed no territorial ecclesiastical jurisdiction in Britain.[16]

Journeying northwards, it was not until nine months later, probably towards the end of April 597, that Augustine with his monks embarked on the north coast of Gaul for Britain, and landed at Ebbsfleet in the isle of Thanet on the east coast of Kent.[17]

As soon as they had landed Augustine sent a message to the Bretwalda Aethelbert informing him that 'he had come from Rome, and had brought the best of messages, which promised without a doubt to those who obeyed it eternal joy in heaven and a kingdom that would last without end with the living and true God.' [18] Augustine's reference to a kingdom showed his wisdom in using such a term which would be well understood by Aethelbert, whom Bede describes as the king of Kent 'who had extended the frontiers of his empire as far as the boundary of the great river Humber.' Some knowledge of the Christian way of life was already possessed by the king because of his conscientious adherence to his undertaking to Bertha, his wife, that she should have freedom to practise her religion. It was within the context of this political and religious

situation that Augustine made his two-fold approach; a recognition
of the high kingly authority of Aethelbert; and the imparting of a
message which informed him of the kingdom which was eternal.

Giving directions that Augustine and his companions should remain
on the island where they had landed, Aethelbert supplied them with
life's necessities, and some days later he visited the island and commanded them to attend a conference at which, by his orders, they
preached to him and his attendants the 'Word of Life.' In the king's
reply is to be seen the fair and open minded way in which he considered the true import of their preaching. His reply was of far-
reaching significance for upon him alone rested the decision whether
he should allow them to remain in his kingdom. The success or failure
of the whole evangelistic enterprise was basically dependent on
Aethelbert's reply, which was as follows: 'Fair, indeed, are the words
and promises which you bring; but because they are new and uncertain, I cannot give assent to them and abandon those which I along
with all the nation of the English have followed for so long time.
But because you have come from far hither as strangers, and, as I
conceive, have desired to impart to us also those things which you
yourselves believe to be true and best, we do not wish to harm you;
rather, we will receive you with friendly entertainment, and supply
you with things necessary for your sustenance; nor do we forbid you
to gain to your religious faith all whom you can by your preaching.' [19]
From these words the missionaries readily understood the com-
prehendingly favourable outcome of the conference. Not only were the
king's words straightforward and fair but they also displayed a
wonderful generosity. Willingly he granted to Augustine, his forty
monks and Frankish interpreters accommodation, supplies for their
maintenance, and freedom to gain converts.

King Aethelbert resided in 'the city of Canterbury, which was the
metropolis of his whole realm,' [20] the former site of the Roman town
of Durovernum. Within his royal city the king appointed them a
residence at the Stable-gate, 'in the parish of St. Alphege, over
against the King's Street on the north.' [21] Without undue delay they
moved into the quarters provided for them by the king and, on
entering the city, they formed themselves into a procession chanting
in unison as they went 'We beseech Thee, O Lord, in all Thy mercy,
that Thy wrath and indignation may be turned away from this city,
and from Thy holy house, for we have sinned. Alleluia!' [22] As they
settled down, Bede records, 'they began to imitate the apostolic life of
the primitive Church; that is, by serving God with continual prayers,
vigils and fastings, preaching the Word of Life to whom they could,
despising all things of this world as not their concern, receiving from
those whom they taught, only the things necessary for their sustenance;

themselves living in all things according to what they taught, and ever ready to suffer adversity or even to die for the truth which they preached.'

There was already a church in Canterbury, dedicated in honour of St. Martin, which was used by Queen Bertha for her devotions, where Bishop Liudhard customarily ministered. Augustine and his companions were allowed to share the use of it, and it was here that they initiated and carried forward their evangelistic work which included the regular chanting of the psalms, prayer, celebration of the Mass, preaching and baptizing converts. Not a few inhabitants were attracted, in the first instance, to the Christian Faith through admiration 'of the simplicity of their innocent way of life and the sweetness of their heavenly doctrine.' [23] Queen Bertha, doubtless, had been able to give the missionaries encouragement and, mindful of the words in the letter which she had received from Pope Gregory I, had fulfilled her 'Christian duty to bring her husband to an acceptance of the Christian Faith.' Early in June 597, within a few weeks of their landing in Kent, Aethelbert accepted the Faith and was baptized by Augustine probably in St. Martin's church. His profession of the Faith created a profound impression on his people, many of whom followed his example. Although the king made no attempt to compel his subjects to become Christians it soon became evident that he was more kindly disposed towards those who, like himself, had accepted the Christian Faith. This in itself acted as an incentive to others to become Christians. Describing this, Bede wrote 'greater numbers began daily to flock to hear the Word, and abandoning their heathen rites to join themselves by faith to the unity of the Holy Church of Christ.' [24]

By the baptism of Aethelbert the initial stage of the mission led by Augustine had been crowned with success, and by the conversion of large numbers of the people the future success of the missionary enterprise seemed to be assured. Kent itself, the kingdom in which Aethelbert dwelt in his royal city of Canterbury, was not completely evangelized but there was every prospect that before long it would be. In view of this the scope of the mission's activities would have to be extended and other territories sought in which to labour. Aethelbert exercised his *imperium* over territories extending as far north as the river Humber. Since he was now a Christian there was every reason to hope that his influence would facilitate opportunities for the Christian religion to spread throughout the neighbouring kingdoms. Such expansion would of necessity confront Augustine with the problem of establishing some form of organization for the newly founded Church, and it was to this problem he now turned.

CANTERBURY BECOMES A METROPOLITAN SEE

It should not be imagined that Aethelbert's pagan beliefs, which he held prior to his acceptance of the Christian Faith, found expression in a primitive form of administration in his kingdom. Bede's reference to Canterbury as 'the metropolis of his whole realm' implies the existence of ordinary urban life and an administration relevant to the needs of town-dwellers. This form of urban administration at this period was without parallel in any part of Saxon England.[1] In this respect Augustine's initial task in establishing the organization of the Church was simplified to some extent. His mission had its head-quarters not in some strong encampment but in an ancient city where the king had his court. Here in the royal city of Canterbury he was now able to take the first steps towards establishing the organization of the newly founded Church in accordance with the traditional pattern of an urban based episcopate. Moreover, if the expansion of the Church were not to be retarded, then without further delay Augustine perceived that the time had come when he must follow the direction given to him by Pope Gregory I that he should receive consecration to the episcopate.[2] Crossing over to Gaul, Augustine made his way to the metropolitan see of Arles where Virgilius, with his suffragans, in November 597, duly consecrated him bishop or, as Bede records, 'archbishop of the nation of the English.'[3] In giving this title 'archbishop' Bede was reading back into the beginning of the Church in Kent the title and situation current in the Church at the time when he wrote his history. To bestow the title of archbishop upon a newly consecrated bishop or, indeed, upon a metropolitan bishop, was completely at variance with the policy of Pope Gregory I. Throughout his pontificate Gregory disallowed metropolitans to be designated 'archbishop,' with very few exceptions, because of its patriarchal implications.[4]

During the absence of Augustine in Gaul the work of the Church advanced so rapidly that on his return he found a great number of converts awaiting baptism. Writing to inform the pope of his consecration he also told him of the remarkable occasion which occurred on Christmas Day 597, when he baptized more than ten thousand persons. In a letter to Eulogius, bishop in Alexandria, Gregory recounts details of the success of the mission to the English people and asks for the bishop's prayers for its continued success.[5] It would appear, therefore, that Gregory regarded the vast number of converts, which included the king, as the hallmark of success of the evangelistic enterprise which had been undertaken at his direction. Not until three years after Aethelbert's baptism did Gregory write to him in 601, and likened him to another Constantine who together with his people had been converted.[6]

Before Augustine's departure for Gaul to seek consecration the king was aware of the needs of the mission and the necessity for making provision for its development and future well-being. According to Bede's record it would appear that Aethelbert was fully acquainted with the need of a bishop having his seat in a city. 'He granted to his teachers a place for their see, suitable to their degree, in his capital of Canterbury, along with possessions of various kinds that were necessary for them.'[7] The full significance of these provisions was later to be seen, when Bede explicitly states 'Augustine had received an episcopal see in the royal city.'[8] With the support of the king an old church, built during the Roman occupation, was restored and dedicated 'in the name of the Holy Saviour our Lord and God Jesus Christ' (Christ Church), and in this church Augustine set his *cathedra,* and adjoining the church he established a residence for himself and his successors. As will be seen later, this was the actual beginning of the primatial see of Canterbury, never to be transferred to any other city, although attempts were made to do so. Further encouraged and assisted by King Aethelbert monastic buildings, including the church of St. Peter and St. Paul, were erected to the east of the city for the use and permanent accommodation of the *familia* of Augustine, which included monks and probably a number of priests.

While all these developments were in progress Augustine sent Laurentius the priest and the monk Peter to Rome carrying letters to Pope Gregory I informing him of his consecration to the episcopate, the progress of the mission to the English people, and a lengthy inquiry concerning a variety of matters relating to the episcopal office and ecclesiastical administration. There was some delay before Laurentius and Peter returned bearing the pope's answers to Augustine's inquiries. With a full realization of the needs of the expanding Church, Gregory sent more helpers, among whom were Mellitus, Justus, Paulinus and Rufinianus, who accompanied Augustine's two messengers on their return to Kent. They carried with them sacred vessels, vestments, ornaments, relics of holy apostles and martyrs and many books. Most important of all, however, they carried back with them letters from Pope Gregory I, addressed to Augustine, which were destined to shape the structure and ecclesiastical administration of the Church in England down to the present day. One of these letters accompanied the *pallium* which Gregory conferred on Augustine 'only for the performing of the solemn service of the Mass.' Another

B

letter set forth at some length Gregory's conception of and directions
for the constitution of the Church in Britain. Subjected to attack on
many occasions, it has been the centre of controversy whenever the
jurisdiction of the metropolitan see of Canterbury has been called
in question. Since this letter, embracing what may be called the
Gregorian Plan, arises in various historical contexts in this study it is
given in full as follows:

'To the most reverend and most holy brother and fellow-
bishop, Augustine: Gregory, servant of the servants of God.
Although it is certain that the unutterable rewards of the eternal
kingdom are reserved for those who labour for Almighty God,
yet it is necessary that we bestow on them the distinction of
honours so that by this reward they may more effectively devote
themselves to their spiritual work. And, because the new church
of the English, through the goodness of the same Lord and your
labour, has been brought to the grace of Almighty God, we grant
you the use of the *pallium* in the same church, only for performing the solemnities of the Mass; so that in several places you
may ordain twelve bishops who shall be subject to your authority,
so that the bishop of London in the future shall always be consecrated by his own synod, and receive the *pallium* of honour
from this holy and apostolic see which, by the will of God,
I serve. But we desire you to send to the city of York a bishop
whom you shall determine to ordain; yet, so that if that city with
the adjoining places shall receive the Word of God, he also is to
ordain twelve bishops, and to enjoy fully the dignity of metropolitan; because, if we shall live we design, by the favour of
God, upon him also to bestow the *pallium;* nevertheless, we wish
him to be subject to the direction of your Brotherliness. But after
your death he is to preside over the bishops whom he shall have
ordained, so that in no way shall he be subject to the jurisdiction
of the bishop of London. But in the future let this distinction of
honour be between the bishops of the cities of London and York,
so that he may have precedence who was first to have been
ordained. But let them by common counsel and agreed action
unanimously arrange whatever is to be done in zeal for Christ;
let them rightly decide and then carry out their decision without
disagreement among themselves.

'To you, however, Brotherliness, by the authority of God and
our Lord Jesus Christ, shall be subject not only those bishops
whom you shall ordain but also those who shall be ordained by
the bishop of York, and also all the bishops of Britain, so that
from the words of and life of your Holiness they may learn the

form of right belief and good living and fulfilling their office with faith and morals, when it shall please the Lord, they may attain the heavenly kingdom.

'God keep you safe, most reverend Brother. Given this 22nd of June in the nineteenth year of the reign of our most pious lord, Mauricius Tiberius Augustus, the eighteenth year after the consulship of the same lord, the fourth indiction.' [9]

Pope Gregory's plan as outlined here conformed to the accepted constitutional pattern of ecclesiastical government which had become established in the Church, by which the chief episcopal see was erected in the metropolis of the civil province or kingdom.[10] In setting out his plan for the administration of the newly established Church in Britain Gregory specifically directed that London and York should be the cities in which should be the seat of a metropolitan bishop. It is significant that in designating these two cities he did not follow the *Notitia Dignitatum* containing details of Diocletianic arrangement of Britain when it was divided into five provinces. This would seem to suggest that there was in existence an earlier *Notitia* available in the papal library which recorded the details concerning the division of Britain into two provinces by the Emperor Severus during the Roman occupation. These were constituted by his *Britannia Superior* (Upper Britain), the capital of which was London, and *Britannia Inferior* (Lower Britain, i.e. farther away from Rome), of which York was the capital city.[11] It is evident, in his direction that London should be the see city of a metropolitan bishop, Gregory had not fully grasped the political situation in southern Britain. The old Roman city of *Londinium* at that time was situated in the territory of the East Saxons over which the sub-king Saberht ruled. To have established a metropolitan bishopric in the capital city of a sub-kingdom and not in the metropolis of the kingdom of the chief ruler, King Aethelbert, would not have been in accord with the traditional and accepted practice concerning the erection of metropolitan sees. Moreover, the East Saxons had not yet been evangelized and this in itself precluded the erection of a bishopric in Saberht's kingdom. Nevertheless, the precise terms in which Gregory designated the cities of London and York to be the seats of metropolitan bishoprics appear to confirm that he had access to some form of *Notitia,* which included the names of the metropolitan cities of the civil administration of the two provinces in Britain during the time of Severus, similar to the *Notitia Dignitatum* in which references are made to the metropolitan cities of Gaul.[12]

London as a city, at this time, possessed no great political importance as the chief city of the sub-kingdom of the East Saxons, and

even when they accepted the Christian Faith the consecration by
Augustine of Mellitus to preach to them and to have his see in
London clearly indicated that Augustine had not entertained the idea
of transferring his *cathedra* from Canterbury to London in order to
fulfil the literal directions of Gregory's plan.[13] Having resided in the
metropolis of the kingdom of Aethelbert for nearly eight years,
together with the king's generous provision of buildings and maintenance for the newly established Church, and the continued growth
of the Church in the city and kingdom, a quality of permanence
had already attached itself to the metropolitan bishopric with its
cathedra in the ancient city of Canterbury (Durovernum). There can
be no question of the rightness of Augustine's decision to continue his
cathedra in the royal city of Canterbury. In doing so he acted in
full conformity with the principle enunciated by the council of
Chalcedon, as early as the year 451, 'let the arrangement of ecclesiastical sees conform to the civil and public standards.' [14]

The continuance of Canterbury as the centre of ecclesiastical
administration where Augustine had set his *cathedra* gave a stability
to the Church in Kent and the whole of Aethelbert's kingdom which
has often been under-estimated, and later attempts to remove the
metropolitan see to London met with failure. With the reception of
the *pallium* there was conferred upon Augustine metropolitan
authority, but the immediate difficulty which confronted him was how
and in what circumstances should he exercise this authority. The constitution of the newly established Church and the lines upon which it
should be developed would conform to the traditional and accepted
pattern. But the situation in which he now found himself was in some
respects exceptional. He was now a metropolitan bishop, with his
see in the royal and ancient city of Canterbury, of a province devoid
of defined territorial boundaries and without dioceses and suffragan
bishops. Even with the growth of the Church this situation remained
unchanged during the lifetime of Augustine and his immediate
successors before a diocesan system of administration was established.

Some of the problems which confronted Augustine are reflected
in the questions which he submitted to Gregory. His replies or
Responsiones incorporated by Bede in his *Ecclesiastical History* have
been the subject of much study and research by eminent scholars
who have reached the conclusion that 'the *Responsiones* are in a loose
sense Gregorian,' and that the last two, which need not be considered here, 'are more probably of Canterbury than of direct
Gregorian origin.' [15] Laurence the priest and the monk Peter had
carried to Rome a communication from Augustine to Pope Gregory I
which contained three distinct but related matters. First among these
were given details concerning the nation of the English who had

received the Christian Faith; secondly, the information that Augustine had been consecrated bishop; and, thirdly, a request for answers to the questions which Augustine considered to be urgent. To all these elements of Augustine's communication the pope made definite acknowledgement. First, he rejoiced with Augustine on the success of the English Mission; secondly, he acknowledged with eminent approval Augustine's consecration by conferring upon him the honour of the *pallium,* the symbol of metropolitan authority; and, thirdly, in his *Responsiones* he answered at some length the questions and problems concerning which Augustine sought the pope's counsel and guidance.[16]

Bishop Augustine's first question concerned the relationship of a bishop to his clergy, and the problem of the distribution of the offerings of the faithful. In his reply Gregory first considered the inquiry in its relation to the revenues of the Church. He informed Augustine that it was the custom of the Apostolic See to direct that bishops newly consecrated should divide the offerings of the Church into four parts: one part for the bishop and his household; another for the clergy; the third part for the poor and the fourth for the repair of churches.[17] Gregory in his reply informed him that the personal life of a bishop could not be unrelated to his practical administration of the affairs of the Church over which he ruled. Although he had received consecration to the episcopal office he was still the abbot of his community of monks, and under obligation to live in accordance with the requirements of his monastic order. Here, then, in the first decade of the life of the newly founded Church, Augustine was confronted with an exceptional situation upon which he sought the counsel of the pope. There were a few isolated instances in Italy of monk-bishops; also in Gaul there were monk-bishops whose *familiae* were monks of the Martinian tradition.[18] On travelling northwards through Italy and Gaul on his way to Britain, Augustine may have become acquainted with such circumstances and would have regarded them as exceptional and not the rule. His household or *familia* at the outset was, for the most part, composed of his community of monks and one or two clerks in orders, who were probably the Frankish interpreters, whom he had brought with him.

The needs of the missionary church of the English would of necessity affect Augustine's administration, but Gregory left him in no doubt about his manner of life. Although he was now a metropolitan bishop he was to continue to live communally with his *familia,* having all things in common after the manner of the early Church. His companions on their ordination, as members of the *familia* at Christ Church, were to live a communal life with him.[19] It would appear that all the monks who accompanied him to Britain were ordained by him in order to meet the progressive requirements of the expanding Church. Clerks below the subdiaconate who were married were allowed to live separately from the *familia,* and to receive their stipends. But they remained subject to ecclesiastical rule and were under obligation 'to lead a holy life, give attention to chanting the psalms, and to preserve by God's grace their hearts, tongues and bodies pure from every forbidden thing.' [20] Although Augustine lived communally, i.e. in refectory and dormitory, with his *familia,* the character of his episcopal office was different from that of the monk-bishop of the Celtic Church in Britain who was a member of a monastic community and seldom its head. His episcopal functions were exercised in and through the monastery of which he was a member and the family or tribe, which was composed of the monastery itself and any lesser houses or cells which it possessed.[21] The bishop of the Celtic Church, therefore, exercised his office within the limits of his tribe and not on the basis of territorial boundaries similar to Augustine's metropolitan authority over a province, later to be sub-divided into dioceses each ruled over by a suffragan bishop.

Gregory's answer to Augustine's first question shows the emphasis which he placed upon spiritual matters for the Church—bishops, clergy, monks and laity. In his dual office as abbot and bishop, Augustine's life was to be the major influence in his relationships with his *familia,* and his personal life was to be governed by his adherence to the disciplines of communal life with his *familia.* This mode of life of necessity involved a specific method of financial administration, required of all bishops, by which due provision was made for the bishop himself, clergy, monks, the poor and the maintenance of church buildings. Here then was the pattern of episcopal administration for the newly founded Church; first at the centre in the city of Canterbury where Augustine had his *cathedra* and later throughout his entire province as the Church expanded. But in Gregory's plan, in which he gave details of the constitution of the Church, were envisaged the creation of episcopal sees and the consecration of bishops to rule over them. A peculiar problem therefore confronted Augustine which impelled him to seek the pope's counsel. 'May a bishop,' he asked, 'be consecrated without other bishops being present when, on account of great distance between them, they could not easily assemble?' This was a real problem because the canon law of the Church since the council of Nicea in 325 had required that at least three bishops should take part in the consecration of a bishop.[22]

If the canon law of the Church were to be observed how then could he consecrate his suffragans? Bishop Liudhard, Queen Bertha's chaplain, in all probability by this time had died or was too infirm to take any part in a consecration. Evidently Augustine, by his inquiry, completely ignored the existence of British bishops as did Gregory in his answer. If he alone was the consecrator, when other bishops could not attend because of the great distance away of their sees, would the consecration be valid? This problem of distance was a real one. It was impracticable for bishops to cross from Gaul for a consecration. Not only would the question of distance arise, if it were attempted, but also the question of time and uncertainty. Gregory set Augustine's inquiry in the context of the situation of the Church in England. Since he was the only bishop in England it was permissible for him alone to consecrate a bishop in the absence of other bishops unless some came over from Gaul to participate in the consecration. The pope was careful, however, to preclude any possibility of this precedent being made the rule contrary to the law of the Church. He therefore advised Augustine that in the erection of sees they should be arranged in such a way that bishops could without difficulty assemble for the consecration of a new bishop. In due course Augustine consecrated a bishop in accordance with the pope's counsel. The situation of the Church in England was such that in the succeeding quarter of a century it was found necessary for a bishop alone to consecrate in order that the episcopate should continue.[23]

As Augustine contemplated the progressive implementation of Gregory's plan for the Church in Britain he inquired concerning the bishops over whom he should exercise metropolitan authority. 'How are we to deal with the bishops of Gaul and Britain?' he asked. This question inevitably implied not only bishops but also the territorial area in which they exercised their episcopal functions. To this inquiry Gregory replied with singular clarity so that no misunderstanding could arise in the mind of Augustine. There was no intention to confer upon him even the slightest authority over the bishops of Gaul. Indeed, Gregory himself, in accordance with the practice of his predecessors, had conferred the *pallium* upon Virgilius, bishop of Arles, and had appointed him his Vicar in Gaul, and it was not his intention to deprive him of any of the authority which he had received. There is little doubt that this inquiry by Augustine concerning the bishops of Gaul was prompted by his knowledge of the slackness in ecclesiastical discipline and irregularities which were prevalent at that time in Gaul.

Gregory was no less aware of the irregularities of the Church in Gaul and, on appointing Virgilius his Vicar, had urged him to take every measure possible to extirpate simony.[24] However, if Augustine should happen to visit the province of Gaul he would have an opportunity to co-operate with Virgilius in amending any faults among the bishops, and if Virgilius himself were slack in maintaining discipline then Augustine's zeal would provide a helpful corrective for him. Similarly, the bishop of Arles would be able to assist him so that any behaviour of bishops contrary to God's commands could be put away. Any action which Augustine was authorized to take in order to amend ecclesiastical abuses in Gaul was by advice, exhortation and example. 'Of your own authority,' wrote Gregory, 'you shall not be able to judge the bishops of Gaul, but by persuading, smooth speaking and showing good works for them to imitate you shall reform perverse minds so that they desire the sanctity of life.' He also informed Augustine that he had written to Virgilius bidding him to accept the advice offered and asking that both bishops should unite in an endeavour to suppress abuses.[25]

At the same time Gregory made it abundantly clear that although Virgilius was his Vicar in Gaul his Vicariate did not include Britain, nor could he claim Augustine to be one of his suffragans because he had consecrated him. It was implicitly stated by Gregory in his reply that each metropolitan possessed no authority whatsoever in the province of the other but mutually they should encourage and assist each other, whenever Augustine was in Gaul, to maintain episcopal discipline.

It may be recalled that a missionary relationship had existed between Britain and Gaul in the fifth century at the time of the heresy of Pelagius. Germanus, bishop of Auxerre, and Lupus, bishop of Troyes, visited Britain and succeeded in stamping out the heresy and confirmed Britain in the true Faith.[26] Under the leadership of Augustine, however, an evangelistic mission sponsored by Rome was established in Britain and there is no evidence to show that the see of Auxerre made any claim that Canterbury was subject to its bishop. Augustine's extensive metropolitan authority was clearly defined by Pope Gregory I. He began his answer to Augustine's question with the unequivocal statement 'We give you no authority over the bishops of Gaul.' At the end of his answer he gave a definitive statement of the extent of Augustine's jurisdiction as metropolitan bishop in Britain, as follows : 'However, we commit to your brotherly care all the bishops of Britain, so that the unlearned may be taught, the weak strengthened by persuasion and the perverse corrected by your authority.' [27]

THE EXPANSION OF THE CHURCH IN ENGLAND

The *Responsiones* of Pope Gregory I have been the subject of much critical study and research, and in the most recent scholarly investigations it has been suggested that the last sentence of Gregory's reply to Augustine's inquiry concerning the bishops over whom he should exercise authority may be 'a later gloss or an apt quotation.' [1] This conclusion is based on the difference of the language used in the *Responsiones* from that used in the authentic letter in which Gregory set forth his plan for the constitution of the Church in Britain. In his plan he explained why all the bishops of Britain should be subject to Augustine. It was 'so that from the words of life of your Holiness they may learn the form of right belief and good living and, fulfilling their office with faith and morals, they may, when the Lord shall please, attain the heavenly kingdom.' [2]

According to the *Responsiones,* however, the purpose of the committal of all the bishops of Britain to Augustine's care was 'so that the unlearned may be taught, the weak strengthened by persuasion and the perverse corrected by authority.' [3] In comparing these two passages it is evident that the tenor of the language of Gregory's reply to Augustine's inquiry is stronger than the parallel passage in his letter. But it should be observed that Augustine's inquiry had raised the whole question of his authority as metropolitan bishop of Britain.

Gregory, in his reply, used the word authority *auctoritas* no less than four times. On the first three occasions he used the word with reference to the specific limitations of Augustine's authority. But in the fourth and final use of the word he expressed in positive definitive terms more clearly than in his letter the purpose and scope of the authority which Augustine possessed in the exercise of his care of all the bishops of Britain. Although the authority conferred by Gregory upon Augustine was extensive it did not extend to any vicarial authority or privileges, for nowhere in his correspondence with Augustine did he at any time make the slightest reference to him being Papal Vicar of Britain.

Augustine did not long delay his approach to the British bishops in an endeavour to bring them within the organization of the newly founded Church. The initial exercise of his authority was in making friendly overtures to them, but the difficulties which he subsequently encountered indicated that Gregory had not been fully informed concerning the bishops of the British Church over which he possessed no effective control. His commission allowed Augustine, as metropolitan bishop, to pursue those measures which he considered to be most advantageous for the unification of the Church throughout his province of Britain. In these initial measures Aethelbert gave his fullest assistance, as he had been enjoined by the pope, in helping to arrange a conference between the bishops and Augustine.[4] To the British Aethelbert was the powerful Bretwalda who in bitter and relentless fighting had driven them from their territory westwards. One commendable feature, however, had since emerged; Aethelbert had confessed the Christian Faith. This in itself may have encouraged the British bishops to meet Augustine, putting behind them the old hostility and looking forward to a more peaceful country in which the Christian religion would be deeply rooted. At all events, whatever Aethelbert's influence may have been, in what Bede describes as 'the nearest province of the Britons,' it was of sufficient consequence for Augustine to journey in safety to the valley of the river Severn, on the borders of the Hwicce and West Saxons. There, at a place known in Bede's day as 'Augustine's Oak,' Augustine met in synod the British bishops and doctors. In his office as metropolitan bishop of Britain, Augustine presided and began the proceedings 'by brotherly admonitions to persuade them in order that, having Catholic peace with him, they should undertake the common labour for the Lord by preaching the Gospel to the people.'[5]

Bede then records that the British bishops did not observe Easter at the proper time and did many other things which were contrary to ecclesiastical unity. As a result of these differences, which were not primarily of theological concern but of traditions firmly held, Augustine became involved in a long and tedious argument. After lengthy discussion the British representatives would neither yield to the entreaties, nor exhortations, nor rebukes of Augustine and his companions. They asked for another synod to be convoked at which more of their representatives could attend.

Having acceded to their request for a second synod, probably held in the same place as the first, the Britons were represented by seven bishops and many learned men from their most important monastery of Bangor-Iscoed in Flintshire, the abbot of which was Dinoot. The presence of seven bishops may suggest organization of the British Church beyond that of claustral bishops. But Bede, in mentioning the number 'seven,' is careful to observe that he is giving what was traditionally accepted and qualifies his statement by the words 'as it is asserted.' At the time when the bishops attended the synod convoked by Augustine there is no reason to assume that the British or Celtic Church possessed an administration and organization similar to the system of ecclesiastical government which had been established throughout Europe and the East. It is evident that when he convoked the second synod there is little doubt that the episcopate of the British Church was organized on a monastic basis, and the delegation would appear to confirm this. Dinoot was the abbot of the most important monastery of the Church and was amongst the learned representatives who accompanied the bishops when they met Augustine at the second synod. It is probable that Dinoot was a bishop-abbot since he claimed to be the 'overseer' of the British bishops, and on this ground disdainfully refuted the claim of Augustine to be the metropolitan bishop of Britain having authority over 'all the bishops of Britain.' [6]

Before meeting Augustine for the second time the British representatives sought the counsel of an anchorite who was known for his sanctity of life and wisdom. Of him they inquired whether they should desert their own traditions at the preaching of Augustine. He replied, 'If he is a man of God, follow him.' They answered, 'And how can we prove that?' Quoting the words of the Gospel the anchorite replied, 'The Lord says, "Take my yoke upon you and learn of me, because I am meek and lowly in heart".' [7] He then advised them how to act in order that they could determine whether Augustine bore Christ's yoke. 'Contrive,' he said, 'that he may first arrive with his company at the place of the synod, and if on your approach he rises to meet you, hear him submissively, knowing that he is a servant of Christ; but if he despises you, and will not rise in your presence, when you are more in number, let him also be despised by you.'

Following the advice of the anchorite they entered the place of the synod and saw Augustine sitting in a chair from which he did not rise to receive them. Immediately their anger was aroused and, charging him with pride, proceeded to contradict everything he said. Finally, Augustine, summing up the situation, told them that they did many things contrary to the custom of the universal Church, but if they would agree with him on three matters he would quietly tolerate the other usages which were contrary to the practices of his Church. The three matters upon which he sought their acceptance were, first, to observe Easter at the proper time (i.e. according to the observance of the Roman Church), secondly, to complete the ministry of baptism according to the custom of the holy Roman and Apostolic Church and, thirdly, to join with him in preaching the Word of God to the nation of the English. It would appear that Augustine neither attempted to show that the British Church observed Easter on the wrong date nor did he try to prove to them that the date on which the festival was observed by the Roman Church was the right one. Augustine asserted without argument that the observance of the Church, of which he was the chief representative in Britain, was at 'the proper time,' and requested that the British Church should abandon their established custom and observe Easter with the Roman Church. This dogmatic requirement may seem strange in view of the fact that as late as 455 there was a difference of a week in the observance of the Alexandrian and Roman Easter, and not until 525 was the Alexandrian date accepted by the Roman Church and adopted in the West.[8] The computation of the date long established in the Celtic Church for the observance of Easter must now be abandoned if Augustine's proposal were to be accepted. In this the British delegation remained obdurate and refused to change the date.

The second requirement, to complete the ministry of baptism according to the custom of the holy Roman and Apostolic Church, involved more than Church order. It brought into question the teaching of the British Church and the validity of their usage in relation to the entire sacrament of initiation. Trine immersion in general had been the practice in early times in the Church, but in the sixth century single immersion appears to have become a mark of orthodoxy because of the continued use of trine immersion by the heretical Arians. There is no doubt, however, of the accepted practice of the Roman Church during the pontificate of Pope Gregory I. In his reply to Bishop Leander of Seville in 591 he wrote, 'By our practice of three immersions we signify the sacramental mystery of the three days' entombment, so that when the infant is taken from the water the third time, the resurrection on the third day is symbolized. And if anyone should think that the trine immersion is in honour of the Holy Trinity, yet even so there is no harm in immersing the infant only once, since in the Three Persons there is but One Substance. Hence it is a matter of indifference whether we use a single or threefold immersion, for the first represents the Unity and the second the Trinity of the Godhead.' [9]

Whatever Augustine may have meant in his request for the British Church to administer the sacrament of baptism in accordance with the practice of the Roman Church, he did not mean acceptance of either trine or single immersion for both forms were permissible and regular. Of all matters, this practice of the mode of the administration of the sacrament of baptism, namely, admission into the Christian Church, would have been one upon which he would have been fully informed as the leader of an evangelizing mission. It must be concluded, therefore, that the completion of the sacrament which Augustine required of the British Church was related to confirmation. At that period the Roman ritual included three unctions or anointings with oil. The first two were administered by a priest, the first before immersion and the second with the chrism. The third was administered by the bishop in confirmation on the forehead with the chrism, although in the east it was administered by presbyters.[10] This part of the administration performed by the bishop was probably the part of the sacrament of baptism not administered by the British Church. However, no certainty can be attached to this but, when Augustine used the word *compleatis* in his second requirement, confirmation was considered to be the completion of baptism. Was it this rite of confirmation, therefore, which in Augustine's judgment was lacking in the administration of the sacrament of baptism by the British Church? Here then was a matter of difference between the two Churches which involved a question of sacramental belief and practice. It was not merely a matter of tradition or long established practice. If it had been only this it would not have weighed so heavily with Augustine since he accepted the principle laid down by Pope Gregory I in a letter to another metropolitan bishop, 'So long as there is unity of faith difference in customs is not detrimental to the Holy Church.' [11] However long the question of the completion of the sacrament of baptism may have been discussed the outcome was the same as that which met Augustine's first request concerning the observance of Easter. The British Church representatives were not prepared to comply and refused Augustine's overtures. His third request was of pivotal importance and its content most persuasive. He asked them 'to preach together with us the Word of God to the nation of the English.' The dominical command 'to preach the Gospel to every creature' [12] was to all Churches, British and Roman alike, and this was their primary duty. His own commission from the pope was to preach the Word of God to the English race, and the representatives now before him belonged to a Church with a long and distinguished history of missionary enterprise, but no missionary from the Church in Cumbria, Wales and Cornwall had attempted to evangelize non-Celtic people. [13] The hostility of the Britons towards the Anglo-Saxons influenced the Church so deeply that they never ventured to preach the Gospel to their enemies. This inactivity impelled the historian Gildas to lament that the Britons never preached the Faith to the Saxons (English) who dwelt among them. [14] It was this attitude of mind which still persisted in the representatives of the British Church who now listened to Augustine's appeal for them to join with him in preaching the Word of God to the Anglo-Saxons. But this request was met with the same refusal as the other two requests.

There is no reason to believe otherwise than that Augustine up to this point had been patient and pacific in his approach to the delegation. He was prepared, as he told them, calmly to tolerate all the other things which they did contrary to the customs of the Roman Church. One difference between them which was clearly visible was the tonsure. The Celtic monk had the front of his head shaved from ear to ear with his hair hanging down his back whereas Augustine and his companions had a tonsure of a circular crown according to the Roman customs. [15]

But of this difference Augustine made no mention. Similarly no mention was made of the practice of the British Church to consecrate bishops by one bishop only. By the Roman rite three or four bishops were required to take part in the consecration of a bishop unless exceptional circumstances arose. Augustine himself was in such an exceptional situation when Bishop Liudhard died, for he was the only bishop of the Roman Church in Britain and in consequence, in the absence of other bishops, would find it necessary by himself alone to consecrate bishops. Understandingly, it may be argued, Augustine was quite prepared to tolerate their tradition of the consecration of bishops. More important, however, than this, was, that in the *Responsiones* of Pope Gregory, Augustine found justifiable grounds for regarding the consecration of bishops by one bishop alone as one of the customs of the British Church which he was prepared 'calmly to tolerate.' [16] There were also certain elements in the ritual of the Mass and Ordinal of the British Church which differed from the Roman Church. But here, too, the *Responsiones,* as it will be seen later, supplied grounds for regarding them as non-essential.[17] The content of Augustine's three requirements, of which he sought acceptance of the delegation, was essentially one of unity. He asked for Church order in the observance of the principal Christian Festival of Easter; unity of faith and practice in the sacrament of Christian initiation; and unity of purpose and action in preaching the Gospel to the English people. Through these three requirements ran the thread of the essential teaching of the Christian Faith. In asking for the completion of the sacrament of baptism there was the deeper significance of the symbolism of the resurrection of our Lord. So, too, the date on which Easter should be observed was wholly concerned with the commemoration of the historic fact of the resurrection. And Augustine's invitation to the British Church to join him in preaching the Christian Faith to the English people was a recognition of the fundamental doctrine of Christianity, for without the resurrection there would have been no Christian Faith to teach.[18] These three minimum requirements reveal the discerning wisdom of Augustine as a great missionary. The traditions and practices of the British Church could be tolerated but these three requirements must be accepted, nor could they be separated from each other. Indeed, there could be no joint enterprise in missionary activity unless the first two conditions were accepted, for their acceptance was 'in order that together with us you may preach the Word of God to the nation of the English.' He did not ask them to 'join with him' but 'with us' *nobiscum*—Augustine and his companions—and in this there was no emphasis on his authority as metropolitan bishop of Britain. To their total refusal to comply with Augustine's requests was added in unequivocal terms their opposition to Augustine himself, when they told him that they would not have him for their archbishop.[19]

By their reply the representatives of the British Church put into effect the counsel which they had received from the anchorite. While their wisdom in following such counsel may be questioned it is evident that their complete and hostile refusal of Augustine's over-tures rested on something more substantial. From whatever sources, oral or written, Bede had obtained his information about these events it must be borne in mind that he wrote at a period when the anchoretic way of life was esteemed more highly than the monastic. It was this predominating influence, doubtless, which impelled him to portray the counsel of the anchorite as far more acceptable and authoritative than any moderating wisdom of the bishops and Abbot Dinoot with his monks from the great monastery of Bangor-Iscoed. Quoting from the New Testament the anchorite had spoken of the One, who was 'meek and lowly in heart,' thereby making humility the sole criterion of judgment. But this was an over-simplification of a deeper conflict between the ancient traditions of the Celtic Church and the inheritance from the 'age of saints,' and the Roman Church.[20] This was clearly shown by the result of the two synods at which, from the beginning, Augustine as leader and spokesman of the Roman Church had spoken and acted throughout on the assumption that the doctrine, practice and customs of his Church alone were right and true. The delegation perceived that acceptance of Augustine's pro-posals for unity would mean first, an admission that in some respects their Church was in error; secondly, that their Church would lose its identity and independence; and thirdly, that they would become subject to a metropolitan bishop and a Church from which they differed in many things. Filled with anger and dismay at the com-plete refusal of his appeal to join with him and his companions in evangelizing the English people, it is said that Augustine began to foretell future judgment upon them for their refusal. 'If they would not preach the Way of Life to the nation of the English, they would undergo the vengeance of death at their hands.' Within little more than a decade King Aethelfrith of Northumbria, at the battle of Chester in 615, slaughtered twelve hundred monks from Bangor-Iscoed who had gone to the scene of battle there to pray for the victory of their countrymen.[21] Bede saw in this calamity the literal fulfilment of the final words of Augustine uttered in reproof of the manifest and expressed hostility of the representatives of the British Church.

The long narrative, in which Bede records the unsuccessful efforts of Augustine to bring the British Church into union with the Roman Church, is recorded in the style of a saga in three episodes which he evidently derived from oral tradition.[22] Not until a generation after Bede's death did the Church in Wales, and in Cornwall not until the tenth century, accept the authority of the Church of Rome, and by this, recognition of the archbishop of Canterbury as their metropolitan bishop.[23]

CHURCH PROBLEMS RESOLVED BY POPE GREGORY I

The unsuccessful efforts of Augustine to bring the British Church into unity with the Roman Church have been attributed to his attempts at the two synods to impose his own personal authority as metropolitan bishop upon the British Church. Augustine's commission in Britain was clearly defined by Pope Gregory I in his plan for the constitution of the Church in Britain and more specifically in the *Responsiones* in which he wrote, 'As for all the bishops of Britain, we commit them to your care.'

Welsh tradition maintains that the British bishops who met Augustine on the banks of the river Severn in the Forest of Dean were the bishops of Caerfawydd (Hereford), Teilo (Llandaff), Llanbadarn Vawr, Bangor, Llanelwy (St. Asaph), Weeg and Morganwg (Margam).[1] These bishops, whether attached to monasteries or not, were all committed to his care; this care extended to Bishop Liudhard, the bishops whom Augustine himself should consecrate and, if the see of York were established in his lifetime, all bishops consecrated by its metropolitan. In the fulfilment of his pastoral office Augustine journeyed westwards through territories of which Aethelbert was overlord where the people had not yet received the Christian Faith, and he travelled farther to the west into territory over which Aethelbert possessed no sovereignty. To suggest that the motive which lay behind this arduous, if not perilous journey or journeys was merely one of self-seeking will not bear scrutiny. Any such interpretation of Augustine's action is wholly contrary to the facts and ignores the pioneering success of the work of evangelisation in Kent which had been achieved under the inspiration of his leadership. Evidence of his zeal for the conversion of the English nation is to be found on all sides and not least in his approach to the British Church in order that their efforts united with his and all the resources of the Roman Church would accomplish the urgent task of 'preaching the Word of Life to the race of the English.'

By the refusal of the representatives of the British or Celtic Church to recognize the authority of the Roman Church they also rejected Augustine as their metropolitan. But this issue was not decided on the acceptance or rejection of a person. The British Church, on the one hand, was determined to adhere to its ancient traditions and practices and thereby to maintain its spiritual independence; on the other hand, by its zealous and progressive missionary enterprise, the Roman Church sought to establish the unity of the Churches and its

33

own supremacy in order to secure the continuous expansion of Catholic Christianity throughout the whole of Britain.

With the co-operation of the British Church evangelizing from the west and moving eastwards and he himself with his band of missionaries working westwards from Kent the inhabitants of a vast area would have been taught the Christian Faith. But any large scale plan for evangelization of this kind was now impossible because the British Church had refused to unite with the Roman Church in this enterprise. While it is difficult to fix with certainty the date of Augustine's meeting with the delegation of the British Church, it must have been after he had received the *Responsiones* from the pope. It would appear to be most probable therefore that his return from the second synod in the west of England to Canterbury was late in 602 or early in the year 603.[2] Having returned to his see city Augustine began the consolidation of the work already accomplished, and initiated measures for the further expansion of the Catholic Church without the co-operation of the British (Celtic) Church.

One of the more immediate problems with which he was concerned was the form of the Liturgy. On his journey from Rome northwards through Gaul he had gained new insights into the customs and practices of the Church and in particular the divergences in the mass. 'He had evidently noticed the number of collects in the mass, the frequent variations of the preface, the invocation of the Holy Spirit on the elements, the solemn episcopal blessing pronounced after the breaking of the bread, and before "the Peace" and the communion.'[3] These differences in the Gallican rite from the Roman rite to which he was accustomed raised a complex problem. The use of the Gallican rite had already been established in Canterbury, before his arrival at the royal court in Kent, by Bishop Liudhard, Queen Bertha's chaplain, who, having come from Gaul, celebrated the mass according to the Gallican rite. But Augustine had brought with him to England both the Gelasian and the Gregorian sacramentaries. Some doubt has been cast on whether Augustine actually brought with him a copy of the Gregorian sacramentary because it was a pontifical mass book, and the date of its compilation is thought to have been not earlier than 592.[4] Archbishop Egbert of York, however, early in the eighth century asserted that when in Rome he saw both the sacramentary and antiphonary attributed to Gregory which Augustine had brought to England.[5]

In addition to the use of the Gallican rite by Bishop Liudhard in the church of St. Martin, Canterbury, Augustine was also aware that the rite of the Celtic Church, which had been derived from both Gallican and Spanish sources, differed from the Roman rite. The Celtic rite, however, did not complicate the situation since the Celtic

Church would not unite with the Roman Church. But the immediate problem remained in Kent, indeed in the royal city of Canterbury, where he had his *cathedra,* for within the city itself both the Gallican and Roman rites were used. What action should he take towards the common use of a rite for the newly established Church? If he attempted, on the one hand, to impose either the Gelasian or Gregorian rite upon Bishop Liudhard the probability was that Queen Bertha would object to any change of the rite to which she had been accustomed all her life. This would inevitably cause division. On the other hand, would it not be divisive of Church unity if more than one rite were used? Here then was a dilemma which Augustine felt unable to resolve without the counsel of Gregory of whom he inquired 'Seeing that the Faith is one, why are the customs of the Churches diverse, and one custom of masses held in the holy Roman Church and another in the Gallican churches?' In his reply he told Augustine that he was free to choose rites and customs from the Roman, Gallican and any other Churches and in this way to compile a rite for use in the Church of the English. Be guided throughout on the principle, wrote Gregory, 'not to value things on account of places, but places on account of things.' And added 'Choose, then, from the various Churches such customs as are godly, religious and right, and bind them as it were into a bundle and place them in the minds of the English for their use.' [6]

No contemporary or later record gives any indication that Augustine compiled a sacramentary particularly for use by the Church of the English. Everything seems to point to the fact that he was so completely immersed in the administration and expansion of the Church that for the sake of unity he did not interrupt the use of the Gallican rite at St. Martin's, Canterbury or anywhere else where it may have been introduced in the city. At all events the two rites continued to be in use in England during the seventh and the greater part of the eighth century, and Theodore during his archiepiscopate was well aware of the use of the Scots in England of the Gallican rite.[7] Following the acceptance of the Roman Easter the Gallican and other rites gradually fell into disuse until the Roman rite finally established itself throughout Britain. There can be little doubt that Augustine continued the use of the Roman rite to which he was accustomed, probably adding to it for variety and enrichment appropriate material from the Gallican rite.

Augustine's evident concern about the marriage traditions and practices of the English people raised issues which prompted questions four and five in which he sought Gregory's counsel. Gregory's reply to his fourth question, whether two brothers could marry two sisters, was short and to the point: such a marriage was lawful and there was nothing in holy writ which would appear to contradict this. But in the fifth of the *Responsiones* concerning prohibited degrees of marriage a more complicated issue was raised. Latest research has discerned what is concluded to be an interpolation by the editor of the text, the priest Nothelm, when he supplied Bede in the eighth century with a copy of the *Responsiones,* for inclusion in his history, from the *scrinium* in Rome.[8] This additional material raised the doubts of Boniface, archbishop of Mainz, and questioning the Gregorian authorship he wrote in 735 to Nothelm, who had now become archbishop of Canterbury, about the matter for it would appear that he possessed the *Interrogationes et Responsiones* contained in Bede's history.[9] Inquiries which Augustine made concerning regulations relating to ceremonial purity were replied to at some length in eight and nine of the *Responsiones.* Critical examination of these has arrived at the conclusion that 'It seems much more probable that these are discourses given at Canterbury.'[10] These inquiries made by Augustine must be set in the context of the pastoral and administrative problems which would of necessity arise among the thousands of converts to the Christian Faith who were members of the newly founded Church of the English people. Even the problem of theft from the Church had become so acute that Augustine consulted Gregory by asking the question 'What punishment should be inflicted if anyone steals anything from the Church?' In the third of the *Responsiones* the pope replied in some detail informing him that the standing of the thief would indicate how he ought to be corrected. Some, though they have substance, commit theft while others transgress in this way through want. It is necessary, therefore, that some be corrected with fines, others with stripes, some with more severity and others more mildly. But the measure of correction should not go beyond the rule of reason. Moreover, those who have committed the theft should make restitution to the Church of the things they have stolen. When this restitution is made the Church should neither receive back more than the value of the stolen property nor make any gain out of the apparent losses.[11]

It is probable that in the newly founded Church the operation of this law was antecedent to the laws promulgated by King Aethelbert during Augustine's metropolitanate. The first of his laws dealt with the property of the Church in the following terms: 'The property of God and the Church (shall be restored) twelve-fold; a bishop's property, eleven-fold; a priest's property, nine-fold; a deacon's property, six-fold; a clerk's property, three-fold; "church-frith," two-fold; "minster-frith," two-fold.'[12]

A closer examination of the inquiries of Augustine submitted to Gregory shows that all of them in varying measure involved some question of law. It may be assumed that Augustine and his monks on coming to Britain carried with them, in addition to the Scriptures and liturgical books, a collection of the canons and decretals of the Church with which to administer the Church they hoped to establish. Towards the end of the fifth and beginning of the sixth century Dionysius Exiguus, a Scythian monk, compiled the most important collection of canons and decretals of all the collections made in Rome. His collection *Dionysiana* was the first important attempt in western Europe to provide the Church with a uniform system of law.[13] Gregory's *Responsiones* imply the operation of the law and in some instances the delivery of judgments by Augustine.[14] These judgments would inevitably be based on the *Dionysiana,* a corpus of law known to both Gregory and Augustine, by which the new Church in England was governed by its metropolitan bishop at Canterbury. To some extent, therefore, Gregory's replies were confirmatory of Augustine's judgments and interpretations of the *Dionysiana.* That Augustine was in possession of and used the *Dionysiana* appears to be confirmed by the council of Hertford in 672 over which Archbishop Theodore presided and produced a book of canons which may have been the *Dionysiana.* From this book the council adopted ten canons all of which are based on canons contained in the *Dionysiana.*[15] It would appear, therefore, that it was this corpus of Church law which Augustine and his successors for seventy years after his death had used.

No record has survived relating to the operation of ecclesiastical law upon any specific case during Augustine's metropolitanate. But there is every reason to believe that, although Church courts as such were not at this period constituted in the missionary Church, Augustine, as abbot of the monastery in chapter or as head of his *familia* in council, considered grave transgressions of canon law. This had its counterpart, as Bede records, when Aethelbert established 'with the advice of his counsellors judicial decrees after the example of the Romans.'[16] This was probably the first witenagemot in English history although this word is not used to describe the king's meeting with his counsellors. Here then was the parallel emergence of Church law in the missionary Church and secular law for the whole of Aethelbert's territories, but probably effectively operative only in the kingdom of Kent. From these beginnings of the Church in Kent, as it expanded and increased its power, gradually developed Church courts.

To the canon law were added papal directives which had the force of law and were issued when circumstances required them. This was to be seen in Augustine's time when there arose the problem of providing churches in which the multitude of converts could worship. The pope wrote to Aethelbert and urged him to be zealous for the

conversion of his subjects and pressed upon him the urgency of
destroying idols and heathen temples. 'Hasten to spread the Christian
Faith among your subjects,' wrote Gregory, 'increase your righteous
zeal for their conversion, suppress the worship of idols, cast down the
buildings of their temple.' [17] After the bearers of this letter, accompanied by additional workers, chief of whom were Mellitus, Justus,
Paulinus and Rufinianus, had left Rome, Gregory wrote a letter and
sent it by special messenger to Mellitus as he journeyed northwards
to Britain. In this letter he requested Mellitus to inform 'Our most
reverend brother, Bishop Augustine,' of his second thoughts concerning
the question of the heathen temple. 'Tell him I have decided after
long deliberation that the idol temples of the English ought not to be
destroyed but only the idols. Let consecrated water be sprinkled in
the temples, altars erected and relics placed there for, if the temples
are well built they should be converted from the worship of devils
to the service of the true God.' [18] Augustine did not hesitate to act
in accordance with the direction given by Gregory in which Aethelbert
gave his practical support. The heathen temple in which the king
had worshipped outside the walls of Canterbury, after its idols had
been destroyed, was converted in the ritual required by the pope into
a Christian church and dedicated by Augustine in the name of
St. Pancras the Martyr.[19] Nearby this church and outside the city
walls to the east Augustine initiated the building of a monastery of
which Peter, the priest, became the first abbot. It was first known as
St. Peter's and later as St. Augustine's, within which, on Augustine's
advice, Aethelbert began the erection of the church of St. Peter and
St. Paul to which he made large gifts. Here it was intended to bury
the metropolitan bishops of Canterbury and the kings of Kent. This
church was not completed in the lifetime of Augustine but on its
completion was consecrated by his successor, Laurentius.[20] Some time
before this, in the early days of the mission, near to the residence
assigned the missionaries by Aethelbert, Augustine had located the
remains of a church within the walls of the city which had been in
use in Roman-British times. With the king's permission and help the
church was rebuilt and dedicated in the name of the Saviour our God
and Lord Jesus Christ—Christ Church—which was the most important church in the city of Canterbury.[21] Another church of Roman-
British origin, St. Martin's, was already in use as the chapel where
Queen Bertha's chaplain, Bishop Liudhard, said mass some years
before the arrival of Augustine in Kent.[22] Augustine also witnessed
the foundations being laid for the church of St. Andrew in Rochester
about twenty-four miles west of Canterbury where Bishop Justus had
his *cathedra*.

In the reconstruction of some churches and the erection of others, in Canterbury, London and Rochester, is to be seen how closely the secular power in the person of Aethelbert co-operated in every possible way to consolidate the work of the newly founded Church under the guiding hand of Augustine. Roman-British remains in the churches of St. Martin and St. Pancras would undoubtedly have been of stone, and it is reasonable to assume that the monastic church of St. Peter and St. Paul and Christ Church would have been erected in no less durable materials. Provision of such a permanent character for Christian worship in Canterbury indicates something of the mind of Augustine. He planned for the continuance of his *cathedra,* as metropolitan bishop, remaining in the royal and metropolitan city of Canterbury irrespective of the constitution laid down in the Gregorian plan by which, in the south, London should be the see city of the metropolitan bishop.

In the extension of the missionary work it was the restraints of the political situation rather than any lack of zeal on the part of the adherents to the newly established Church which made it necessary for Augustine to delay the evangelization of the East Saxons until Aethelbert indicated that the time was opportune. Having consecrated Mellitus bishop in 604 he was commissioned by Augustine to preach the 'Word of Truth' in the province of the East Saxons. So successful were the immediate efforts of this missionary bishop that Aethelbert built in the city of London a church dedicated in the name of St. Paul the Apostle in which Mellitus and his successors should have their episcopal seat.[23]

In this phase of the expansion of the Church it is significant that both Justus for Rochester and Mellitus for the East Saxons were consecrated bishops by Augustine, thus giving to each in his respective missionary enterprise episcopal authority and consequently a greater independence than that which he himself possessed on his arrival in Kent. The order in which Augustine consecrated Laurentius, Mellitus and Justus can only be a matter of surmise. Bede mentions first the consecration of Laurentius and then the consecration of Mellitus and Justus, probably at the same time, but it would be unwise to attach any chronological order to his record of these consecrations.[24] But now an unprecedented situation had arisen since Bishop Liudhard had died, by which the continuance of the episcopate in the Catholic tradition in Britain could only be assured by Augustine himself being the sole consecrator. Augustine therefore proceeded to consecrate Laurentius in order that he should succeed him in the metropolitan see, 'lest on his death the state of the Church, so far untried, should begin to falter if destitute of a pastor but for an hour.'[25]

In recording Augustine's consecration of Laurentius it is apparent

that Bede was conscious of it being uncanonical, and justified
Augustine's action by referring to the tradition that St. Peter consecrated Clement to be his assistant and at the same time his successor
at Rome.

By his consecration of Laurentius, Mellitus and Justus the episcopal
constitution of the southern province began to take shape in accordance with the Gregorian plan. In his lifetime, however, he had only
three suffragan bishops. There was no diocesan system in the modern
sense of the term but each bishop was the head and leader of a
missionary centre or station from which to evangelize the people within
the territory or kingdom over which he had the pastoral care. Bishop
Mellitus had his centre in his see city London, the capital of the
kingdom of Essex over which the sub-king Saberht ruled. Similarly
Bishop Justus exercised his missionary activities from his see city of
Rochester. The founding of this bishopric, not far distant from
Canterbury, may indicate the former existence of a separate kingdom
of the West Kentings. Kent at this period 'was the most civilized, and
probably the most populous, of all the English kingdoms.' [26]
Thousands of the people in Kent had been converted to the Christian Faith, and it is reasonable to assume that a bishop would be
required at Rochester in order fully to organize and establish Church
life among the numerous converts in a populous area. Although the
boundaries were ill-defined of these kingdoms, the territory of each
bishopric at this time was regarded as co-extensive with the kingdom
in which its see city was situated.

During the last year of his metropolitanate Augustine adopted
realistic measures for the consolidation, continuance and expansion of
the Catholic Church within the territories over which Aethelbert had
sovereignty. Augustine's consecration of Laurentius assured the continuance and consolidation of the newly founded Church's activities
in the see city of Canterbury and the kingdom of Kent, while the consecration of Mellitus and Justus as missionary bishops provided for
the expansion of the Church in unevangelized territory, especially in
Essex. This mission to the East Saxons headed by Bishop Mellitus
evidently had the encouragement and support of Aethelbert as is
shown by his royal munificence in founding the church of St. Paul
in London. There is every reason to believe that Mellitus did not
delay after his consecration but journeyed forthwith into Essex there
to begin preaching the Christian Faith. Since Augustine died in 604
or early in 605 he must have lived long enough to see the firstfruits
of the East Saxons in the conversion of the sub-king Saberht and
some of his people as the first members of the Catholic Church in
Essex.[27] At the time of his death, therefore, the conversion of the
English people, for which he had been commissioned and sent to

Britain by Pope Gregory I, was still proceeding under Mellitus while the consolidation of the newly founded Church was under the guidance of Justus at Rochester and Laurentius at Canterbury.

In making any assessment of the founding of the Catholic Church in Kent and the metropolitan see of Canterbury it cannot be separated from Augustine himself, the leader of the mission to the English people. He possessed no great gifts of leadership and when power was placed in his hands he lacked the wisdom to use it to the best advantage of the Catholic Church. On meeting the bishops and other representatives of the British Church in synod it was not only their determination to preserve the historic traditions of their Church but also his authoritative demeanour, as metropolitan bishop, which contributed to their total rejection of his overtures, despite the simplicity of his appeal for them to join with him in preaching the Christian Faith to the English people. After his failure with the British Church it would appear that he perceived his own limitations. His supreme gifts lay in pioneer missionary work, and even his ignorance of the language of the people was not allowed to impede his labours. Evidence of these distinctive gifts were to be seen in the persuasive and convincing eloquence with which he preached the Christian Faith before Aethelbert and his courtiers. After the king's acceptance of the Faith his example and influence gave such a momentum to the missionary work of Augustine and his workers that when writing to the pope he was able to inform him of the baptism of ten thousand converts. By his devoted and self-sacrificing labours the Catholic Church was firmly established in Kent with its metropolitan see at Canterbury. He made no effort to remove his *cathedra* from Canterbury in order to conform to the plan of Pope Gregory I by which the *cathedra* of the metropolitan bishopric should be in London, even though London had become the see city of Bishop Mellitus. Canterbury was the royal and capital city of the territories over which Aethelbert ruled and it had now become the established centre of the newly founded Church's organisation. Moreover, he had consecrated Laurentius as his successor so that the Church which was still 'untried' would not be without episcopal leadership and care even for an hour. In such circumstances Augustine realized that any attempt to transfer the metropolitan see to London, which would have meant removing it from the immediate influence and support of Aethelbert, would have weakened the Church and jeopardized its future. Augustine's burial near the unfinished church of St. Peter and St. Paul and later the interment of his remains in the north porch of the church sealed for all time the city of Canterbury as the see city of the metropolitan bishop.[28] Throughout successive centuries the metropolitan see of Canterbury experienced ecclesiastical and political assaults upon its authority and location but its survival to the present time indicates how well its foundations were laid by its first metropolitan bishop Augustine.

THE GREGORIAN PLAN IMPLEMENTED BY CANTERBURY

During the eight years of Augustine's metropolitanate at Canterbury there gradually emerged a mutual understanding and trust between him and King Aethelbert which contributed immeasurably to the successful mission of the Catholic Church.[1] This was in reality the beginning of the relationship between Church and State in England which has continued in various forms down to the present day except for the disruptive period during the Commonwealth. The dependence of the Church upon secular power, in the person of the king, was to be seen when Aethelbert gave his permission to Abbot Augustine and his missionary band to remain in his kingdom for, without that permission, any attempt to evangelize would have proved futile. Aethelbert's willingness with his courtiers to hear Augustine preach the evangel further indicates how dependent the missionaries were upon the goodwill of the king, who knew something about the Christian religion from his wife, Queen Bertha. They were also dependent upon the king for accommodation and food which he provided for them in his royal city of Canterbury until the Church was sufficiently self-supporting to maintain Augustine and his workers. After his acceptance of the Christian Faith the king generously founded churches and made provision for their maintenance. Canons for Church government and administration which Augustine had carried with him from Rome were applied by him with such good effect on the thousands of converts in the newly founded Church that it inspired Aethelbert to compile a code of laws for his people. A significant feature of these laws, promulgated by the king in Augustine's lifetime, is that the first law is concerned with the protection of the bishops and clergy and the property of the Church.[2]

While it would be difficult to determine the extent to which the Church was dependent upon the influence and support of the king during the metropolitanate of Augustine, it is evident that Augustine, himself, had doubts about the inherent strength and stability of the Church in Kent. The Church had not yet been tested outside the protecting influence of Aethelbert. In consequence, Augustine had consecrated Laurentius to be his coadjutor and successor so that the Church, for even one hour, would not be without the guiding hand of a spiritual leader and pastor. Future events proved the foresight of Augustine to be correct.

Under the wise direction of Bishop Laurentius the see of Canter-

bury was considerably strengthened by building truly upon the foundations laid by Augustine. Remarkable success also attended the efforts
of Bishop Mellitus in the evangelization of the East Saxons after
Saberht had accepted the Christian Faith. At the same time the work
of the Church was more firmly established by Bishop Justus in the
bishopric of Rochester. At this juncture the successful administration
and expansion of the newly founded Church provided the opportunity
for Laurentius with his two suffragans to initiate measures for bringing
the Scotic and British Churches into union with the Catholic Church.

Having been visited by a certain Bishop Dagan from Ireland he had
learned that the Scottic Church possessed the same traditions and
followed the same practices as the British Church, which had rejected
Augustine's overtures for unity. Such was the hostility against the
Catholic Church that on visiting Canterbury he refused to eat with
Laurentius and his suffragans.[3] There can be little doubt that Mellitus
and Justus as they journeyed through Gaul in 601 heard of the
controversy in which Abbot Columban was involved with the Gallican
clergy because of his support of the Celtic Easter and tonsure.[4] The
expression of dismay on the part of the three bishops, in their letter
to the bishops and abbots of the Scotic Church, at Bishop Dagan's
information concerning the practices of the Scotic Church and his
open hostility to them, may have been a conciliatory gesture by which
they strove to make a more tactful approach for Catholic unity.
A similar letter was also addressed to the British bishops in an effort
to bring them into conformity with the Catholic Church. This
approach by the three Catholic bishops was completely rejected as
were Augustine's earlier overtures. Perplexed by the obduracy of the
Celtic Church, Laurentius, following the example of his predecessor,
turned to the pope for counsel, and commissioned Bishop Mellitus to
visit Rome. At the time of the arrival of Mellitus in Rome in 610
a synod of the bishops of Italy had been convoked.[5] Bishop Mellitus
joined the synod and its agenda included the problems which confronted the Church of the English people. It is most probable that the
difficulties created by the persistent refusal of the Celtic Church to
accept the Catholic observance of Easter came under review. Elmham
explicitly says the object of the visit of Mellitus to Rome was to
obtain papal privileges for the monastery of Christ Church.[6] Because
of the doubtful validity of the decree and documents purporting to
have been issued by this council some doubt has been cast on the
council as a whole, and particularly so because it seems that Bede is
the only authority for recording this council. [7] Even the letter purporting to have been sent by Pope Boniface IV to Aethelbert does
not escape suspicion,[8] while other documents concerned with the

claims of the primacy of the see of Canterbury are characteristic of a later period.[9]

However, there is no reason to doubt the record relating to one item of business which Mellitus brought before the council concerning the official ministry of the Church. Augustine, after his consecration, continued to live in accordance with the requirements of his monastic order, as advised by Pope Gregory I, but his *familia* in addition to monks included secular clergy. Laurentius had not been cucullated but from the priesthood had been consecrated bishop by Augustine. While it could not be said that Laurentius was predisposed in favour of the secular clergy, his action in ordaining monks to the priesthood caused much jealousy and dissension. Although his predecessor Augustine, both monk and bishop, provided a good precedent for ordaining monks to the priesthood it did not put an end to or diminish the rivalries between the clergy and monks. The situation was made more acute by the new monastery of St. Peter and St. Paul which was nearing completion at Canterbury. On returning from Rome, Bishop Mellitus was the bearer of letters to Laurentius and all the clergy, and to Aethelbert and the English nation from Pope Boniface IV. The letter to Laurentius has not survived but it would appear that the pope fully approved of the action of Laurentius in ordaining monks to the priesthood. No reference is to be found of Mellitus bringing the *pallium* to England for Laurentius nor is any mention made of the pope conferring it upon the metropolitan bishop of Canterbury, but, doubtless, Laurentius did receive the *pallium* from Pope Boniface IV.

Soon after the return of Mellitus the monastery of St. Peter and St. Paul founded by Aethelbert was consecrated in 613 by Bishop Laurentius and shortly after the remains of Augustine were removed from the grave outside the church and re-interred in the north porch of the monastery where, says Bede, all his successors were interred with the exception of Theodore and Berhtwald. Within three years Aethelbert was laid to rest in the church which he had founded. By his death was brought to a close the opening chapter in the history of the beginning and expansion of the Catholic Church in England, which was now to be tried and tested as never before by hostile forces.

On the accession of Eadbald, Aethelbert's son, the whole climate of the existence of the Church rapidly deteriorated. Eadbald had refused to embrace the Christian Faith and openly demonstrated his adherence to pagan practices by marrying his late father's wife.[10] Those who 'either for favour or from fear of King Aethelbert' had been baptized into the Catholic Church quickly followed the new king's example and lapsed into their former pagan beliefs and practices. The imme-

diate effect of this not only militated against the work and witness
of the Church in Canterbury but also extended to Rochester where
Bishop Justus had been diligently labouring to bring the people into a
full acceptance of the Christian Faith.

Later in the same year in which Aethelbert had died or early in
617 King Saberht of the East Saxons died and his three sons inherited
the kingdom.[11] They professed and followed their pagan beliefs and
granted freedom to the people, who had professed the Christian Faith,
to return to their former paganism. People who firmly adhered to the
Catholic Church were observed regularly practising their religion by
receiving the holy eucharist. Seeing this, the sons of Saberht required
Bishop Mellitus to administer the sacrament to them although they
had not been baptized. On being met with a definite refusal by the
bishop they angrily ordered him with his followers to leave their kingdom. On his expulsion, Mellitus returned to Canterbury in order to
confer with his fellow-bishops Laurentius and Justus. Bede makes no
mention of Augustine bringing his three suffragan bishops Laurentius,
Mellitus and Justus together in synod, but now was held the first
English provincial synod, not convoked by the metropolitan, Laurentius, but assembled by the urgent compulsions in the threat of the
newly founded Church being confronted by the hostility of kings,
and the return of many people, who had professed the Christian
Faith, to paganism. There was only one matter before this synod,
namely, what should they do in this entirely new and tragic situation?
All three bishops agreed that it would be better for them to return
to their own country there to serve God with a free mind than to
remain to no purpose among barbarians who had renounced the
Christian Faith.[12] Without delay both Bishop Mellitus and Bishop
Justus crossed over to France intending to await there the outcome
of events. Bishop Laurentius was about to leave Britain, following
Mellitus and Justus, but the night before his planned departure,
according to Bede's account, he was visited by St. Peter who scourged
him and with apostolic sternness asked him why he was forsaking
the flock which he had committed to him or to what shepherd was
he leaving Christ's sheep who were in the midst of wolves? Bishop
Laurentius in the morning visited King Eadbald telling him of his
vision and showing the scars of the scourging. Deeply stirred at the
sight and alarmed when he heard from the bishop the details of his
sufferings at the hands of St. Peter, the king cursed all idolatrous
worship, renounced his unlawful marriage and accepted the Christian
Faith. After being baptized Eadbald did his utmost to advance the
well-being of the Church. Not only did he give every support to
Laurentius at Canterbury but he also concerned himself with the
missionary work of the Church which had been initiated with the

encouragement of his father, by sending to France and bidding both Justus and Mellitus to return to their bishoprics. By the time they returned they had been absent from their sees a year and although Bishop Justus was able actively to renew the work of the Church at Rochester, chiefly because it was territory under the direct rule of Eadbald, Mellitus found himself confronted with insurmountable difficulties in London. After Bishop Mellitus had fled from his bishopric the whole of Essex had been overrun by the Gewisse or West Saxons. Eadbald had never been able to exercise the same authority over the East Saxons as his father had done and now that the West Saxons had occupied the territory his power there had become ineffectual. The people of London, in particular, refused to allow Mellitus to return to his see city, and Eadbald's efforts were of no avail against the pagans who opposed the bishop's return.

The renewal of the work and witness of the Church in Kent under the guidance of Laurentius, made possible by the king's support, was further strengthened in the metropolitan see city of Canterbury by the king's foundation and erection of the church of St. Mary, which was dedicated later during the metropolitanate of Bishop Mellitus. Since Mellitus was unable to enter his bishopric it is most probable that he journeyed to Canterbury in order to consult his metropolitan bishop, Laurentius, and remained there to assist in the work of the Church in the city and its environs. Despite the additional help of Mellitus ministering among the people there is no evidence that the Church was able to extend its work even in Kent where Eadbald exercised a Christian influence and gave his support. Indeed, when Bishop Laurentius died in 619 and was succeeded by Mellitus the Catholic Church in England was in a precarious condition. Encouraged by letters from the pope, Mellitus laboured diligently notwithstanding his physical disability caused by gout.[13] The erection of St. Mary's Church within the monastery of St. Peter and St. Paul was a tangible expression of the king's goodwill towards the Church and of the pious hopes of Mellitus who dedicated it.

There is no record of Mellitus receiving the *pallium* nor of his consecration of bishops. When he died in 624, Bishop Justus without delay moved from his bishopric of Rochester to Canterbury and assumed metropolitan authority, afterwards consecrating Romanus to succeed him at Rochester.

A letter purporting to have been addressed to Justus by Pope Boniface V makes reference to letters received from Eadbald and to the influence of the bishop who brought the king to the acceptance of the Christian Faith. It is evident from the contents of the letter that it is composite and includes at least parts of two letters written on separate occasions and probably by two different persons. The

first part of the letter is addressed to more than one person giving
to them words of encouragement and exhortation. In the second
part of the letter one person is addressed throughout, and it is
evident that the writer is Pope Boniface V, who informs Bishop
Justus that he has sent him the *pallium* for 'use in the celebration
of the sacred mysteries; and granting you likewise the ordination of
bishops when occasion shall arise.' [14] Having received the *pallium*
from Pope Boniface V Justus was thereby confirmed in the office,
to which he had moved from Rochester, of metropolitan bishop of
Canterbury.

Although much progress in the work and witness of the Church
could not be made in Kent, Justus was ever watchful for an opportunity to extend the missionary work of the Church in territories where
the people had not accepted the Christian Faith. Such an occasion
arose when a marriage was arranged between Aethelberga, the sister
of Eadbald, king of Kent, and King Edwin of Northumbria. King
Edwin was not a Christian but he pledged himself to give every
facility for Aethelberga and her companions to practise their religion
and also to consider becoming a Christian himself. Having been
assured that there would be no hostility shown to the Christian religion
but rather a favourable regard for it because of Aethelberga, Justus
consecrated Paulinus bishop to accompany the future queen and to be
her chaplain in Northumbria.[15] By this action Justus took positive
measures to implement the plan of Pope Gregory I to send a bishop
to the northern parts of Britain who should have his seat in the city
of York. Many months were to elapse before King Edwin was converted to the Christian Faith, but on the eve of Easter in 627, with
many of his people, he was baptized by Bishop Paulinus in a wooden
church which the king had built in York. In this city of York Edwin
appointed Paulinus, his 'teacher and bishop,' his episcopal seat.
Tangible evidence of the increasing strength of Christianity in
Northumbria was to be seen by the king's initiation of the erection of
a stone built church to replace the wooden structure in which he had
been baptized.

Paulinus in his evangelizing efforts extended the work of the
Church, beyond the kingdoms of Bernicia and Deira, southwards
across the river Humber into the territory of Lindsey over which King
Edwin ruled as overlord. The mission of Bishop Paulinus was so
successful that Blaecca, the governor *praefectus* of the city of
Lincoln, and his family were converted to the Christian Faith. Before
the year 627 ended a stone church was erected in Lincoln, which was
the chief city of Lindsey.

At that time Bishop Romanus of Rochester was sent by Justus on a
mission to Pope Honorius I, most probably to inform him of the

success of the Church in Northumbria. From this mission to Rome Romanus never returned for he was drowned at sea. In Kent, however, the work of the Church was static and any progress was most difficult. Undaunted, however, the missionary zeal and initiative of Justus had brought into being, in relation to the north, what Pope Gregory I had envisaged in his letter to Augustine setting forth the constitution of the Catholic Church in Britain. 'We desire,' wrote Gregory, 'you to send to the city of York a bishop whom you shall determine to ordain; yet, so that if that city with the adjoining places shall receive the Word of God, he also is to ordain twelve bishops and to enjoy the dignity of metropolitan, because, if we shall live we design, by the favour of God, upon him also to bestow the *pallium*.' [16] Augustine had been able to extend the Church in Kent and Essex, but later political changes revealed how insecure were the foundations of the new church. Neither Laurentius nor Mellitus was able to do little more than consolidate the work and witness of the Church still weak in Kent, and the major part of the episcopate of Justus at Canterbury was concerned with maintaining the life of the Church. His great achievement, however, was to seize the opportunity of sending a Christian mission to Northumbria when the marriage had been arranged between the Christian princess, Aethelberga of Kent and Edwin, king of Northumbria. In appointing the city of York for the seat of Bishop Paulinus, King Edwin in reality revived a bishopric of which York had been its see city in the fourth century.[17] On this occasion, however, the succession was not of British bishops who formerly occupied the see, but a new line of succession was begun by Paulinus of the Roman tradition in conformity with the Gregorian plan.

When Justus died in 627 the Catholic Church was making great progress under the guidance of Paulinus throughout the territories of King Edwin from whom he received the fullest support. Justus was the only surviving bishop in Kent after the death of Romanus of Rochester, and when Justus died Paulinus of York was the sole survivor of the episcopate of the Catholic Church in Britain.

One of the original company of missionaries who landed in Kent with Augustine or one of the later company, which included Justus, Mellitus and Paulinus sent by Pope Gregory I to strengthen the mission, named Honorius, was still alive. There is no ground for the statement made by one writer, that Honorius was sent from Rome in 628.[18] Bede identifies Honorius quite explicitly and describes him as 'one of the disciples of the blessed Pope Gregory, a man eminently instructed in ecclesiastical matters.' [19] Bishop Paulinus, in establishing the work of the Church in Lindsey, evidently made the city of Lincoln the centre of his missionary activities, and it was to this city that

Honorius journeyed in order to acquaint Paulinus with the grave situation which now confronted the Church in Kent owing to the death of Justus. Immediate measures were taken by Paulinus so that the Church in Kent would not be without episcopal leadership, and in the same year 627 in the newly erected church in Lincoln he consecrated Honorius metropolitan bishop of Canterbury.[20] During the early years of his metropolitanate, not on his initiative but later with his active co-operation, Christianity spread throughout East Anglia. Sigeberht, who had lived in exile in France where he had been baptized, had succeeded to the throne in East Anglia and, recognizing the metropolitan authority of Bishop Honorius, asked him for help in establishing the Catholic Church in his kingdom. Honorius sent Felix a Burgundian, who may have been consecrated bishop in France and known to Sigeberht. Sigeberht desired to set up good institutions similar to those he had seen in France, and established a school in which boys were instructed in letters, being assisted in this by Bishop Felix. On entering England Felix went to Canterbury and submitted himself to Honorius who commissioned him if already a bishop, but more probably consecrated him and then sent him to East Anglia where King Sigeberht gave Felix Dunwich to be the seat of his bishopric.

The extension of the Catholic Church in Sigeberht's kingdom and the specific work accomplished by Felix in the school established by the king reveals the progressive work of the Church in Kent during this period. As the Church's educational activities developed in East Anglia Felix obtained teachers and masters from Canterbury to give instruction after the 'manner of the Cantuarians.' [21] Since no reference to the Church's development of education in Kent is to be found before this, it shows that one of the major contributions to the life of the Church made by the metropolitan Honorius was the development of the educational side of the Church's work to such an extent that it was able to supply teachers and masters for the Church in another part of Britain. From the beginnings of the missionary labours of Felix in East Anglia in 631 until late 632 or early in 633, for the first time in the history of the Catholic Church in Britain, two metropolitan bishops, Honorius of Canterbury and Paulinus of York, in their respective areas laboured with unparalleled wisdom and vigour by their leadership to extend the teaching of the Christian Faith among the English people. Bishop Paulinus, receiving every support from King Edwin throughout his territories, baptized converts as far south in the river Trent at Littleborough in Nottinghamshire and as far north in the river Swale in Northumbria.

It was extremely difficult to consolidate the work of evangelism so widely spread and in consequence the Christian Faith had but a tenuous hold on the people, which resulted in a lack of strength and stability in the Church to enable it to withstand any sudden hostility or change in the political situation. A change of this character arose suddenly in 632 when Edwin was slain in the battle of Hatfield and the combined forces of Penda, king of Mercia, and Cadwallon, king of North Wales, defeated his armies and devastated Northumbria.[22] For the safety of Queen Aethelberga, her children and himself, Paulinus fled with them by sea, and were safely conducted by a thegn of the late king to the court of the queen's brother, Eadbald, king of Kent. In his flight from Northumbria Paulinus had vacated his metropolitan bishopric of York. Soon after his arrival in Kent, Bishop Honorius, metropolitan of Canterbury, with the concurrence of King Eadbald, appointed him to the see of Rochester which had been vacant since the death of Romanus.[23]

CANTERBURY AND THE CELTIC CHURCH

One of the last acts of King Edwin before the battle of Hatfield was to address a petition to Pope Honorius I requesting him to bestow the *pallium* upon Paulinus. At the same time King Eadbald of Kent also petitioned the pope for the bestowal of the *pallium* on Honorius of Canterbury. It would appear that the two kings acted together in this matter and made a joint approach to the pope. From the terms of the pope's reply it is evident that he was not aware that Edwin had been slain and that Paulinus had fled from York, for he informed Edwin that he had sent a *pallium* to each of the metropolitans, Honorius and Paulinus, and also congratulated him on his conversion to the Christian Faith.[1] In the same year, 634, the pope sent a letter to Honorius together with the two *pallia* to which he had made reference in his letter to Edwin. These two letters were undoubtedly issued at the same time and were carried by the same messengers to Britain. They both contain the same information and directions concerning the use of the *pallium,* which is referred to as the symbol of papal authority bestowing upon the recipient the delegated authority of the pope which enabled him to consecrate bishops. Because of the distance from Rome a papal directive was also given that if one of the metropolitans should die then the survivor possessed full authority to consecrate a successor to the vacant metropolitan bishopric. Pope Honorius I, in giving this directive, conformed to that which Pope Gregory I had given in his *Responsiones* to Augustine, in which he said that since Augustine was the only bishop of the Catholic Church in Britain he could not do otherwise than consecrate a bishop in the absence of other bishops, although ordinarily a consecration should not take place without the presence of three or four bishops.[2]

The significance of the *pallium* may here be observed since it arrived for Paulinus after he had vacated the metropolitan see of York. By his reception of the *pallium,* Paulinus who was now bishop of Rochester and a suffragan of Bishop Honorius, metropolitan of Canterbury, did not receive metropolitan authority because he was no longer in occupation of his metropolitan see. Augustine was the first bishop in Britain to receive the *pallium,* and in bestowing it upon him Pope Gregory I granted it for use only at the mass, but in the letter conferring it he spoke also of the consecration of bishops. Although it is not clearly expressed in so many words, it is evident that Gregory, in bestowing it, confirmed Augustine's authority as a metropolitan bishop to consecrate bishops for his own province and by implication full authority to discharge all the functions attaching to the office of metropolitan bishop. Pope Boniface V clarified the position in sending the *pallium* to Justus of Canterbury for, in the letter accompanying it, he gave permission for Justus to use it in the 'celebration of the holy mysteries,' and continued with the words 'also granting to you the ordinations of bishops.'[3] At this period the metropolitan bishop in Britain who received the *pallium* understood quite clearly that authority was derived from the pope and that it was the visible symbol of the possession of that authority. For Paulinus, therefore, the *pallium* which he had received was the symbol of an office and authority upon which he had turned his back and forsaken when he fled from his see. No second opportunity occurred for Bishop Honorius to send a missionary bishop to the north nor was Paulinus able to return to his see of York. When stable government had been established in Northumbria by King Oswald he adopted measures for the evangelization of his people by seeking a bishop from the isle of Iona where, during his days of exile, he had been taught the Christian Faith. By 635 Bishop Aidan of the Celtic Church with his band of monks, from the Iona monastery, had begun his missionary labours, having for his seat not the city of York but the isle of Lindisfarne.

Paulinus occupied the see of Rochester for eleven years and when he died in 644 Bede records 'in that church he left the *pallium* which he had received from the Roman pope.' Any plan which Honorius as metropolitan bishop of Canterbury may have had for reviving the metropolitan see of York by the return of Paulinus came to an end when Paulinus died, and any further attempt by Honorius to implement the Gregorian plan in Northumbria was precluded by Oswald's appointment of Aidan, whose missionary labours were remarkably effective. In East Anglia Bishop Felix, whom Honorius had commissioned, exercised a successful ministry in establishing the Catholic Church in the kingdom of King Sigeberht. On the death of Felix in 647 Honorius consecrated Thomas to succeed him but within five years Thomas died and Berctgils, surnamed Boniface, was consecrated to his see of Dunwich.[4] Honorius had already consecrated in 644 Ithamar for the bishopric of Rochester. By the consecration of Ithamar, Thomas and Berctgils, all of whom were natives of England, Honorius advanced the process of transforming more completely what was originally a mission from Rome into an indigenous Church of Britain. In the same year that Pope Honorius I recognized Bishop Honorius as the metropolitan of Canterbury by conferring upon him the *pallium* he appears to have acted in a manner which completely disregarded the bishop's metropolitan authority. Both in the letter addressed to King Edwin and in the one sent to Bishop Honorius the pope stated that he was sending two *pallia* for the metropolitans Honorius and Paulinus, and thereby set his seal of approval on the Gregorian plan for the constitution of the Church in Britain. Acting in a manner contrary to this plan and disregarding the metropolitan Honorius, the pope commissioned a certain Birinus for missionary work in Britain, and there is no evidence that he informed the bishop of his intention to send Birinus into his province. It may be urged that the pope was exercising his authority as patriarch of the West in much the same way as did his predecessor Pope Gregory I when he sent Augustine to Britain and Felix to Sardinia. On the latter occasion, however, Gregory, in accordance with his usual custom, first informed the metropolitan of Sardinia, Januarius, concerning the personnel and purpose of the mission led by Bishop Felix.[5]

Birinus, having pledged himself in the presence of the pope 'that he would sow the seed of the Holy Faith in the remotest inland regions of the English, where no teacher had preceded him,' was advised by the pope to go to Britain. He also advised Birinus to receive episcopal consecration from Asterius, the metropolitan of Milan, at the time resident in Genoa. On arriving on the south coast of Britain among the West Saxons, he found the people were pagans. Confronted with the necessity of preaching the Christian Faith to these people he remained among them and did not proceed farther inland. In complete independence of Honorius of Canterbury, Bishop Birinus initiated his evangelistic work as a missionary or regionary bishop with freedom to preach the Christian Faith in accordance with his pledge to the pope.[6] Birinus proved himself to be a gifted evangelist, and within a year of his arrival Cynegils, king of Wessex, was baptized and shortly after other members of his family accepted the Faith. Between the daughter of Cynegils and Oswald, the Christian king of Northumbria, a union had been effected and, united in family relationships, political interests and religion, the two kings jointly appointed Bishop Birinus his episcopal seat in Dorchester.[7] Cynegils' successor, King Cenwalh, having been baptized, founded a church at Winchester in 648 which Birinus consecrated. Two years later when Birinus died, he was succeeded by Bishop Agilbert, a native of France, who, after having studied in Ireland, visited the court of Cenwalh and was appointed by him to the see of Dorchester. It would appear that Agilbert, after ten years in Wessex, was unable to speak the language of the West Saxons, much to the king's dissatisfaction. In consequence Cenwalh brought into his kingdom Bishop Wini, who had been consecrated bishop in France and was able to speak the language of the West Saxons. In order that Wini should have a see he appointed Winchester for his see city, Agilbert remaining with his seat at Dorchester. Affronted by the king's action in dividing his bishopric, Agilbert withdrew from the see of Dorchester and went to Northumbria. In 664 he was present at the synod of Whitby and later, returning to France, became bishop of Paris.

While much progress was being made by the Catholic Church in Wessex the Celtic Church under Bishop Aidan's leadership extended its work of evangelization beyond the kingdom of Northumbria. Although the traditions and practices of the Celtic Church differed in some respects from those of the Catholic Church there was no open conflict between the two traditions. Perhaps the most evident of these differences was the date of the observance of Easter. In this particular respect the differing traditions were to be seen in the royal household of King Oswiu who, on the death of his brother Oswald in 641, had become king of Bernicia and later by force of arms had established himself king of Northumbria and overlord of the southern English people and the Mercians. Like his brother he followed the tradition of the Celtic Church whereas his wife, Eanfled, the daughter of King Edwin of Northumbria, who had been slain, had been nurtured in the Roman tradition at the court in Kent. In consequence, Easter was observed on two different dates in accordance with the two traditions at the court in Northumbria. During the lifetime of Aidan, however, the difference concerning the observance of Easter, as Bede records, 'was patiently tolerated by all.' [8] Honorius, the fourth metropolitan bishop of Canterbury in succession to Augustine, was, under the terms of the Gregorian plan, bishop of all Britain since York had not yet been constituted a metropolitan see. But within his extensive province the Celtic Church and the mission led by Bishop Birinus in Wessex were completely independent of his metropolitan authority. The only extension of the Church under the authority of the metropolitan see of Canterbury was the mission in East Anglia for which Bishop Honorius had commissioned Felix, who was given Dunwich for his seat by King Sigeberht.

Through the relationship which existed between the royal households of Kent and Northumbria, Honorius would have learned of the progress made by the Celtic Church under Aidan, and in consequence he held him in high esteem for his diligent and successful missionary labours, for Aidan's 'faith, piety and love' were widely known.[9] Under Aidan's leadership the Celtic Church was firmly established throughout the regions in which Bishop Paulinus of the Roman tradition had formerly laboured. This tradition, which had been growing weaker in the face of the missionary activities of the Celtic Church, received an infusion of strength by the presence of the Christian Queen Eanfled which acted as a moderating influence on the more extreme elements of the Celtic Church. As a result there gradually emerged a measure of toleration based on understanding and goodwill during

Aidan's lifetime, but when he died in 651 and was succeeded by Finan, the vigour with which the new bishop pursued his policies effectively destroyed much of the goodwill which existed.

The East Saxons, who had expelled Bishop Mellitus of the Roman tradition from their territory, were a generation later governed by King Sigeberht. Through his friendship with Oswiu, the Christian king of Northumbria, Sigeberht requested him to send missionaries to his territory. Oswiu sent to him Cedd and another priest from the Middle Angles, and when Sigeberht with many of his followers accepted the Christian Faith they were baptized by Bishop Finan. Cedd was later consecrated bishop by Finan and two other bishops to continue his work among the East Saxons, and he established centres of missionary activity at *Ythancaestir* and Tilbury.[10] Cedd is nowhere referred to as bishop of London, but throughout his life Cedd remained bishop to the East Saxons although, later in life, he retired to Lastingham where he founded a monastery on a site which he received from his friend Aethelwald, sub-king of Deira.

Throughout the continued expansion of the Celtic Church in Northumbria, among the Middle Angles and East Saxons, there is no evidence to show that, as metropolitan bishop, Honorius made any attempt to bring the Celtic Church into union with the Catholic Church. This was partly due to his recognition of the inherent weakness of the Catholic Church in Britain which made it impossible for him to speak from a position of strength and influence to the Celtic Church which was strong and ever increasing and expanding its missionary activities. It was due chiefly to the pattern of Church organization at this period. Bishops in Britain were not bishops of cities with dioceses as on the Continent. They exercised their episcopal ministry from a mission station within an area coterminous with the territory in which they were allowed to minister by the ruler. This situation created insuperable difficulties for Bishop Honorius. By the terms of the Gregorian plan for the constitution of the Church he was the metropolitan bishop of Britain. At this juncture, however, he was powerless to implement the plan in those territories where, with the support of the rulers, the Celtic Church was actively ministering among the people.

A similar situation existed in Wessex where the Catholic Church had been established in complete independence of the metropolitan Honorius. He must have been aware of the successful missionary labours and of the founding of the Catholic Church by Bishop Birinus among the West Saxons. There is no evidence to show that he endeavoured to co-operate with or to bring Birinus and his activities under the metropolitan authority of Canterbury. For the suggestion that, in sending Birinus to Britain without informing Bishop Honorius, the pope was administering a 'tacit rebuke' to the head of the Canterbury mission for his failure to bring the British bishops into union with the Catholic Church, there is no ground whatsoever.[11] In the same year when Birinus began his missionary labours in Wessex Pope Honorius I had conferred the dignity of the *pallium* upon the metropolitan Honorius. This badge of honour and delegated papal authority rules out any thought of a papal rebuke.

Pope Honorius I, when sending the *pallium* to Bishop Honorius, also sent one for Paulinus of York thereby showing that he had full knowledge of the Gregorian plan for the constitution of the Church in Britain. Despite the lack of the expansion of the Catholic Church from Canterbury it should not be assumed that it was inactive. No similar opportunity for expansion presented itself to Bishop Honorius as it had done to his predecessor, Justus, who had sent to Northumbria as chaplain to Aethelberga, Bishop Paulinus whose missionary labours abruptly came to an end when King Edwin was slain. A similar situation emerged, in some respects, seventeen years later when another princess, Eanfled, left the court at Canterbury and journeyed north to marry King Oswiu of Northumbria. But that is as far as the similarity goes. King Edwin was a pagan at the time of his marriage to Aethelberga, hence the opportunity for missionary enterprise seized by Bishop Justus. But King Oswiu had already accepted the Christian Faith before his marriage to Eanfled and he actively supported Bishop Finan of the Celtic Church in his territories. There was therefore no need for Honorius to send a missionary bishop to Northumbria which was under a Christian ruler and where the Celtic Church was established and expanding.

The counsel of Bishop Honorius, undoubtedly, would have been sought by King Eadbald when the proposed marriage of Eanfled and King Oswiu was under consideration, and this Christian king from the north could not have failed to have found much in common with Honorius although of differing Church traditions. At the court in Canterbury, Honorius, as metropolitan bishop in his own see city, had found a sphere of work and witness for the Catholic Church which, in addition to the immediate good, was destined to bear much fruit in later years. His diligent religious work at the royal court was not interrupted by the death of King Eadbald in 640, for his son Eorcenberht, who succeeded him, endeavoured to relate the teaching of the Catholic Church, of which he was a member, to the government of his kingdom. Augustine's administration of the Church which he founded in Kent was in accordance with the principles of canon law, and had without doubt influenced Aethelbert in his promulgation of laws for his territories in which he made provision for the protection of all members of the Church and its property.[12] King

Eorcenberht, however, was the first English king to enact laws enforc-
ing under penalty the relinquishing and destruction of idols throughout
his kingdom.[13] His laws also made compulsory the observance by his
people of the forty days' fast before Easter. No further details of the
code of laws enacted by Eorcenberht have survived with the exception of these two which relate to the development of the Catholic
Church.[14] A quarter of a century had elapsed since the people had
returned to paganism during the first year of Eadbald's reign, and a
new generation instructed in the Christian Faith, found remaining
in their homes the idols of their parents and elders. These idols were
now by law to be forsaken and destroyed.[15] King Eorcenberht's laws
had a twofold effect. First, the destruction of idols removed tangible
evidences of paganism and apostasy and, secondly, it strengthened
the new generation in its practice of the principles of the Christian
Faith in which they had been instructed by teachers from the schools
in Canterbury.[16]

Territorially, the authority of the metropolitan bishopric of Canterbury was limited to the confines of the kingdom of Kent, and the
area north of the Thames in East Anglia in which Bishop Berctgils
laboured. But its influence extended far beyond these limits. In
Northumbria the young Queen Eanfled worshipped in the Cantuarian
or Roman tradition. James the deacon, who remained in Northumbria
after the flight of Paulinus, in spite of his age still had the freedom
to teach the Christian Faith according to the Catholic tradition among
people who were under the episcopal rule of the Celtic Church. This
was possible through the tolerant attitude of King Oswiu towards
his queen's Church tradition—a toleration which, without doubt, he
had learned from the sagacious and tolerant Bishop Honorius when
visiting Canterbury.

Although Bishop Birinus had laboured in Wessex in complete
independence of the metropolitan of Canterbury there is reason to
believe that the influence of the metropolitan was no less strong in
Wessex than in Northumbria. This was partly attributable to the
friendly relationship which existed between the courts of Northumbria
and Wessex; for both King Oswald and King Cenwalh had appointed
Dorchester to be the see city for Bishop Birinus. This friendly relationship also extended to the court of Canterbury where King
Oswald's brother Oswiu found his future queen, Eanfled. These three
royal families contributed immeasurably to the religious tolerance
between the Catholic and Celtic Church in which Honorius had taken
an influential part. When the metropolitan Honorius died in 653
there were only two bishops who had been under his immediate
authority; Berctgils of Dunwich and Ithamar of Rochester. An
interregnum of eighteen months could not fail to impair the authority

of the metropolitan bishopric but, at the same time, it would appear that it was conducive to a more intimate understanding with the bishopric of Dorchester. Boundaries separating the two kingdoms of Kent and Wessex in no way impeded ecclesiastical relationships, and especially so since both kingdoms held the Catholic Faith. Indicative of the relationship which existed between the clergy was the significant fact that Frithonas, a priest who was a native of Wessex, was chosen to succeed to the vacant metropolitan see of Canterbury.[17] Bishop Ithamar alone consecrated Frithonas at Canterbury who on consecration took the name Deusdedit.[18] Little is recorded concerning the activities of Bishop Deusdedit beyond his consecration of Damian, a South Saxon, to succeed to the see of Rochester on the death of Bishop Ithamar. No longer did any member of the mission from Rome occupy the metropolitan bishopric nor, indeed, any other bishopric. Deusdedit and his two suffragans, Berctgils or Boniface and Damian, were natives of England. With its episcopate being drawn from the people of the land the Catholic Church in England had become for the first time truly indigenous and in consequence could hope for its further expansion. There was, however, no evidence of this during the metropolitanate of Deusdedit. Nevertheless, the Catholic Church received a new impetus as a result of the council or synod of Whitby in 664 over which Oswiu, king of Northumbria, presided. Since the chief business of the council was to decide whether Easter should be observed according to the tradition of the Celtic Church or the Catholic Church it might have been expected that Deusdedit, as metropolitan bishop of Canterbury, would have been in the forefront as the protagonist for the Catholic Church since Colman the leading Celtic bishop attended to present the claims of the Celtic Church. Many probable reasons may be advanced for his absence. Within a few months of the synod Deusdedit died and it may well have been that at the time of the synod he was unable to travel to Northumbria because of ill-health. Or again, did his central work of the Catholic Church in Canterbury, both ecclesiastical and educational, demand his continued presence in his bishopric? Consideration must also be given to the probability that Bishop Agilbert, after withdrawing from his see of Dorchester, went to reside in Canterbury and, with his knowledge of the schools in both France and Ireland, assisted bishop Deusdedit in the educational work of the Church. Possessing a widely known reputation for learning and experience in Church affairs, there is little doubt but that Agilbert was requested by Deusdedit to represent the Catholic Church at Whitby. Agilbert's inability freely to speak the native language was surmounted. He was accompanied by his brilliant pupil the priest, Wilfrid, who with outstanding eloquence convincingly presented the claims of the Catholic Church.

This great assembly of bishops, clergy and among others the Abbess Hilda, over which King Oswiu presided, was not a synod in the sense that the bishops and clergy were allowed to cast their votes on any matter which had been considered. It was a prolonged discussion which at times developed into a vehement debate, and did not exclude plausible arguments between the representatives of the two Church traditions—Celtic and Catholic. King Oswiu finally decided that the Roman or Cantuarian date for the observance of Easter should be followed and to this decision assent was given.[19] Bishop Colman, on realizing that the traditions and practices of the Celtic Church had been rejected in favour of the Roman observance of Easter, immediately vacated his see of Lindisfarne and journeyed northwards into Scotland accompanied by his supporters. It is significant that the Catholic tradition was soon implemented in Oswiu's territory when Tuda, a bishop consecrated among the southern Scots and resident in Northumbria, who observed the Catholic tradition, was appointed to succeed Bishop Colman.

As early as 656 Bishop Finan had consecrated Diuma bishop to the Mercians and Middle Angles over whose territories Oswiu was over-lord. On Diuma's death he was followed successively by Ceollach, Trumhere and Jaruman, who probably had their seat at Lichfield although in those parts no clearly defined diocesan boundaries had yet emerged. Both Trumhere and Jaruman had been consecrated by Scottic bishops and, like Tuda, observed the traditions of the Catholic Church. King Oswiu's influence, and that of his son Alhfrith, in establishing the Catholic Church tradition in his territories was to be seen still further in Wilfrid's nomination to the bishopric of York. Doubting the validity of consecration by bishops in England and probably wishing to be consecrated by his former tutor, Wilfrid visited France and received consecration at the hands of Agilbert and other bishops at Compiègne. His return to Northumbria to assume the duties of the bishopric of York was delayed by his stay in France and his being shipwrecked on his voyage home. Dissatisfied by the delay and probably influenced by those favourably disposed to the Celtic Church tradition Oswiu nominated the priest, Chad (the brother of Cedd of Lastingham) to the unoccupied see of York and sent him, accompanied by another priest, Eadhed, to Canterbury there to be consecrated by the metropolitan bishop Deusdedit. The king neither sent him to Bishop Jaruman at Lichfield, which was much nearer to York, nor did he send him to the senior bishop by consecration, Berctgils of Dunwich in East Anglia. The see of Rochester was more accessible than Canterbury where Bishop Damian was probably still alive. But to none of these three bishops was Chad sent. By sending Chad to Canterbury it is evident that King Oswiu's knowledge and recognition of the see during the metropolitanate of Honorius, at the time of his marriage to Princess Eanfled, had in no way diminished. Indeed by his royal direction for Chad to seek consecration at the hands of the metropolitan bishop Deusdedit Oswiu implicitly recognized the primacy and authority of the metropolitan see of Canterbury. On his arrival in Kent Chad found that Deusdedit had died and the see was vacant. He therefore journeyed into Wessex and received consecration at the hands of Bishop Wini of Winchester, and two British bishops who had accepted and observed the tradition of the Catholic Church.[20] Returning to York, Bishop Chad occupied his see and discharged the duties of his episcopal office with pastoral devotion and zeal similar to Bishop Aidan whose disciple he had been. On returning and finding his bishopric occupied by Chad, Bishop Wilfrid withdrew to his monastery at Ripon.

THE UNIFICATION OF THE CHURCHES

The departure of Bishop Colman from his see of Lindisfarne with his followers for Scotland, after the synod of Whitby, was in reality the end of the mission of the Celtic Church in England, which had begun in 635 when Oswald, king of Northumbria, asked the monastery of Iona to send him a bishop to evangelize his people. Within thirty years, Bishops Aidan, Finan and Colman successively fulfilled their evangelistic and pastoral mission and had taught and practised the traditions of the Celtic Church of which they were bishops. For many years elements of the traditions of the Celtic Church survived, especially in the north. Nevertheless, 664 may be regarded as the year in which the unification of the Church became so effective that throughout England the Catholic Church had become the Church in England.

Illustrative of this new found unity was the consecration of the monastery of Medehamstede in 664, as recorded by the Peterborough version of the *Anglo-Saxon Chronicle*,[1] when bishops from various parts of the land assisted the metropolitan bishop Deusdedit of Canterbury. Taking part in the service of consecration were Deusdedit with his suffragan, Ithamar, bishop of Rochester, Jaruman, bishop of the Mercians, Tuda, bishop of Lindisfarne, both of whom had been consecrated by Irish bishops who held the Catholic Faith, Wini, bishop of Wessex and Wilfrid the priest. An occasion of such significance may suggest that this minster, of which the nobly-born Saxwulf became the first abbot, witnessed an implicit recognition by the Bishops Wini, Jaruman and Tuda of the metropolitan authority of the metropolitan see of Canterbury. In the same year Deusdedit had died, King Eorcenberht of Kent died on the same day, both probably falling victims of the plague which raged in England at that time. King Eorcenberht's legislation to stamp out idolatry, combined with the diligent teaching and pastoral administration of Bishop Honorius and Deusdedit in Canterbury were to be seen in the full measure of the strength of the work and witness of the Church in Kent as Egbert, another Christian king, ascended his late father's throne. The new king together with King Oswiu of Northumbria virtually possessed the overlordship of England and both of them endeavoured to advance the work of the Catholic Church throughout the land. But after the battle of Hatfield in which King Edwin had been slain and Queen Aethelberga had fled for safety to Kent, his successor Oswald supported the Celtic Church in which he had been nurtured.

Some years later when another marriage between the two families was effected King Oswiu accepted the traditions and practices of the Catholic Church of which his wife, Queen Eanfled, was a member. In consequence the relationship and friendship which existed between the two royal houses was further strengthened by their united allegiance to the Catholic Church.

Both kings recognized the central importance of the see of Canterbury and, on the death of Deusdedit, consulted together concerning the appointment of a successor. They also sought the counsel of the people and 'with the choice and consent of the holy Church of the race of the English' the English priest, Wighard, one of Deusdedit's clergy, was chosen bishop. The two kings sent him to Rome in order to receive consecration at the hands of Pope Vitalian and to receive the bestowal of the *pallium* in order that 'he might be able to consecrate bishops for the churches of the English people throughout Britain.' Bede's statement that the Kings Egbert and Oswiu sent Wighard to Rome is neither qualified by his statement in his *Historia Abbatum* that King Egbert alone sent him [2] nor by the pope's letter addressed alone to King Oswiu. [3]

While modern implications of democracy should not be read into the joint action of kings and people conferring together and electing a new metropolitan bishop, it is of sufficient importance to observe that this democratic expression of the will of kings and people emerged in the context not of the secular but of the ecclesiastical administration. It is evident, therefore, that the unifying factor, in its initial development, found both its origin and tangible effectiveness in the Church of the land united in its teaching and practices, and in consequence considerably assisted in creating a unity of purpose which until this time had not existed between kings and people and between the English kingdoms. Nevertheless, although formally united, by its acceptance of the Catholic Easter, the Church of the English people had yet to be united in its administration. This could only be effected by the consecration of bishops to fill the vacant sees, and one of the chief functions of a new metropolitan bishop of Canterbury would be the consecration of bishops. Doubtless, to obviate any question of the authority of the future metropolitan bishop of Canterbury, Wighard, a priest of the late metropolitan's *familia,* was not sent to a metropolitan bishop in France but to Rome there to be consecrated by Pope Vitalian himself. Conforming to the traditionally accepted practice each letter would contain a petition from the kings and people, accompanied with thank-offerings, requesting the *pallium* to be conferred by the pope upon Wighard, their nominee, who presented himself for consecration. After having delivered the letters and gifts Wighard had died before receiving consecration. An unprecedented situation was therefore created of which Pope Vitalian did not hesitate to take full advantage for the exercise of his papal authority. Vitalian at this period was still chafing under his subjection to the Eastern Emperor Constans II, and the power of the papacy was at a low ebb, and any opportunity for the papacy to exercise its unfettered authority was eagerly grasped.[4]

Addressing his letter alone to King Oswiu the pope acknowledged the letters which had been sent by both kings, Oswiu and Egbert and the people, and thanked him for the gifts which included gold and silver vessels. With his letter were sent personal gifts of relics to Oswiu and a special present to Queen Eanfled, which could only be regarded as reciprocal gifts to those which he had received. By regarding the gifts from the kings and people as personal gifts Pope Vitalian dissociated them from any impression that they were the traditional offerings made at the bestowal of the *pallium,* which they were intended to be. At the same time he made it appear that the import of the letters which he had received from England was nothing more than a request that he should find a suitable bishop for the Church of the English people. 'We have not been able now, considering the length of the journey, to find a man apt and qualified in all respects to be a bishop, according to the tenor of your letters. But as soon as a suitable person shall be found we will send him instructed to your country.'[5] In his efforts to fulfil this obligation Vitalian was confronted with a most difficult problem. Canterbury's remoteness and the long journey which would have to be made from Rome to this most northerly of metropolitan sees combined with the perils of crossing France with its uncertain political conditions were sufficient to daunt the most zealous of good men. Turning for counsel to others, diligent inquiries were made and Vitalian decided that Hadrian, a native of Africa, who was abbot of the Niridian monastery near Naples should be sent to Britain. On arriving in Rome, Hadrian was ordered by the pope to accept the bishopric and go to Britain. He declined on the grounds of his unworthiness for so great a dignity, and recommended a monk, named Andrew, who because of infirmity was unable to be consecrated bishop. The pope then turned again to Hadrian and urged him to accept the bishopric, but the abbot asked for more time so that he would have further opportunity to find another who might be consecrated. At that time Theodore, a Greek from Tarsus in Cilicia, a friend of Hadrian's, was in Rome. He was a monk like Hadrian and they had many interests in common. Both were well-versed in the Scriptures; both possessed a thorough knowledge of Latin and Greek. Theodore's uprightness of character was widely known and he was sixty-six years of age. He had a good knowledge of secular literature but was not as fully conversant with monastic and ecclesiastical discipline as Abbot Hadrian, who duly recommended him to the pope for the bishopric. The pope decided to consecrate Theodore but laid down certain conditions which required that Hadrian, who on two former occasions had travelled through France and had sufficient men of his own to provide an escort, should conduct Theodore to Britain. The second condition imposed by Vitalian was that on arrival in Britain Hadrian should remain there with Theodore, and discharge what was probably a confidential papal commission, because of his special knowledge of monastic and church disciplines and traditions which Theodore lacked. By this commission Hadrian was not only to advise Theodore but also to exercise restraint upon him should he at any time attempt to introduce any Greek perversities of Eastern Church teaching into the Church in Britain. It is evident in making this latter condition the pope desired to be certain beyond all doubt that Theodore was in no way influenced in his teaching of the Faith by the waning Monophysite heresy or the Monothelite heresy which at that period corrupted the Eastern Church.[6] These conditions were accepted by Hadrian who, in due course, with Theodore set out from Rome for Britain. Having been ordained sub-deacon, Theodore had to delay four months, since he had the eastern tonsure, for him to receive the Roman tonsure. There was no further delay in Rome and on Sunday, 26th March, 668 Theodore was duly consecrated bishop by Pope Vitalian.[7] Two months later he set out from Rome accompanied by Hadrian and Benedict Biscop, a friend of Wilfrid of Ripon, carrying with them commendatory letters from the pope to facilitate their passage through France. Arriving at Marseilles they journeyed to Arles where they were hospitably entertained until Archbishop John had obtained a pass for them to travel through France from Ebroin, mayor of the palace of Neustria. After having received the pass Theodore visited Agilbert, bishop of Paris, with whom he lived for some time, and there is little doubt that it was from Agilbert Theodore gained much detailed knowledge of the people and conditions in England, which greatly assisted him when he assumed the responsibilities of metropolitan bishop of Britain. Meanwhile, Abbot Hadrain visited the bishops of Sens and Meaux. On learning that Theodore was making but slow progress on his journey through France, King Egbert of Kent sent his reeve, Redfrith, to conduct him safely to Britain. With Ebroin's permission Redfrith accompanied Theodore to Quentavic at the mouth of the Canche and, after some delay caused through illness, sailed for Britain arriving in Canterbury in May 669. On Hadrian's arrival in Kent, Theodore in obedience to the pope's injunction made provision in his diocese for him and his followers, and immediately appointed him abbot of St. Peter's monastery, Canterbury, which

E

had been held for two years by Benedict Biscop, who taught Theodore English.[8] The metropolitan bishopric had been vacant for nearly five years by the time Theodore had entered into his see. Bishop Berctgils of Dunwich alone had remained of the episcopate of the Catholic Church in the tradition begun by Augustine and he had died during the interregnum. By his death was severed the last link in the chain of episcopal succession from Augustine the first metropolitan bishop of Canterbury. The Gregorian plan which envisaged a metropolitan bishop in the south and in the north, each having twelve suffragan bishops, still remained but a plan and nothing more. There had been every indication of the progressive realization of the plan when the metropolitan bishop Justus consecrated Paulinus bishop and sent him to Northumbria where he was given York for his see city by King Edwin. Political upheavals and the fortunes of war brought this enterprise for the expansion of the Church in Northumbria to a close. Later, even with the kingdoms of Kent and Northumbria growing together in political understanding through the influence of the Church, no opportunity for the development of the Church in accordance with the plan of Pope Gregory I had emerged.

Although every attempt to implement the Gregorian plan had failed it would be a mistake to conclude that ecclesiastical organization began to disintegrate. Bishop Deusdedit's death and the prolonged interregnum did not interrupt the continuance of the educational work of the Church in Canterbury. In the schools men were still trained for the sacred ministry but their ordination had to be delayed until the arrival of a bishop. This occurred by accident when Bishop Wilfrid, returning from his consecration at Compiègne, was shipwrecked on the coast of Sussex. Being driven away by the pagan South Saxons he finally landed safely at Sandwich in Kent within twelve miles of Canterbury. On arrival there he was summoned by King Egbert to visit him. Later the bishop was requested to ordain those who were awaiting ordination. Acceding to this request he exercised his episcopal office for the first time in his own country and ordained both priests and deacons. Among those whom he ordained to the priesthood was Putta, who subsequently became bishop of Rochester.[9] Without undue delay in Kent, Wilfrid then journeyed northwards to take possession of his bishopric at York, but withdrew to Ripon on finding Chad in occupation of his see.

More than a year after his consecration Theodore arrived in Canterbury and took possession of the metropolitan see. For the first time in the life of the Church in England since its foundation by Augustine who, like Theodore, had been chosen by the pope, a metropolitan bishop of Canterbury had been consecrated by the pope. Although this act of consecration by the pope established a precedent there is no evidence to show that it was used to extend papal authority in the Church of the English people. Theodore did not hesitate to let it be known that in some sense he regarded himself to be the delegate of the Apostolic See in Britain because he had been appointed metropolitan bishop by the pope. Nowhere however is any reference to be found of the pope having appointed him his Vicar in Britain.[10]

Having acquainted himself with the organization of the Church in his see city of Canterbury, Theodore was confronted with the problem of episcopal administration throughout his vast province. The see of Rochester was vacant and the extensive territories of Mercia, Wessex and East Anglia were without bishops. From the Channel northwards to the river Humber there was only one bishop and his authority was not without question. This was Bishop Wini who, after having been expelled from the see of Winchester by King Cenwalh, simoniacally occupied the see of London which he had purchased from Wulfhere, king of Mercia.[11] In the north beyond the Humber Wilfrid was exercising his episcopal ministry in Deira with his seat in his monastery at Ripon, while Bishop Chad served the rest of Northumbria having his seat in the city of York.

In order to be fully informed of the condition of the Church in Britain Theodore began a visitation of the English people wherever they were settled. Accompanied by Abbot Hadrian he was well received and attentively heard. He instructed the clergy concerning the obligation which rested upon them to observe the right rule of life and to celebrate Easter according to canonical custom. Bede waxed eloquent in his description of the early years of Theodore's metropolitanate when the kings of Kent and Northumbria, in their adherence to the Church, gave it their fullest support, and wrote 'There were never happier times since the English came to Britain.' [12] It was the first time that a metropolitan bishop of Canterbury had visited his province so extensively and with such thoroughness. His scholarship did not cloud his understanding of men and his friendly yet authoritative demeanour gained for him the support of those who formerly had held the Celtic Church tradition in addition to those of the Catholic Church. So completely was Theodore accepted as the metropolitan bishop of Britain for, 'This was the first among the archbishops whom the whole Church of the English agreed to obey.' [13] The attainment of the unity of the Church in Britain in the person of Theodore, irrespective of the Gregorian plan for the creation of two provinces, preceded by three hundred years any similar expression of unity in the political sphere. At a later period, this unity of the Church under Theodore was used in support of the claim that the primacy of Canterbury extended over all England.[14] But what can only be regarded as legendary is the record given by Thorn in which

Theodore appears as possessing legatine authority throughout England, Scotland and Ireland.[15] Theodore's later action in failing to comply with papal directives sufficiently indicated that he was not an apostolic legate in Britain.

During his visitation he journeyed to Northumbria where he found the complicated problems of the see of York awaiting him. Wilfrid had been nominated by the sub-king Alhfrith of Deira with Oswiu's concurrence to the see of York, and had left the country for consecration in France. Meanwhile Alhfrith had fallen under the displeasure of his father, King Oswiu. Taking advantage of this situation and the long delayed return of Wilfrid, the ageing Oswiu needed little persuasion by those who were still inclined towards the Celtic Church tradition to nominate Chad to the bishopric of York. Undeterred by the political and ecclesiastical issues involved, with two bishops claiming the same bishopric, Theodore immediately grappled with the problem. From his extensive knowledge of canon law he saw that Chad's occupancy of the bishopric contravened the conciliar decrees of both Nicea and Ephesus that there should not be two bishops in the same city and that no bishop should take possession of another's see.[16] On these grounds alone Bishop Chad could have been removed from the bishopric, but another matter emerged which affected Chad deeply and personally. He had received consecration from Wini, bishop of Winchester, and two British bishops. His consecration was therefore irregular because the two British bishops possessed episcopal orders which were considered to be irregular by the Catholic Church. In all humility Chad accepted Theodore's judgment concerning his consecration thus making a gesture of obedience which evidently pleased Theodore to such an extent that he completed Chad's consecration in accordance with the requirements of the Catholic Church, and at the same time deposed him from the see of York. Subsequently Wilfrid was installed in the see of York for which he had been consecrated. Chad too had received his irregular consecration in order to occupy the same see. Because of this Eddius, Wilfrid's biographer, makes the grounds of Chad's deposition 'the sin of being ordained to another's see by the Quartodecimans' and makes it appear that he regarded not only Chad's consecration as being invalid but also his orders.[17]

During the period in which Chad had occupied his see, Wilfrid, on frequent occasions, at the invitation of Wulfhere, king of Mercia, exercised his episcopal ministry in Mercia. This now ceased on Wilfrid regaining his bishopric, but the need of a bishop in Mercia still remained. Diuma, Ceollach, Trumhere and Jaruman, Celtic bishops by consecration, successively had ministered among the Mercians, and it was during the episcopate of bishop Jaruman that Wilfrid had assisted in King Wulfhere's territories. On the death of Jaruman in 669, Wulfhere asked Theodore to provide a bishop for him and his people. Bishop Chad, after his deposition from the see of York, had retired to his monastery at Lastingham in Oswiu's kingdom. Theodore therefore consulted Oswiu concerning Chad and with the king's agreement sent him to Wulfhere. Having received from Wulfhere Lichfield for his see city, Bishop Chad exercised his episcopal ministry in the extensive territories of Lindsey and Mercia.

The circumstances of Chad's episcopate set in bold relief the mutual understanding and relationship which Theodore had so soon established between kings and himself. He had removed Chad from the see of York and had installed Wilfrid. Later he had consulted Oswiu and had obtained his agreement to Chad's appointment to the Mercian bishopric. Wulfhere's request for Theodore to send him a bishop for his kingdom was a recognition of the ecclesiastical authority of the metropolitan bishop of Canterbury which, until Theodore's metropolitanate, had not been so clearly shown.

The vast stretches of country through which Theodore journeyed on his visitation, the great distances separating centres of Christian activity, and the insuperable difficulties which confronted the small number of bishops in their efforts to minister effectively to the people, were decisive factors in shaping his policy for the future organization of the Church in Britain. In consequence he set himself the task of creating, out of the mission centres under the leadership of bishops from which the Christian Faith was preached and the Church received its ministrations, a unified form of administration. To give effect to this Theodore initiated a plan by which his province would be divided into dioceses. Some of these in their territorial extent coincided with the boundaries of a kingdom while others, where the kingdom was too large for effective pastoral oversight, were created by subdividing the kingdom, invariably on a tribal basis of division. His immediate problem, however, was to maintain and expand the episcopate, and on the death of Bishop Damian he consecrated Putta to succeed him in the see of Rochester and Bisi in 669 to Dunwich vacant by the death of Berctgils. The bishopric of Winchester still remained vacant after King Cenwalh's dispute with Bishop Wini who had bought appointment to the bishopric of London from King Wulfhere of Mercia. Cenwalh of Wessex desiring to restore the Christian way of life for himself and his people requested Agilbert, bishop of Paris, who had formerly occupied the see, to return, but refusing, commended as worthy of a bishopric his nephew, the priest Leutherius. Both king and people welcomed Leutherius and requested Theodore to consecrate him as their bishop. Visiting Winchester, probably for the first time, Theodore consecrated Leutherius, of whom it is recorded that he administered his bishopric by synodal authority.[18]

Until the time of the consecration of Leutherius by Theodore, the Church in Wessex, beginning with the missionary Birinus, and continuing with Bishops Agilbert and Wini, had been episcopally governed in complete independence of the metropolitan of Canterbury. This independence gradually disappeared during the episcopate of Leutherius. The invitation of Cenwalh and his people to Theodore asking him to visit Winchester there to consecrate Leutherius bishop, was a tacit recognition of the metropolitan authority of the see of Canterbury. Further recognition of this authority was shown three years later when in 672 Leutherius accepted and responded to Theodore's summons to attend the synod of Hertford.[19]

During the year preceding the synod Chad had died and Wynfrid, who had served for some time in the office of deacon, was chosen to succeed him. Wynfrid was consecrated bishop by Theodore to have the episcopal oversight of the territories of the Mercians, Middle Angles and Lindsey over which Wulfhere ruled. Theodore's arrangement for the synod to meet at Hertford on the main road northwards to Northumbria shows that he chose a place as accessible as possible to all representatives of the Church both from the north as well as the south. In keeping with the practice of bishops of the Graeco-Roman world, who had their own notaries, Theodore had brought with him from Rome his own notary, Titillus. Tribute is paid by Theodore to the assistance given by his notary in the record of the synod which 'I dictated to be written by Titillus our notary.' [20] The bishops who obeyed Theodore's summons to the synod are recorded in the following order: Bisi, of the East Angles, Wilfrid of the Northumbrians represented by his deputies, Putta of Rochester, Leutherius of the West Saxons and Wynfrid of the Mercians.[21] These six bishops including Theodore constituted the whole episcopal college of the English Church at that time. The exclusion of Bishop Wini shows how effectively his expulsion from the bishopric of London, which he had simoniacally obtained, deprived him of all episcopal privileges and functions as he spent the remaining years of his life in penitence in the monastery at Winchester.

With the bishops also assembled 'many other teachers of the Church who loved and knew the canonical decrees of the Fathers.' [22] Since it was a provincial synod, the constituent members of which were bishops, the 'teachers of the Church' were present as advisers and consultants and probably King Ecgfrith was the only layman present.[23] Having addressed the synod Theodore inquired of each in turn whether they agreed to observe the canonical decrees of the fathers. On receiving the assurance of his bishops, Theodore produced the book of canons, doubtless the compilation of Dionysius Exiguus, and directed their special attention to the ten parts which he considered to be particularly necessary for the Church in England, and requested that they should be the more carefully received by all. After discussion the definitive form of the canons was agreed. The first of these confirmed the Catholic observance of Easter, and the tenth Church law relating to Christian marriage. Canon four directed that monks should not move from the monastery where they had been professed without the permission of the abbot. Specific reference to the clergy was made in canons five and six. None of the clergy was to leave his own bishop for another without commendatory letters from him. In the sixth canon, however, bishops are coupled with the clergy and are directed that when travelling they should be content with the hospitality offered them. Furthermore, when travelling they were forbidden to exercise their priestly ministry without first obtaining the permission of the bishop of the diocese in which they were at the time.

The control of the movement of both clergy and monks would effectively bring a continuity of ministry and religious activity to the scattered Christian settlements which would create a stability and unification of Church organization which hitherto it had lacked. Theodore perceived, however, that canons which alone concerned the clergy and monks were insufficient without episcopal authority to see that the canons were obeyed, although in the case of monks it would largely depend on the relationship which existed between the bishop and the abbots in his diocese. To this end, therefore, no less than four canons are concerned with the episcopate. It was decreed by canon two that no bishop should intrude into the diocese of another bishop but that he should be content to govern the people entrusted to his pastoral care. Protection was also given to the monasteries for canon three laid it down that no bishop should interfere with the monasteries dedicated to God nor should he remove by force any of their possessions. No bishop impelled by ambition should claim precedence over another bishop but should observe the rule of seniority of consecration enjoined by canon eight. It was also decreed in canon seven that a synod should be held twice a year, but because of various hindrances it was approved that the bishops should meet annually on the first of August at 'the place which is called Clofeshoh.' [24] This was the first synod convoked by a metropolitan bishop of Canterbury at which were set forth positive constructive measures for the government of the Church in Britain. Laurentius, when metropolitan bishop of Canterbury, met his two suffragans, Bishops Justus and Mellitus, in council to consider what action should be taken in the face of the return to paganism by the people of Kent and the East Saxons. It was in reality a provincial council held at Canterbury in 616, the first one of the English Church, at which the future policy of the Church at this critical juncture was determined.[25] The synod of Hertford, however, was of greater importance because it reflected more than an ecclesiastical unity of representatives drawn from Northumbria, East Anglia, Mercia and Kent. It was in reality 'the first of all national gatherings for such legislation as should affect the whole land of the English, the precursor of the Witenagemots and the Parliaments of one indivisible imperial realm.' [26]

Of all the ten parts of the canons which Theodore had marked especially for the synod's consideration one of the *capitula* which concerned the increase of the episcopate was passed over. Bede, in recording the proceedings of the synod, quotes what Theodore had dictated to his notary, Titillus, as follows: 'The ninth *capitulum* was discussed in common: "That more bishops should be made as the number of the faithful increased"; but we passed over this matter for the present.' [27] It was evident from the discussion which ensued that personal interests were involved. It was improbable that the bishops would welcome any proposal for the division of their dioceses and the consequent diminution of the extent of their influence and authority. The proposal for the increase of the episcopate may have been regarded by the bishops as irrelevant to the immediate requirements of the administration of the Church because of the presence in the country of non-diocesan bishops who formerly observed the Celtic tradition. At the same time, the bishops present would have realized that they were unable to make a firm decision on a matter which was not exclusively ecclesiastical but which possessed political implications which were in themselves decisive. This, without doubt, was the overriding consideration with the synod on this canon which was 'passed over for the present.' Theodore had succeeded in ventilating the matter at the synod for he knew that it would be futile to attempt to divide a diocese without first obtaining the concurrence of the ruler of the kingdom in which the diocese was situated. What was still more important, unless that concurrence was expressed by the ruler in a practical manner by a grant of land for the endowment of the proposed see it could not be erected. Although the synod dispersed without accepting in principle Theodore's policy for the increase of the episcopate and the sub-division of large dioceses, each bishop was fully aware of his metropolitan's plans for the future administration of his extensive province. Until this time a ruler had invariably taken the initiative in choosing a bishop for his kingdom. But now Theodore's policy brought the influence of the Church, through its metropolitan bishop, into the formation and extent of dioceses and the nomination of bishops. This was to be seen in the initial implementation of his policy soon after the synod of Hertford. Bisi, bishop of the East

Angles, who had his see at Dunwich, on his return from the synod was unable to administer his diocese because of ill-health. Seizing this opportunity, Theodore, with the support of Aldwulf, king of East Anglia, adopted immediate measures for the division of the large diocese. There were good grounds for doing this. It would relieve the incapacitated Bisi and place the diocese under efficient pastoral care. These measures provided for two bishops, Aecci and Baduwine, who, after election, were consecrated by Theodore in 673 to have the oversight of the diocese.[28] Bishop Aecci had his see at Dunwich but the northern part of the diocese was separated to form the new diocese of Elmham where Bishop Baduwine had his seat. By this division Theodore followed the tribal boundaries which still remained in Aldwulf's kingdom. Dunwich was destined to survive as a bishopric for little more than two hundred years but in nineteen hundred and thirty-four it was revived as a suffragan bishopric in the diocese of St. Edmundsbury and Ipswich. Elmham, although its line of succession is uncertain, continued down to the Norman Conquest, after which it was transferred to Thetford for a short period before finally being established in 1091 at Norwich which has remained the see city down to the present time. Thetford was revived, however, in 1963 as a suffragan bishopric in the diocese of Norwich.

Having completed the initial step in his policy for the division of the large dioceses, Theodore turned his attention to the diocese of Mercia. After Ecgfrith of Northumbria had defeated Wulfhere of Mercia he annexed the territory of Lindsey to his kingdom in 671, or at least at some time before the synod of Hertford in 672. Lindsey was therefore under the pastoral care of the bishop of York. Bishop Wynfrid, whom Theodore had consecrated a few months earlier to the see of Mercia, was present at the synod. It is probable that Theodore assumed that the newly consecrated bishop would accept his counsel and favour his proposal for the division of his diocese. However, in 675 he was deposed from his bishopric by Theodore for disobedience.[29] What his disobedience was is unknown for there is no record relating to it, but it may be assumed that his removal from the see of Mercia was caused by his refusal to co-operate with Theodore, his metropolitan, in the reorganization and division of his diocese. Without opposing Theodore, Wynfrid vacated his bishopric and withdrew to his monastery at Barrow.

This was not the first occasion on which Theodore took action against a bishop. In his office as metropolitan bishop of Canterbury, he had shown his strong disapproval of Bishop Wini's occupancy of the see of London, which he had purchased from Wulfhere, king of Mercia, so that in penitence he vacated the see. Neither on this occasion nor in deposing Wynfrid is any reference to be found to synodal action. On both occasions Theodore acted alone. It was required by the Apostolic Canons, when any accusation was brought against a bishop, that he should appear before a synod of bishops,[30] and that the president should not take any action without the consent of the synod.[31] Under Justinian's law, however, a metropolitan possessed the power to hear causes himself on appeal being made to him, and instances are recorded when a metropolitan deposed suffragans without recourse to a provincial synod.[32] There always remained the right of the suffragans to appeal over the head of the metropolitan to the provincial synod of which the metropolitan himself would be the president. This procedure was invariably unsatisfactory and was productive of many appeals to the Roman See.[33] Precedents for metropolitan action independent of synodal authority, and metropolitan action pending synodal confirmation were available. With his extensive knowledge of canon law, as shown at the synod of Hertford, Theodore would be fully informed concerning the principles of ecclesiastical government by metropolitans which received definitive formulation at the council of Turin in 398. These were sufficiently wide to cover his action in deposing Wynfrid.[34] In giving effect to the canon law it was within the competence of a metropolitan bishop to require his suffragans to give due obedience to the law which he communicated to them.[35] Theodore's action was therefore not contrary to canon law. At the same time it is evident that without Wulfhere's approval he would have been unable to depose Bishop Wynfrid. The metropolitan possessed the king's fullest confidence. Earlier, at the king's request, he had provided him with Bishop Chad for his kingdom. With Wulfhere's support he had been able to remove Bishop Wini from the see of London.

To succeed Wynfrid Theodore consecrated Saxwulf, the abbot and founder of Medehamstede (Peterborough). Probably at the same time he consecrated Earconwald, who had founded the monastery of Chertsey, and the nunnery at Barking for his sister, Aethelberga, to the bishopric of London. After Bishop Saxwulf had occupied the bishopric of Mercia there was some delay before any definite measures were taken for the division of his see. Indeed, before the first year of his episcopate was ended Wulfhere died, and the whole political situation was changed. For this reason, no doubt, Theodore considered it wise to defer any immediate reorganization. King Wulfhere's brother Aethelred within a few months of succeeding him marched his forces into Kent and amidst the general destruction the city of Rochester severely suffered. Bishop Putta of Rochester was absent from his see at the time. On learning that his cathedral church had been despoiled and feeling unable to undertake the restoration of his bishopric he did not return to his see city but went to Mercia. Without delay Theodore consecrated Cwichelm to the vacant see, but the newly consecrated bishop found his see so impoverished that he resigned. Thereupon, Theodore consecrated in 678 Gebmund to succeed him.

On arriving in Mercia Putta visited Bishop Saxwulf at Lichfield, who appointed him a church with a small estate at Hereford. Bede speaks of Putta as 'serving that church alone,' and then adds that the bishop accepted invitations in the diocese to teach church music. It is evident, therefore, that his ministry extended beyond the area surrounding the church where he resided. In such circumstancs there can be little doubt that Saxwulf permitted Putta to exercise his episcopal office in that remote part of his diocese north of the river Wye. Out of the political situation, which delayed Theodore advancing his own policy, virtually came the initial step towards the division of the Mercian bishopric by Saxwulf placing Putta at Hereford, which later became the see city of a bishopric.[36]

Any plans which Theodore may have entertained for the division of the bishopric of the West Saxons had to be set aside because of the unstable political situation in the kingdom. King Cenwalh unsuccessfully divided his kingdom into two bishoprics, at the time when Bishop Agilbert occupied the see of Dorchester by establishing Bishop Wini at Winchester. Cenwalh's plan soon collapsed when Agilbert took offence at the division of his bishopric, vacated his see and left the kingdom. This situation did not long remain a problem for the king of Wessex because Dorchester was in territory which the king of Mercia annexed, and the see was held by Bishop Aetla. During the political upheaval in Wessex following the death of Cenwalh the see of Winchester fell vacant through the death of Leutherius.[37] Theodore took full advantage of the situation and tried to bring the bishopric under his metropolitan see of Canterbury. This was not accomplished, but he achieved much by the personal relationship which existed between himself and the successor of Leutherius, Haeddi, priest and abbot of Breedon in Mercia, who was his friend. Probably Haeddi had been a member of Theodore's school at Canterbury since he is described as a friend of scholars, although not himself distinguished in learning.[38] Theodore did not visit Winchester as he had done to consecrate Leutherius but consecrated Haeddi in London assisted no doubt by Bishop Earconwald in 676. It was during Haeddi's episcopate that the see of Wessex was finally established at Winchester. This was largely achieved by his removal of the remains of Birinus, the first bishop of the West Saxons, from the church in Dorchester and their re-interment in his cathedral church at Winchester. The bishopric of the West Saxons, among whom Birinus had laboured in complete independence of the metropolitan bishop of Canterbury, under the commission of Pope Honorius I, in effect became a diocese within Theodore's jurisdiction during Haeddi's episcopate since both Leutherius and Haeddi had been consecrated by him and both had obeyed his summons respectively to attend the synods of Hertford and Hatfield.[39]

VIII

THEODORE'S ADMINISTRATION OF THE PROVINCE OF ALL BRITAIN

During the ten years which had passed since his consecration in Rome and his subsequent arrival at his see city of Canterbury in 669, Theodore by his great gifts had won the confidence of both rulers and ruled. Progressively the metropolitan see of Canterbury attained an importance in the life of the English people which it had never before possessed. The frequently changing political conditions and the consequent readjustment of the boundaries of kingdoms militated against Theodore's efforts to create a stable and efficient ecclesiastical administration throughout his province. To him Kings Egbert and Hlothere of Kent, Wulfhere and Aethelred of Mercia, Oswiu and Ecgfrith of Northumbria and Cenwalh of Wessex had turned for counsel in secular and ecclesiastical affairs and especially on occasions when they required a bishop to serve in their respective kingdoms. Whenever an opportunity arose he advanced his policy for the increase of the episcopate and the sub-division of the large dioceses.

On Aethelred's return to Mercia, from his invasion of Kent, the unsettled state of his own kingdom made it impossible for Theodore to attempt any ecclesiastical reorganization there, and in consequence he deferred his plans for the division of the Mercian diocese. In Northumbria, however, difficulties had arisen which affected the well-being of the Church throughout the territories of Ecgfrith who had expelled Wilfrid from his see of York. This was also a contributory cause for the postponement of Theodore's plans for Mercia. The precise sequence of events which led to Wilfrid's expulsion is obscure. He was the spiritual adviser of Ecgfrith's queen, Aethelthryth, who refused to consummate her marriage, and was encouraged by Wilfrid to lead the life of a religious. Finally she left her husband and entered the nunnery of Coldingham, where Ecgfrith's aunt Aebbe was abbess, and received the veil at the hands of the bishop. This caused a breach between the king and Wilfrid which became wider when the king married Eormenburgh. Although the second marriage was legal by Church law it was evident that Wilfrid looked with disfavour, if not hostility, on the marriage. From the outset the new queen, knowing how the bishop had come between husband and wife, took a dislike to him and succeeded in increasing Ecgfrith's enmity against him to such a degree that he adopted measures to humiliate Wilfrid and to diminish his power.[1] Finding these measures ineffective the king's hostility reached its culmination in the expulsion of the bishop from

77

his see of York. Both king and queen united in inviting Theodore to visit them, and Wilfrid's biographer unworthily adds that they bribed him 'to help them in their madness.' [2] By the time Theodore arrived in Northumbria the vast diocese, co-terminous with the kingdom which at this time included Lindsey, had been without a bishop for some months. Although Wilfrid had been banished from his bishopric by the king he still remained *de jure* bishop of York. Theodore was aware that Wilfrid was unable to administer his diocese now that he had been expelled by Ecgfrith. Because of this the responsibility for the pastoral care of the diocese devolved upon him as metropolitan bishop of the province which included all the northern territories. Ecgfrith conferred with Theodore concerning the measures which should be taken for his kingdom to have the pastoral care which he desired. In doing this it is evident that the king was determined that any future bishop in his kingdom should not become as powerful as Wilfrid. The immediate outcome of the conference between king and metropolitan was a policy by which to humiliate Wilfrid, not merely by minimising his authority in Ecgfrith's territories but by taking positive action as if he were no longer bishop of York.

Theodore was not in ignorance of the Gregorian plan for the bishopric of York to become a metropolitan see in complete independence of the metropolitan see of Canterbury. Moreover, he had not failed to observe the implications of independence in Wilfrid not obeying his summons to attend in person the synod of Hertford. Any proposals made by the king to reduce the bishop's authority would, in the circumstances, receive Theodore's practical support. Theodore saw that this could be achieved to the king's satisfaction by the sub-division of the vast diocese over which Wilfrid had ruled. Both king and metropolitan therefore agreed that the diocese of York should be sub-divided to form three dioceses. These would be the kingdom of Deira with its see city at York; the kingdom of Bernicia with its see city either at Lindisfarne or Hexham; and the recently conquered territory of Lindsey with its see city probably at Lincoln. Without delaying to summon bishops from the province to assist him in the consecration of bishops he proceeded by himself to consecrate at York three bishops: Bosa was consecrated bishop for the diocese of Deira; Eata, prior of Lindisfarne, for Bernicia; and Eadhed for Lindsey. In consecrating these bishops without other bishops assisting him, Theodore was well aware that such consecrations were irregular although valid. He also knew that by his action in placing other bishops, with the king's full co-operation, in Wilfrid's diocese, he had broken canon two which had been endorsed at the synod of Hertford over which he had presided. Urged by Ecgfrith, however, to implement these measures, regardless of the irregularities they involved,

Theodore was content to know that Wilfrid no longer exercised episcopal authority in Northumbria, and that his own policy had been advanced on the largest scale so far for the efficient administration of the Church in his province.

On learning what had been done Wilfrid fearlessly re-entered his bishopric and confronted both Ecgfrith and Theodore. From the account of Eddius it would appear that Wilfrid found himself before some kind of council. The bishop asked for what reason he had been deprived of his possessions. Publicly *coram omni populo* they replied 'We do not ascribe to you any criminal offence in any injurious act, but we will not change our settled judgments concerning you.'[3] Wilfrid realized that his first line of appeal against this judgment must be to a provincial synod. But the futility of any such appeal was apparent. Theodore, as metropolitan bishop, would preside at the synod and there would be little likelihood of a synod reversing the considered judgment of its own president which was also the judgment of the powerful Ecgfrith, king of Northumbria. After taking counsel with his fellow-bishops Wilfrid decided to visit Rome, there personally to present his appeal at the papal court. By making this appeal against the judgment of Theodore, his metropolitan bishop, he was doing nothing canonically irregular. The Sardican canon of 343 establishing the right of a bishop to appeal to Rome had later received the confirmation of imperial authority during the pontificate of Leo the Great.[4] Moreover, he had sought the advice of his fellow-bishops which did not deter him.[5] Wilfrid did not arrive in Rome until 679. At that time a council under Pope Agatho's presidency was in session, and it would appear that the agenda of the council was extended and the council kept in session in order to consider Wilfrid's appeal. This was the first occasion in the history of the Church in England that a bishop of that Church had made an appeal to the Apostolic See. Added importance was given to the appeal because it called in question the administration of Theodore, metropolitan bishop of Canterbury, who had been chosen, consecrated and sent to Britain by Pope Vitalian to rule over the province of the whole of Britain.

Before Wilfrid arrived at the papal court Theodore's messenger, Coenwald, had arrived there and had submitted a general report of the Church in Britain including details concerning Wilfrid's appeal and claims relating to the bishopric of York. Pope Agatho took no immediate action on Theodore's communication conveyed to him by Coenwald but awaited the arrival of the appellant, Wilfrid, from Britain. This delay was also prompted, no doubt, by Agatho's hope that Theodore, himself, would arrive in Rome to attend the council, at which one hundred and twenty-five bishops were present, which

had been convened for the purpose of condemning the heresy of the
Monothelites. There is reason to believe that Theodore had been
summoned to attend the council but had been excused on the grounds
of age and infirmities. In the pope's synodical letter to the emperor
the excuse for its late arrival was the delay caused by his expecting
Theodore, archbishop of Britain, to join the synod.[6] It would appear
that prior to the general council, and the special session at which
Wilfrid's appeal was heard, probably during the intervening period
between the arrival of Coenwald in Rome and the later arrival of
Wilfrid, a special council was convened by Agatho at which seventeen bishops and thirty-five priests were present. In his presidential
address to the council Pope Agatho defined the business which he
desired the council to consider with him as 'the state of the Church
in the island of Britain in which, by the grace of God, the multitude
of the faithful has greatly increased and where dissension has recently
arisen.' [7] Two bishops opened the discussion by saying the Church in
Britain needed pontifical succour because of the dissension between
Archbishop Theodore and other prelates of the same province. This
is the first reference to any disagreement with bishops other than
Wilfrid. Was the Apostolic See informed of Theodore's action in
depriving Bishop Wynfrid of Mercia of his bishopric because of his
disobedience? 'Other prelates' in this context seems to imply other
bishops in addition to Wilfrid and Wynfrid with whom Theodore
had been in dispute. It was agreed that apostolical authority, with
the help of God, alone could assuage and remove the fuel of dissension.
Substantially Pope Agatho and his synod confirmed the Gregorian
plan but omitted all reference to the number of provinces. It was
decreed that 'every kingdom constituted in the Island of Britain have
bishops of their provinces so placed in proportion to their dominion;
that all the prelates of the Churches together with the archbishop be
twelve in number.' [8] It was also decreed that the archbishop for the
time being who had been honoured with the *pallium* (in this instance
Theodore) should promote and consecrate bishops who should be
subject to him alone, and that no bishops should interfere with the
rights of another bishop. The decision was also made to inquire concerning the observance of ecclesiastical statutes, the succession of
bishops, their assent to the Catholic Faith and the orthodoxy of the
Church in Britain. All the decrees were to be carried to Britain, under
Pope Agatho's authority, by John, precentor of St. Peter's, Rome and
abbot of the monastery of St. Martin, to 'Theodore, the most reverend
and holy archbishop of the Kentishmen' in order that Theodore
should convoke a synod in accordance with the papal missive carried
by Abbot John.

In addition, the pope directed that John should carry with him the decrees of the council held by Pope Martin in 648–9, which condemned the Monothelite heresy, for acceptance at the synod which should be convoked by Theodore.[9] In all the papal documents of the councils held at Rome at this time reference was made to Theodore not as metropolitan bishop but as 'archbishop.' This was the first occasion that a bishop of the Church in England had been given this title. Bishop Wilfrid in his petition adopted the terminology of the papal court and referred to Theodore as the 'most holy archbishop.' [10]

On receiving the papal letters from Abbot John, Theodore, in complete obedience to the pope's directive, convoked a synod which assembled at Hatfield in 680 and issued a statement of full acceptance of the Catholic Faith and condemnation of the Monothelite heresy.[11]

It is significant, however, that Theodore, adopting the language of the papal missive, described himself as 'archbishop' and indicated the extent of his province. By the use of this title the metropolitan bishop of Canterbury was given the title 'archbishop' for the first time in a document of the Church in England. After reference to the kings reigning in Britain at the time of the synod there follow the words: 'Theodore, by the grace of God, archbishop of the Island of Britain, and of the city of Canterbury, being president, and the other venerable bishops of the Island of Britain sitting with him . . . expounded the true and orthodox faith.' [12] These words describing Theodore's office and province were identical with the words of the papal missive which Abbot John carried from the pope directing that such a synod should be convoked. They show conclusively that the Gregorian plan for two provinces in Britain was no longer in mind but, following the commission given to Theodore on his consecration by Pope Vitalian, both in Rome and Britain the province of Canterbury was regarded as the province of the Island of Britain.

Abbot John, at the conclusion of the synod, departed for Rome bearing an account of its proceedings and a copy of its decrees. While travelling across France he died and was buried at Tours, but others carried the document to Rome where it was received 'with the greatest satisfaction by Pope Agatho and others who heard it or read it.' [13] In his appeal Wilfrid stated, what is not found elsewhere, that the decision to divide the diocese of York was made by Theodore and other bishops assembled with him. In pronouncing judgment, the synod presided over by Pope Agatho regarded Theodore's division of the diocese as regular.[14] His action in placing three bishops in the diocese in Wilfrid's absence without his consent was unlawful and the bishops must be removed from their sees. Wilfrid was given authority to nominate fellow-bishops, with whom he could live peaceably, whom Archbishop Theodore should consecrate.[15]

At the conclusion of his appeal, Wilfrid, because of the absence of

F

Theodore, was summoned by the pope to take his seat with the other bishops for the closing session of the council of Rome. He was also required to declare his own faith and 'the faith of the province, or island, from which he had come.' Knowing that he was not the accredited delegate of the whole ecclesiastical province of Britain he made a declaration of faith only for that territory over which he considered himself to be bishop, namely, 'all the northern part of Britain and Ireland, and the islands which are inhabited by the nations of the English and Britons, as well as the Scots and the Picts.' [16] When the final report of the council was prepared for the emperor, Wilfrid, in subscribing to it, endorsed Pope Agatho's expressed hope that Archbishop Theodore would have been present. In these two instances it may be recognized that Wilfrid did not attempt to detract from the authority of the metropolitan archbishopric of Canterbury but by his two subscriptions positively affirmed its authority and the position of Archbishop Theodore. In the documents relating to Wilfrid's appeal no mention is made of Ecgfrith nor is the king mentioned as being solely responsible for the bishop's expulsion from his see, as indeed he was. In the papal judgment which Wilfrid received, deprivation and curse were placed upon any bishop who flouted the judgment, and excommunication was pronounced upon priest, deacon, cleric and monk and 'upon a layman of whatever degree, even a king.' Basically his petition, while mentioning his uncanonical ejection from his see, turned upon Theodore's actions in dividing his diocese without his consent and the consecration of bishops to rule over the subdivisions which were constituted new dioceses. On his arrival in Britain, Wilfrid did not first visit his metropolitan archbishop as would have been expected, but according to Eddius he journeyed to the Northumbrian court there to show the papal bull to Ecgfrith. The king did not delay until Theodore arrived at his court but summoned 'all his chief counsellors and the servants of God,' Bishops Bosa, Eata and Eadhed, before whom the papal judgment was read. Both king and council rejected the papal document as having been obtained by bribery from the Apostolic See to serve his own ends. [17] Bishop Wilfrid now received another judgment which condemned him to solitary imprisonment, a judgment with which the three bishops who occupied his divided bishopric approved. On his release from prison after nine months, Wilfrid for a short time found hospitality in Mercia and then journeyed southwards, finally establishing a mission centre at Selsey, where he founded a monastery, from which with much zeal and success he evangelized the people of Sussex.

In 679 war had broken out between Northumbria and Mercia and, at a decisive battle near the river Trent, Aethelred of Mercia defeated Ecgfrith of Northumbria and regained the territory of Lindsey which

Ecgfrith had annexed during Wulfhere's reign. After this battle Theodore intervened with such acceptance that as a result of his mediation the two kings made peace. Out of the chaos of war Theodore found the opportunity to bring an ordered form of Church administration to the large diocese of Mercia. With Aethelred's approval he consecrated Aethelwine to succeed Eadhed in Lindsey. Any opposition which Bishop Saxwulf of Mercia may have shown formerly to the proposed sub-division of his large diocese had ceased. It is probable that at the time of Aethelwine's consecration Archbishop Theodore also consecrated Bosel, bishop of the Hwicce, with his seat at Worcester and Cuthwine, bishop of the Middle Angles, with his seat at Leicester.[18] There is also reason to believe that Theodore made it the occasion for regularizing Bishop Putta's ministry among the 'Magonsaetan' with his seat at Hereford. With the assistance of Aethelred Theodore had now arranged Church government throughout Mercia on a wise administrative basis, preserving old tribal frontiers in such a manner that they formed the boundaries of the new dioceses. There were now five dioceses in the Mercian kingdom : Bishop Saxwulf of Mercia had his seat at Lichfield ; Aethelwine of Lindsey probably had his seat at Lincoln ; Cuthwine of the Middle Angles had his seat at Leicester ; Bosel of the Hwicce at Worcester and Putta of the 'Magonsaetan' at Hereford.

There remained, however, the problem of Eadhed who was now without a see after his expulsion by Aethelred from Lindsey. It was to the problems of the northern part of his province to which Theodore now turned. Bishop Eadhed had returned to Northumbria and 'was made bishop of Ripon,' but the extent of his diocese is not known.[18] Since Wilfrid was unable to return to his see it remained the responsibility of Theodore to make provision for the pastoral care and efficient administration of the extensive diocese of York. King Ecgfrith's success in subduing the Picts provided an opportunity for their evangelization. To meet this need Theodore consecrated Trumwine, who had his seat in the monastery of Abercorn near the Firth of Forth.[19] Within four years of his consecration the Picts became free of Ecgfrith's overlordship when he was slain in 685 at the battle of Nechtanesmere. No longer could Trumwine remain in his see and, entering the monastery of Whitby, the bishopric became extinct. Bishop Eata had now established his seat at Lindisfarne thus leaving the monastery of Hexham as a separate seat for a bishopric to which Theodore consecrated Tunberct. This further sub-division of the diocese of York, with the king's approval, accorded with the report which Coenwald, on his return from Rome, had made to Theodore concerning the proceedings at the papal court relating to the appeal of Wilfrid. These proceedings had made reference to a province in

Britain having twelve bishops inclusive of the archbishop. The papal judgment had pronounced as regular Theodore's action in creating new dioceses but the appointment of bishops within another bishop's diocese without his consent was a contravention of canon law. Nevertheless, Wilfrid, although *de jure* bishop of York, was powerless to exercise any episcopal authority within the diocese of York.

When Theodore entered his see city of Canterbury in 669 the vast territories of East Anglia, Wessex and Mercia had no bishops. Bishop Wini, expelled from Winchester, by simony occupied the see of London, while in Northumbria the see of York was irregularly occupied by Chad, and Wilfrid, the rightful bishop, exercised his ministry from his monastery at Ripon. The success of Theodore's policy for the sub-division of the larger dioceses and the establishment of smaller dioceses with the consequent increase of the episcopate immeasurably advanced the efficient administration of the Church in Britain. By the year 681 there were no less than sixteen dioceses in Britain including the metropolitan see of Canterbury to which all were subject.[20]

While attributing to Theodore the highest motives for his zeal efficiently to provide for the pastoral care of his whole province, his sub-division of the diocese of York suggests that he was influenced by other motives which were not so commendable. Both Ecgfrith and Theodore were united on the common ground of their hostility towards Wilfrid. The king, because of the wealth and power which Wilfrid had possessed in his kingdom of Northumbria; the archbishop, because Wilfrid had openly challenged his metropolitan authority by his appeal to the papal court. In his consecration of Tunberct and Trumwine respectively to the dioceses of Hexham and Abercorn Theodore had again contravened canon law and actively had shown his rejection of Pope Agatho's decrees, and the papal judgment which Wilfrid had carried back to Britain. Despite his knowledge of the Gregorian plan Theodore chose to act upon that part of Agatho's decrees which implicitly recognized him as metropolitan archbishop of the province of Britain. In his letter to Augustine setting out the constitution of the Church in Britain Pope Gregory I had written 'We desire you to send to the city of York a bishop whom you shall determine to ordain; yet, so that if that city with the adjoining places shall receive the Word of God, he also shall ordain twelve bishops, and to enjoy fully the dignity of metropolitan; because, if we shall live we design, by the favour of God, upon him also to bestow the *pallium*.' 'York and the adjoining places had received the Word of God,' but the bishopric of York had been made neither a metropolitan see nor had Theodore taken the slightest measures to implement this part of the Gregorian plan. He had every reason to regard Gregory's plan as having been abrogated, first by the terms of the commission which he had received from Pope Vitalian and, secondly, by the directive given in Pope Agatho's judgment of Wilfrid's appeal in which he was directed to consecrate three bishops to serve in the sub-divided diocese of York.

At this juncture Archbishop Theodore's attitude towards papal decrees was clearly shown. He accepted and implemented those parts which confirmed his authority and strengthened his position as archbishop of Canterbury and metropolitan of the province of the whole of Britain, but completely disregarded any part of a decree which in any way appeared to assail or weaken his own authority.

The whole of Britain was one vast province, the metropolitan archbishop of which had for his see city Canterbury and not London as Pope Gregory I had planned. The archbishopric of Canterbury in both the political and ecclesiastical spheres had never before possessed such widespread recognition of its authority. Documents, recording royal grants, to which Theodore subscribed, and the joint presence of king and archbishop at synod or witan testify to the relationship which now existed.[21] Outstandingly illustrative of this was the synod of Burford in 679 at which a grant of land was made by sub-king Berhtwald of Mercia to Abbot Aldhelm and the abbey of Malmesbury[22]; and in the same year a synod in Northumbria at which King Ecgfrith and bishops confirmed a privilege granted by Pope Agatho to the monastery at Wearmouth.[23] When, however, Prior Cuthbert of Lindisfarne was elected bishop in 684 at the synod of Twyford, now identified as Alnmouth, both Ecgfrith and Theodore were united in a common purpose for the well-being of the people.[24] After the king with Bishop Trumwine had visited Lindisfarne and entreated Cuthbert to accompany them he was unanimously elected bishop. Bishop Tunberct having been deposed from the see of Hexham, Eata was translated from Lindisfarne and, at Easter in 685, Cuthbert was consecrated in the presence of Ecgfrith at York when six bishops took part with Theodore in the consecration. The far-reaching influence and authority of the archbishopric of Canterbury in the seventh century had now reached its zenith.

By the death of Ecgfrith of Northumbria in 685 Wilfrid's most powerful enemy was removed, and increasing age and infirmity compelled Theodore to see the futility of his continued hostility towards Wilfrid, who was continuing his great missionary work among the South and West Saxons. Theodore was well aware of the remarkable success of Wilfrid's missionary work. In his old age he had lost none of his magnanimity and could not have failed to have had a high regard for Wilfrid's evangelistic zeal and labours. Moreover, now that Ecgfrith had died Theodore felt freed from any sense of obligation to adhere to Ecgfrith's policy of hostility towards Wilfrid. Desirous of being reconciled to Wilfrid the archbishop summoned him to meet him in London. Present at this meeting was also Bishop Earconwald of London. Before these two bishops Eddius portrays Theodore as making his confession and receiving absolution from Wilfrid. In his confession Theodore admits that he did wrong 'in consenting to the kings who robbed you (Wilfrid) . . . and drove you into exile.' [25] Theodore is also made to say 'Agree to me appointing you, while I am still alive, to my archiepiscopal see as my successor and heir.' Wilfrid, however, desired that with Theodore's consent the question of a successor to the archbishopric of Canterbury should be considered in a 'greater council.' For himself his chief desire was to have some part of his possessions and his see restored to him in accordance with the directive of Pope Agatho. Without delay Theodore adopted measures to bring about Wilfrid's restoration by writing letters to King Aldfrith, who had succeeded Ecgfrith in Northumbria, King Aethelred of Mercia and Abbess Aelffled of Whitby telling them of his reconciliation with Wilfrid and urging that the bishop should be restored according to the terms of the papal bull which Ecgfrith had cast aside as having been fraudulently obtained.[26] Aldfrith was greatly influenced by the letter which he had received from the archbishop of Canterbury, and by his invitation to Wilfrid to visit him, he took the initial step for his restoration to his bishopric in accordance with the archbishop's request. By the time he arrived in Northumbria the see of Hexham had fallen vacant by the death of Eata. This monastery and see the king restored to him. Later, after Bishop Bosa of York and Bishop Eadhed of Ripon had been deprived or induced to resign their sees, Wilfrid regained possession of his monastery of Ripon and his see of York. Bede makes only a brief reference to these events and dismisses them with the words 'he recovered his see.' [27] This was not precisely true, for the decree of Pope Agatho was not fully implemented. The see of Lindisfarne which Theodore had originally established retained its separate identity and a year after Cuthbert's death Theodore consecrated Eadberht as his successor. It would appear that Wilfrid on removing from Hexham to York found himself unable to administer the see of Hexham to which John of Beverley was consecrated in the same year as Eadberht in 688, and probably on the same occasion.[28] This total disregard of the papal decree in these two instances indicates that Theodore's policy for the subdivision of the larger dioceses had proved itself to be administratively successful. The maintenance of this policy by king and archbishop reflected a further rejection of papal directives and the increasing acceptance of the independent authority of the archbishopric of Canterbury. This was destined soon to be more pronounced and later to become more evident of an independence distinctively characteristic of the Church in England until the eleventh century.

Archbishop Theodore's relationship with the monasteries of Britain was one of wise understanding and tolerant regard for their established traditions. His knowledge of monastic life and its disciplines was not theoretical but had been gained from practical experience for he himself as a Basilian monk had been chosen and consecrated by Pope Vitalian for the office which he now occupied. His consecration to the episcopate could neither change the Byzantine influences which had helped to shape his outlook nor could the monastic traditions under which he had been nurtured in Eastern Christendom be lightly set aside. In the Eastern Church double monasteries were considered to be uncanonical and to this principle Theodore adhered. Throughout his province, however, there existed double monasteries among which were those of Bardsey, Barking, Coldingham, Ely, Repton, Wenlock, Whitby and Wimborne. Of these Whitby Abbey, ruled over by the Abbess Hilda, was the most distinguished for sanctity of life and learning. While he regarded their existence as uncanonical and looked upon them with disapproval he made no attempt to transform them into single monasteries. Even the distinctive qualities of Whitby Abbey in no way changed his attitude towards the double monasteries though it seems likely that, to some extent, he was influenced by the abbey's remarkable achievements. In his Penitential, which is a collection of answers to questions on penance, ecclesiastical law and discipline, the greater part of which were received from Theodore by Eoda, a priest, and edited by a native of Northumbria, one of the archbishop's pupils, the problem of the double monasteries was resolved. This was clearly shown by the words : 'It is not lawful for men to have women as nuns, nor for women to have men as monks. Nevertheless, we for our part do not disallow that which is customary in this country.' [29] In these words may probably be discerned the moderating influence of Abbot Hadrian who, at Pope Vitalian's request, had accompanied Theodore to Britain in order to restrain him from introducing any Greek doctrine and custom contrary to Roman orthodoxy into the Church in England.

Nevertheless, he introduced measures of reform for the well-being of the monasteries. His chief reform concerned monks who, without their abbot's permission, left the monastery where they had been professed for another monastery. This was strictly forbidden at the synod of Hertford. At the same synod under Theodore's presidency a canon was received which set definite limits to a bishop's authority in monasteries. The bishop's spiritual jurisdiction still remained over the monasteries in his diocese, but he was forbidden to interfere with their internal affairs and to remove by force any of their property. At his own monastery at Canterbury, during the abbacy of Hadrian, Pope Agatho in 675 had confirmed privileges granted to the monastery by Pope Boniface IV, probably as early as 610.[30] These privileges conferred no exemption from episcopal jurisdiction and expressed an anathema upon both secular and ecclesiastical persons who at any time should invade the property of the monastery or interfere with its normal life. Similar privileges were bestowed by Pope Agatho upon the monasteries of Peterborough, St. Paul's, London, and Chertsey, while Benedict Biscop carried back from Rome 'a letter of privilege from the venerable Pope Agatho' for his monastery of Wearmouth and Jarrow, which he had obtained at the request of King Ecgfrith of Northumbria.[31] After accompanying Theodore from Rome at the pope's command, Benedict Biscop remained in Canterbury for two years as abbot of St. Peter's monastery.[32] During that period a lasting relationship was established with Theodore's flourishing school which Benedict maintained on his return to his monastery of Wearmouth and Jarrow either by visits to or correspondence with Canterbury's centre of learning. This was in some measure due to Ceolfrid, whom Benedict appointed to be abbot of his twin-monastery because of his frequent absences abroad, for Ceolfrid himself had been educated in Kent.[33]

Amidst all the preoccupations of his office it is evident that Theodore had a deep concern for the financial stability and well-being of the Church over which he ruled. The gifts of the faithful offered at the mass were the only direct financial support which the newly founded Church received.[34] King Aethelbert had promulgated laws for his territories during Augustine's episcopate which made provision for compensation for the loss of property of a bishop, priest, deacon and clerk, and for Church property.[35] This assurance of restitution in no way meant that financial support for the Church and its officers had been provided, although this may have been the first step towards the payment of 'church-scot,' which became obligatory shortly after Theodore's archiepiscopate.[36] Records still survive which show that at least thirty-eight grants of land or other gifts were bestowed upon the Church in England during Theodore's long administration of twenty-two years at Canterbury.[37] Provision of this kind for the work of the Church could hardly have been an isolated case. But for the general work of the Church there can be little doubt that tithes were paid to the Church in England during the last decade of Theodore's archiepiscopate. Archbishop Boniface, the papal legate in Germany, wrote a letter in 747 to Archbishop Cuthbert of Canterbury, in which he made reference to the payment of tithes in the English Church.[38] Born in Crediton in 680, Wynfrith, later named Boniface, was brought up in close acquaintance with the activities of the Church, having entered as a boy of seven years of age into the monastery of Exeter. It would appear that during his boyhood tithes were voluntarily and fully paid. This seems to be confirmed by the laws of Ine, king of the West Saxons who, following the advice of his father Cenred, Haeddi, bishop of Winchester and other counsellors, in the year 690 in which Theodore died, promulgated laws which directed that 'church-scot' should be paid at St. Martin's Mass (11th November).[39] Theodore, in his Penitential, laid down certain principles which would preserve and if possible expand the financial support of the Church. Provision for the poor, however, remained a first obligation. In the erection of churches by owners of land there had emerged the problem that they might divert their traditionally given tithe to other purposes. Because of this and the needs of the Church in the whole of his province he enjoined that it should be lawful to give tithe to the poor and strangers, and for the laity to give tithe to their churches.[40] His reference to law possessed no element of compulsion other than the sense of obligation on the part of the faithful in the conscientious fulfilment of their Christian duties, for at that time there was no secular law by which the payment of tithes could be enforced. Not until the mid-tenth century, however, did the payment of tithes become obligatory by law.[41]

Theodore's last public act at Canterbury as metropolitan archbishop was the consecration of Eadberht and John of Beverley to serve in King Aldfrith's kingdom of Northumbria. Although unable to visit the northern parts of his province, owing to the infirmities of old age, the benefits of his ecclesiastical administration still remained. Aldfrith insisted that Wilfrid should conform to the policy and arrangements laid down for his diocese by Theodore and not to the requirements of Pope Agatho's decrees.[42] The king's demand that Theodore's policy should be implemented serves to underline the archbishop's outstanding gifts by which he gave to the Church in England organization and unity. He had whenever possible administered his vast province through regularly convoked synods as required by canon law. Nevertheless, when occasion arose, he did not hesitate to exercise his provincial authority as metropolitan archbishop of Britain in complete independence of any synodal precept. He initiated his policy for the sub-division of the larger diocese without any synodal authority and in the face of adverse criticism and at times opposition. Nevertheless, his policy brought lasting benefits to the Church in England which have remained down to the present time. But according to Bede, in his letter to Bishop Egbert of York in 734, the division of larger dioceses and the increase of the episcopate was still greatly needed for the efficient administration of the Church.[43] Theodore's policy concerning the sphere of the ministry of the individual priest is not so clearly discernible as that for bishops. Early indications of a

priest exercising his ministry in a defined area are to be found in the
missionary labours of Bishop Cedd among the East Saxons after his
consecration in 654.[44] Certain passages in Theodore's Penitential
indicate that he had established some kind of system by which a
district or defined area was under the spiritual care of its own priest.
How extensive this system was it is difficult to determine with certainty.
But in Kent, not too far distant from his own see city of Canterbury,
he had initiated a plan by which an individual priest exercised his
ministry in an assigned district, which may have included a village
with a church, for which he was pastorally responsible to the archbishop.[45] In the northern parts of his province a similar scheme formed
a part of the pastoral administration in the diocese of York. Bishop
Wilfrid's biographer records of him that 'he ordained in all parts
numbers of priests and deacons to assist him.' [46] Bede was well aware
of the need for the revival of such arrangements when, forty-four years
after Theodore's death, he wrote to Bishop Egbert of York impressing
upon him the urgency of 'ordaining priests and instituting teachers,
who may devote themselves to preaching the Word of God, and
especially to performing the rites of holy baptism, whenever opportunity arises.' [47] Theodore's unhurried journey across France, on his
way to Canterbury after his consecration, had provided ample opportunity for him to learn of parishes with their own priests and churches,
for this had been an integral part of ecclesiastical organization in
France since the sixth century.[48] No originality, therefore, may be
attributed to his plan which possessed the embryo-elements later to
develop into the parochial system. But Elmham, writing in the fifteenth
century, was mistaken in attributing to Theodore the founding of the
parochial system.[49] King Egbert of Kent in 669 gave Reculver to the
mass priest Bassa, there to found a clerical minster.[50] Later, like
Reculver, the minsters of Dover, Folkestone, Lyminge, Sheppey, Hoo,
Upminster and South Minster came to be regarded as mother churches
in Kent. Evidence of elements which provided the basis for the
parochial system similar to those in the diocese of Canterbury were to
be found in the northern parts of his province beyond the Humber.
Since Theodore himself was so deeply involved in ecclesiastical
administration there is every reason to believe that this subject found
a place in the curriculum of his school at Canterbury. Two of his
most brilliant pupils later were distinguished not only for sanctity of
life but also for their administrative gifts in their respective spheres :
Abbot Aldhelm in his monastery at Malmesbury and Bishop John of
Beverley successively in the dioceses of Hexham and York. Bishop
John evidently sought to give effect to the instruction which he had
received from his master in assigning a defined area or district to the
charge and ministry of one priest. During his episcopate John con-

secrated churches, built by thanes in villages on their estates, which were served by their own priests.[51] Archbishop Theodore's administrative gifts had provided his vast province with dioceses of manageable size, but he did not live to see the dioceses divided into small defined areas served by individual priests so that the common people could have the fullness of the pastoral care which the Church could give. Many years were destined to elapse before a system which could be claimed to be truly parochial came into being throughout the country.

THE AUTHORITY OF CANTERBURY ACKNOWLEDGED

The authority of the metropolitan archbishopric of Canterbury was fully recognized and accepted throughout Britain during Theodore's archiepiscopate. His rule did not go unchalleneged, but even Bishop Wilfrid's successful appeal to the papal court failed to diminish the authority of the metropolitan see. There was, however, before the end of Theodore's archiepiscopate a perceptible decline in the effective administration of his province. As early as 680, after having occupied the archbishopric for ten years and having reached his seventy-seventh year, it was assumed that his absence from the council of Rome was due to the infirmities of old age. But evidence of his active pastoral oversight of his province was to be seen in his visit to one of the most northerly parts of his province for the synod of Twyford in 684 and his consecration of Cuthbert early in the following year at York. Two months later King Ecgfrith of Northumbria was slain in battle. By this time Theodore had journeyed southwards to Canterbury where he remained until his death in 690. A year after his return to his see city, in his letter to King Aethelred of Mercia telling him that he had 'made peace in Christ with the venerable Bishop Wilfrid,' he referred to his infirmity of old age and that before long he would be 'departing from this world.' He suggested to the king that he might make the journey to Canterbury to see him. And quoting the words of the patriarch Isaac, he wrote 'I would that my eyes could see your pleasant face and that my soul might bless you before I die.' [1] Theodore lived for another four years after this letter, reaching the age of eighty-eight years and, from the date of his conscration, having occupied the archbishopric for twenty-two years. His infirmity of old age was not the only cause of the decline in the ecclesiastical administration of the province. Even if Theodore had been physically active during the last few years of his archiepiscopate it would have been extremely unlikely that he would have been able to journey beyond the confines of his see city because of the invasion of Kent by Caedwalla and Mull of the West Saxons in 686. In the following year Caedwalla again ravaged Kent with his forces but the city of Canterbury emerged from these ravages of Kent unscathed, probably because Caedwalla had accepted the Christian Faith and consequently had some regard for the Church and its property. Theodore's diocese which comprised the greater part of Kent was still suffering from the inroads of the West Saxons when Ine succeeded to rule over them. But four years after the archbishop's death the Kentishmen were further impoverished when they were compelled to pay a great sum in compensation to the West Saxons for the death of Mull.[2]

Briefly summing up Theodore's rule as metropolitan archbishop Bede observed that 'The churches of the English received more spiritual advantage in the time of his episcopate than they ever could before.'[3]

There was an interregnum of two years before another archbishop was appointed to the vacant metropolitan see. This delay was doubt-less due to the unsettled state of the kingdom of Kent, but inevitably the delay adversely affected the immeasurable benefit, described by Bede, which Theodore, during his archiepiscopate, had bestowed upon the archbishopric of Canterbury and the ecclesiastical province of Britain. Finally, Berhtwald, abbot of the monastery of Reculver in Kent, was elected to the vacant see on the first of July, 692.[4] In recording Berhtwald's election the Anglo-Saxon Chronicle makes the noteworthy observation that 'Hitherto there had been Roman bishops; afterwards they were English.'[5] Bede's record appears to imply the concurrence of the two kings of Kent, Wihtred and Swaefheard, with the election of Berhtwald, who is described as 'trained in the know-ledge of the Scriptures, and deeply learned in ecclesiastical as well as monastic discipline, yet not to be compared with his predecessor.'[6] Contradictory records relating to Berhtwald's consecration have given rise to much speculation concerning their validity and the true his-torical facts. The *Liber Pontificalis* states he was consecrated by Pope Sergius I.[7] Confirmation of this is to be found in a papal letter preserved by Eadmer and William of Malmesbury[8] addressed to the three kings, Aethelred of Mercia, Aldfrith of Northumbria and Eadulf of East Anglia, 'kings of the English,' in which the pope urges them to receive Berhtwald 'the chief pontiff of all Britain.'[9] Similar terms were used by the pope in 693 in his letter to the bishops of Britain. In his commendation of Berhtwald to the bishops he reminded them that Berhtwald had been elected their archbishop to succeed Theodore in accordance with ancient custom retained by the Church since the days of Pope Gregory I. He further informed them that he had invested Berhtwald 'primate of all the churches of Britain' by means of the sacred usage of the *pallium* and holy dalmatic for which Berhtwald had petitioned, and exhorted them to render due obedience to him as primate.[10] These letters, it has been contended, breathe the spirit of a later age when the heat of controversy raged between the sees of Canterbury and York. While the apparent emphasis on the primacy of the archbishopric of Canterbury might make them suspect, on closer scrutiny their factual contents show that they cannot lightly be set aside as unauthentic. The letter to the three kings is suspect because it omits any reference to King Ine of the

West Saxons. But this omission is explained by the political situation at that juncture for Ine's war against East Anglia and Kent had ended in his defeat. Boehmer's searching criticism of this letter reached the conclusion that it is authentic and that no valid objection could be made against the designation 'chief pontiff of all Britain' for Archbishop Berhtwald, since both Eddius and Waldhere, bishop of London, used similar terms.[11]

West Saxon hostilities against East Anglia and Kent precluded any possibility of bishops safely journeying to Canterbury for his consecration. Therefore, leaving Kent for France, he received consecration at the hands of Godwin, archbishop of Lyons in July, 693.[12] Archbishop Berhtwald of Canterbury, in addition to being the first Englishman to occupy the chair of Augustine, was the first archbishop of Canterbury to carry the threefold title of 'metropolitan archbishop and primate of all England'; a title which has remained unchanged down to the present day for the one who occupies the highest ecclesiastical office in the Church of the land.[13]

Nearly three years had elapsed since the death of Theodore before his successor actually entered into his archbishopric. Inevitably the long vacancy adversely affected the Church, for the archbishopric of Canterbury was the centre from which the Church in England expected guidance and leadership. During the interregnum Bishop Wilfrid of York made persistent efforts to recover his property and to merge the dioceses established by King Ecgfrith and Archbishop Theodore into the diocese of York from which they had been taken. This policy brought Wilfrid into conflict with Aldfrith, king of Northumbria, who demanded that he should adhere to the arrangements which had been made during Theodore's archiepiscopate. On refusing to accede to the king's demands he was for the second time expelled from the kingdom and, journeying to the Mercian court, was well received by King Aethelred who asked him to exercise his episcopal ministry among the Middle Angles.[14] It is very probable that during the vacancy at Canterbury, he consecrated Aetla, with his see at Dorchester which, at the time, was under Mercian influence, and Haedda for the see of Lichfield. It was at Aethelred's request, about this time, that Oftfor was consecrated by Wilfrid to succeed the aged Bosel in the bishopric of Worcester.[15] While Berhtwald was in Lyons for consecration by the metropolitan Godwin, Swidberht was sent to Friesland to Wilfrid for consecration for missionary work among the Frisians.

On entering his archbishopric Berhtwald could not fail to be aware of the influence of Wilfrid on ecclesiastical affairs, while expelled from Northumbria, and of the friendship which existed between King Aethelred and the bishop. He found that his first major administrative problem centred round Bishop Wilfrid. It is not without significance that Theodore's first major problem of administration, but in different circumstances, also was concerned with Wilfrid. Having informed himself of the condition of the Church in Northumbria and particularly of the see of York, Berhtwald initiated measures calculated to resolve primarily Wilfrid's expulsion from his bishopric. For this purpose he convoked his first synod which assembled at Edwinspath or Austerfield in Yorkshire in 702–3 at which King Aldfrith and the bishops were present. After heated debate the synod demanded that Wilfrid should abide by the former 'judgments of Archbishop Theodore.' [16] On his refusal the synod decreed that he should be deprived of all his temporalities with the exception of the monastery at Ripon, which he had built, where he should live and not leave without the king's permission, and should give an undertaking not to exercise his episcopal office. He completely refused to accept the synod's judgment and said that he would appeal to the Apostolic See. On learning of Wilfrid's rejection of the synod's decree and his determination to appeal to the papal court both King Aldfrith and Archbishop Berhtwald considered Wilfrid had condemned himself by refusing the judgment of his metropolitan archbishop and comprovincials, and by appealing to a court outside his own country. Although seventy years of age Wilfrid did not hesitate to set out for Rome with his supporters in order to plead his cause in person before the papal court. Messengers from Archbishop Berhtwald arrived in Rome at the same time as Wilfrid carrying with them 'written accusations' against him. Pope John VI and his synod received Wilfrid's petition in which he prayed for the confirmation of Pope Agatho's decree and for the pope to urge the two kings, Aldfrith and Aethelred, to fulfil the decree. Wilfrid added that he was content to leave to the judgment of the pope the question of the government of the monasteries and of the bishopric of York and 'would accept and fulfil the decrees of the Apostolic See with the utmost goodwill.' [17] The messengers representing the archbishop of Canterbury were given the opportunity of choosing any part of their accusations against Wilfrid and of addressing the court upon it. They stated that Wilfrid had contumaciously refused and despised in the presence of the synod (Austerfield) the judgments of 'Berhtwald, archbishop of the Church of the Kentishmen and of all Britain.' [18] After a prolonged hearing of the appeal, judgment was delivered and Wilfrid was acquitted of any reproach of guilt and the decisions of Agatho, Benedict and Sergius concerning him were confirmed. Addressing a letter to the kings Aldfrith and Aethelred the pope informed them that he had directed Berhtwald to convene a synod at which the bishops Wilfrid, Bosa and John of Beverley would be present, and if the archbishop was able to bring the dispute to a satisfactory conclusion then he, himself, would also be satisfied. To the kings he also wrote 'lend your aid and assistance' so that the matters under dispute may be resolved to good effect. Bearing letters to the kings and one to the archbishop Wilfrid departed from Rome, described by Eddius as, 'victorious and altogether free from guilt.'

It is significant that the chief pleading of accusation made by Berhtwald's representatives at the papal court against Wilfrid was his open disobedience of his metropolitan archbishop in rejecting his terms of settlement of the dispute at the synod of Austerfield. This pleading weakened their case for it showed that Wilfrid, in rejecting the archbishop's terms for a settlement, had decided to accept and to adhere to the former decree of the papal court pronounced by Pope Agatho. It also revealed Berhtwald as setting aside a papal decree in favour of his own authoritative decision. In consequence the papal court could not condone nor accept the active repudiation of a papal decree by a metropolitan archbishop.

Despite the lengthy consideration of Wilfrid's appeal, it is evident that the court had failed to understand the political situation. The pope addressed the two kings in the same letter; Aldfrith, who had exiled Wilfrid and Aethelred, who had received him in exile; and appealed for their help in resolving the dispute. Further evidence of this was to be seen in the readiness with which Aethelred accepted the papal letter and enjoined Cenred, who was to succeed him as king, to obey the precepts of the Apostolic See. King Aldfrith, how-ever, having received the papal letter, was determined that the decision agreed upon by himself and Berhtwald concerning Wilfrid should remain, and declared that 'as long as I live I will never change because of writings sent from the Apostolic See.' [19] But underlying the dispute in which Wilfrid was involved was the larger issue of the authority of the metropolitan archbishop of Canterbury and the province of all Britain over which he ruled. The pope's direction to Berhtwald that he should convene a synod at which to settle the dispute and, failing a settlement, that the parties should appear again at the papal court was, in itself, a reassertion of the pope's authority over the metropolitan archbishop of Britain. The terms of settlement had been given in the appellate court's judgment, namely, that the decree of Agatho should be implemented. There was no room for compromise between this decree and the decision of the synod of Austerfield which had accepted the agreed policy of Aldfrith and Berhtwald. It meant that whenever the archbishop complied with the pope's direction and convoked a synod he would be compelled openly in all obedience to the pope to receive and implement the findings of the papal court or to reject them and thereby show his disregard for the authority of the pope. Acceptance of the papal judgment would mean a reversal of the decree of the synod, attended by King Aldfrith, over which Berhtwald had presided and a consequent undermining of his own authority as metropolitan archbishop of Britain. On their return from Rome his representatives had given a report of the proceedings at the appellate court by which he was so deeply moved that he promised to mitigate the severity of the decrees which his own synod had pronounced against Wilfrid. Afterwards he met Wilfrid and the two were reconciled and journeyed together joyfully from Canterbury to London.

The year 705 in which Wilfrid returned to Britain was a momentous year for him, Northumbria and the Church in England. In the kingdom of Northumbria events followed in rapid succession. Within a few months of Aldfrith's total rejection of the pope's letter he died at Driffield and was succeeded by Eadulf, who was deposed after two months, and Aldfrith's son Osred became king. In the first year of his reign with his chief men he was present at a synod convoked by Archbishop Berhtwald in obedience to the pope's directive, on the banks of the river Nidd in Northumbria.[20] Three bishops, without doubt John of Beverley, Eadfrith and Bosa respectively of the sees of Hexham, Lindisfarne and York, with their abbots were present and the Abbess Aelffled. Papal documents which had been received by Berhtwald and Wilfrid were produced and the synod's permission was given for them to be read. After they had been read, Berhtfrith, next in rank to the king, asked for the documents to be translated. To this the archbishop replied that they were expressed in circuitous and ambiguous terms but that he would explain in brief the bare sense of the writings. He told them that there were two choices before the bishops, either 'to restore to Wilfrid those parts of the churches he formerly ruled as wise counsellors and myself shall settle; or, altogether to go to the Apostolic See, there to be judged in a greater council.' The bishops resisted the papal decrees and said 'Who can anywise alter that which was once decided by our predecessors, Archbishop Theodore, who was sent from the Apostolic See, and King Ecgfrith; and what we and the bishops of almost the whole of Britain and in your excellent presence, archbishop, afterwards decreed with King Aldfrith in the place called Austerfileld?' The final outcome of the synod was the making of a complete peace with Wilfrid, which was kept thoughout their lifetime, and the restoration to him of the important monasteries of Ripon and Hexham with all their revenues.[21] By this decree the synod completely set aside the pope's directive that the decrees of Agatho, Benedict and Sergius should be implemented. Berhtwald, the first Englishman to be archbishop of Canterbury, had disregarded papal decrees, like his predecessor

G

Theodore, and had shown an independence of action which was not only accepted but supported by the Church in England.

Out of the conflict with Bishop Wilfrid the metropolitan archbishopric of Canterbury had emerged with increased prestige and authority which were personified in Berhtwald during the early years of his archiepiscopate. With the accession of Osred to the throne of Northumbria the kingdom's greatness came to an end, and this change in the political situation, further complicated by the precocious wickedness of the young king, inevitably affected the Church in Northumbria.[22] In this kingdom there was a progressive decline over the next thirty years,[23] but in the south the archbishopric of Canterbury continued to increase its influence.

From the outset of his archiepiscopate Berhtwald's hand on the helm of the Church was tolerant yet resolute. Before his consecration, but doubtless with his knowledge since he was abbot of Reculver, King Ine of Wessex had promulgated laws which had brought some benefits to the Church of the West Saxons. In the introductory paragraph to his laws Ine refers to the presence at the witenagemot of Bishop Haeddi of Winchester and Bishop Eorcenwald of London and describes each as 'my bishop.' [24] The lack of any reference to Berhtwald is explained by the fact that he had not yet entered into occupation of his see, and the reference to the bishop of London would suggest that when the witenagemot assembled Ine's influence over London had superseded that of Mercia. Of his seventy-nine laws no less than thirteen relate to the life and rights of the Church.[25] Infants must be baptized within thirty nights of birth; the oath of a communicant who 'goes to Housel' is of higher value; there is a distinctive solemnity given to an oath taken before a bishop; payment of church-scot for roof and hearth must be paid regularly. These laws both temporal and spiritual indicate how closely integrated at this time were State and Church. There had existed during the reign of King Ecgfrith close co-operation with Archbishop Theodore in his arrangements for the administrative structure of the Church in Northumbria. But their joint activity could hardly be described as integration between State and Church similar to that which had gradually emerged in Kent since Augustine had founded the Church at Canterbury. King Aethelbert of Kent, after he had accepted the Christian Faith, had enacted laws, some of which provided for penalties for offences against God and the Church.[26] Many years later, c. 684, Kings Hlothere and Eadric of Kent added to the laws of their ancestors but they did not confer any additional benefits by law upon the Church, although Hlothere assisted the Church by his grants of land.[27] Before the close of the seventh century, however, King Wihtred of Kent held a witenagemot at Bearsted, near Maidstone in Kent, in 695, which was attended by nobles and clergy among whom were Gebmund, bishop of Rochester and Berhtwald, 'high-bishop of Britain.' [28] Of the laws promulgated from this assembly, those which bestowed privileges upon the Church and its ministers make the document of singular historical interest.[29] The most important benefits received by the Church were : by law the Church had freedom from taxation ; men were bidden to pray for the king of their own accord ; the penalty for breach of the protection of the Church was the same as that for the king—fifty shillings ; a bishop's word like the king's was to be accepted without an oath. There had existed nothing comparable in any other kingdom of Britain to the kingly protection which the Church in Kent had enjoyed since the days of Augustine. Wihtred's laws had now placed the Church in an almost unassailable position and had inevitably strengthened the tradition and conception estab- lished by Theodore of a centralized administration of the Church at Canterbury. Further evidence of this was to be found in a council held at Bapchild, near Sittingbourne in Kent, in 698, at which King Wihtred and Archbishop Berhtwald presided.[30] From this council came 'the privilege' of Wihtred purporting to grant certain privileges to the churches and monasteries of Kent. The record of it is to be found in a manuscript not earlier than 1220 and its contents are regarded as spurious. It contains some elements of truth for it is stated in a note that it was copied from a very old charter or land book, which may have been the source from which 'the privilege' was copied into the late Canterbury version of the Anglo-Saxon Chronicle.[31] Whatever may be the true import of 'the privilege' there can be little doubt but that the council conferred some further benefits on the Church in Kent, which show the influence of Archbishop Berhtwald upon Wihtred, the Christian king of Kent, who together presided at the council.

At the opening of the eighth century Berhtwald was able to initiate measures for the division of the diocese of Winchester.[32] Archbishop Theodore had planned to divide the diocese when he consecrated his friend Haeddi to rule over it, but the uncertain political situation in Wessex and the needs of the Church in Northumbria prevented at that time the fulfilment of his plans. He had established a friendly relationship with the Church of the West Saxons despite its indepen- dence of the metropolitan see of Canterbury from its first beginnings under Bishop Birinus. King Cenwalh had unsuccessfully attempted to divide his kingdom into two sees, Dorchester and Winchester, and after Dorchester had been conquered by the Mercians it was served by a certain Bishop Aetla.[33] In view of Theodore's zeal for the efficient administration of the Church there can be little doubt but that the question of the division of the West Saxon bishopric arose

when he consecrated Haeddi or soon after. A fragment of a decree
made by Theodore *c.* 679 at a council of unknown location, records
that the bishopric of Winchester should not be divided during Haeddi's
lifetime.[34] Although the authenticity of this document cannot remain
unquestioned, the facts show that the see of Winchester was not
divided in his lifetime nor during the lifetime of Bishop Haeddi who
died in 705. Theodore had a plan for the division of the see and it
would appear that Berhtwald had tried to implement it at a synod,
probably the annual synod at Clofeshoh in 704. The West Saxons
reasserted their independence with sufficient vigour to delay any
division, but they did not escape censure.[35] In less than a year, and
after the death of Bishop Haeddi in 705, at a West Saxon synod over
which King Ine presided, it was decreed that the see should be
divided, and the see of Sherborne established.[36] There had been no
delay in Daniel's succession to Bishop Haeddi and it would appear
that he fully agreed with the division of the see of Winchester and
the election of Aldhelm, abbot of Malmesbury, to be the first bishop
of Sherborne. Of necessity the problem of financing the new bishopric
arose, but whether Aldhelm's election and financial arrangements for
his see were made at the same synod, which may have been 'near
the river Nodder' is not certain. At this place in Wiltshire, however,
suitable provision was made for the newly created bishopric by permission being granted, with the consent of Ine and Daniel, for
Aldhelm to retain the abbacies of Malmesbury, Frome and Bradford-
on-Avon.[37] All these proceedings, whether he was present or not,
were helpful to Archbisop Berhtwald in his efforts to complete his
predecessor's plan for efficient ecclesiastical organization. Aldhelm,
a former pupil at Theodore's school in Canterbury, journeyed to the
primal see for consecration by Berhtwald after which they took
counsel together for the well-being of the Church.[38] The see of
Winchester was further sub-divided by decree of a West Saxon synod,
during the episcopates of Daniel and Aldhelm, when Selsey was
created a bishopric to serve the South Saxons, and about this time
Bishop Daniel was able to include the Isle of Wight within his
diocese of Winchester.[39] Presiding at a synod *c.* 703, Berhtwald had
decreed what course to adopt if proposals for the sub-division of the
bishopric of the West Saxons were not accepted and implemented.
Reference to this synod is made in a letter, which must have been
written in 704, by Bishop Waldhere of London to Berhtwald, at
which it was decreed that there ought to be no intercourse with the
West Saxon Church if fulfilment of the decree relating to bishops
were delayed. So far, Bishop Waldhere observed, the decree had not
been implemented. At this time Bishop Haeddi was still bishop of
Winchester.

This letter reveals many aspects of Church life and organization at that period. Not least, it indicates the important place which the metropolitan archbishopric of Canterbury held in matters relating to the Church and the immense influence it exercised on rulers and their kingdoms.[40] Waldhere had been invited by the kings of Essex and Wessex to attend a council at Brentford in 704, at which the kings, bishops, abbots and counsellors would be present, in order to settle disputes between the kings. These disputes evidently involved the well-being of the Church. The kings undertook to observe the conditions of any agreement which Bishop Waldhere and the West Saxon bishop (Haeddi) devised. As powerful as the bishops were in the counsel which they gave to kings, the letter shows that Waldhere attached much more importance to the authority and influence of the metropolitan archbishopric. Earlier in the same year he had been invited by King Cenred of Mercia to attend a council concerned with 'the reconciliation of Aelfthryth,' but because he had been unable to ascertain the wishes of Berhtwald in the matter he had declined the invitation. Now he had been requested to attend a council of much more importance and it was necessary that he should attend. Knowing of the decree relating to the Church in Wessex he asked Berhtwald to inform him what he ought to do in the matter. Subsequent events after the death of Bishop Haeddi show that whatever political agreements were reached at the council, summoned by the kings of Essex and Wessex, there followed definite action on the part of the king of Wessex to implement the ecclesiastical decree for the sub-division of the diocese of Winchester. This meant that after more than thirty years, Theodore's plan for the diocese finally materialized under the guidance of Berhtwald. The political power of the archishopric had in no way declined since Theodore's archiepiscopate. He had made peace between kings but now, under Berhtwald's wise counsel, two of his suffragans, Bishops Waldhere and Haeddi, had not only settled political disputes between kings but at the same time had resolved a long-standing ecclesiastical problem.

Another element of this remarkable letter is its expression of Waldhere's overwhelming recognition of the authority of the archbishopric and the completeness with which he was willing, without question, to accept Berhtwald's advice. 'I choose what you may choose,' he wrote, 'refuse what you may refuse, and hold the same view as you in all things.' [41] This unquestioning readiness to follow his archbishop's counsel should not detract from the influence which Bishop Waldhere exercised at a time when the East Saxon kings were unable to settle disputes among themselves and their disputes with the king of Wessex. Their request for him to act as mediator and their pledge to accept his terms of settlement of their disputes show their respect for the bishop's office and their confidence in his political judgment. Waldhere's letter, however, shows beyond all doubt that the central authority of the archbishopric of Canterbury had reached so far its highest level of influence although it had been persistently assailed during Theodore's archiepiscopate and the first twelve years of Berhtwald's primacy by Bishop Wilfrid of Northumbria.

Nevertheless, the influence of the archbishopric of Canterbury was increasingly felt in Wessex. Forthere had been consecrated by Berht-wald to succeed Aldhelm in the see of Sherborne. In the presence of the newly consecrated bishop he had requested Beorwald, abbot of Glastonbury, on behalf of her relatives in Kent to accept a ransom for a girl whom he held captive. Contrary to the archbishop's expectation Beorwald would not accede to his request. The girl's relatives again asked the archbishop to use his influence to obtain her freedom and, as a result, he sent a letter by her brother, Eppa, to Bishop Forthere asking him to approach the abbot and to offer a ransom of three hundred shillings. Since no further reference is to be found concerning the matter it is most probable, in view of the high esteem with which Berhtwald was regarded in Wessex, that Forthere was successful in obtaining the girl's release.[42] While undue emphasis should not be placed on this incident it illustrates the ease with which Canterbury in Kent could communicate with far distant Glastonbury in Somerset, and the administrative efficiency of the metropolitan archbishopric in its knowledge of and active interest in personal problems in the province. It also indicates the progressive ecclesiastical integration of the Church of the West Saxons with the province of Canterbury since the division of the see of Winchester and Berhtwald's consecration of Bishops Daniel, Aldhelm and Forthere. Further evidence of this integration was to be seen when a dispute arose concerning what would appear to have been a matter of critical importance to the Church in Wessex. So widespread was dissension that, after consultation between King Ine and church leaders (bishops and abbots), a council was convened at which the matters causing dissension among the West Saxons were fully considered. Agreement was finally reached and it was decided that the conclusions of the council should be submitted verbally by messenger to Berhtwald. The principal member of the embassy sent by the king was Boniface (Wynfrid) of the monastery of Nursling, Hampshire. Bearing in mind that the council feared to make any final decision without the counsel of the archbishop, lest they should be accused of presumption and temerity, Boniface with diplomatic skill and wisdom laid the whole situation before the archbishop as commissioned by the king. Having been given an immediate reply by the archbishop, Boniface returned to Wessex where he gave a full report to the king at a synodal council. King Ine and all present were highly pleased with the approval given by the archbishop to the conclusions which they had reached at their former council.[43] Since the first of these two councils was wholly concerned with ecclesiastical affairs there can be little doubt that the matter upon which they sought Berhtwald's advice and approval was the further division of the see of Winchester by the erection of a bishopric to serve the South Saxons, with its seat at Selsey in the monastery founded by Bishop Wilfrid. The immediate problem would arise concerning the financial maintenance of the new see. Any proposal to divert the finances of the monastery of Selsey in order to maintain a bishopric would inevitably meet with opposition from the monks. This, undoubtedly, brought the monks into conflict with both bishops and priests and caused widespread dissension in Wessex. Any opposition from the monks was brought to an end by the choice of their own abbot, Eadberht, to be the first bishop with his seat in the monastery. He was consecrated sometime between 709 and 711 during which period, it would appear, the two councils assembled.[44] For the bishops of Winchester and Sherborne with the Christian king, Ine, and other ecclesiastics to have countenanced the erection of a new diocese without first seeking the advice and approval of the metropolitan archbishop would have been 'presumptuous and temerarious' as the council described it. But the pleasure and approbation with which the council received the report of Boniface indicated that the independence of the Church in Wessex had finally come to an end in its full recognition of the archbishopric of Canterbury and its consequent integration of the three dioceses of Winchester, Sherborne and Selsey within the province of Canterbury.

One of the great achievements of the archbishopric of Canterbury during Berhtwald's archiepiscopate was the encouragement which it gave to synods. From these can be gathered a more complete picture of the Church and its activities during the first decades of the eighth century. Diverse subjects were the concern of these synods. The settlement of ecclesiastical disputes at the synods on the banks of the Nidd and in Wessex [45]; the consecration of Evesham Abbey at the synod of Alcester [46]; and the policy adopted for persuading adherents to the Celtic Church traditions in Devonshire and Cornwall to observe the Catholic date of Easter, at a West Saxon synod, were matters which received consideration.[47] In this way Berhtwald advanced the tradition established by Theodore and also sought to implement the decree of the council of Hertford that a synod should assemble annually at Clofeshoh.[48] This freedom of synodal government did not supersede his metropolitan authority. His firm hand was ever at the helm, and recognition of this was made by Bishop Waldhere in his letter to him in which he made specific reference to 'your decree about the ordination of bishops,' [49] at what was probably the annual synod at Clofeshoh. Similar recognition, of both Church and State, was to be seen when a West Saxon synodal council delayed any action on its findings until the approval of Berhtwald had been obtained.[50]

It was from this part of the province that Boniface, with the advice and assistance of Bishop Daniel of Winchester, left England for Frisia where he assisted Willibrord, a former monk of Ripon, in his missionary labours. To what extent Boniface influenced the wider work of the Church in England during Berhtwald's archiepiscopate is uncertain. But he was destined to become one of the greatest missionaries of the Anglo-Saxon Church and, as his correspondence shows, he maintained a close and helpful relationship with the Church of his native land.[51]

Although Berhtwald completed Theodore's plan for the division of the larger dioceses, there were at the close of his archiepiscopate the same number of dioceses as in Theodore's time. Of necessity some changes had been made in the sixteen dioceses within the province. Soon after the death of Theodore, during the interregnum, Leicester ceased to exist as a separate diocese. It was merged with the see of Lichfield at the time when Haedda became bishop in 691, but was separated again in 737.[52] Farther south the large diocese of Winchester had been divided and the dioceses of Sherborne and Selsey had been established.[53] In the northern part of the province the bishopric of Ripon had no successor after Bishop Eadhed had occupied the see on his expulsion from the see of Lindsey, which had been conquered by the Mercians.[54] Still farther north the see of Abercorn had been abandoned when the Picts defeated and slew King Ecgfrith. The more distant parts of the province, particularly in the north, had always created much difficulty for effective oversight and administration from Canterbury. After the synod on the banks of the river Nidd in 705, at which Bishop Wilfrid's dispute was finally settled, no record is to be found which would show that Archbishop Berhtwald ever again visited that part of his province north of the river Humber. Bishop Acca in 709 succeeded to the see of Hexham and there is every reason to believe that he journeyed to Canterbury to receive consecration from the archbishop.[55] The bishop's subscription is to be found on documents relating to royal grants in the diocese of Worcester in 709 and 710, and evidence of his presence at the synod of Clofeshoh in 716 indicates that he received and obeyed a summons from his metropolitan to attend the synod.[56] John of Beverley, bishop of York, in nominating and consecrating his priest Wilfrid to succeed him on his retirement in 718, reflected an increasing independence of the archbishopric of Canterbury, and it would appear that Aethelwald, prior of Melrose, was consecrated by Northumbrian bishops in 724 to succeed Eadfrith in the see of Lindisfarne.[57] On the conversion of the southern Picts in Galloway, Pechthelm was consecrated in 730 to serve the restored bishopric of Whithorn where the missionary bishop, St. Ninian, originally had his seat.[58] Pechthelm, its first Anglian bishop, had been deacon and monk under Bishop Aldhelm of Sherborne, and it may be assumed that in view of the close and friendly relationship between Aldhelm, Daniel and Berhtwald, Pechthelm journeyed from Wessex to Canterbury, a year before the death of Berhtwald, to receive consecration at his hands. If so, this was the last consecration by the archbishop of Canterbury of a bishop to serve north of the river Humber before the bishopric of York became a metropolitan see in 735 under Egbert, its first archbishop. It would also appear to be the only occasion during the last twelve years of Berhtwald's archiepiscopate that he was able to exercise some form of administrative oversight from Canterbury of the remotest northern parts of his province. A similar difficulty of administering the Church in the north from the centre of Canterbury had arisen during the closing years of Theodore's archiepiscopate. Towards the close of each archiepiscopate the advanced age of the two archbishops, the remoteness of the northern dioceses and the unstable political conditions, especially north of the river Humber, imposed upon the Church in the north the necessity of independent action in order to preserve its continuity. How this was to be attained was graphically portrayed in Bede's memorable letter to Bishop Egbert of York, which greatly influenced the northern Church.

BONIFATIAN INFLUENCE AND THE REFORMING SYNODS

The political scene changed considerably during the decade preceding the death of Archbishop Berhtwald in 731. Throughout all the changes the central administrative structure of the metropolitan arch-bishopric of Canterbury, firmly based upon Theodore's foundations, had adapted itself to the changing conditions and had expanded under the sure guidance of Berhtwald so that its authority was unquestioned in Britain. Its influence was visibly effective and recognized in the south but this could hardly be claimed for that part of the province north of the river Humber. A contributory cause of this was the beginning of Northumbrian isolation, which had become more apparent since 678 when King Ecgfrith of Northumbria had been defeated near the Trent by King Aethelred of Mercia, and Lindsey had become again a part of the Mercian kingdom. Aethelred's influence greatly strengthened the Church but his two immediate successors, Cenred and Ceolred, did much harm to the Church. Ceolred drove Aethelbald into exile, regarding him as a possible claimant to the Mercian throne. He was given asylum by his kinsman Guthlac at Crowland and finally became king of Mercia in 716. At that time in the south King Wihtred of Kent and King Ine of Wessex still ruled, but on Wihtred's death in 725 and Ine's abdication in 726 their successors within five years recognized Aethelbald as their over-lord. To the west Gwynedd and Powys remained in their strength undisturbed. This was the political situation in England when Berht-wald died. Bede, writing in the same year, 731, recorded that all the 'provinces' south of the river Humber 'with their kings are subject to Aethelbald, king of the Mercians.'[1] So effectively did Aethelbald consolidate his position that within another five years he subscribed to charters under the style 'Rex Britanniae,'[2] as the head of a con-federation of kingdoms which included not only Kent and Wessex but all the kingdoms from the Channel northwards to the Humber. On this political background the immediate future of the Church in England south of the Humber was set, and the powerful influence of Mercia was destined to change the course of the history of the arch-bishopric of Canterbury and of the Church throughout the land. In the election of the Mercian, Tatwine, a priest of the monastery of Breedon, to succeed Berhtwald may be seen the beginning of this influence. It was to Aethelbald's advantage as overlord of Kent to have a Mercian, who was 'renowned for piety and wisdom, and notably learned in the sacred scriptures,' doubtless known to him as the most eminent churchman in Mercia, in the most important office of archbishop of Canterbury. After his consecration in Canterbury by the bishops of Winchester, London, Lichfield and Rochester he received the *pallium,* and in 733 he consecrated two bishops, Alwig for Lindsey and Sigga for Selsey.[3] This is the only recorded activity of his archiepiscopate which was ended by his death in 734. Before his death, however, Egbert, a cousin of Ceolwulf, king of Northumbria, had been consecrated bishop of York, probably by Wilfrid II of York to succeed him on his retirement from the see.[4] In the same year in which Tatwine died the initial step was taken by Bede in sending his historic letter to Bishop Egbert in which, among other matters, he gave the relevant details of the plan of Pope Gregory I for York to become a metropolitan see. This could not be effected until Egbert possessed the *pallium* from the Apostolic See.[5] Following Bede's advice that he should have the support of his royal cousin, King Ceolwulf of Northumbria petitioned Pope Gregory III for the *pallium* to be conferred upon Bishop Egbert. The petition was successful, and the *pallium* was received in 735 by Egbert, who then became the first metropolitan archbishop of York in accordance with the Gregorian plan.

By the implementation of this plan, as it applied to the see of York, the whole course of the history of the Church in England was changed. In possessing the *pallium* during the interregnum at Canterbury, Egbert was in the unique position of being the only metropolitan archbishop in Britain. His newly created province, co-extensive with the territorial extent of Northumbria, included in addition to his own see of York the dioceses of Lindisfarne, Hexham and Whithorn. There was, however, no long interregnum at Canterbury for Nothelm, described by Thorn as 'archpriest of the cathedral church of St. Paul, London,' succeeded to the archbishopric and was consecrated in 735.[6] He was one of the most eminent scholars of the post-Theodoran age and must have been known for his mature scholarship as early as 721. His distinguished researches still survive in the contributions which he gave to Bede for his *Ecclesiastical History.* Taking with him, on a visit to Rome, copies of the letters of Gregory I which were at Canterbury, he evidently checked them in the papal *scrinium* and made copies of Gregorian and other papal letters which he found there.[7] On his return, before Bede had completed his *History* in 731, he journeyed northwards to the monastery of Jarrow, on the advice of Abbot Albinus of Canterbury, and personally delivered into the hands of Bede the copies of the letters which he had found in the *scrinium* at Rome. With full acknowledgements to Nothelm they were incorporated by Bede in his *History,* which at that time must have been near completion.[8]

A year after his consecration in 735 Nothelm received the *pallium* from Pope Gregory III. Of all the metropolitans who had occupied the chair of Augustine none had found himself in a situation similar to that which now confronted Archbishop Nothelm. Already in Britain there was another metropolitan archbishop, Egbert of York, who also had received the *pallium* and had consecrated Frithoberht, bishop of Hexham, as one of his suffragans. Nothelm's immediate predecessors, Theodore, Berhtwald and Tatwine, had all been recognized as metropolitan archbishops exercising their authority throughout the whole of Britain. But now the territory north of the river Humber constituted the ecclesiastical province of York and had received the seal of papal approval by the bestowal of the *pallium* upon its metropolitan. No longer could the archbishop of Canterbury exercise metropolitan authority north of the Humber for beyond that line he possessed no jurisdiction although by right of succession he still held the office of 'primate of the whole of Britain.' Neither protest nor adverse comment by Nothelm is anywhere to be found concerning this new situation. But it should be borne in mind that he was probably the only scholar of that period who possessed detailed knowledge of what should be the constitution of the Church in Britain as set forth by Pope Gregory I in his letter to Augustine, a copy of which with other papal letters he had copied and conveyed to Bede. There is every reason to believe that when Nothelm met Bede at Jarrow they discussed in some detail the Gregorian plan and its implications for the Church in the north of Britain. On this occasion Bede's advocacy for the creation of the province of York in conformity with the plan was undoubtedly urged as a necessity for the well-being of the Church. And it was to this argument he later returned and cogently developed in his letter to Bishop Egbert. In consequence, when Nothelm became archbishop of Canterbury he was already convinced that the implementation of the Gregorian plan in the creation of the ecclesiastical province of York had been the wisest and best course for the Church in Britain. He was also fully aware that he possessed no authority over the metropolitan archbishop of York for Gregory had informed Augustine that after his (Augustine's) death the bishop of York 'shall be in no way subject to the jurisdiction of the bishop of London' (Canterbury).[9] In its territorial extent Nothelm's province embraced the whole of Britain south of the river Humber, although Cornwall and Wales had not yet become subject to the jurisdiction of the archbishopric of Canterbury. Evidence of the independence and separate identity of each province was to be seen in the normal procedure of the two archbishops consecrating their own suffragans. Before Nothelm became archbishop of Canterbury Egbert had consecrated Frithoberht and the following year, 735, in which Nothelm was consecrated, Frithowald was consecrated by the archbishop of York for the see of Whithorn. Similarly, in the same year that he received the *pallium* Nothelm consecrated Bishops Cuthbert, Aethelfrith and Herewald respectively for the sees of Hereford, Elmham and Sherborne. At a synod in 736, which was probably the annual synod of Clofeshoh, convoked by Nothelm, the Church in the south functioned for the first time as an ecclesiastical province since the separation of the dioceses which now formed the province of York. Of the twelve dioceses which constituted the province of Canterbury ten were represented by the presence of their bishops.[10] The two dioceses of Elmham and Dunwich unrepresented, it would appear were vacant at that time. The only recorded business of the synod which has survived is a document relating to a reversion to the see of Worcester.[11] More important business was doubtless transacted which concerned the separation of the see of Leicester from the see of Lichfield. Early in 737, on the death of Bishop Ealdwine, also called Wor, of Lichfield, Leicester once again became a bishopric to which Nothelm consecrated Torthelm or Totta, and Hwitta to the see of Lichfield. This could not have been effected without the concurrence of King Aethelbald of Mercia whose royal court was in the city of Lichfield and whose interest in the well-being of the Church at this time was shown by his grants of land.[12] Nothelm's subscription is to be found on a confirming charter to Aldwulf, bishop of Rochester, of a grant of land from King Eadberht of Kent.[13]

Little more is known about Nothelm's archiepiscopate beyond a letter addressed to him from Boniface, the English missionary to the Frisians, who had been consecrated and invested with the *pallium* by Pope Gregory II for missionary work in Germany. The contents of this letter appear to indicate that Boniface and Nothelm were known to each other and had probably met sometime from 716 to 718 when Boniface was on a visit to England. Boniface had been confronted with a problem concerning the degrees of marriage, and had learned of the answers which Pope Gregory I had given in his *Responsiones* to Augustine's inquiries. Evidently, knowing of Nothelm's researches and, now as archbishop of Canterbury, his access to the archives at Canterbury, Boniface asked him for a copy of Gregory's letter and whether the letter had been proved to be authentic.[14] He also sought Nothelm's advice concerning a judgment he (Boniface) had made in allowing a marriage which, later he had learned, was considered to be irregular. His letter to Nothelm concluded with a request to know 'the year in which the first missionaries sent by St. Gregory came to England.'[15] Boniface's letter to Nothelm was a continuance of a relationship which had already been established between the missionary bishop and Canterbury during Berhtwald's archiepiscopate. And in writing to Nothelm he implicitly recognized the archbishop's scholarship and specialized knowledge, and did not hesitate to show the high esteem with which he regarded his counsel. Whatever information he gave him would appear not to have been conclusive because after Nothelm's death Boniface was still seeking copies of the letters of Pope Gregory I.[16]

In his letters to bishops and others in his native land Boniface invariably asked for books, manuscripts and vestments for his missionary work in addition to their prayers. By this wide correspondence he kept himself fully informed concerning the political situation, and the activities of the Church in England and particularly in the province of Canterbury.[17] From the time of Berhtwald he had personal knowledge of the wide influence exercised by the archbishopric of Canterbury, and was well aware of the problems which confronted Nothelm during his scholarly and wise administration. After the separation of the dioceses north of the Humber the consolidation of the remaining dioceses in the southern province had its difficulties but also its compensations. Under his guidance diocesan administration was efficient and the re-establishment of the see of Leicester was indicative of the wise metropolitan oversight of his newly constituted province. Nevertheless, the relatively short archiepiscopates of both Tatwine and Nothelm was a period of decline in the Church in England. What Bede had written in his letter to Egbert of York, giving a detailed diagnosis of the condition of the Church north of the river Humber, was equally true of the Church to the south of it, in the province of Canterbury. The northern and midland parts of the province had been disturbed during the second year of Nothelm's archiepiscopate when Aethelbald of Mercia invaded Northumbria while King Eadberht was campaigning over his northern border against the Picts. Although Aethelbald did not annex any territory, his power was respected if not feared in the north. Within his own territories as overlord he dominated both ecclesiastical as well as political affairs and his influence may be discerned in the translation of Bishop Cuthbert on the death of Nothelm, from the see of Hereford to the archbishopric of Canterbury. Cuthbert was not a stranger to Kent, having been abbot of Lyminge before his consecration in 736 by Nothelm.[18] His translation came at a time of general decline in religion in England. The province which he ruled as metropolitan archbishop embraced all the territories over which King Aethelbald was recognized as overlord. During the first thirty years or thereabouts of Aethelbald's reign churches and monasteries received generous benefactions from him,[19] but throughout the same period there were occasions when he violated churches and monasteries by the seizure of their property and revenues for his own purposes. He ruled with equity and maintained peace in his kingdom and was regarded as the protector of widows and the poor. On the other hand, having no lawful wife, he indulged in immoral excesses with a complete disregard of the marriage bond in order to satisfy his lust. Nominally he was a Christian and a supporter of the Church yet he acted contrary to the faith he professed and openly rejected the Church's teaching by yielding to his vicious desires. These irreconcilable elements of his character and manner of life inevitably affected the general standards of morality of clergy and people alike.

It was into this difficult and involved situation that Archbishop Cuthbert entered as he took up the reins of ecclesiastical government in his province. He could not fail to perceive that reform measures were urgently needed in the Church if reforms were to be effective among the people. But he realized that any reform measures among the people would need the co-operation of King Aethelbald, and this would demand personal reform in the manner of life of the king himself. Precipitate action would probably antagonize the king and fail to achieve the reforms so urgently needed. Whatever plans for reform he may have had were not put into operation, and disturbing reports of the decline in morals in both Church and civil life continued to reach the English missionary, Boniface, who had now become archbishop and papal legate to Germany. After his departure from England he had maintained contact with his native land, as his correspondence shows, and in consequence was currently well-informed about prevailing political and ecclesiastical conditions. In the Frankish Church he had initiated reforms with the support of the rulers Carloman and Pepin. With their co-operation a synod was convoked over which Carloman, mayor of the palace of Austrasia (who is described by Boniface as emperor of the Franks) presided in 742, followed in the same year by another synod presided over by Pepin, mayor in Neustria.[20] Reforming councils were also held in 743 and 745, and in all the measures for reform which were adopted Boniface had the encouragement and support of Pope Zacharias.[21] The success of the reforms in the Church of the Franks coupled with his deep concern for the Church of his homeland prompted Boniface to take what may well have been the initial steps towards bringing about reforms in the Church in England. Having had the support of Carloman and Pepin in the reform of the Frankish Church Boniface considered it necessary that any reform measures in the Church over which Cuthbert ruled should have the support of Aethelbald whose territories were in the province of Canterbury. To this end, therefore, he sent a letter to Egbert, archbishop of York, seeking his counsel concerning a letter which he and five of his fellow-bishops, three of whom were natives of England like himself, intended to send to

Aethelbald. In seeking the advice of Egbert of royal lineage, who was renowned for his scholarship and learning throughout Europe, it should not be imagined that any ill-will existed between Boniface and Cuthbert of Canterbury. Indeed, at this time they were on most friendly terms and Cuthbert sent to Boniface, by his deacon Cyneberht, 'generous gifts and a delightful and affectionate letter.' At the same time Cyneberht was also commissioned to say how much the fraternal relations between the two archbishops were appreciated by his master.[22]

In order to remove any appearance of interference in the affairs of the English Church Boniface, in his letter to Egbert, informed him that he was acting in obedience to the pope's command to recall erring Christians to the path of salvation.[23] This letter together with the one for Aethelbald was carried by Herefrith, the priest, to York. Boniface requested Egbert to consider the letter to the king and 'if any things are wrongly expressed you may amend them, and those things which are right you may season with the salt of your wisdom and confirm with your authority.' Any attempt to assess the extent to which the letter was amended by Egbert is difficult. While it contains a full acknowledgement of the king's almsgiving, his defence of widows and the poor, and maintenance of stable peace throughout his territories, there are also stern words of rebuke for his adultery, lasciviousness and his seduction of veiled and consecrated women. He is also rebuked for his violation of churches and monasteries and for appropriating their revenues. Egbert's wise counsel may probably be discerned in the way reference is made to Aethelbald's impieties and wrong-doings upon which Boniface had no first hand knowledge. The letter concludes with the words 'I pray you, most dear son, give assent to the wholesome words of God's law and amend your life. . . . May Almighty God so turn your life to better things that you may be worthy from the Lord Himself to attain His eternal grace.' [24] Nowhere are to be found the smooth words of court diplomacy but words of stern rebuke and a plea for amendment of life in this letter which Herefrith now carried to Aethelbald who, on former occasions, had received counsel from this faithful and fearless priest. It was not the first time that the king had received a letter from Boniface, but no record is available of any reply from the king to the two letters.

The fraternal relationship which existed between the archbishop of Canterbury and Boniface would not leave Cuthbert in ignorance of the letter to the king. There was much common ground between the two archbishops because both were confronted with similar problems of Church reform. Any hesitations the archbishop may have had whether the time was opportune for convoking a synod for initiating the reform of the Church were removed when he received a letter from

Pope Zacharias directing him to initiate measures for the reform of the Church and the consequent improvement of the moral life of the people.[25] Without delay a provincial council was convened at Clofeshoh in 746 at which eleven of Cuthbert's twelve suffragans were present. This was the second provincial synod of Canterbury since the creation of the province of York and, as with the first convoked by Nothelm, representatives from the province of Canterbury alone assembled. The prologue to the account of the synod in 746 records that Aethelbald with his princes and dukes was present in addition to Cuthbert of Canterbury and his suffragans, many priests and others of lesser ecclesiastical order.[26] A description of the business transacted is given in general terms as follows: 'to consider and to settle the unity of the Church, the state of the Christian religion and equally to arrange and confirm a peaceful agreement.' At the opening of the synod two communications from Pope Zacharias were publicly read in Latin and then explained in English as directed by him. All people of every rank and dignity of the island of Britain were severely admonished by the pope, who also mentioned the possibility of a sentence of anathema against any who treated his admonitions with contempt. After 'mutual exhortations' the bishops reviewed the obligations of their office as given in the homilies of Pope Gregory I and the canonical decrees of the fathers. Of the thirty decrees made by this synod the first six deal specifically with the episcopate and its functions. Bishops should be ready to defend the pastoral care entrusted to them, and they should devote themselves to peace, sincere charity and perfect agreement concerning the rights of religion in word, work and judgment. Annually a bishop should visit throughout his diocese and should admonish abbots and abbesses to be examples of good life. He should inspect regular monasteries and also visit pseudo-monasteries for the purpose of reforming them. Any necessary reform which a bishop was unable to effect in his diocese should be brought by him to the archbishop in synod. A bishop should not ordain to the priesthood a monk or clerk without first making inquiry about the candidate's former life, present manner of life and knowledge of the faith. Every bishop, abbot and abbess should diligently provide for their *familia,* and a bishop should assemble all priests, abbots and abbesses of his diocese on returning from a provincial synod and make known to them its injunctions. These canons show the reforming zeal of the primatial see, and the way in which it inspired the bishops with high ideals and pastoral knowledge. Cuthbert's reform measures by conciliar action gave to his suffragans guide lines for reforms in their dioceses inclusive of the matters which concerned clergy, monks and laity.

No less than five canons of this synod were concerned with priests

H

and their ministry. In the eighth canon priests are reminded of the basic meaning of their ordination in the words of the Pauline dictum that they are 'God's ministers and stewards of the mysteries of Christ' and that 'it is required of stewards that a man be found faithful.' As far as possible priests were not to be engaged in secular business but faithfully to fulfil their office at the altar and in divine service; caring for the house of prayer and its furnishings; and spending their time in reading, celebrating masses and psalmody. They should discharge their apostolical commission in baptizing, teaching and visiting with diligent care according to lawful rites: they should learn how to construe and explain the sacred words of the mass and baptism; the Creed and the Lord's Prayer. In church they should not speak in the manner of secular poets nor pronounce the sacred words like tragedians but follow the custom of the Church in plain song and holy melody. In the clearest terms it was decreed 'let not priests presume or attempt in any wise to perform any of those things which are peculiar to the bishops in some of their ecclesiastical offices.'

Priests were directed by the ninth canon to exercise their ministry in 'the places and districts of the laity assigned to them by the bishops of the province *in baptizando et docendo ac visitando.*' Although no mention is made of such places and districts being marked out by boundaries, the fact that a priest was to exercise his ministry, among other requirements, 'in visiting' suggests a specifically recognizable area. This canonical directive shows that, since the times of Cedd and Wilfrid, Theodore and Bede's letter to Bishop Egbert of York in 734, there had been a gradual development towards a parochial system which Cuthbert and his suffragans in synod codified as the normal organization of the Church in the province of Canterbury.[27] But it should be borne in mind that the majority of priests were still assistants to abbots and abbesses.

Reform measures for the internal discipline and administration of monasteries were also decreed. Bishops and priests were enjoined to teach the faith to the people, and the faithful regularly should practise almsgiving. Other matters of relatively minor importance but relevant to the major reform measures were also decreed.

On comparing the reforming canons of this synod with the reforms mentioned by Bede in his letter twelve years earlier to Bishop Egbert of York, it appears that there had been some improvement in the ministrations of bishops and priests, but problems relating to pseudo-monasteries had not been resolved. Reform or suppression of these monasteries so-called presented great difficulties as was seen a few years later when the joint efforts of king and archbishop in the northern province proved abortive.[28] In its decrees, however, this synod of 746 carries distinctive evidence of the influence which

Boniface exercised on the life of the Church in England. Many of the reform measures are identical with those adopted for the reform of the Frankish Church which Boniface had initiated under Carloman and Pepin. Further evidence of this is given at length in the letter which Boniface sent to Cuthbert in 747 giving the salient features of his many reform measures.[29] In comparing the Bonifatian reform canons for the Frankish Church with those decreed under Cuthbert there emerge two major differences, which may be described as omissions in the English canons. These omissions are of some historical importance for, while recognizing the authority of the papal see in convoking the synod in obedience to the command of Pope Zacharias, there is to be found no expression or gesture of subservience to the papal see such as that of which Boniface informed Cuthbert in his letter, 'We decreed in our synod,' wrote Boniface 'that we will maintain . . . our subjection to the Roman Church as long as we shall live . . . and that we will be loyal subjects of St. Peter and his Vicar.' The second expression of full submission concerned metropolitans about whom it was decreed that 'our metropolitan bishops shall ask for their *pallia* . . . and in all things shall obey the orders of St. Peter according to the canons.' It was in this context that there is found the only contemporary evidence that Cuthbert had received the *pallium* for Boniface speaks of 'the *pallium* entrusted to us and accepted by us.' By omitting the two foregoing decrees the Church of the English showed that it was an integral part of the Roman Church of which the pope was the recognized head, but at the same time it showed its independence as it had done since the archiepiscopate of Theodore.

A close relationship existed at this period between the English Church and Western Christendom. Students from the Continent were drawn to York there to receive instruction from Egbert, the learned royal metropolitan of the most northern archbishopric in Christendom. And it was from Egbert, with whom he corresponded, that Boniface requested his prayers and books for the centres of learning in the churches which he had founded.[30] His relationship with the archbishopric of Canterbury was more intimate. He had known Berhtwald, Tatwine and Nothelm but it was only Cuthbert whom he described as a friend 'with whom he could speak as with himself.' The friendship which bound the two archbishops together was further strengthened by Cuthbert's deacon, who conveyed by word of mouth to Boniface his master's high regard for the friendship which existed between them. Because of this long and understanding friendship Boniface was able to express himself in his letter to Cuthbert in forceful terms which contained a definite element of reproof. With his knowledge of King Aethelbald's violation of monasteries and churches there can be little doubt but that Boniface had this in mind when he wrote 'any layman, whether he be emperor or king, official or courtier who violated monasteries is to be condemned with the extreme anathema.' Similarly, in emphasizing the individual responsibility of a metropolitan for his province he observes, 'we have undertaken to steer a ship through the waves of an angry sea and can neither control it nor without sin abandon it.' He supports this by quoting one of the fathers: 'The Church makes its own way through the ocean of this world like a great ship, buffeted in this life by diverse waves of temptation, but it is not to be abandoned.' [31] Boniface considered that there had been supine acquiescence with the deteriorating conditions of the Church in England, and that there was an imperative and urgent need for decisively strong leadership in the province of Canterbury, which was Archbishop Cuthbert's particular responsibility.

The tones of reproof, however, are moderated by other considerations. All the information possessed by Boniface about conditions in England was not first hand knowledge. It was gleaned from those who corresponded with him and from others who visited him from England. His missionary zeal and spiritual ideals had accomplished much in the Frankish Church, but from the outset he had been piously supported by Carloman and Pepin in his reform measures. The situation in England and its Church was entirely different from that of the Franks. There was no pious ruler in England to give Cuthbert similar support in his Church reforms. Aethelbald had violated monasteries and churches and despised the moral standards of the Church to which he professed allegiance. Here was a situation of unparalleled difficulty which Boniface from a distance could only partly perceive. But it was to this situation that Cuthbert courageously, with wisdom and statesmanship, addressed himself by convoking the synod of Clofeshoh, about which he informed Boniface. This was in response to Boniface's request that Cuthbert would share the wholesome counsel of his synod with him and give his advice as to what seemed prudent for him to do. And he expressed the hope that the exchange of spiritual counsel between them would continue as long as life should last. With true humility Boniface recognized the high qualities of Cuthbert, and concluded his letter by describing him as one whom 'God had endowed with greater gifts of knowledge and power.' It is evident that Boniface considerably influenced the reform movement in the English Church. But it was a two way traffic. The mutual exchange of information between the two archbishops inevitably meant that the archbishopric of Canterbury exercised considerable influence on Church reform on the Continent in the counsel which Cuthbert gave to Boniface and which he admittedly followed.

During the continuing years of peace following the synod there is every reason to believe that the bishops in their dioceses endeavoured to implement the synod's decrees. From King Aethelbald's activities it would appear that the deliberations of the synod which he had heard and the letter from Boniface and his fellow-bishops had had a good effect on the king's manner of life. To Eadburg, abbess of the minster in Thanet, the king granted in 748 at London half-dues on a ship,[32] and in the following year at Gumley, now in Leicestershire, further benefits were conferred by Aethelbald upon the Church. These benefits, however, were of significant importance because they affected the whole of his territories, and granted to monasteries and churches freedom from all public taxes and secular services with the exception of building bridges and the defence of strongholds against enemies.[33] This immunity meant that no longer would the king violate monasteries and churches, and that firm restraint had been placed upon his ealdormen and thegns who formerly had been guilty of such violation.

Despite the difficult time through which the Church in the province of Canterbury had been passing there are indications that the pastoral ministry of priests had expanded since the archiepiscopate of Theodore.[34] The measures which he had initiated in Kent for some priests to exercise their ministry in a particular place or district for which they were directly responsible to him had now become a widespread feature of the pastoral organization of the Church throughout the province of Canterbury, and was of such importance that it had become the subject of the ninth canon at the synod of Clofeshoh in 746. It was decreed that priests, in parts of estates or districts owned by laymen assigned to them for their ministry by the bishops of the province, should take care to discharge the duty of the apostolic commission in baptizing, teaching and visiting according to lawful rites with great diligence.[35] Bede, in his letter to Bishop Egbert, made specific reference to the need of priests to preach the Word and to celebrate the sacraments in the hamlets and homesteads, but nowhere did he mention visitation by priests. St. John of Beverley, bishop of York (705–718), consecrated two churches on the estates of Puch and Addi where priests could minister. No reference was made to visiting although by implication it may be concluded that it was an active part of the priest's pastoral charge in the village where his church was situated. Now, for the first time in the history of the Church in England, the particular form of the pastoral ministry of priests, described as 'visiting' had been given authoritative recognition by synodal decree. A bishop's annual visitation of his diocese for many centuries had been the subject of canonical direction but a priest's visitation of the area or district assigned to him by his bishop had now become by canonical decree obligatory.

While this synodal action was an indication of progress in the evolution of the parochial system, the assigned area or district in which the priest ministered had not yet been described as a *parochia* or parish. The synod's realistic approach to the pastoral ministry of bishops and priests reflected the discerning leadership which the province of Canterbury received from Cuthbert, whose reforms were more original and detailed than those by Boniface in the Frankish Church.

Since the seventh century synods of Hertford and Hatfield convoked by Theodore no such synod of far-reaching importance had been held until Cuthbert, at the command of Pope Zacharias, convoked the synod of Clofeshoh. But this synod differed from the Theodoran synods because it did not include the sees of the province of York, and in consequence its decrees were applicable only to the province of Canterbury. Nevertheless, it was a tribute to the leadership of Cuthbert, despite the political problems of the time, that the synod, by its comprehensive decrees on the organization, administration and religious life of the Church in his province, made a lasting contribution to the well-being of the Church in England.

From the deliberations and decrees of this synod the Frankish Church also profited for, at Boniface's request for advice, Cuthbert had sent him a full account in order to give him guidance in his Church reforms. The continuing friendship between the two archbishops brought others within its orbit. Bishop Mildred of Worcester in 754 visited Boniface and Lull in Germany. Soon after his return home he learned of the martyrdom of Boniface, and wrote a letter to Lull expressing his condolences and praising the blessed life, the noble work and glorious end of Boniface.[36] This letter has an added interest because it shows that there was an interchange of books between Cuthbert, Lull and Mildred.

After learning of the martyrdom of Boniface in 755 at Dokkum, Cuthbert presided at a synod in that year, probably an annual synod at Clofeshoh, at which it was decreed that a festival day (5th June) on which to celebrate the martyrdom would annually be observed, and that with the blessed Gregory and Augustine, Boniface would be 'our special patron before Christ the Lord.' Cuthbert conveyed this information in a letter from himself, fellow-bishops, priests and abbots to Lull, who had now succeeded Boniface as archbishop of Mainz. He also expressed words of comfort, and recalled that Boniface, whose faithful stewardship had been sealed by a martyr's death, was an Englishman. For this Cuthbert expressed thanks to God that 'the race of the English had been accounted worthy to send forth . . . so distinguished a searcher of the heavenly Scriptures, so famous a soldier of Christ.'[37] Such a tribute to his master and friend could not fail to inspire Lull, for he too was an Englishman to whom it now fell to maintain relations between the Church in England and the Church in Germany, evidence of which is to be found in his letters.

A few years before Boniface's martyrdom Cuthbert's reform measures in parts of his province were halted when the peace which Aethelbald had established and maintained so long was broken by King Cuthred of Wessex who regarded the burden of Aethelbald's overlordship as far too irksome. He successfully challenged in battle his authority and established the independence of Wessex. It would appear that Wessex again became a dependency of Mercia, but in the same year Aethelbald was murdered by some of his bodyguard at Seckington near Tamworth. Beornred usurped the throne for a few months until he was driven out by Offa who established himself king of Mercia in 757.[38]

About this time Cuthbert was stricken by illness from which he died in 758. Before his death he had devised a plan by which to give increased honour and importance to the metropolitical church of Christ Church in which his *cathedra* was set. It had been the traditional practice since Augustine's time for the archbishops of Canterbury to be buried at St. Augustine's abbey in the monastic church of St. Peter and St. Paul with the obsequies being performed by the abbot and monks. Cuthbert had received authority from King Eadberht of Kent to make a change in the place of sepulture for archbishops of Canterbury. Having obtained the king's approval it is said that he received a decree from Pope Gregory III directing that in future archbishops of Canterbury should be buried at Christ Church.[39] Before his death Cuthbert had added the chapel of St. John the Baptist to the east end of his cathedral church, and it was here that he was buried.[40] Not until three days after his death did the tolling of the bell of Christ Church inform the monks of St. Augustine's that the archbishop had died. On arriving to convey the corpse for burial to their monastery they found that the archbishop had already been interred in the newly erected chapel. Rivalries had existed for a long time between Christ Church and St. Augustine's, and at this period there was a larger proportion of secular priests than monks in the archbishop's *familia*. The presence of the seculars was a constant cause of friction and undoubtedly Cuthbert's last act before his death by the change in the place of sepulture was not only to ease any strife between regulars and seculars but also to free the archbishop's *familia* in the future from any dependence upon the regulars of St. Augustine's.[41]

By the death of Archbishop Cuthbert in 758 the first important chapter in the history of the archbishopric of Canterbury, since the creation of the province of York, was brought to an end. It was chiefly due to his wise and far-seeing policy that the authority of the archbishopric, so fully accepted during Berhtwald's archiepiscopate, became a unifying influence throughout the dioceses which constituted the province of Canterbury. At the synod of Clofeshoh in 746 over which he presided the authority of the archbishopric was never questioned but fully accepted by all his suffragans present, and unitedly with Cuthbert they issued their decrees for the reform of the Church in the province. This was all the more significant when the political power and influence of the Mercian supremacy, south of the Humber, had reached its highest point so far during the first half of the eighth century. It was at this time that the archbishopric of Canterbury under Cuthbert's sagacious rule came to be regarded by the Frankish Church as expressing the authentic voice of the Church in England. Parallel with this, the fame of the school at York which Archbishop Egbert re-established had spread so widely that students from the Continent were drawn to York in order to receive instruction from the learned and royal metropolitan of the recently founded archbishopric. Moreover, the ties of friendship and interchange of information concerning conciliar measures of reform between Cuthbert and Boniface had strengthened as never before the relationship of the Church in England with the Church on the Continent, and paved the way for stronger relationships in the future. By his consistently conscientious and discerning administration he arrested the declension in the Church which had positive results on the life of the people and probably on the manner of life of King Aethelbald of Mercia. The closing years of Cuthbert's archiepiscopate were adversely affected by the breakdown of peace which had lasted so long throughout Aethelbald's territories. Wessex freed itself from the Mercian overlordship and King Eadberht of Kent acted with a greater degree of independence which later caused much hostility. These events were not conducive to the Church's well-being and progress but proved to be the prelude to the unleashing of hostile forces which wrought immeasurable harm upon the archbishopric of Canterbury.

OFFA'S DESPOLIATION OF THE ARCHBISHOPRIC

The long reign of forty-one years of King Aethelbald, during which he had established himself as overlord over the whole of Britain south of the Humber probably made him the most powerful king in Britain since King Aethelbert of Kent. Henry of Huntingdon described him as *rex regum*.[1] But the kings who recognized him as their overlord, towards the end of his reign, sat loosely to the ties which bound them to him. It was not surprising, therefore, after he had been murdered, that civil war broke out and his confederation of kingdoms fell apart. Before the end of the year 757, in which Aethelbald had died, Offa established himself king of Mercia. The unsettled political situation did not prevent Offa from taking an interest in ecclesiastical affairs. In the same year that he became king he subscribed his consent to a charter by which the sub-king Eanberht of the Hwicce made a grant of land to Mildred, bishop of Worcester.[2]

When Cuthbert, archbishop of Canterbury, died in October 758, it would appear that Offa had not so far ventured to impose his authority on the kingdom of Kent over which Eadberht continued to rule. After a year's interregnum Bregowine was consecrated to succeed Cuthbert in the chair of St. Augustine. Little is known about him, but from a letter which he sent to Archbishop Lull of Mainz Bregowine made reference to their friendship and their meeting in Rome.[3] Bregowine's letter, it would appear, was in answer to an inquiry from Lull concerning the date of the death of Eadburg who had regularly corresponded with Boniface and by her gifts had supported his missionary work. There is no record of Bregowine having received the *pallium*. At that time the *pallium* and all it signified had been under suspicion since the reported action relating to its bestowal by Pope Zacharias had been questioned by Boniface.[4] This may have been the cause of the delay in Lull's reception of the *pallium*. He had been archbishop of Mainz for eighteen years when, influenced by Tilpin, archbishop of Rheims, his formal petition was made to Pope Hadrian I for its bestowal.[5] Bregowine could not have been unaware of Lull's attitude and that of other archbishops on the Continent towards the *pallium*. He would also have been aware that the synod of Clofeshoh in 746 did not issue a decree, similar to that of which Cuthbert had been informed by Boniface, requiring all metropolitan bishops to seek the *pallium*.[6] In this context it would be quite understandable that Bregowine took no initial steps to have the *pallium* conferred upon him and in consequence did not receive it. Nevertheless, this did not deter him from consecrating bishops to the sees of Leicester, Lichfield and Selsey in his province when they became vacant.[7]

One of the chief factors which influenced Bregowine's archiepiscopate was the continued instability of the political situation under King Offa as he strove to gain the overlordship in the territories which Aethelbald had possessed. Aethelbald's overlordship in the kingdom of Kent had visibly weakened by the increasing independence of the Kentish kings. In his tentative approaches to Kent there can be little doubt that Offa came to the conclusion that the archbishop of Canterbury would be of no help to him if he tried, even peacefully, to establish his overlordship in Kent. This perhaps explained Offa's action in appropriating the monastery of Cookham in Mercia. This was the only assailable property of Christ Church, Canterbury, within his territories. It had been granted by Aethelbald to Canterbury during Cuthbert's archiepiscopate. By this despoliation was revealed Offa's frustration at finding how powerful was the archbishopric of Canterbury by its influence in the Kentish kingdom and in his own territories. Archbishop Bregowine regarded Offa's action as one of hostility against the Church as a whole, and in consequence convoked a synod at Clofeshoh at which the injuries sustained by Christ Church were the subject of complaint and consideration.[8] This in no way prompted Offa's restoration of the property nor did it change his attitude towards the archbishopric and the kingdom of Kent. The continued retention of Cookham was later considered at another synod of Clofeshoh during the archiepiscopate of Jaenberht, Bregowine's successor.[9]

In his attempts to establish his overlordship in Kent, like his predecessor, Offa realized that he had dual powers with which to contend. Although the succession of Kentish kings at this period is confused, since some of them appear to have reigned concurrently, he was confronted by their political power and the archbishopric of Canterbury which exercised a powerful influence throughout its ecclesiastical province which included the Mercian territories over which he ruled. Moreover, the influence of the archbishopric extended to the Continent where Offa sought friendship with the Frankish rulers for his own political purposes. His hostile action against Bregowine and the archbishopric of Canterbury was the cause of much concern to Eardulf, bishop of Rochester, whose diocese was the gateway from the north to the diocese of Canterbury. He perceived the political implications of Offa's hostility and his concern for the future was shared by one of the Kentish kings, Eardulf. Together, the two Eardulfs, bishop and king, addressed a letter to Archbishop Lull of Mainz.[10] In it they made no specific reference to any political or ecclesiastical events but the whole tenor of the letter cannot hide their forebodings as they entreat Lull for his prayers on their behalf. Bishop Eardulf received grants of land from Kentish kings, and from King Offa land on the Medway.[11] When receiving this grant from Offa in 764, the charter to which both Bregowine and King Eadberht subscribed, in addition to Offa, it is probable that Bishop Eardulf learned more of Offa's attitude towards the archbishopric of Canterbury and of his ambitions concerning the kingdom of Kent, which may have prompted the joint letter to Archbishop Lull.

Since Bregowine approved the grant of land made by Offa, in subscribing after the king to the charter issued in 764 at Canterbury, it is evident that there was no open breach between the archbishop and king, nor was there any sign of hostility by the inhabitants of Canterbury towards Offa at that time. Nevertheless, Bregowine's archiepiscopate did not escape unscathed by the uncertainties created by Offa's territorial ambitions. But the archbishopric of Canterbury, under Bregowine's wise and statesmanlike leadership throughout the province acted with a common mind through synodal consultation and in consequence the bishops, in their respective dioceses, maintained to the fullest extent the Church's work and witness amidst the difficulties which arose from the unstable political situation. At this time, therefore, the Church was the strongest unifying element in the life of the people south of the Humber despite the prevailing adverse conditions. Bregowine fully agreed with his predecessor's action in changing the tradition for the archbishops of Canterbury to be interred at St. Augustine's monastery and made arrangements for his burial in his cathedral of Christ Church. On his death his *familia* followed the same stratagems used when Cuthbert died. Frustrated and dismayed, violence was threatened by the monks for not only had St. Augustine's lost the distinctive honour of being the burial place of the archbishops but the monastery had been deprived of 'soul-scot' at the time of burial, and the offerings of pilgrims at the tombs of the archbishops. Elmham records that Jaenberht and his monks decided to petition the pope for the restoration of their former privilege, but before their decision was carried into effect their abbot was elected to the vacant archbishopric.[12]

A charter by which King Egbert of Kent granted land to Bishop Eardulf within the castle walls of his see city of Rochester gives some indication of the extent of Offa's overlordship in Kent at the time of Jaenberht's election. Two Kentish kings, Egbert and Eadberht, Jaenberht and others subscribed to the charter which was then carried to Offa with Eardulf's petition for its confirmation. He gave this in the monastery of Medehamstede and extended the charter's provisions by granting to the bishop the right to alienate the property.[13] On the second of February 766, the year after Bregowine's death, Jaenberht was consecrated by three of the bishops of his province; Ecgwulf of London, Cyneheard of Winchester and Eadberht of Leicester [14] and in due course received the *pallium* from Pope Paul I.[15] On the day of his consecration a charter issued by Offa shows that the king was in Canterbury on that day, and probably attended the consecration, since he subscribed to the charter 'with the consent of my bishops and all my ealdormen.' In view of the later conflict with the kingdom of Kent and the archbishopric of Canterbury this charter, by which Offa granted land in Worcestershire to Mildred, bishop of Worcester, possesses political and ecclesiastical significance. King Offa's overlordship of the kingdom of Kent had been established already to such a degree that no king of Kent subscribed to the charter, and Offa, in his own subscription, could refer to the newly consecrated Archbishop Jaenberht and three consecrating bishops as 'my bishops,' and to 'all my ealdormen' with whose consent he subscribed. Jaenberht, in subscribing, stated that he did so 'on the day of my ordination (consecration) with the bishops.' [15] Towards the end of the year 766 Friothoberht of Hexham and Archbishop Egbert had died, leaving only the bishops of Whithorn and Lindisfarne in the northern province. Albert, Egbert's *defensor clerici,* on election to the vacant archbishopric, received consecration at the hands of Jaenberht, archbishop of Canterbury. For the first time since the creation of the province of York the primate of all England visited the cathedral church of York and consecrated Albert, the second archbishop of York, and with him Ealhmund for the see of Hexham, Ceolwulf for Lindsey, in his own province, and Aluberht to be a missionary bishop to the Old Saxons.[16]

Having journeyed to the northern limits of his province and beyond, it would appear that on his return southwards he attended Offa's court at Lichfield and with the king and two local bishops, Cuthfrith of Lichfield and Eadberht of Leicester, subscribed to a charter granting land by Offa to Abbot Stidberht.[17] In 772 the archbishop was again, no doubt at Offa's court, in Mercia when the king granted land in Kent to Jaenberht's successor, Abbot Aethelnoth, of St. Augustine's monastery, Canterbury. To this charter Offa, Queen Cynethrytha, their son Ecgfrith with some ealdormen subscribed; Jaenberht subscribing himself for the first time as 'archbishop and rector of the Catholic Church.' [18] Offa, described himself as *rex Anglorum* in a charter of 772 by which he granted land to Oswald, bishop of Selsey, with reversion to his bishopric. The large number of persons who subscribed to the charter, including Offa, the kings of Kent and Wessex, four ealdormen, Jaenberht, the bishops of Selsey, London, Leicester and Rochester, Abbot Botwine with seventeen others suggests that the charter was issued at a witenagemot probably held at Medeshamstede or Canterbury.[19]

Offa granted land for the first time to Jaenberht in 774. Two charters granting land in Kent, and a third granting land to his *familia* at Christ Church, Canterbury, appear to have been issued at a witenagemot or synodal council since the first two charters carry the subscriptions of Offa and his queen, Jaenberht, the bishops of Lichfield, Leicester, Lindsey and Worcester, five abbots and eleven of Offa's chief men.[20] Because of the increasing hostility of Kent to Offa's overlordship these charters were probably issued at Lichfield or Medeshamstede, and Jaenberht's presence clearly shows that at this period he was active in his province outside his own diocese of Canterbury. For the first time Offa described himself as 'king of all the country of the English.' [21] Such a claim could not fail to add fuel to the fire of the Kentishmen's resentment and appearing in a charter by which Jaenberht received a royal benefaction, the archbishop may have regarded it as a warning that Offa considered his own power, even in Kent, to have been fully equal to his claims. At Gumley in Leicestershire Offa held another witenagemot at which in 775 he granted land at Evenlode with reversion to the monastery of Breedon. To this charter, in addition to Offa, six bishops subscribe including the bishops of London and Rochester. Since Jaenberht's subscription does not appear it suggests that the political situation in Canterbury demanded his presence.[22] The climax was reached in 776 when the Kentishmen fought the Mercians at the battle of Otford. Of the outcome of this battle no definite record can be found, but later events show that whatever measure of success Offa obtained in battle his complete overlordship in Kent was long delayed.

The succession of kings in Kent at this period is obscure. For some years kings had reigned concurrently—Sigered and Eanmund; Egbert and Eadberht—each of the two kings ruling over a part of Kent.[23] After the battle of Otford this dimidiated situation came to an end since Egbert II alone is to be found subscribing to charters as king of Kent.[24] It was to Egbert II that Jaenberht, doubtless a Kentishman himself, and a kinsman of the king's reeve in Canterbury, gave his loyal support. The archbishopric of Canterbury possessed a great and influential heritage, both political and ecclesiastical, into which Jaenberht had entered with all his gifts and devotion to his archbishopric, the kingdom of Kent and his province. His gifts of leadership brought added strength to Egbert's rule and inspired him and the people of Kent to consolidate the independence which they had gained by freeing themselves from Offa's overlordship. They fully recognized the importance of the archbishopric and Jaenberht's position among them as a courageous leader. He possessed his own coinage,[25] and his coins are the earliest to be found of an archbishop of Canterbury, the circulation of which could not fail to increase his influence and authority in Kent. But the archbishop's influence was far more extensive than the kingdom of Kent. The whole of Offa's territories lay within the province of Canterbury, and although Jaenberht's loyalty to Offa was in question his freedom to visit the dioceses within his province was in no way restricted. Nevertheless, after 776 no charter issued by Offa carried Jaenberht's subscription until 780. During that period the only charter to which the archbishop subscribed was one by which a grant of land was made to Diora, bishop of Rochester, by Egbert II of Kent.[26] In 780 Offa held a witenagemot at Brentford in Middlesex, where it would appear that he had his court at that time, since the charters issued carry the subscriptions of Offa, his queen and six ealdormen, also the three Mercian bishops of Leicester, Lindsey and Worcester and 'Jaenberht, archbishop of Canterbury.' [27] All these charters, however, were concerned with grants of land made by Offa for the benefit of the Church in the diocese of Worcester during the episcopate of Tilhere who died in the same year as the grants were made. In view of the synod of Brentford held in the following year 781 these grants suggest that Offa was preparing the ground for his claim to property held by the monastery of Worcester, which formed the business of the synod.[28] By the time the synod was convoked Jaenberht had consecrated Heathored for the see of Worcester against whom Offa laid his claim to the monastery of Bath and certain other lands. King Aethelbald had granted the land in 736 to his ealdorman Cyneberht upon which to erect a monastery. No sooner had Heathored become bishop than he was confronted with this royal claim to property held by his *familia*. The bishop resisted Offa's claim and a dispute arose. In consequence a synod was convoked to settle the matter. The conduct of the synod's business is clearly shown in the final paragraph of the synod's findings which show that Jaenberht alone did not preside, 'Archbishop Jaenberht presiding along with me' (Offa). Offa's presence and sharing of the presidency of the synod at which his claim was considered would not have deterred the archbishop from supporting the claim of a bishop of his province, and it was probably here that Offa realized that from Jaenberht he would have little support in his political ambitions and even less in ecclesiastical affairs which affected the well-being of the Church in the province of Canterbury. Heathored finally agreed that Offa should have the land at Bath and in compensation for the adjacent land of thirty hides he should concede the one hundred and eleven hides to the *familia* of Worcester. This compromise in settlement was reached after the synod had 'considered and pondered about the peace and condition of the Church.' [29] This was the last synod at which all the bishops of the province of Canterbury attended with Jaenberht before initial measures were taken by King Offa for the division of the province and the setting-up of the province of Lichfield. There was no open breach, however, between Jaenberht and Offa. Synodal administration continued without interruption with a synod at Oakley in 782, and two synods at Chelsea in 785 and 786 at which both subscribed to charters by which Offa made grants of land.[30] At each of the synods at Chelsea nine of Jaenberht's suffragans subscribed in addition to Offa's queen and son, and four ealdormen, and it is probable that at the synod in 785 Offa made his grant of land at Aldenham to the church of St. Peter, Westminster.[31] Despite the weaknesses of his political system Offa had established such an understanding relationship with the emperor Charlemagne, as the correspondence between them shows, that he was able to treat on equal terms with this most powerful ruler in Europe. It should be borne in mind, however, that for many years there had existed a friendly relationship between the ecclesiastical provinces of Canterbury and York and the Church in the kingdoms over which Charlemagne now ruled. This relationship had been maintained during Lull's archiepiscopate at Mainz as in the days of his predecessor Boniface. Political relationships now used the much travelled paths of ecclesiastical relationships with the Continent to the detriment of the Church in England. It is evident that Offa in his dealings with the archbishopric of Canterbury, its archbishops and the bishops of the province, had assimilated the policy and methods used by Charlemagne in his dealings with the Church throughout his kingdoms.

Offa's failure to establish his supremacy over Kent made him well aware that Jaenberht's sympathies were with King Egbert II of Kent and not with him. He realized, too, that Jaenberht as metropolitan archbishop of Canterbury was the spiritual leader throughout the province of Canterbury, in which his territories were situated and that inevitably such powerful influence would affect any political situation which might arise. Moreover, the centre from which this powerful influence came was the archbishopric with its seat in the royal city of Canterbury in a kingdom which had prevented or destroyed his overlordship and a kingdom to which he had no access. In order to overcome these difficulties Offa tried to persuade Jaenberht to transfer his archiepiscopal seat from Canterbury, the capital city of Kent, to Lichfield, the capital city of Mercia, where he had his royal court.[32] By this means the predominating influence of Jaenberht would have been removed from Kent, and the possibility for Offa to bring the Kentishmen into submission to his overlordship would have been increased. Furthermore, with Jaenberht at Lichfield in Mercia his political influence would have been contained if not nullified. But the archbishop who, when abbot of St. Augustine's, had shown his fiery zeal for maintaining the established privileges and traditions of his monastery, was openly hostile to the proposal. First and foremost he was metropolitan archbishop of the primatial see in the city where Augustine had placed his chair; the royal city where his predecessors had been interred; and the city confirmed by papal authority as the primatial see of the Church in England. Offa's proposal was resolutely rejected by Jaenberht. This refusal, the hostility of the people of Kent and the reluctance of the episcopate to give any open support to Offa's proposal precluded any possibility of the king attempting to remove Jaenberht by force from his archbishopric.

Impelled by what Alcuin described as 'an immoderate desire for power' [33] and his desire to dignify his royal city and to adorn the scene of his triumphs with a metropolitical cathedral and with the dignity which an archbishopric and primacy could confer,[34] Offa sought another expedient to give effect to his plans. His knowledge of the manner in which Charlemagne exercised his authority over the Church in his empire undoubtedly set the pattern for Offa's erection of another archbishopric. The emperor independently created bishoprics and metropolitan sees in his kingdoms and exercised a dominating influence over Pope Hadrian I. So complete was Charlemagne's control over ecclesiastical appointments that a contemporary writer described him as *episcopus episcoporum*.[35] In much the same way Offa now determined to exercise his authority over ecclesiastical affairs by the arbitrary division of the archbishopric of Canterbury for the purpose of establishing a third metropolitan see in the city of Lichfield. Future events seem to indicate that Pope Hadrian I possessed some knowledge of Offa's plans to despoil the archbishopric. In contemplating such revolutionary action against the Church in England Offa may have informed the pope of his intentions in the hope of obtaining his approval but had been met with a rebuff. If so, this would have provided ample ground for the rumour which had reached Hadrian that Offa with Charlemagne was conspiring to depose him from the papal throne.[36] It was about this period, however, that the friendly relations which had existed between the two rulers became strained and misunderstanding had arisen because Charlemagne had granted asylum to exiles from Offa's territories. At this juncture Jaenberht, fearing that Kent would be unable successfully to repel Offa's forces, should he invade his archbishopric, turned for help to Charlemagne, and assured him that if he were to invade Britain he would receive him with goodwill, give him support and would grant him free entrance into his archbishopric.[37] While this action by the archbishop has been described as treacherous it should be borne in mind that Offa possessed no complete overlordship of

Kent. Jaenberht in this way was giving support to Egbert II, king of Kent, and making a last desperate attempt at all costs to preserve the integrity of his see from Offa's proposed plans for the despoliation of his archbishopric.

Never before in the history of the Church in England had such a crisis arisen, which threatened irrevocably to damage the efficient administration and spiritual well-being of the Church of the province of Canterbury, extending from the channel to the Humber. This critical situation provided Pope Hadrian I with an opportunity for intervening with some show of authority into matters which involved archiepiscopal administration, and an occasion for correcting any irregularities which had found their way into the Church. He therefore sent Theophylact, bishop of Todi to the court of Charlemagne where George, bishop of Ostia, was residing, commanding him to go with Theophylact as legates to England 'to renew the faith and peace which St. Gregory had sent by Augustine the bishop.' For the first time in its history the Church in England was now visited by papal legates. Charlemagne commissioned Abbot Wigbod as his ambassador to accompany the legates, and with them also journeyed the English scholar Alcuin from the emperor's court and Pyttel. On arrival in England the legation was received by Archbishop Jaenberht at Canterbury 'where St. Augustine rests in the body.' While staying with the archbishop they 'advised him of those things which were necessary.' Journeying northwards the legates were received with 'the sacred letters . . . and with great joy and honour' by King Offa at his court 'on account of his reverence for the blessed Peter and your apostolate.' Subsequently Offa and Cynewulf, king of Wessex, met in a council at which the legates presented the pope's 'holy writings,' after which the kings made promises of reforms. While Bishop Theophylact remained in the southern province Bishop George and Wigbod, accompanied by Alcuin and Pyttel, visited the province of York where they met in synod at Finchale, near Durham, Archbishop Eanbald I of York, Aelfwald, king of Northumbria, and other ecclesiastical and secular representatives. To the synod the legates submitted the papal letters, and the proposed decrees which were duly accepted. In substance the decrees covered much the same ground as the canons issued by the synod of Clofeshoh in 746. The fourth canon was significant because for the first time in the history of the Church in England clergy who were canons were mentioned and a distinction drawn between them and monks. It directed that 'bishops shall diligently take care to see that all canons shall live canonically, and monks shall live according to their rule.' [38] In effect it meant that the clergy of the bishop's *familia* should live communally with him, thus accepting a semi-monastic rule of life, and those who lived in

I

accordance with this rule or canon were called *canonici*, canons. A total of twenty decrees were accepted at the Finchale synod and the document recording them carried the subscriptions of the archbishop of York, his suffragans, abbots, the king of Northumbria and some of his ealdormen. This document was then taken to the southern province by Alcuin and Pyttel, acting as representatives of the king and the archbishop of York, who arrived with Bishop Theophylact and Wigbod for the 'council of the Mercians.' At this council held at Chelsea 'the glorious king Offa had come together with the senators of the land, along with Jaenberht, archbishop of the holy church of Canterbury and the other bishops of those parts.' The document was read in Latin and the vernacular and expounded in both, and then was unanimously approved and accepted. It is significant that Jaenberht subscribed first in order before the king, then followed the subscription of Hygeberht, bishop of Lichfield and the subscriptions of the other eleven of Jaenberht's suffragans, four abbots and four ealdormen.[39] This was the first time in the history of the English Church that the archbishops of Canterbury and York subscribed to a document promulgating canons which had been accepted by their respective synods in their own provinces. When this business had been completed the synod continued in session at which the papal legates, Bishops George and Theophylact, were present. King Offa then made a vow that 'he would send every year as many mancuses as the year had days, that is, three-hundred and sixty-five, to the same Apostle of the Church of God for the support of the poor and the provision of lights' for St. Peter's, Rome.[40] This munificent benefaction, ostensibly made in thanksgiving for his victories, cannot be dissociated from the traditional offerings made in Rome when a royal petition was presented requesting that the *pallium* should be bestowed upon a metropolitan. At the same time that he made his votive gift it would appear he made known his plan for the division of the province of Canterbury in order to establish the metropolitan archbishopric of Lichfield.[41] Having disclosed his plan to the synod, Offa was immediately confronted with fierce opposition from Jaenberht, who produced the letter of Pope Gregory I to Augustine which contained the plan for the Church in Britain. He showed that in conformity with the plan provision had been made for two metropolitan sees, Canterbury (London) and York. With irrefutable evidence he argued for no deviation from the Gregorian plan, and with vehemence defended the rightful possessions of his archbishopric and claimed his retention of the dioceses within his province and pastoral jurisdiction. Jaenberht was supported by some of his suffragans and the chief men of Kent in his defence of the integrity of his archbishopric. Offa was obdurate in his determination to reduce to a minimum the archbishop's influence in his territories and, heedless of all pleadings and arguments, he declared that he would divide the province of Canterbury and forthwith designated Hygeberht, bishop of Lichfield, a metropolitan.[42] The king then gave details of the territorial extent of the new province and the dioceses which would remain in the province of Canterbury.

All dioceses north of the Thames were to be separated from the province of Canterbury. This meant that the territorial extent of the southern province would extend from the Channel no farther northwards than the river Thames. Under its impaired constitution it now contained six dioceses including Jaenberht's own diocese of Canterbury and the dioceses of London, Winchester, Rochester, Sherborne and Selsey. Offa's biographer omits the diocese of Selsey,[43] and William of Malmesbury's Gesta Pontificum Anglorum, whose record of bishoprics of this period is unreliable, omits the diocese of Sherborne.[44] The Anglo-Saxon Chronicle tersely records 'In this year (787) there was a contentious synod at Chelsea, and Archbishop Jaenberht lost a certain part of his province, and Hygeberht was chosen by King Offa, and Ecgfrith was consecrated king.' For Offa this synod had been politically and ecclesiastically successful, and his satisfaction at the outcome may have found expression in the hallowing of his son Ecgfrith, probably by the papal legates, and in formally associating him in his kingship. In this may be seen a significant parallel to the action of Charlemagne who had his two sons Pepin and Louis anointed to kingship with him by Pope Hadrian I. Indeed, Offa had already shown by his creation of another metropolitan see and the appointment of an archbishop that he was following the emperor's ecclesiastical policy.[45]

On their return to Rome the papal legates submitted to the pope their report concerning the Church in England, and informed him of Offa's power and influence and, doubtless, commended for approval and recognition the king's action in dividing the province of Canterbury and establishing another metropolitan see. By their report the pope was reassured that any rumour of Offa's hostility toward him was unfounded, and in addition this powerful king in Britain had made a generous gift for the Church in Rome. The papal legates, it would appear, were accompanied by Offa's embassy carrying his petition for the bestowal of the pallium upon Hygeberht and the offerings which he had vowed. In 788 Hygeberht received the pallium and charter of bestowal from Pope Hadrian I, which were the tangible evidence of papal approval and confirmation of the division of the province of Canterbury and of departure from the Gregorian plan for the Church in Britain. Jaenberht evidently recognized the overwhelming forces against him and his archbishopric at the synod, and in consequence there is no evidence that he appealed to the pope for the restoration of the dioceses separated from his province.

When the see of Hereford fell vacant in 788 the responsibility for the consecration of Ceolmund to fill the vacancy rested with Archbishop Hygeberht, since Jaenberht now possessed no jurisdiction in the dioceses north of the Thames. Having effectively curtailed Jaenberht's influence in his territories some measure of reconciliation came about between king and archbishop. Concurrently the hostility of the Kentishmen subsided and Offa attained an insecure overlordship in Kent. Keeping the sphere of influence of the archbishopric of Canterbury ever in mind, Jaenberht, towards the end of the year 788, was to be found at the court of the king subscribing with Hygeberht to a charter by which Offa made a grant of land in Kent to the church of St. Andrew, Rochester.[46] In this charter Jaenberht rightly had precedence in his subscription by virtue of his seniority both in consecration and archiepiscopal dignity. The two archbishops from this time onwards are to be found subscribing in the same order to no less than four charters with bishops drawn from both provinces of Canterbury and Lichfield.[47] All these charters were issued at Chelsea just north of the boundary of the Canterbury province. King Offa was present and at the council in 789 in his presence 'the two archbishops Jaenberht and Hygeberht presiding together' agreement was reached between Bishop Heathored of Worcester and a certain Wulfheard concerning land in the diocese of Worcester.[48] This anomalous position of the archbishop of Canterbury sharing in the presidency of a council concerned with matters relating to one of his former bishops in one of his former dioceses was evidently approved by Offa. It shows that the administrative wisdom of the archbishopric of Canterbury in ecclesiastical affairs was still needed in a diocese separated from it, and Jaenberht willingly gave his help and guidance although the diocese had been taken from his province. On all these occasions the king was present when the two archbishops worked together in council.

Having attained his objective of establishing a metropolitan archbishopric in the city of Lichfield, Offa's hostility towards Jaenberht subsided, and in ecclesiastical affairs he received his help irrespective of the provincial boundaries which he had made. It is also evident that Jaenberht, having been unsuccessful in preserving the integrity of the archbishopric of Canterbury, zealously laboured for the well-being of the whole Church in England and showed no resentment against his former suffragan, Hygeberht, who had been appointed a metropolitan. Hygeberht was not in any way assertive of his new archiepiscopal authority but appeared to welcome the counsel of Jaenberht in matters affecting dioceses so recently under his pastoral jurisdiction; counsel which Jaenberht willingly gave for the peace of the Church. Although his province only had half the number of dioceses which it formerly possessed, the synodal government of his province was not relaxed. Quite apart from the councils of Chelsea, at which he was present, Jaenberht held a synod at Oakley south of the Thames,[49] and another at Clofeshoh, probably in the last year of his archiepiscopate.[50] At this synod, like his predecessor Bregowine at a former synod, he protested unsuccessfully against the retention of the monastery of Cookham and other properties belonging to Christ Church, Canterbury, which Offa had seized.

Before his death in 792 Jaenberht had given instructions that on his decease he should be buried at St. Augustine's monastery of which he had been abbot. In this way be vindicated the protest he had made against archbishops of Canterbury being buried at Christ Church and the discontinuance of the long tradition of them being interred at St. Augustine's. He was, however, the last of the archbishops to be buried at St. Augustine's monastery. It is a great tribute to Jaenberht that when his province was despoiled by Offa and untold harm done to the administration of the Church, the influence of the archbishopric of Canterbury in ecclesiastical affairs was still recognized by the king, the archbishop of Lichfield and his suffragans. The charters of the synodal councils after 787 amply testify to this. But they also show that Jaenberht's political influence was effectively diminished by the division of his province, and Offa's overlordship in Kent increased although later it proved to be insecure.

Jaenberht's removal by death now gave Offa the opportunity to co-ordinate political and ecclesiastical policy for the unification of Kent with his Mercian kingdom. He therefore took immediate steps to secure the election to the vacant archbishopric of someone who would advance his plans for the closer integration of Kent with his other territories. Abbot Aethelheard of Louth, a Mercian, was chosen but when the people of Kent learned that he was a Mercian they openly showed their hostility by refusing him entry into his cathedral. Previously the men of Kent by force of arms had prevented Mercian supremacy in Kent. Now they used force to prevent a Mercian archbishop-elect from peacefully entering into possession of his archbishopric. It may appear to have been short-sighted on the part of Offa to send a Mercian to Kent. This was, however, in conformity with his plan; first to achieve the ecclesiastical unification of Kent and Mercia and then, as subsequent events proved, to use this as a basis for political unity. By nominating the Mercian Aethelheard he was assured of the co-operation of the Mercian archbishop, Hygeberht, and his province of Lichfield. For the king the situation grew more complex because there now arose the problem of the consecration of an archbishop whom the people refused to receive. The election of

Aethelheard had been forcefully challenged and he could not risk the possibility of his consecration being challenged. Should Abbot Aethelheard receive consecration at the hands of Archbishop Hygeberht, Archbishop Eanbald I of York, his future comprovincials of the province of Canterbury or should he visit Rome and seek consecration by the pope? Offa was confronted with these alternatives, any one of which might retard the advance of his ecclesiastical policy. Finally he sought the advice of Alcuin, the English scholar from York, who was now resident at the court of Charlemagne. Friendship existed between king and scholar because Offa had provided pupils for one of the distinguished young scholars whom Alcuin had sent to him, and Offa was regarded by Alcuin as 'the glory of Britain.'[51] He informed Offa that an archbishop should be consecrated by an archbishop and that after consecration the *pallium* should be sent by the pope.[52] The only reference which can be found to Aethelheard's consecration is in the Worcester Chronicle under the year 793, and the precise terms of this reference suggest that it is a copy from a calendar, probably of Lichfield Cathedral, 'Consecration of Archbishop Aethelheard 12th August.'[53] It would appear, therefore, that the new archbishop was consecrated by Hygeberht in his cathedral at Lichfield. After his consecration Offa adopted measures, irrespective of Kentish opposition, to place Aethelheard in full possession of his archbishopric. From that time onwards the whole attitude of the king changed towards the archbishopric of Canterbury and expressive of this change was the generous benefactions of land to Christ Church, Canterbury.[54] Offa was assured of Aethelheard's co-operation as he strove to implement his policy of bringing the kingdom of Kent into close unity with his other territories. To a charter by which Offa granted land to Worcester Cathedral in the province of Lichfield, Hygeberht's subscription does not appear. There are, however, the subscriptions of two of his suffragans, Worcester and Leicester, preceded by Archbishop Aethelheard's which follows the royal subscriptions.[55] Offa, it would seem, did not consider it irregular for the archbishop of Canterbury to approve his benefactions within a province under the jurisdiction of the archbishop of Lichfield. The absence of Hygeberht's subscription may indicate Offa's approval, if not support, of Aethelheard's immediate measures to bring the dioceses which had been separated from the province of Canterbury once again within the jurisdiction of his archbishopric. Now that Offa had a Mercian archbishop at Canterbury his interest in the metropolitan archbishopric at Lichfield which he had established seemed to decline. The apparent ease with which Aethelheard successfully used every occasion for the gradual unification of the dioceses of the Lichfield province with the province of Canterbury, from which they had been taken, seems to suggest that Aethelheard and Hygeberht, who were both former abbots, came to some kind of understanding by which all the dioceses from the Humber to the Channel would again be under the sole jurisdiction of the metropolitan archbishopric of Canterbury. This was the situation during the last three years of Offa's reign, and when he was succeeded by his son Ecgfrith in 796 he purposefully followed his father's policy. Although Ecgfrith's reign lasted but five months there continued the strengthening both politically and ecclesiastically of the archbishopric of Canterbury and the consequent progressive weakening of the metropolitan see of Lichfield. Charters relating to ecclesiastical matters during his short reign which carry his subscription with that of Aethelheard are all concerned, with cne exception, with land in the province of Lichfield.[56] In none of these charters does Hygeberht's subscription appear though some of his suffragan bishops subscribe as they do to a charter relating to land in the province of Canterbury.[57] Ecgfrith, like his father, took good care to secure the goodwill and co-operation of the Church throughout his Mercian kingdom, and there can be little doubt that the diocesan bishops of the Lichfield province were in accord with the policy for the unification and restoration of the authority of the primatial see of Canterbury. Before he had been archbishop a year, Aethelheard had been recognized on the Continent as the leader of the Church in England. Because of this and partly on account of his friendship with Charlemagne he was invited to attend, with Bishop Ceowulf of Lindsey, the council at Frankfort in 794 to consider the *filioque* clause.[58] Sometime after his return to Canterbury the emperor wrote to the archbishop and Ceowulf asking them to intercede with Offa for some English exiles to whom he had given asylum 'for the sake of reconciliation, not out of enmity.' [59] Charlemagne was well-informed about the Church in England by Alcuin, who in April 796 wrote to tell Offa that the emperor was sending a letter accompanied with gifts to him to inform him that he had sent envoys to Rome 'for the judgment of the apostolic pope and of Archbishop Aethelheard.' [60] It was on this occasion, no doubt, that Aethelheard received the *pallium*. In his letter to Offa is disclosed by Charlemagne the business which had been remitted for judgment by Aethelheard and the pope at Rome. It concerned an English priest, named Eadberht, whom Offa wrongly thought had gone to the emperor's court to inform against him. In consequence he did not wish to return to England although the emperor declared Eadberht's innocence. Charlemagne also assured Offa that although pilgrimages to Rome through his kingdoms had been exploited for commercial gain, genuine pilgrims from England to Rome could be assured of peaceful travel and exemption from the payment of toll.[61] To Offa he sent gifts of a belt and Hunnish sword with two silk palls, and from his 'dalmatics and palls' the emperor sent a gift to every bishopric in Offa's kingdom. Shortly after Aethelheard had returned to Canterbury Offa died and his son Ecgfrith, who succeeded him, was driven out after five months by Cenwulf, a distant kinsman, who seized the throne. Taking advantage of the political upheaval the people of Kent once again asserted their independence, finding a leader in Edward Praen, a brother of a former king of Kent. Under the pressure of Offa's overlordship he had entered a monastery and received the tonsure.[62] But at the call of the Kentishmen he left the monastery and rallied them to arms under his standard in their fight for independence. Having broken his monastic vows and taken up arms Aethelheard placed him under ecclesiastical censure which was fully confirmed when Pope Leo III excommunicated Edward Praen, 'accounting him like Julian the Apostate.'[63] Aethelheard, who had already experienced the hostility of the Kentishmen, found their hostility renewed with greater intensity against him for excommunicating their leader. The situation became so dangerous that on the advice of his community of clergy at Christ Church he fled from his archbishopric, despite the fact that Alcuin had written to him urging him not to desert his archbishopric and to the community urging them to persuade their archbishop to remain.[64] In safety on the Continent, probably at the court of Charlemagne, he was able to consider the letter which Alcuin had addressed to him advising him to return to his deserted see.[65] 'You are yourself aware for what cause you left your see,' he wrote, 'yet, whatever the cause, it seems good, that penance be done for it . . .' Alcuin said that the people should do penance also, having already urged them to recall their archbishop.[66]

It is evident from this letter to Aethelheard that the uncertainty of the political situation in Kent over many years had adversely affected the work of the Church at Canterbury. Consequently, Alcuin requested Aethelheard 'to bring to the house of God the zeal for reading, that there may be there young men reading, and a choir of singers, and the study of books, that the dignity of that holy church may be renewed by your diligence.' He also urged the archbishop to address his bishops in synod so that they would give more attention to their episcopal ministrations. Alcuin's letter had the desired effect, and before long Aethelheard was again in occupation of his archbishopric at Canterbury initiating plans for the unification of the southern province and adopting measures for Church reform.

THE REHABILITATION OF THE ARCHBISHOPRIC

In response to Alcuin's advice Archbishop Aethelheard had returned to Canterbury where the unsettled political conditions had changed little since his flight to the Continent. Not until two years after his accession to the Mercian throne in 796 was Cenwulf able to suppress the revolt of the Kentishmen and, as a gesture to their independence, he gave them his brother Cuthred to be king of Kent. By this means Cenwulf's authority was recognized in Kent as it was in East Anglia, Essex and Sussex.

It was in this political context that Aethelheard laboured to bring the dioceses of the province of Lichfield once again within his own province of Canterbury from which they had been separated. One of Alcuin's pupils, before leaving Canterbury to rejoin his master at St. Martin's, Tours, had been commissioned by the archbishop to explain to Alcuin the problems involved if the unification of the two provinces were to be achieved. Alcuin then wrote to Aethelheard advising him how he should proceed 'in order that the unity of the Church, which is in part torn asunder, may be peacefully united and the rent repaired, if it can be.' Even Alcuin was hesitant and unsure because of the complicated situation. Amidst the matters of ecclesiastical organization and administration there was the personal problem of Archbishop Hygeberht and his suffragan bishops. Aethelheard was advised that Hygeberht should not be deprived of his *pallium* during his lifetime, nor should he exercise the authority it conferred in the consecration of bishops : the consecration of bishops should revert 'to the holy and original see.' Before acting on this advice Alcuin requested Aethelheard to take counsel with his community of clergy at Christ Church and also with the archbishop of York. By implementing Alcuin's advice which both the *familia* of Christ Church, Canterbury, and the archbishop of York had confirmed as the best course to adopt, Aethelheard initiated the peaceful unification of the two provinces of Lichfield and Canterbury. But he had already acted on a policy to bring the consecration of all bishops south of the Humber back to the archbishopric of Canterbury and, since Hygeberht made no effort to restrain him, it must be assumed that Hygeberht agreed, or at least acquiesced in his policy. During the short reign of Ecgfrith to two charters, not carrying Hygeberht's subscription, Eadulf, bishop-elect of Lindsey, in the province of Lichfield, subscribed with Aethelheard. One of these charters related to land in the province of Canterbury.[1] Following the normal procedure Eadulf should have presented himself to Hygeberht for consecration but instead he sought consecration from Aethelheard. Prior to consecrating Eadulf, Aethelheard devised a means by which the archbishopric of Canterbury would be in a position to retain the allegiance of its suffragan bishops even if confronted with a situation similar to that created by the division of the province of Canterbury by Offa. For the first time in western Christendom a metropolitan archbishop required from a bishop, before he proceeded to his consecration, a profession on oath of canonical obedience to him and his successors and a confession of faith. This unprecedented action by Aethelheard not only reflected his tenacity of purpose to bring about the unification of the two provinces but also increasing authority of the archbishopric of Canterbury. Eadulf formerly had been a pupil of Aethelheard, but any admiration or respect for his former master could hardly account for the generous and submissive terms of his profession of obedience to him and his successors in perpetuity. Its unequivocal character shows that Eadulf was in full accord with Aethelheard's innovation to such an extent that he added to his profession of canonical obedience his own judgment that 'not only he himself but all bishops should look to the seat of St. Augustine from which the canon of ecclesiastical authority is given.' [2] A profession of orthodoxy and oath of canonical obedience had been required of Boniface on his consecration to the episcopate in 722 by Pope Gregory II.[3] Later, when he became the papal legate to Germany it was decreed among the reform measures of the council of Soissons in 744 that metropolitans in seeking their *pallium* should make a profession of faith and an oath of canonical obedience to the pope.[4] Aethelheard's originality of action was to be found in his adaptation of that which already existed between the pope and metropolitans and bishops consecrated by him to the relationship of himself as metropolitan archbishop to bishops whom he consecrated. Seventy years later in the Church of France, following the action of Aethelheard, Archbishop Hincmar of Rheims found it necessary to demand a similar profession from his suffragan, Bishop Hincmar of Laon.[5] No exception to this requirement was permitted by Aethelheard, even of bishops-elect to dioceses south of the Thames, and before Wigberht, bishop-elect of Sherborne, was consecrated he made his profession of canonical obedience to his archbishop.[6] Similar confessions of obedience were made, before their consecration, by Deneberht, Tidferth and Wulfheard, appointed respectively to the sees of Worcester, Dunwich and Hereford in the province of Lichfield.[7] By the year 801 there remained only the dioceses of Elmham and Leicester of the dioceses separated from the archbishopric of Canterbury, excepting Lichfield, to which Archbishop Aethelheard had not consecrated bishops. Since the subscription of Bishop Unwona of

Leicester is not to be found after 799 it would appear that for some reason, probably age and infirmity, he took no active part in provincial affairs. There remained only Bishop Alcheard of Elmham, and he favoured the return of his diocese to Canterbury.[8] The consecration of bishops to vacant sees in the province of Lichfield by Aethelheard could not have taken place without the consent of Archbishop Hygeberht. This confirms previous indications that Hygeberht was agreeably co-operative with Aethelheard in the progressive return of the dioceses to the province of Canterbury. By his assiduous and resolute action Aethelheard had extended the influence and authority of his archbishopric considerably beyond the confines of the mutilated province to which he was consecrated in 793. In 799 King Cenwulf, in a charter by which he restored land in Kent to Christ Church, Canterbury, described him as 'primate of all Britain' a title first used of Archbishop Berhtwald.[9]

The complete return of the separated dioceses to the province of Canterbury was now in sight, but the situation still remained complicated. There remained the anomalous position of the bishops who had made a profession of canonical obedience to the archbishop of Canterbury by whom they had been consecrated yet they exercised their episcopal ministry in another province and under another archbishop. However much Aethelheard's influence affected the Church north of the Thames, he was unable to exercise any archiepiscopal authority in the dioceses over which the bishops, who had professed canonical obedience to him, had the pastoral charge. Moreover, Hygeberht had received the *pallium* and by its bestowal had confirmed Offa's action in dividing the archbishopric of Canterbury in order to erect a new archbishopric. Hadrian's action had abrogated the constitution of the Church in Britain as laid down by Pope Gregory I, and instead of the two metropolitan sees of Canterbury and York had approved the addition of a third, Lichfield. It was, therefore, only by papal action that the third metropolitan see could be dissolved and the Gregorian plan re-established in Britain.

With much foresight Aethelheard had written a letter in the presence of his suffragans to Pope Leo III outlining the situation and seeking his guidance, but neither his letter nor a reply from the pope has survived. King Cenwulf in 797 with the bishops sent Abbot Wada as an embassy to the papal court concerning the same matter but through incompetence the embassy was a failure. The urgency with which Cenwulf regarded the unification of the two provinces undoubtedly sprang primarily from political considerations, for Kent was not yet a province of Mercia. With the restoration of the province of Canterbury to its former position, under a friendly archbishop, Cenwulf realized that the Church would give a unity to his territories which politically it had not so far attained. In the same year, 798, that he had crushed the revolt in Kent and established an uneasy peace, Cenwulf sent a letter with a gift of one hundred and twenty mancuses to Pope Leo III carried by 'Byrne, the priest, Cildas and Colberht my thegns.' [10] Reference was made in this letter to the two former approaches to the papal court made by the archbishop and king. He then informed the pope that 'our bishops and certain most learned men among us say that against the canons and apostolic decrees which were established for us by the direction of the most blessed father Gregory, as you know, the authority of the metropolitan of Canterbury has been divided into two provinces.' Cenwulf then referred to the city of London mentioned in the Gregorian plan, which provided for 'the highest pontifical dignity' to be appointed to that city with the honour and ornament of the *pallium*. But this honour and dignity was for Augustine's sake bestowed on Canterbury. This was done 'because Augustine, of blessed memory, who by Gregory's order preached the Word of God to the nation of the English, and presided most gloriously over the churches of the Saxon land, died in the same city, and his body was buried in the church of the blessed Peter, Prince of the Apostles, which his successor Laurentius consecrated, it seemed to all the wise men of our race that the metropolitan dignity should remain in that city where rests in the body he who planted in these parts the truth of the faith.' The king then briefly outlined Offa's action in dividing the province of Canterbury and that of Pope Hadrian I in bestowing the *pallium*. Finally, he implored the pope 'that the coat of Christ, woven without seam, may not suffer the rent of dissension among us, but may as we wish be brought to the unity of true peace by your sound teaching.' Pope Leo III did not delay to send his reply to Cenwulf. He acknowledged that his predecessor, Hadrian, 'diminished contrary to custom the authority of the bishop of Canterbury, and by his authority confirmed the division into two archiepiscopal sees.' [11] But he did this solely because Offa had testified in his letter that it was the united wish and unanimous petition of the people, and because of the vast size and the extension of his kingdom, and many more reasons. It was because of all these reasons advanced by Offa that Hadrian had sent the honour of the *pallium* to the bishop of the Mercians. King Cenwulf's reference to London, mentioned in the Gregorian plan, was interpreted by the pope as an inquiry concerning the possibility of London becoming the seat of the archbishop of the southern province. Many political advantages would have accrued to the king, and ecclesiastically there may have been benefits in the metropolitan see becoming more accessible to the whole of his province. Uninfluenced by the history and traditions of Canterbury Cenwulf probably considered the time was opportune since, it would appear, the bishopric of London was vacant. The unequivocal terms of the reply of Pope Leo III could have left King Cenwulf in no doubt of the ecclesiastical position, for he wrote : 'As for what was said in your letter asking us if the authority of the supreme pontificate could by canonical consent be situated in the city of London . . . we by no means dare to give them the authority of the supreme pontificate; but as the primacy was established at Canterbury, we concede and pronounce it by our decree the first see. . . .Therefore, according to the canons it is right that it should be, and be called, the primacy, and in the order that was arranged by our predecessors, thus be venerated and honoured as the archiepiscopal see in all things.'

From the letters of Cenwulf and Aethelheard the pope had fully grasped both the political and ecclesiastical situation, but in his reply to the king he issued neither directive nor counsel but only an implied accord with their desire for the unification of the two ecclesiastical provinces within Cenwulf's territories. Beyond a reference to 'the bishop of the Mercians' Lichfield is not mentioned by the pope. But his emphatic statement that Canterbury was the primatial see excluded not only London but any other city, including Lichfield, from possessing the primacy. Neither his nor Cenwulf's letter from Pope Leo III gave Aethelheard any authoritative mandate to dissolve the metropolitan archbishopric of Lichfield and to unite its dioceses once again with the province of Canterbury. Until a papal mandate was obtained even the consecration of bishops reverting to Canterbury for the dioceses separated from it was nothing more than a preparatory step towards unification. It is evident that when Aethelheard sought the advice of Eanbald II of York they had agreed that it was necessary for Aethelheard to appear in person at the papal court and there present his petition for the rehabilitation of his archbishopric. Although Eanbald at the time was involved in political problems in his own province, he showed a real interest in the well-being of the Church throughout Britain by sending Torhtmund, the chief nobleman of Northumbria, to accompany Aethelheard to Rome. Aethelheard had been praised by Pope Leo III 'because he had endangered his life for the orthodox faith,' when he placed Edward Praen under ecclesiastical censure, therefore the archbishop had ground for confidence in the successful outcome of his mission. In addition to Torhtmund he was accompanied by Ceolmund, a former thegn of Offa, and two bishops, one of whom was Cyneberht, bishop of Winchester.[12] In his journey across the Continent he called upon Alcuin at his cell of St. Judoc. The great scholar was not there but had left a letter for Aethelheard in which he expressed his satisfaction at the meeting of the two archbishops of Canterbury and York as he had advised, and gave Aethelheard an invitation to visit him at St. Martin's, Tours, on his journey homewards from Rome. Knowing the attractions of the splendour and magnificence of the papal court, Alcuin, once again in fatherly fashion, gave advice to Aethelheard and urged him not to delay his return from Rome after he had completed his mission. 'Return, return, holy father, as soon as your pious embassy is finished to your lost sheep' he wrote. 'As there are two eyes in the body, so I believe and desire that you two, Canterbury and York, give light throughout the breadth of Britain. Do not deprive your country of its right eye.' [13] Here was Alcuin's conception of the structure of the Church in the land of his birth. He regarded the Gregorian plan as authoritative and that it should not be assailed or altered in any way. For him there were only two ecclesiastical rulers in Britain and the only distinction between them, the 'two eyes' of the body politic of the Church, was that Aethelheard was the 'right eye' since he was the occupant of the primatial see of Canterbury. He was most anxious that the arch-bishop's mission should be successful and knowing the great influence which Charlemagne had over the pope he wrote to his patron telling him of Aethelheard's journey to Rome and of his intention to visit the imperial court. Friendship between the emperor and archbishop had existed for some years, and it was Aethelheard's intention to visit Charlemagne, on his journey to Rome, for he was well aware that a friendly relationship with the most powerful ruler in Europe could not fail favourably to impress the papal court. Alcuin told the arch-bishop that he had written commending him to the emperor. Using the sobriquet by which he was called by Charlemagne, Alcuin wrote: 'I have been informed that certain of the friends of your Flaccus (Alcuin), Aethelheard, to wit, metropolitan of the Church of Canter-bury and pontiff of the primatial see of Britain. . . . Ceolmund and also Torhtmund desire to approach Your Grace.' [14] No records have survived of the meeting with Charlemagne, and of Aethelheard's personal meeting with Pope Leo III there are no details. Evidence is not lacking, however, to show that the archbishop's petition for the restoration of his archbishopric to its former state was the subject of thorough investigation. From the documentary records of the sacred archives was found confirmatory evidence of the statements and claims which Aethelheard made concerning his metropolitan archbishopric of Canterbury. William of Malmesbury alone gives the letter which Aethelheard received from Pope Leo III in January 802. After the customary greetings and introduction the pope wrote: 'We . . . advise and instruct your brotherly goodness, for the sake of the dioceses of England committed to you, that is, of the bishops and the monasteries, whether monks, canons, or nuns; just as your church held them in ancient times, as we have learnt from investigations in our sacred archives, so we confirm that they should be held by you and your successors. The holy and noble preacher Gregory ordained and confirmed according to orthodoxy, that all the churches of the English were to be subject for ever to blessed Archbishop Augustine, his chaplain, by the sacred use of the *pallium*. And, therefore, by the authority of the blessed Peter, Prince of the Apostles, . . . and, moreover, according to the established judgment of the holy canons, we, holding without merit the office of the same Peter, keeper of the keys of heaven, concede to you Aethelheard and to your successors all the churches of the English just as they were from former times, to be held for ever in your same metropolitan see by inviolable right, with due acknowledgement of subjection. And if anyone, which we do not wish, shall attempt to contravene the authority of our decision and apostolic privilege, we have decided by apostolic authority that, if he is an archbishop or bishop, he is cast out from the order of the episcopate. Likewise if it be a priest or deacon or other minister whatever of the sacred ministry, he is to be deposed from his order. And if it is one of the number of laymen, whether king or prince, or any person of high rank or low, he is to know himself separated from participation in the sacred communion. We grant by the authority of the blessed Peter, Prince of the Apostles, whose ministry we discharge, the document of the privilege to you, Aethelheard, and to your successors to be held for ever.' [15] This historic document was written on the pope's instructions and was based squarely on the plan which Gregory had conceived, and the threefold reference to it in different forms in this document removed any doubt as to its import. Pope Leo III neither made reference to the archbishopric of Lichfield nor to the action of Pope Hadrian I in bestowing the *pallium* upon Hygeberht. An exceptional feature, however, was his specific mention of 'an archbishop,' which could mean none other than Hygeberht, in which he ordered the deposition from the episcopate of 'an archbishop or bishop' if he should attempt 'to contravene the authority of our decision and apostolic privilege.' There was no delay since no opposing plea had been entered, and judgment on the archbishop's appeal having been received Aethelheard remained no longer than was necessary in Rome. Carrying with him the papal judgment which was completely in his favour he was eager that it should be implemented as soon as possible in his own country. As he travelled across the Continent he did not delay to visit Alcuin at St. Martin's, Tours, as he had been invited. He was not unmindful of the advice which he had given and which he had followed so he wrote to Alcuin telling him of the successful result of his appeal at the papal court. [16] In due course Alcuin sent a letter of congratulation to Aethelheard on the restoration 'to its ancient dignity of the most holy see of the first teacher (Augustine) of our native land.' While he recognized the unique position of the archbishopric of Canterbury he saw the whole Church in Britain, which included the archbishopric of York where he had been nurtured, and expressed his satisfaction at the friendly relationship which existed between Aethelheard and Eanbald II. 'By the operation of divine grace, the unity of the members is held together in the proper head, and priestly dignity rejoices in its ancient honour; and brotherly peace shines forth between the highest pontiffs of Britain. And one will of piety and concord flourishes under the two cities of the metropolitans of Canterbury and York, as I perceive in the letters of Your Beatitude.' [17]

After Aethelheard's departure from Rome it would appear that the pope received another letter and gift from Cenwulf which the pope acknowledged in effusive terms. Once again the pope paid tribute to the archbishop who pleased him 'in all holiness and manner of life,' and informed the king on what grounds he had granted Aethelheard's petition, concluding with the words : 'But concerning Archbishop Aethelheard of the Church of Canterbury, to whom reference has already been made, since the surpassing merit of your bishops has urgently requested of us that we do him justice concerning his own dioceses, and of bishops as well as of monasteries, of which he has been illegally deprived, which he held a little time ago, as you know, and which have been taken from his venerable see. Having investigated without prejudice all particulars we have found in our sacred repository that our predecessor St. Gregory delivered that province to his co-adjutor archbishop, St. Augustine, and confirmed to him the right of consecrating bishops to the extent of twelve in number. Whence, having discovered this truth, in right of our apostolic authority by ordinance and confirmation we have restored them to him in their entirety as they were in former times. And we have delivered to him the privilege of confirmation which is to be observed by his Church according to the judgment of the sacred canons.' [18]

Aethelheard received the privilege in January 802, but it was not until eighteen months later that a synod was convoked at Clofeshoh in October 803 at which he presented the papal privilege. It is probable that the delay in convening the synod was caused by the unsettled conditions after the Northumbrian invasion by King Eardulf of Cenwulf's northern territories and the political upheaval caused by the defeat of the Hwicce after they had invaded Wiltshire. However, before the synod assembled Cenwulf and Aethelheard consulted together about the business of the synod since elements from the letter which they had received from the pope appear in the synod's decrees. All the bishops and abbots from the dioceses of the province of

Canterbury prior to its division attended and also Cenwulf with his chief counsellors. Although there are no records of the proceedings of the council, the introductory decree, which expanded and interpreted the papal document which the archbishop presented, sufficiently reflects their outcome and gives some details how the division of the archbishopric of Canterbury was effected. The decrees were as follows: 'Glory to God in the highest, and peace on earth to men of goodwill. We know indeed because it is known to many who faithfully trust in God, and yet nevertheless nothing in it seems pleasing to those who are of the English peoples, that Offa, king of the Mercians, in the days of Archbishop Jaenberht with great fraud presumed to divide and cut asunder the honour and unity of the see of our father, Saint Augustine, in the city of Canterbury; and how, after the death of the aforesaid pontiff, Archbishop Aethelheard, by the gift of the grace of God, his successor, after the course of years happened to visit the thresholds of the Apostles and the most blessed Pope Leo of the Apostolic See concerning many rights of the churches of God. Among other necessary embassy matters he also told that the division of the archiepiscopal see had been unjustly made; and the Apostolic Pope, as soon as he heard and understood that it had been done unjustly, immediately made a decree by the privilege of his own authority and sent it to Britain and directed that the honour of the see of St. Augustine with all its dioceses should be completely restored, according as St. Gregory, the apostle and teacher of our race, had arranged, and should be restored in all things to the honourable Archbishop Aethelheard when he returned to his country; and Cenwulf, the pious king of the Mercians, with his counsellors, thus gave effect to this in the year of our Lord's incarnation 803, the eleventh indiction on the twelfth of October.

'I, Archbishop Aethelheard, with all the twelve bishops subject to the holy see of the blessed Augustine, in a synod which was held by the apostolic decrees of the lord Pope Leo in a famous place called Clofeshoh, with the unanimous counsel of all the holy synod, in the name of Almighty God and of all His saints and by His terrible judgment, command that neither kings nor bishops nor princes nor men of tyrannical power presume to diminish or divide to the slightest degree the honour of St. Augustine and his holy see; but that it shall always remain most fully in all respects in the same honour and dignity in which it is now by the constitution of the blessed Gregory and in the privileges of his apostolic successors, and as appears to be right by the decrees of the holy canons.

'Now, also, with the co-operation of God and the lord apostolic, Pope Leo, I, Archbishop Aethelheard, and others our fellow-bishops and with us all the dignitaries of our synod, with the standard of the

K

cross of Christ, unanimously confirm the primacy of the holy see. And writing with the sign of the holy cross, decreeing this also that the archiepiscopal see from this time onward shall never be in the monastery of Lichfield nor in any other place except only in the city of Canterbury where is the Church of Christ and where first in this island the Catholic Faith shone forth, and where Holy Baptism was celebrated by St. Augustine.

'Moreover, with the consent and licence of the lord apostolic, Pope Leo, we pronounce that the charter sent from the Roman see by Pope Hadrian concerning the *pallium* and the archiepiscopal see in the monastery of Lichfield to be of no validity because it was obtained by deception and misleading suggestion. And, therefore, we have decreed by the manifest signs of the heavenly king, with canonical and apostolical supports, that the primacy of archiepiscopal rule is to remain where the Holy Gospel of Christ was first preached in the province of the English by the blessed father Saint Augustine, and then by the grace of the Holy Spirit widely spread abroad.

'If, indeed, any one contrary to these apostolic decrees and all those of ours dare to rend the garment of Christ and to divide the unity of the Holy Church of God, let him know that unless he makes worthy amends for what he has wickedly done against the sacred canons then he is eternally damned.

'Here are the names of the holy bishops and abbots who confirmed the above written document by engrossment in the synod held at Clofeshoh in the year from the coming of the Lord 803, with the sign of the holy cross of Christ.' [19] To this historic document Aethelheard first subscribed followed by two abbots and three priests of his diocese of Canterbury, and for the first time in any English ecclesiastical document there is to be found the subscription of an archdeacon, by name Wulfred.[20] The twelve bishops of the restored province then subscribe and after each bishop's subscription the abbots and some priests of his diocese subscribed. Among the subscriptions of the diocese of Lichfield, after that of Bishop Ealdwulf is to be found the subscription of a certain Abbot Hygeberht.[21] Since Hygeberht's subscription does not appear in any contemporary documents either as archbishop or bishop after 801 it would seem that Hygeberht had consecrated Ealdwulf as his co-adjutor bishop, with right of succession, and then relinquishing his see had withdrawn to the seclusion of the monastery of Lichfield of which he became abbot.[22]

In all the documents relating to the restoration of the archbishopric of Canterbury there is a significant emphasis on the plan of Pope Gregory I for the constitution of the Church in Britain. In his mandatory letter to Aethelheard and in his letter to Cenwulf Pope Leo III made it clear that he regarded the Gregorian plan as canon law, irrespective of the fact that during Theodore's archiepiscopate the plan was set aside. Nevertheless, the Gregorian plan as it was in operation before the division of the province of Canterbury was acknowledged by the council of Clofeshoh in 803 as a part of the legally constituted plan for the administration and government of the Church in Britain. The two parts of the archbishopric of Canterbury created by Offa were, in another council, territorially united by his successor Cenwulf. This action of the two kings, the one dividing and the other uniting territories over which they ruled in order to determine the extent of ecclesiastical provinces indicates how far their royal authority, at this period, vitally influenced for good or ill the administrative functioning and spiritual well-being of the Church. Nevertheless, there remained a continuity of episcopal ministry which had an effective bearing on the years of division and unsettlement. When Cenwulf sent his letter in 798 to Pope Leo III seeking the restoration of the archbishopric of Canterbury he mentioned not only the concurrence of the ealdormen but also of the bishops. He was aware that the suffragan bishops of Jaenberht, who were arbitrarily separated from the archbishopric of Canterbury by Offa, still looked with reverence to the primatial see with its Church traditions from the days of Augustine. But this separation of the bishops, north of the Thames to the Humber, from the jurisdiction of the archbishop of Canterbury could not destroy their loyal devotion to the fount from which they had received consecration nor their veneration for the Church founded by St. Augustine. In this it seems was the strongest element upon which Aethelheard was able to build his policy for the restoration of his archbishopric. Evidence of the importance with which he regarded the loyal support of the bishops is to be seen in his requirement of a profession of canonical obedience. No expression of reluctance to make the profession is to be found but rather a willingness to do so. The professions of the bishops vary in their length and substance. Each, it would appear, was an original composition possessing first a confession of Catholic orthodoxy and, secondly, a profession of canonical obedience to Aethelheard and his successors.[23] Their confessions of faith are similar to those made by metropolitans before receiving from the pope the dignity of the *pallium*. And they compare favourably with the confession of faith made by St. Boniface before his consecration by Pope Gregory II.[24] By these confessions of faith and professions of canonical obedience Aethelheard dealt with a twofold divisive influence. He assured himself that, during the political upheavals which had disrupted the work and witness of the Church, the disintegrating and destructive power of heretical teaching had not crept into the Church. And, secondly, the continuity of the relationship of bishops to the primatial see had been established on an oath of obedience to him and his successors. Moreover, the papal decree which Aethelheard had obtained in Rome regularized all that he had done for the restoration of his archbishopric. His desires and those of Cenwulf, his ealdormen and the bishops were finally fulfilled by the acceptance of the papal decree and its endorsement by the promulgation of the Church's own decree in 803 at the council of Clofeshoh.

While the council was still in session Aethelheard initiated a long overdue reform of the monasteries. By decree it was decided that 'In the name of Almighty God, and by His awful judgment, I enjoin, as I have the mandate from Pope Leo, that from this time none dare to choose themselves lords over God's heritage from laymen and seculars.' [25] For the first time in the English Church a measure excluding seculars in this way, although they themselves may have conformed to a semi-monastic ordering of their life, made the difference yet more distinct between the seculars and the monks. Other business transacted at the council included an agreement between the bishops of Worcester and Hereford by which monasteries in Gloucestershire were conveyed to Bishop Deneberht of Worcester by Bishop Wulfheard; Bishop Deneberht in turn conveyed the pasturage of their land to Aethelheard for his lifetime. [26] Aethelheard also subscribed to a charter by which the kings Cenwulf and Cuthred granted land to the convent of Lyminge in Kent, [27] and in the same year, 804, he consecrated the last of his suffragan bishops, Beornmod, after he had made his profession of canonical obedience to him, to the see of Rochester. [28] Aethelheard's greatest concern during the last years of his archiepiscopate, of which there is any record, was the future well-being of his *familia* at Christ Church. A *mensa* had been made possible for the *familia* in 774 by Offa's grant to Jaenberht and another to the *familia,* but so far there was no communal life. [29] By Aethelheard's recovery of land of which the *familia* had been wrongly deprived and by his own grant, it would appear that he tried to establish a form of communal life which would conform more closely to the monastic pattern, but his death in May 805 prevented this reform.

Aethelheard's archiepiscopate of fourteen years covered one of the most critical periods in the life of the English Church, which had been the most constructive unifying force in England until it had been disrupted and torn apart to serve the political ambitions of Offa. Aethelheard's greatest achievement was the restoration of the archbishopric of Canterbury. Beginning with the disadvantage of the hostility of the Kentishmen who prevented him on his consecration from entering his cathedral of Christ Church, Canterbury, and later being compelled to flee to the Continent for his own safety, he finally triumphed in his struggle to regain the dioceses north of the Thames which had been separated from his archbishopric during Jaenberht's archiepiscopate. His introduction of a profession of canonical obedience from bishops-elect before they were consecrated brought a unifying principle into the episcopate which has remained a part of the life of the Church to this day. The city of Canterbury which had grown into the great administrative centre of the Church in the southern province had also become a centre of learning and scholarship of widespread influence and known throughout western Christendom. But these had suffered immeasurably amidst the unsettled conditions of the country, particularly in Kent, during the reigns of Offa, Ecgfrith and Cenwulf. The standards of learning and priestly ministrations had reached such a low level towards the end of the eighth century that the scholar, Alcuin, in writing to Aethelheard urged him personally to 'bring into the house of God' a revival of learning and to undertake measures for the pastoral ministry of the Church to be renewed. Aethelheard possessed the friendship of Charlemagne, the great Christian emperor, and of Alcuin, probably the greatest scholar of his day. He also maintained amicable relationships with kings Offa, Ecgfrith, Cenwulf and Cuthred, and won the allegiance of the episcopate. All these qualities together with his indomitable labours for the Church indicate some of the gifts with which he enriched the archbishopric of Canterbury. Fully involved in his unremitting work for the territorial restoration of his archbishopric, all reform measures had to be delayed until after the council of Clofeshoh in October 803. From then until his death eighteen months later the greatest of his reforms for the Church began to emerge but were never accomplished by him. Nevertheless, his spiritual rule and leadership, having found expression in his administrative gifts, preserved and enhanced the veneration and loyalty of bishops, clergy, monks, nuns and laymen to the Mother Church of Canterbury where the Catholic Faith was first preached and where Holy Baptism was first celebrated in England by St. Augustine.

THE COMMUNITY OF CHRIST CHURCH: CONFLICT BETWEEN KING AND ARCHBISHOP

The continuity and consolidation of the great work of Archbishop Aethelheard for the restoration of his archbishopric was assured when Wulfred, his archdeacon, was chosen to succeed him. Wulfred was present at the council of Clofeshoh in 803 and subscribed as archdeacon to the decree which endorsed the papal mandate restoring the archbishopric of Canterbury to the position which it had held in former times. From the appearance of Wulfred's subscription it would appear that he had been appointed archdeacon sometime before the council in order to assist Aethelheard with the restoration of the archbishopric, and for that purpose was a metropolitan archdeacon possessing archidiaconal authority in all the dioceses of the province of Canterbury.[1] While the archbishop attended to the spiritual administration he would have commissioned Wulfred to co-ordinate and to have the oversight of the temporalities of the province. In the prevailing conditions at the time it would have been a difficult task since it involved, in part, giving effect to the papal mandate for reuniting with the province of Canterbury the dioceses between the Thames and Humber which had been separated in order to erect the archbishopric of Lichfield.

Before his consecration he was present at a synodal council at Oakley in 805 and subscribed as *Wulfredus electus*. Within a few days, at what may have been another session of the same council, he received as archbishop a grant of land in Kent from Cuthred, king of Kent, the charter of which carries the subscription of Cenwulf, king of Mercia.[2] Since all the bishops who subscribed to this charter also subscribed to another charter of the same year at Oakley there can be little doubt that, while all the bishops were present, Wulfred was consecrated at Canterbury, Oakley being not far distant, between two sessions of the council. At the time of his consecration Pope Leo III occupied the papal throne, from whom Aethelheard had received the mandate for the restoration of his see. Conciliar action had been taken on the authoritative mandate without any questioning of the papal authority by bishops or reigning monarch, and the pope now required Wulfred to visit the apostolic see to receive the *pallium,* as is evident from a fragment of a letter of protestation which the bishops of Britain addressed to the pope. Precedents were cited by the bishops from the time of Augustine showing that the *pallium* had been sent to the archbishops in Britain, and an excerpt was included from the letter sent by Pope Honorius I to Honorius of Canterbury which accompanied the two *pallia* for Bishops Honorius and Paulinus. Reference was also made to the counsel given by Alcuin to Offa at the time of the erection of the archbishopric of Lichfield, that 'the *pallium* ought to be sent to him (the archbishop) from the lord apostolic.' [3] Nothing further concerning the letter is to be found, but it is recorded in the Chronicles that Wulfred received the *pallium* in 806.[4]

By his good relations with the king and the people of Kent Wulfred's influence extended to political as well as ecclesiastical affairs in his own diocese of Canterbury and in his province. Unlike his predecessor, Aethelheard, who minted his own coins which carried the name of Offa or Cenwulf on the reverse, Wulfred issued coins which had no name of a royal overlord upon them. For the first time the tonsured effigy of an archbishop appeared on the obverse with Wulfred's name and title, and on the reverse the place of mintage or the name of the moneyer and the place of mintage in monogram form.[5] Coinage of such a character reflected in some measure the archbishop's independence and, by his omission of King Cenwulf's name from his coins, probably little regard for his authority.

Wulfred had continued his work for the recovery of property which belonged to his archbishopric and province, but not without coming into conflict with Cenwulf. It was at this period that Archbishop Eanbald II of York, with whom Cenwulf sympathized, succeeded in driving King Eardulf from Northumbria, who found asylum at the court of Charlemagne. Learning that Eardulf had fled to the emperor's court, Eanbald, Cenwulf and Wada, the powerful ealdormen of Northumbria, sent an embassy to Charlemagne in order to vindicate themselves. Having knowledge of this embassy and the situation in the northern archbishopric of York, Pope Leo III wrote a letter to Charlemagne in which he mentioned that peace between Cenwulf and Wulfred did not exist.[6] This reference was not to strained relations but to a state of hostility between king and archbishop, a report of which was of sufficient importance to have reached Rome. Was this hostility caused by Wulfred's marked independence or increasing influence in political affairs? Or was it caused by his interest in Bishop Aethelwulf of Selsey and Bishop Wigthegn of Winchester, whom he had recently consecrated, whose dioceses were in the kingdom of Wessex over which King Egbert ruled?[7] Or was it Cenwulf's fear that a situation might arise between him and the archbishop comparable to that which arose between Offa and Jaenberht or that which then existed between Archbishop Eanbald II and King Eardulf of Northumbria? Whether it was any or all of these things Cenwulf and Wulfred were so far reconciled in 809 that 'Cenwulf by the grace of Christ king of the Mercians and of the

province of Kent' granted to him land in Kent, the grant being confirmed a year later at Canterbury by the nobles of the people of
Kent.[8] The breach having been healed king and archbishop together
are to be found subscribing to charters until 817. In this year the
early series of Cenwulf's charters abruptly ended when a dispute
unparalleled in the history of the English Church arose between him
and Wulfred. King Cenwulf continued his benefactions to the Church,
and at the council of London in 811 he made a grant of land in Kent
to Bishop Beornmod of Rochester.[9] From the same council came
another charter showing Wulfred, the possessor of land in his own
right, having a business transaction with the king.[10] Earlier in the
same year Wulfred had exchanged some of his lands for lands belonging to his *familia,* much to its benefit. The charter recording the
exchange is of special interest because of those who subscribed.
Wulfred and Beornmod first subscribe and then follow the subscriptions of three priest-abbots, seventeen priests, seven deacons and two
of an inferior order.[11] On such an occasion involving the exchange of
property belonging to the *familia* it would be expected that all members would subscribe to the charter. On this occasion such a large
number of subscriptions including three priest-abbots indicate that
more than the clerks of Wulfred's *familia* subscribed. Since Bishop
Beornmod subscribed there can be little doubt that the priest-abbot
and others of his own *familia* subscribed. Wernoth, another priest-
abbot, who subscribed also appears in the list of abbots of St. Augustine's monastery.

During Cuthbert's archiepiscopate the Bonifatian reform movement
on the Continent was reflected in the decrees of the synod of
Clofeshoh in 746 and in the subsequent efforts of the Church to
conform more closely to canonical requirements. The two synods
attended by the legates of Pope Hadrian I decreed among other
things that 'bishops shall diligently take care to see that all canons
shall live canonically; and that their monks and nuns shall live according to their rule.' [12] Although the *familia* had a *mensa,* from the
time of Jaenberht's grant in 774, there is no evidence that the *familia*
of Christ Church lived communally or under canonical rule.[13] By the
recovery of land and by his own gift 'to the holy church of Christ
as its own possession' Aethelheard had initiated preparatory measures
for communal life at Christ Church but his efforts were cut short by
his death. The secular chapter or *familia* of Christ Church now
possessed endowments, separate from those of the archbishopric, which
had been generously augmented by Wulfred, who also restored and
adapted the buildings in which his *familia* resided so that they would
be able to live canonically.

Bishop Chrodegang of Metz, following Boniface's reforms, 'drew up

a rule for canons by which all members of the *familia* were to lead
a communal life in dormitory and refectory, young lectors were to
be trained by a brother of proven life, the canons (among whom the
young lectors are included) were allowed to retain the disposition of
their patrimony, and in certain cases to receive special stipends.' [14]
It was now that Wulfred probably achieved his greatest work for the
archbishopric of Canterbury by shaping the life of his *familia* in
accordance with the principles enjoined by Boniface and Chrodegang.
Wulfred's charter of privileges also carried obligations for his *familia*
as laid down in the following terms : 'For the honour of God I have
caused to be rebuilt, renewed, and restored the holy monastery of the
church of Canterbury, for the presbyters, deacons, and all clergy
serving God together. I, Wulfred, gave and grant to the *familia* of
Christ to have and to enjoy the houses which they have built for
themselves at their own cost by the perpetual right of inheritance,
during their own lifetimes, or of those descendants to whom each
shall have free power to leave or grant them within the said monastery,
but not to any external person without the congregation (i.e. the
possibly married canons who have received stipends, and lived in
their own houses, may bequeath them to sons or relations trained in
the Christ Church *familia,* as the canons had probably received them
themselves, but not to their other children). But under this condition,
that they sedulously frequent the canonical hours in the church of
Christ. . . . And that they frequent together the refectory and
dormitory, and that they observe the rule of the discipline of life in a
monastery. But if any one of them . . . dare to gather together feasts
for eating and drinking or even sleeping in their own cells (houses),
let him know, whoever he be, that he shall be deprived of his own
house and it shall be in the power of the archbishop to hold and to
grant to whomsoever it shall please him.' [15]

To this charter there are only a third of the number of subscriptions
compared with the charter recording the exchange of lands with
Christ Church. Among the subscriptions are those of a priest-abbot,
eight priests and three inferior clerks.

Wulfred's twofold compulsory requirement of the use of a common
dormitory and refectory by the members of his *familia* did not place
them under full monasterial discipline. Although reference was made
to 'canons' in the conciliar decrees at Clofeshoh in 787 it was not
until now that they actually became 'canons.' Before the end of the
eighth century there had been such a decline at Canterbury in the
spirit and disciplines of monasticism that it was deplored by Alcuin in
his letter to the clergy and nobles of Kent.[16] Some of the members
of the community had lived independently in houses near the cathedral, but since Wulfred's reform measures required communal life

in refectory and dormitory these residences could no longer continue for the canons themselves. Mention is made in a later charter of 'Dodda the monk,' probably a member of the *familia,* whose house and garden held by him were now to be used at the discretion of the community of Christ Church for sick and aged canons who were unable to bear the rigours of communal life.[17]

As successful as Wulfred's reform measures at Canterbury appear to have been, there is no evidence to show that similar measures were adopted by his suffragans in their own dioceses, for they could not have been unaware of their archbishop's reforms of the community of Christ Church. Of these they would have learned in fuller detail when he called them in 816 to a council at Chelsea, attended by Cenwulf and twelve magnates, which promulgated eleven decrees, three of which made special reference to communities. A bishop should have the power in his own diocese, it was decreed, of electing abbots and abbesses with the consent of the *familia,* but neither bishop nor the community could act alone in this matter but only conjointly.[18] Bishops and the heads of monastic houses were guardians of the lands and property belonging to communities. Already lands had been diminished by the depredations of the Danes and other causes and now they must guard against any further loss of land lest the monks be at risk of perishing through poverty. So uncertain had the survival of monasteries become that the decree enjoined bishops not to surrender them but to 'defend the flock of Christ.' However, if a monastery through poverty or the rapacity of seculars was unable to continue then it should not by any means 'be made the property or residence of seculars.' [19] In the light of these decrees there is little doubt, in view of his reforms at Christ Church, that Wulfred was striving not only to arrest the decline of monasticism within his own see city but throughout the whole of the province of Canterbury. His reform measures within his own archbishopric were not merely to secure the endowment of his *familia* but also to ensure that the canonical rule of life which he had established at Christ Church would survive even if monasticism with its regular rule of life disappeared, as indeed it did, as a result of the raids of the Danes, before King Alfred came to the throne.

A problem which had confronted the archbishopric of Canterbury was the influx of priests ordained by bishops of the Scotic Church. These priests had evidently entered England in consequence of a decree of the council of Châlons convoked in 813 at the direction of Charlemagne.[20] Although this council was concerned with heresy and simony throughout the empire it also decreed that the ordination of priests and deacons who had received ordination from those who claimed to be Scotic bishops was null and void. Priests and deacons of this tradition, it would appear, had entered dioceses in the province of Canterbury and exercised their ministerial functions without episcopal licence or authorization. This irregular situation was now dealt with by Wulfred and his suffragan bishops in council by a decree expressly forbidding all who had been ordained in the Scotic tradition to exercise the functions of their office in any diocese of the province. Two reasons for this conciliar action were given by the council. First, there was no certainty how or by whom they had been ordained and, secondly, because the Scotic Church had neither the order of metropolitan nor any regard for it.[21] The council also considered the extent of the metropolitan archbishop's authority in his province. Since the restoration of the archbishopric of Canterbury under Aethelheard it had become evident that Offa's division of the province had made uncertain what authority the archbishop possessed in the dioceses of his province. The profession or canonical obedience rendered by each bishop-elect to the archbishop did not cover this matter. Wulfred, at this council, had the matter clarified and stated in unequivocal terms in the decrees. It was made obligatory for every bishop to have a record of any judgment concerning his diocese given by a provincial council. This record had to give the year, by what archbishop and other bishops the judgment had been reached and confirmed. The bishop was also required to carry to his diocese two copies of the judgment; one for himself and the other for the person concerned in the sentence. By this decree the council strengthened the bishop in his diocesan administration, obviated any personal element in the judgment pronounced and gave to the archbishop his rightful place as president of the court which gave judgment.[22] Reference was made by the council to Theodore's canon 'no bishop shall invade the parish (diocese) of another.'[23] This was reaffirmed and expanded, decreeing that no bishop should exercise his office in the consecration of churches and in ordinations which rightly belong to another bishop, but these things could be done by the archbishop 'because he is the head of his own bishops.'[24] Moreover, any bishop who transgressed in this respect became subject to the judgment of the archbishop unless a reconciliation was effected with the bishop of the other diocese. For the first time in the English Church, that which formerly had been accepted as belonging to the office of a metropolitan archbishop, based on conciliar statements from the council of Nicea in 325 onwards, was given canonical definition. By virtue of his office as 'head of his own bishops' he had authority to visit all dioceses within his province, and he possessed authority to consecrate churches and to ordain priests and deacons in all the dioceses over which his suffragan bishops ruled. The authoritative statement in these canons relating to the provincial spiritual authority of the archbishop indicates that out of the disruption during the archiepiscopates of Jaenberht and Aethelheard there had emerged an element of episcopal independence which did not fully recognize the extensive authority of the metropolitan archbishop of Canterbury. These canons had received the unanimous approval of Wulfred's suffragans and the ground had now been prepared for more efficient administration of all dioceses in his province.

Progress was halted, however, in the following year when a conflict of the utmost gravity broke out between Cenwulf and Wulfred. The powerful influence of Wulfred in Kent, his friendliness with King Egbert of Wessex, and his unremitting efforts in claiming the restoration of property which formerly belonged to the archbishopric of Canterbury undoubtedly had caused friction between king and archbishop on earlier occasions. This situation, the king's jealousy aroused by Wulfred's friendship with the Emperor Louis and his concern for the well-being of the Church, probably impelled Wulfred in 814 to visit Rome, accompanied by Wigthegn, bishop of Winchester, there to seek the counsel of Pope Leo III.[25] Papal counsel may have found expression in the archbishop convoking the last of the great ecclesiastical councils in 816, during the supremacy of Mercia, when there appeared to be an amicable relationship between king and archbishop. At this council there were written into the canon law of the English Church some particulars of the extensive authority of the archbishop of Canterbury throughout his province. Cenwulf, having been present at the council, could not have failed to realize the immense authority wielded by Wulfred. This, with some unrecorded happenings within a few months of the council, aroused the unrestrained hostility of Cenwulf who seized the monasteries of Reculver and Southminster within the archbishopric of Canterbury.[26] Wulfred had regained Reculver which had been previously possessed by Cenwulf during the turmoil caused by the despoliation of the archbishopric of Canterbury. The re-possession of the monastery of Reculver probably roused Cenwulf's anger to such an extent that not only did he retake it but also seized Southminster. This act of aggression against the Church seems to have provoked Wulfred to take ecclesiastical action with which to punish the king. Much obscurity and uncertainty surround the sequence of events at this period. Cenwulf's series of charters ceased in 817 and none appeared again until 821.[27] The only record in which the quarrel between Cenwulf and Wulfred is to be found is in a Canterbury document which records that 'The whole race of the English for nearly six years were deprived of primordial authority and the ministry of sacred baptism.'[28] Some confusion has been caused by this statement because of its rhetorical element. Wulfred was not deprived of his primatial authority since he continued to consecrate bishops during the period of the interdict. Were 'primordial authority' and 'the ministry of holy baptism' two parts, related to each other, of the interdict placed upon the people by Wulfred? The sacrament of baptism is the first in order and the first in time. It was administered by the Apostles to the first converts to the Christian Faith and similarly Augustine, the first metropolitan bishop of Canterbury, was the first to administer the first sacrament to the first converts of the mission to the English. As successor, in the chair of St. Augustine, Wulfred possessed the authority to administer the sacrament of baptism as did the bishops, priests and deacons within his province. And it may have been this primordial authority which none could exercise because of Wulfred's interdict. There must remain some doubt whether the interdict affected the kingdom of Wessex over which Egbert ruled and with whom the archbishop was on friendly terms. The whole race of the English, therefore, must be taken to mean the people in that part of the province of Canterbury co-terminous with the territories of Cenwulf, or perhaps only Wulfred's diocese since the interdict is unrecorded elsewhere. On the other hand the deprivation of primordial authority may mean retaliatory action by Cenwulf against Wulfred for depriving him and his people of holy baptism. This would have meant that, while Wulfred continued to exercise his primatial authority in the consecration of bishops, he was placed under some form of restraint by the king which prevented him from visiting any part of his province beyond the boundaries of his own diocese of Canterbury. Cenwulf laid a charge against Wulfred at the papal court. But the only knowable ground upon which he would have been able to make a charge against Wulfred would have been the ecclesiastical interdict laid upon him and the people of his kingdom. Both Pope Paschal I and the Emperor Louis were acquainted with the quarrel between the king and Wulfred, and it seems that both agreed with the archbishop in the action he had taken. Whatever may have been the charges against Wulfred at Rome they would most likely have been rejected in Wulfred's favour. A tradition since the third century, later confirmed by the pseudo-Isidorian decretals, made it difficult for a bishop to be accused.[29] A presumption of innocence in a legal sense was always attached to a bishop and any accuser who brought a charge against a bishop, by that act, was himself presumed a wrongdoer and worthy of punishment. It is most improbable, therefore, that the pope would have acted in Cenwulf's favour contrary to the tradition which Pope Fabian had maintained was initiated by the Apostles, and which had been accepted for so many centuries.[30] In any case papal reproof of an archbishop would not have been to punish the laity, for the pope had power to punish an archbishop by depriving him of the *pallium*, of all metropolitan and archiepiscopal authority and of his archbishopric.[31] But Pope Paschal I took no such action against the archbishop of Canterbury. During the early years of the interdict Cenwulf summoned a witenagemot in 821 to assemble in London at which he cited Wulfred to appear. In his determination to settle the quarrel between them Cenwulf demanded from Wulfred an estate of three hundred hides, and the payment of a fine of £120 for which he declared that he would clear Wulfred of the charges which he had brought against him in the papal court. The king also agreed that if he failed to establish Wulfred 'innocent before the pope' he would refund to him the fine. On such terms the archbishop was unwilling to agree to a settlement. He was then threatened by the king that if he would not agree to a settlement on the terms he had laid down he would be despoiled of all his possessions and would be banished from his archbishopric and the country, from which exile he would refuse to receive him back even though the pope or emperor intervened on his behalf. Under the pressure of such threats Wulfred finally agreed to the settlement demanded, but it neither brought about a reconciliation nor did it bring to an end the interdict.[32] Shortly after the witenagemot Cenwulf made, what may have been a gesture of reparation to the Church, a grant of privileges to Abingdon Abbey, land to the bishop of Worcester and a grant of land made in felicitous terms 'to the venerable and most beloved in Christ Archbishop Wulfred.'[33] In the same year while leading his forces into Wales Cenwulf died in Flintshire. Kenelm, his seven year old son, succeeded him but after a reign of a few months he was assassinated and his uncle Ceolwulf was chosen king of Mercia. He was consecrated king by Wulfred and in a charter recording this Ceolwulf conveyed a gift of land in Kent to Wulfred for 'the work of the monks of the church of Christ in Canterbury.' As Church land it was freed from taxes and charges with the usual exceptions to which was added the condition of 'military service against pagan enemies,' a reference to the constant fear of invasion by the Danes. The charter concludes with further reasons why this gift was made to Wulfred as 'chiefly for the love of God, and for the venerable degree of the aforesaid pontiff, and also of my consecration which, through the grace of God, I have received from him the same day, and also for his acceptable money, that is, a gold ring containing seventy-five mancuses, as I received it from him.'[34] On Ceolwulf being deposed Beornwulf, a powerful ealdorman, gained the throne and his authority was recognized in Kent, Essex and Middlesex. Within two years he became the most powerful figure in southern England. No record is to be found indicating that the interdict had been lifted and the problems created by its continuance now confronted Beornwulf.

Wisely he sought the support of Wulfred by taking initial steps to resolve the dispute which had arisen when Cenwulf seized property in Kent belonging to the Church. Beornwulf had shown his willingness to help at the council of Clofeshoh in 824 over which he presided, 'Archbishop Wulfred directing and guiding that meeting,' when property unjustly held by Cynethrith, abbess of Southminster, was recovered for the archbishopric, and the dispute between the bishop of Worcester and Berkeley Abbey over an inheritance was settled.[35] This council in some respects was preparatory to the more important synodal council of Clofeshoh in 825 at which some of its business was confirmed, and the whole question of the properties of the archbishopric of Canterbury which had been seized by Cenwulf was considered. The settlement of his quarrel with Wulfred by his threat to banish the archbishop did not restore any property, and three years later the archbishopric was still deprived of money and rents from various properties including Southminster in the diocese of Canterbury. King Beornwulf, probably at Wulfred's wish, convoked the council, and it is evident that he was determined to see that Wulfred received justice. Cynethrith, abbess of Southminster, the daughter of Cenwulf, had inherited all her father's personal property. In consequence, the most important business of the council was Wulfred's claim against Cynethrith for the restoration of all the Church property belonging to his archbishopric which her father had unjustly seized. His claim was successful in the recovery for his see of the monasteries of Reculver and Southminster and other properties held by Cynethrith, and in the subscription to the charter of settlement both Wulfred and Cynethrith refer to the settlement as a 'reconciliation.' The central importance of the archbishopric of Canterbury is reflected in the representative attendance of Church and State. King Beornwulf with eleven of his ealdormen, the Abbess Cynethrith, Archbishop Wulfred with his twelve suffragan bishops, abbots and clergy, making sixty-five persons in all, subscribed to the deed of settlement.[33] While Beornwulf had been fully occupied in establishing his authority in southern England and settling problems involving the archbishopric of Canterbury, Egbert, king of Wessex, had overrun Cornwall and brought it into his kingdom. So strong had he become that when Beornwulf invaded Wessex in 825 he was decisively defeated by Egbert at Ellandun. Egbert finally established his supremacy over Mercia in 829 and in the same year, after his invasion of Northumbria, his overlordship was recognized by King Eanred's submission to him at Dore. Throughout these changes progress was made towards the political unity of the English peoples but the military exploits of Egbert adversely affected the efficient administration of the Church in the province of Canterbury. This was not because of any hostility of Egbert towards the Church. Indeed, he was a great supporter and had made many benefactions to the Church in Wessex and as other kingdoms came under his rule so too the Church in them received benefactions from him.[37]

Wulfred's success in recovering property rightfully belonging to the archbishopric of Canterbury was implemented by his own benefactions which he continued to make to his *familia* at Christ Church.[38] His kinsman the priest, Werhard, made a testamentary disposition of his property for the benefit of the *familia* of Christ Church. 'The substance and lands which, by God's grace, and the help of Archbishop Wulfred my kinsman, I have acquired, I give back to Christ Church and the monks my brothers who serve God there, all the lands within Kent and without which I have heretofore held of the said archbishop and the consent of the aforesaid *familia* of Christ Church. I also grant . . . to Christ Church . . . thirty-two hides of my patrimony, which I may grant to whom I will . . . and another land. . . . Let the monks of Christ Church remember my soul because I freely restored what I ought to restore, and I have offered to Christ devoutly what was my own.'[39] Since this grant was made in 832, the year in which Wulfred died, it indicates that the reforms which he had made in 813 were effectively established to such an extent that Werhard, himself a priest and member of the *familia*, described those who with him led the *vita canonica* as monks although they were actually secular canons. These reforms proved to be one of the most enduring elements of his archiepiscopate for by this means he sought to rekindle the lamp of sound learning and scholarship in his see city of Canterbury, and to make it once again the centre of efficient ecclesiastical administration for his extensive province.

His continuance of the practice initiated by his predecessor of requiring from every bishop-elect before his consecration a confession of faith and a profession of canonical obedience strengthened the archbishopric of Canterbury. Of the nineteen bishops whom he consecrated no less than ten of their professions have survived.[40] United in a common allegiance to him his suffragans sustained his metropolitan authority and their profession of orthodoxy gave the assurance of leadership in Christian doctrine among the clergy and people of their dioceses.

Throughout his long archiepiscopate of twenty-seven years Wulfred laboured diligently and courageously to repair the breach in the fabric of the archbishopric of Canterbury made by Offa's action in dividing the province. Aethelheard's work, so ably initiated for the recovery of property which rightfully belonged to the archbishopric, was continued by Wulfred with such zeal and vigour that it brought him into open conflict with Cenwulf. Out of the quarrel between them arose one of the most disastrous periods in the history of the English Church when king and people were under interdict. The settlement of the quarrel under the king's threat to banish Wulfred from his archbishopric and from the country reveals that in the humiliation and indignity which he received from the king he was indefatigable in the courageous and statesmanlike manner with which he defended his archbishopric and the Church in his province. When Cenwulf died the effects of his aggression against the Church still remained, and before it could recover it was confronted with the rapidly changing political situation throughout the whole of England. Archbishop Wulfred by his spiritual leadership, dignity and strength of character gained the support and friendship of Kings Ceolwulf, Beornwulf and Egbert all of whom in turn enriched the Church with their benefactions.

Within a month of Wulfred's death in March 832, Feologeld, a priest-abbot, was elected to succeed him. Little is known about him except that he was present at the council of Clofeshoh in 803 and attested its findings and many charters some of which related to Christ Church.[41] This may suggest that he was probably priest-abbot of Christ Church or of some abbey within or near the city of Canterbury itself. He was consecrated in June 832 and died at the end of August in the same year.

It was not until the following year that Ceolnoth was elected and consecrated archbishop, receiving the *pallium* in 834.[42] One of the Chroniclers describes him as 'dean' of Christ Church. In the use of this title, however, there is some confusion although it seems that he may have been priest-abbot of the community.[43] The Canterbury Chronicle records that during Ceolnoth's first year as archbishop a devastating sickness assailed the monks at Christ Church from which only five survived. Finding it difficult to fill the vacant places caused by death Ceolnoth admitted secular clerks to the monastery. Since this statement is a late insertion into the Chronicle it is of doubtful authenticity and especially so because contemporary documents nowhere confirm this and its whole tenor is entirely contrary to the known situation within the community of Christ Church during the archiepiscopates of both Wulfred and Ceolnoth. Christ Church was probably the scene of Archbishop Ceolnoth's greatest achievement by the expansion of the community which was his *familia,* and by his insistence of adherence to the reforms which Wulfred had made.

Within a year of his consecration his archbishopric and province were the prey of Danish invaders who descended in great force on Sheppey in 835, and for a period extending over the next thirty years, the greater part of Ceolnoth's archiepiscopate, the Danes made at least twelve separate invasions in various parts of the country.

L

THE DANISH INVASIONS AND DECLENSION
IN THE CHURCH

It was not only in Kent but wherever the Danes made war in England that the work of the Church of necessity was disorganized. Anticipating further difficulties of freely moving about his diocese on his archiepiscopal duties Ceolnoth increased his number of archdeacons from one to four as their subscription to charters shows.[1] Archbishop Wulfred, who had vacated the office of archdeacon under Aethelheard, continued the office by his appointment of Cynehard to succeed him. Both Wulfred and Cynehard, in succession, had shown the administrative value and effectiveness of their office, and when the Danes descended upon Sheppey in 835 Ceolnoth already had his four archdeacons to assist him.

The archdeacon, as his title indicates, was the chief of the deacons. Invariably, however, he was in priest's orders but his duties in the *familia* did not conflict with those of the archpriest who was chief of the priests. Indeed, his duties were much more important and extensive than those which he exercised in the *familia*. He was the chief assistant to the bishop in all diocesan affairs, with the exception of distinctive ministerial functions attaching to the order of the episcopate, and was aptly described as *oculus episcopi*.[2] On the Continent the office of presbyter archdeacon was recognized as an office in accord with the tradition and usage of the Church, and archdeacons were chosen from among the presbyters as shown by the *Capitula* of Archbishop Hincmar of Rheims.[3] In his commission in 874 to his archdeacons he gave directions for the regulation of their ministry in his diocese wherever they exercised their office.[3] Nowhere is there any evidence that he assigned to them any particular territorial area in which to function. The tradition that Heddo, bishop of Strasbourg, about this period allocated to each of his archdeacons a precisely delineated district in which to exercise his office, has proved to be unfounded.[4]

It is improbable that Ceolnoth's archdeacons remained with the *familia* in the city of Canterbury. Owing to the turmoil caused by the invading Danes and their settlement in some parts of the diocese stable Church organization had virtually ceased to exist. Conditions such as these demanded Ceolnoth's use of the administrative assistance which his archdeacons could give to the best advantage which would most likely require their residence in different parts of the diocese. The presence of Danes severely restricted the mobility of the archdeacons and inevitably they functioned in the area where they resided. Evidence is insufficient, however, to conclude that each archdeacon was assigned a specific territorial district comparable to the present day clearly defined boundaries of an archdeaconry.

During the archiepiscopate of Ceolnoth's successor, Aethelred, Swithulf, bishop of Rochester, possessed an archdeacon who subscribed with other clergy to a document in 889 by which the bishop made a grant of land to a certain Biorhtulf.[5] Archdeacon Ciolmund's appointment was the first recorded instance of a suffragan bishop of the English Church having appointed an archdeacon. Nowhere after 889 does any reference to an archdeacon appear until 1011 during the archiepiscopate of Aelfheah of Canterbury when mention is made by Florence of Worcester of archdeacon Aelfmaer in the city of Canterbury.[6] Since the office of archdeacon appears to have been in abeyance in England for more than one hundred and twenty years it would be unwise to conclude without evidence that the office was continued during that period. Evidence is not lacking to show that in the province of York during the first quarter of the eleventh century the office of archdeacon had been established and was effectively exercised. Under a document entitled 'The Laws of the Northumbrian Priests,' probably of 1020–1023, a priest was to be fined twelve ores for neglect of the archdeacon's summons and a fine of the same amount for celebrating mass when prohibited by the archdeacon.[7]

Since the administrative difficulties of the Church still remained, the discontinuation of the office of archdeacon in the archbishopric of Canterbury appears to indicate that Ceolnoth's plan of having the assistance of four archdeacons did not prove effective. The question therefore arises whether the archbishop, in his advancing years, re-established the office of *chorepiscopus* in order to have assistance in distinctly episcopal functions? In a fragment of a document which mentions Archbishop Lanfranc's suppression of the chorepiscopate at Canterbury, it is recorded that Theodore, with the authority of Pope Vitalian, ordained a bishop in the church of St. Martin, Canterbury, who acted with full authority in the absence of the archbishop.[8] During the first half of the ninth century *chorepiscopi* had had a chequered existence but Pope Nicholas I by his decretal sent to Rodulf, archbishop of Bourges, in 864, vindicated the office of the *chorepiscopus;* the decretal superseding for more than twenty years the conciliar decrees of Aix-la-Chapelle (802), Paris (829) and Meaux (845).[9]

By a charter which issued from a council of Canterbury in 867, bearing the subscriptions of Aethelred, Ceolnoth and others, the king granted to a certain priest, Wighelm, *unam sedem* in a place which is called the church of St. Martin.[10] The doubt which has been expressed concerning the existence of a *chorepiscopus* at Canterbury is attributed to the translation of *unam sedem* rather as a 'residence' than a 'see,' in the same sense of the Anglo-Saxon 'seat' or 'setl.' [11] In the charter of grant to Wighelm he subscribes as 'presbyter,' [12] and in another charter of 863 to 870 there is to be found the subscription of a bishop named 'Whelm'—a shortened form of Wighelm.[13] This subscription immediately follows the subscriptions of Ceolnoth and one of his suffragans, the traditional position assigned to those ranking as *chorepiscopi,* followed by the subscriptions of the *familia* of Christ Church, Canterbury.

Although no record can be found of Wighelm's consecration, a bishop of that name subscribed to a document in 904 and his subscription is to be found no less than seven times in documents of 909.[14] Gervase of Canterbury, referring to Lanfranc's abolition of the office of *chorepiscopus* observed that during the archiepiscopate of Aethelnoth, from 1020 to 1038, the archbishop of Canterbury was accustomed to have 'a *chorepiscopus* who dwelt in the church of St. Martin without Canterbury.' [15] At this time the *chorepiscopus* possessed authority to bestow holy orders, consecrate churches, confirm children and to exercise other episcopal functions. In the archbishop's absence he exercised full episcopal authority both in the city and diocese of Canterbury.[16] It would appear, therefore, that any decretal or decree for the abolition of the office during the ninth century which may have been effective on the Continent had not been accepted by the Church in England.

Ceolnoth had entered his archbishopric at a time of political turmoil which inevitably affected his administration of the archbishopric and province of Canterbury. Subsequent events suggest that he was a West Saxon and that Egbert, king of the West Saxons, after he had subdued the kingdom of Kent, had secured the election of Ceolnoth with the intention of gaining the influential support of the powerful metropolitan archbishopric. Credence is lent to this by the friendly relationship which was established between king and archbishop. This relationship undoubtedly facilitated the extension of the authority of the archbishopric into Cornwall or West Wales which earlier had been subdued by Egbert, who had granted one tenth of his gains of conquest to the Church. For this new diocese Ceolnoth consecrated Kentsec, bishop of Cornwall, and duly received from him a profession of canonical obedience.[17] Three years before Egbert's death in 839 the political situation was sufficiently stable to allow Ceolnoth and eleven of his bishops, including the bishops of the dioceses of London, Rochester, Sherborne and Selsey, to attend a council at Croft in Leicestershire. By this time Mercia once again exercised a powerful influence in the province of Canterbury.[18]

The resurgence of the power of the Mercian throne put an end to Egbert's overlordship of the southern English. Egbert and his son Aethelwulf therefore did their utmost to strengthen the friendly relationship which already existed between them and Ceolnoth. Such was this relationship that the archbishop was able to treat on equal terms with the two kings at the council of Kingston in 838. At this council Egbert and Aethelwulf restored to the archbishopric land at Malling which Baldred, a former king of Kent, had granted to Christ Church, and to the see of Winchester land in the Isle of Wight.[19] This restoration of Church property was the basis upon which a treaty of alliance was made of lasting friendship between Ceolnoth and the community of Christ Church and his successors and Egbert and Aethelwulf and their heirs. Aethelwulf considered the treaty to be of such importance that on the death of his father a year later it was confirmed by Ceolnoth and his bishops when a council was held 'aet Astran.'[20]

Although the meaning of the document recording the treaty between the two kings and the archbishop is obscure in parts, it clearly shows the high regard which they had for Ceolnoth, and the importance they attached to the authority and influence of the archbishopric of Canterbury.

A year before his death in 839 Egbert had gained a decisive victory at Hingston Down over the combined forces of the Danes and Welsh. Aethelwulf succeeded him in the kingdom of Wessex and made his son Aethelstan sub-king of Kent, the East Saxons, Surrey and the South Saxons. In the same year the Danes stormed London, Rochester and the city of Canterbury where they caused extensive disorganization at the ecclesiastical centre of the southern province.

Later in his reign King Aethelwulf, before his departure on a pilgrimage to Rome, handed over the government of the kingdom of Wessex to his son Aethelbald. When he returned in 856 the political situation had changed so that in order to maintain peace, Aethelbald continued to rule over Wessex while he himself ruled over Kent, Surrey, Sussex and Essex until his death in 858. These kingdoms then passed to his second son Aethelbert who, when he succeeded Aethelbald as king of Wessex in 860, reunited them to the kingdom of Wessex, but within five years he died and was succeeded by his brother Aethelred.

Throughout this period of war and political changes the archbishopric of Canterbury was considerably restricted in its provincial administration and its central activities in Canterbury also suffered. Nevertheless, Ceolnoth contrived to visit distant parts of his province, and at a witenagemot in 862 at Wellesbourne he subscribed to a charter by which King Burgred of Mercia granted immunities to the monastery of Gloucester.[21] A year later at Canterbury a royal gift of land was made to the monastery of St. Augustine. To this charter after Ceolnoth's subscription are to be found those of the clergy in Canterbury at that time. These included two priest-abbots, six priests, four archdeacons, one sub-deacon and nineteen of the lower orders.[22] These subscriptions indicate that the numerical strength of the clergy in Canterbury had not declined during Ceolnoth's archiepiscopate. From this witenagemot issued the document by which King Aethelred granted a 'sedes' or 'setl' to Wighelm in St. Martin's, Canterbury. Subscribing to this document after the archbishop were one priest-abbot, twenty-one priests, three archdeacons and four sub-deacons.[23] Since Ceolnoth, three years after becoming archbishop, had at least twenty-seven members of his *familia,* there is every reason to assume that the twenty-nine persons who subscribed with him at Canterbury were members of his *familia.*[24] That Ceolnoth should maintain his *familia* at the centre which had experienced the full force of the depredations of the Danes is a tribute to Ceolnoth's courageous leadership. But this was only made possible by the uneasy peace which had been purchased by the people of Kent from the Danes. When they returned for more money with a further promise of peace it seems likely in his efforts to protect the inhabitants and to continue the ministrations of the Church in his archbishopric that he used the treasure of his cathedral for minting coins with which to buy a further period of peace. This would probably account for the numerous coins which have been found bearing Ceolnoth's name.

Because Ceolnoth's *familia* was able to survive in such numerical strength within his see city, it cannot be inferred that similar conditions were to be found in the sees throughout the province. Indeed, the extensive invasions of the Danes militated against this. Even at the time when peace was procured in Kent the Danes ravaged the eastern part of the kingdom. In the same year they invaded Northumbria and seized York. Returning south across the Humber in 869, after a further assault upon York, the Danes then crossed Mercia into East Anglia, and defeated the army of King Edmund, who was slain, making their winter quarters in 870 at Thetford. These warlike activities wrought much havoc on the Church. Royal benefactions to the Church declined and a large increase of lands granted to thegns is shown by the charters of the period. Clergy were unable in many parts of the country to continue their ministrations to the inhabitants in the minsters and village churches, the lands of which often became the property of thegns with which to provide the means to support and maintain forces to fight against the Danes.[25] Owing to the impoverishment of the Church its organization in many parts of the country collapsed, episcopal administration became impossible and many *familiae* of bishoprics ceased to exist. The see of Dunwich disappeared; the succession in the sees of Lindsey and Elmham was broken; and in 874 the bishop of Leicester removed his seat to Dorchester-on-Thames. At Worcester and in Wales, parts not overrun by the Danes, it would appear, the episcopal *familiae* had survived and learning still flourished though restricted because of conditions in other parts of the province.[26]

Throughout the whole of Ceolnoth's archiepiscopate his province was hardly ever free from hostilities. Nevertheless, although this hindered the efficient administration of the archbishopric of Canterbury in its wider work in the province much encouragement and help were given to the Church by benefactions of successive kings as shown by the numerous contemporary charters which have survived.[27] Despite the turmoil and political upheaval caused by the Danes, Ceolnoth's consecration of bishops to serve in his province shows that any vacancy in a see was not unduly prolonged and that dioceses were not deprived of episcopal oversight. Contact with the Apostolic See was maintained by pilgrimages and infrequent correspondence. About the year 850 Pope Leo IV addressed a letter to all the bishops of Britain, doubtless received by Ceolnoth, in which he inveighed against simony.[28] On the Continent at one period the influence of kings on episcopal appointments had sometimes led to simony,[29] but no evidence of simony in the English Church can be found since the time of Bishop Wini *c.* 666, who purchased the see of London from Wulfhere, king of Mercia. Any possibility of simony at this period in the province of Canterbury could be ruled out by Ceolnoth's archiepiscopal administration. It is inconceivable that in receiving a confession of faith and a profession of canonical obedience from a bishop-elect the archbishop would have proceeded to consecrate him if there had been the slightest suspicion of simony. Many of the professions made by the bishops whom he consecrated have survived, all of which possess an inevitable sameness of content and expression. Helmstan's profession attracts attention by its remarkable difference from the others. It is made solely to Ceolnoth and not to his successors, and opens with the declaration that he had been elected by the pope, the congregation of the city of Winchester, King Aethelwulf, the bishops, nobles and all the people of the West Saxons. Special reference is also made by Helmstan to the Apostolic See and the primacy of the Roman Church.[30] It appears that the king had already chosen him for the see of Winchester, or as Florence of Worcester records, he succeeded to the see 'by command of the king' prior to setting out on an embassy to Rome where the pope signified his approval of the king's nomination. On his return from an apparently successful mission Helmstan was duly consecrated by Ceolnoth.

After the English forces had made peace with the Danes at Nottingham in 868, a witenagemot was held at which Burgred of Mercia confirmed lands and privileges to Crowland Abbey. To the document of confirmation are to be found the subscriptions of the king, Ceolnoth, the bishops of London, Sherborne, Winchester, Lichfield and Hereford; the abbots of Evesham, Medeshamstede and St. Albans; King Aethelred and his brother Alfred and other nobles.[31] At the same council it is likely that Burgred confirmed the foundation deed of the monastery of St. Peter, Gloucester. In both these documents appear the last subscriptions of the archbishop, with the exception of another of uncertain date.[32] During his long archiepiscopate of thirty-seven years the archbishopric of Canterbury, by his wise leadership and administrative gifts, had not only survived amidst the hostilities of the Danes but had maintained its position of influence and authority although as a centre of learning it had declined. His reforms and the development of ecclesiastical organization had been hindered and in many parts of the province destroyed by the invasions of the Danes, their raids over wide tracts of the country and their battles with the English armies.

While they wintered at Thetford in 870, in February of the same year, Archbishop Ceolnoth died and was buried in his cathedral church in the city of Canterbury.[33]

On leaving Thetford the Danes defeated the English at Reading in Wessex, and then crossed into Berkshire where they were defeated at Ashdown by King Aethelred and his brother Alfred. Within two weeks, however, the Danes gained the victory at Basing and shortly after at 'Meretun,' where Heahmund, bishop of Sherborne, was slain. In the same year Aethelred died and his brother Alfred succeeded to the kingdom of Wessex. One of his last acts with his brother was to appoint Aethelred, bishop of Winchester, to the archbishopric of Canterbury. In due course Aethelred received from Pope Hadrian II the *pallium*,[34] and in 871 his subscription to a charter is to be found by which King Alfred granted to him and the monastery of Christ Church land at Chartham in Kent in exchange for land at Croydon. In the same year Alfred made a grant of lands at Donhead to the abbey of Shaftesbury. Two years later the archbishop and the monastery of Christ Church sold land in Kent to a certain Liaba,[35] and in the two following years Aethelred subscribed to other charters. These documents are indicative of the way in which the administrative work of the archbishopric continued to function despite the unsettled conditions in the country. Communication having broken down between Rome and York would probably account for Pope John VIII addressing a letter received by Archbishop Aethelred, 'To our reverend and holy fellow-bishops Aethelred of Canterbury and Wulfred (Wulfhere) of York, archbishops, and all bishops, priests and deacons appointed throughout the land of England,' and in this way keeping in contact through Canterbury with the archbishopric of York, about which little or no information concerning ecclesiastical affairs would have reached beyond Northumbria owing to its occupation by the Danes and the flight of Wulfhere from his see. Only a fragment of this letter has survived in which the pope says he had been informed by English residents in Rome that the clergy in England wore lay attire. After discusssion with these residents he advised that the clergy should voluntarily discard laymen's dress, which was 'voluminous and short,' and wear 'after the Roman fashion tunics reaching down to the ankle.' Neither the pope nor those with whom he had discussed the matter could have been aware of the disastrous effects of the Danish invasions, for it is inconceivable that a minor question about the dress of the clergy would have received such attention when the Church in England was engaged in a struggle for its survival.[36] Shortly after Wulfhere had returned to Northumbria, Burgred was driven from his kingdom by the Danes, and in his place they made Ceolwulf 'a foolish king's thegn' ruler over Mercia.[37] Although his territory was later reduced by Danish occupation, he proved himself acceptable to the Mercians and supported the Church by his grants of privileges and land to the diocese and community of the church of Worcester.[38]

Within a few months of each other Aethelred had ascended the chair of St. Augustine and Alfred had ascended the throne of Wessex. Each assumed his responsibilities of office at a period when the Danes threatened the survival of both archbishopric and kingdom. Aethelred's see city had twice been occupied by the Danes, and the work of the archbishopric with depleted resources was difficult to maintain and its property to defend. Similarly, on becoming king, Alfred possessed no financial resources with which to arm and support his forces to fight the Danes. Although possessing extraordinary gifts he created difficulties for himself at the beginning of his reign by his impatience and lack of consideration for his subjects who sought his aid and relief from those who oppressed them. His unconciliatory attitude and impatience brought a sharp rebuke from his relation St. Neot, who described his actions as tyrannical, and enjoined him to 'depart entirely from thy unrighteousness and thy sins : with alms and tears abolish them.'[39] There is little doubt that the archbishop, advanced in years and of wide experience in affairs both ecclesiastical and political, did not take kindly to the young ruler whose actions were at times hostile to his subjects and unfriendly to his supporters. It is likely that the archbishop, widely known for his wisdom and piety, advised him to be more conciliatory and to moderate his actions. Initially, this may have caused friction between the two which later made a breach in their relationship and developed into open conflict.

Alfred engaged the Danes both on sea and land but towards the end of 875, after attacking Wessex, they ravaged the country around Cambridge and Wareham. Amidst this critical period of hostilities a dispute arose between him and the archbishop. Nowhere in precise terms are details of the quarrel recorded, and all that is known about it is found in a letter from Pope John VIII, in reply to a letter which he had received from the archbishop, which clearly shows that the property of the archbishopric was involved. Whether the archbishopric, because of its impoverished condition, had failed in its obligations to maintain bridges and fortresses on its lands, and for that reason Alfred had adopted oppressive measures to enforce their fulfilment; or whether in extreme circumstances when threatened by the Danes, Alfred had taken lands and property belonging to the archbishopric in order to maintain his forces against the Danes is not known. Whatever may have been the cause, the situation had become so serious that Aethelred wrote to the pope seeking his counsel. From his reply it is clear that the king had trespassed upon the rights of the archbishopric, which the pope regarded as hostility against the Church. Aethelred was advised by the pope to be 'as a wall to the House of the Lord,' and not to cease 'to resist strenuously not only the king but all who wish to do any wrong against the Church.' [40] The pope also informed Aethelred that he had already written an admonitory letter to the king in which he had exhorted him to be obedient to the archbishop and to help him in all things 'beneficial to the Holy Church.' After this letter, written in either 877 or early 878, no further reference is to be found to the dispute. Alfred was a deeply religious man and it would appear he heeded the pope's admonition and in consequence an abiding friendship grew up between archbishop and king as they laboured together for the well-being of the Church.

A decisive victory over the Danes in 878 at Edington by Alfred was followed by a treaty between him and King Guthrum, which was soon broken but was later confirmed in 886. Recognizing that the Danes were now permanent settlers in the land Alfred took the first measures towards fusing the Danes and the Anglo-Saxons into one people. It was agreed that the Danes should occupy the Midlands including East Anglia and the northern parts of the country; Alfred ruled over the southern parts of Mercia, Kent, Wessex and south of the Thames; also London and the surrounding territory over which he placed ealdorman Aethelred.

It is significant that Alfred perceived no true and stable peace could be formulated with the worshippers of Woden, who had frequently broken their oaths, but only on the common basis of the Christian Faith. Not only did this reflect Alfred's personal religious faith but the extent to which the Church, under Aethelred's guidance, had made its impact on the political life of the kingdom. Three weeks after peace had been made Guthrum with thirty of his chief men received baptism, doubtless at the hands of the archbishop, at Wedmore, Alfred standing sponsor for Guthrum who received the name of Aethelstan. Subsequently their baptism was followed by the ceremony of chrysom-loosing.[41] An alliance was also made with Guthrum by which any of his followers should be fined or punished if they failed to conform to ecclesiastical discipline and the authority of the bishops, or failed to pay tithes and other ecclesiastical dues.[42]

Aethelred now enjoyed the complete confidence of Alfred which could not fail effectively to strengthen the influence of the archbishopric in political affairs as well as matters ecclesiastical which were his immediate concern. Some time between 873 and 888 when 'inquiring about the needs of my soul and about my inheritance which God and my ancestors gave to me' for the purpose of making his will, Alfred's sole consultant was the archbishop. This he acknowledges in the opening words of his will : 'I, King Alfred, by the grace of God and on consultation with Archbishop Aethelred and with the witnesses of all the counsellors of the West Saxons . . .'[43] Further evidence of the assistance given by the primatial see was to be seen at the time when Alfred called his counsellors together in consultation for the preparation of laws which he purposed to promulgate. Chief among his counsellors was Aethelred from whom, no doubt, he gained information from the books recording earlier synods to which he refers in his prologue.[44] In the laws of King Aethelbert and Wihtred of Kent and Ine, king of the West Saxons, specific reference had been made to bishops; now for the first time recognition of the important place the archbishopric of Canterbury possessed in the life of the kingdom was made by certain provisions in the laws relating to the archbishop. Breach of the archbishop's surety or of his protection carried a fine of three pounds as compared with a fine or compensation of two pounds for another bishop. Anyone fighting or drawing a sword in the presence of the archbishop had to pay compensation of one hundred and fifty shillings but for another bishop one hundred shillings : while forcible entry into the archbishop's residence demanded compensation of ninety shillings as compared with sixty shillings for another bishop.[45]

From a detailed study of these laws there is portrayed, for the territories over which Alfred ruled, a true picture of the inter-relationship of Church and State as conceived by the king with the counsel of his archbishop and other counsellors. Evidence of this is to be seen in the law which required payment of compensation of one hundred and twenty shillings by anyone who neglected 'the rules of the Church in Lent without permission.' This is further illustrated by the obligatory holidays required by law, strangely reminiscent of modern statutory holidays, that there should be given to all free men twelve days at Christmas, seven days before and after Easter, at harvest-time the whole week before the feast of St. Mary, one day on the feasts of St. Peter and St. Paul, St. Gregory, All Saints and the day commemorating the victory of Christ when tempted by the devil in the wilderness.[46]

The detailed comprehensiveness of Alfred's laws was manifestly based, for the most part, on his own observations and knowledge of conditions which were predominant throughout the length and breadth of the land where he had fought against the Danes, in which law and order had virtually ceased to exist. He perceived, therefore, that the most effective means of restoring law and order was the observance of true religion. For this reason he gave an important place in his code of laws to the Church and its ministrations; its archbishop, bishops and clergy in relation to the lives of his subjects. To effect this he made the underlying concept of his laws appropriate for a Christian kingdom, which he desired his kingdom to be, having its sure foundation on the laws of Christ.

King Alfred's government of his kingdom, in which religion and law went hand in hand, impelled seven minor kings of South Wales to seek his protection and friendship. In receiving him as their overlord all their petty rivalries and disputes came to an end. South Wales already possessed a Church with its own metropolitan administration to which Asser refers, mentioning his relation Archbishop Novis who had been expelled from his see of St. Davids by Hemeid, the most formidable of the minor kings.[47] This addition to Alfred's territories had not suffered the havoc wrought by the Danes as in other parts of his kingdom and, except for Hemeid's hostility, the life of the Church had remained unimpaired. In much the same way as Ceolnoth had extended the jurisdiction of his archbishopric in Cornwall and West Wales after King Egbert had established his lordship over them, so now when South Wales accepted the overlordship of King Alfred, the archbishopric of Canterbury, under the guidance of Aethelred, extended its ecclesiastical jurisdiction in these territories which became an integral part of the southern province. Therefore, without delay, when bishoprics fell vacant Aethelred of Canterbury consecrated bishops Lunverd to the see of St. Davids and Cimeliauc to the see of Llandaff.[48]

One of the most remarkable achievements of Alfred's reign was that his laws were enacted at a time when his chief concern was the assiduous maintenance of his sea and land forces to meet any contingency.

The loss and suffering caused by the depredations of the Danes had fallen heavily upon the Church throughout the whole country. Having emerged from a Church working on a mission station basis it had firmly established itself with diocesan bishops with their *familiae* which included monks and clergy. Now, however, many centres of diocesan activity had been plundered and burned by the Danes, and smaller minsters and churches in the larger villages had been destroyed. In the province of Canterbury the great minsters of Malmesbury, Medeshamstede, London, Rochester, Selsey, Wimborne and Canterbury itself, like those of Glastonbury, Sherborne and Winchester ten or twenty years before, had been left in ruins; bishops' sees overrun and their *familiae* scattered. As a result many monks abandoned their vocation and, in order to survive, sought other means for a livelihood, some joining the armies fighting against the Danes. The clergy, too, were affected and laboured under great difficulties to fulfil their restricted ministrations to the people. No longer could clergy receive instruction since the monastic schools of learning had been destroyed. This decline in learning impaired the efficiency of the clergy although they laboured with zeal and self-sacrifice, wherever possible, to exercise their ministry. By this means the witness to the Christian Faith was maintained even in those parts of the country where the Danes had settled and many of the English people had lapsed into the paganism around them.

How far west the Danes penetrated is uncertain, but it would appear that Worcester, situated in the Severn valley, remained unscathed by the hostilities. This undoubtedly explains the survival of the community at Worcester as a centre of learning, continuing its functions when others were destroyed.

THE REVIVAL OF LEARNING UNDER KING ALFRED

King Alfred's reign was never completely free from war or its threat by the Danes. This rendered his reforms more difficult and more significant. The just administration of his laws was sometimes hindered by the ignorance of those who administered them. For this the king reproved them telling them to study wisdom in order to administer the law correctly with justice or to vacate their office.

His insistence on knowledge and desire for learning had dominated his life since he was a boy of twelve and his insatiable desire for knowledge was not set aside amidst his warlike activities. He acquainted himself with the history of his country, and in the prologue to his West-Saxon version of 'Gregory's Pastoral Care' he vividly described the situation in England in his own day. Formerly there were wise men both of spiritual and lay orders. 'The spiritual orders,' he wrote, 'were zealous both about teaching and learning and all the services which they should do for God . . . and foreigners came hither to this land in search of knowledge and instruction.' The position had now so completely changed that it was necessary to bring wise men from abroad, adding that 'learning had decayed in England so that there were few men on this side of the Humber who could apprehend their services in English or even translate a letter from Latin into English, and I think that there were not many beyond the Humber. There were so few of them that I cannot recollect a single one south of the Thames when I succeeded to the kingdom.' He also recalled 'before everything was ravaged and burnt, the churches throughout all England stood filled with treasures and books, and likewise there was a great multitude of the servants of God. And they had very little benefit from those books, for they could not understand anything in them, because they were not written in their own language.' [1] Alfred also lamented that the monasteries had 'lost both wealth and wisdom,' and of Christians in general he wrote, 'we possessed only the name of Christians, and very few possessed the virtues.' His Prologue shows that he had informed himself in some detail of the decline in learning, the decay of monastic life and the ineffectiveness of the Church's ministrations covering the whole of England south of the river Humber, namely, the southern province of Canterbury, over which Aethelred was metropolitan. In giving such graphic details of the conditions which existed in the Church, everything appears to point to the fact that although he possessed some personal knowledge of these matters in his own territories, he must have obtained information about other parts of the country south of the Humber from another source. The only person who would have such knowledge of the province of Canterbury could be none other than the archbishop himself, and from him without doubt the king gained his information so that he could refer to conditions in England south of the Humber. Confirmation of this may be found in Alfred's order that a copy of his version of 'The Pastoral Care' should be sent together with an extremely valuable book-marker [2] to every bishop. [3] Here again, knowledge in the possession of the archbishopric of Canterbury would have been drawn upon, for there alone would information be found of the whereabouts of the bishops of the province, some of whom had been compelled to leave their sees after the destruction of their cathedrals. Further evidence of King Alfred and Archbishop Aethelred working in close co-operation is to be seen as the king formulated his plans for the revival of the Church, learning and cultural pursuits in his kingdom. For this purpose Alfred formed a group of distinguished scholars at his court, seven of whom are known by name, to devise the best means for the revival. From the bishopric of Worcester was summoned by Alfred to his court Waerferth, whom Aethelred had consecrated to that see in 873. Drawn from the same centre of learning were Werewulf, a member of Waerferth's *familia* and the priest Aethelstan. Also from western Mercia was summoned the hermit Plegmund, a Mercian by birth, who was a most distinguished scholar. It is significant that among those whom he summoned to his court there was not a scholar of sufficient merit in his own kingdom with the exception of Aethelred, whose contribution was undoubtedly of counsel behind the scenes, since to him was not given any special task of scholarship. From his friend, Fulco, archbishop of Rheims, Alfred obtained the services of Grimbald, a learned priest and monk of St. Bertin at St. Omer; and the priest and monk, John of Corbie, was also summoned to Alfred's court. Probably one of the last scholars summoned was the priest, Asser from St. Davids, who later became Alfred's close friend and biographer. Having assembled these scholars at his court Alfred obtained their assistance in his own work of translation. 'I began,' he wrote, 'in the midst of the other various and manifold cares of this kingdom to turn into English the book which is called in Latin *Pastoralis* and in English "Shepherd-book" sometimes word by word, sometimes by a paraphrase; as I had learnt it from my Archbishop Plegmund, and my Bishop Asser, and my priest Grimbald and my priest John. When I had learnt it, I turned it into English according as I understood it and as I could render it most intelligibly.' [4] This translation was the first of Alfred's books and was probably completed by him in 894 since it is not mentioned by Asser. But the firstfruits of the literary labours of the king's group of scholars came from the pen of Bishop Waerferth who had been commissioned by Alfred to translate from the Latin into the English tongue *The Dialogues of Pope Gregory the Great*.

Church reform in his kingdom did not make the Church self-centred. Alfred, doubtless, with the counsel of Aethelred, fulfilled his promise to send alms to Rome and received from Pope Marinus 'some wood of the Cross' in acknowledgement. Later the same pope freed from taxation the English quarter or school in Rome.[5] Towards the close of Aethelred's archiepiscopate the revival of the English Church found remarkable expression in its missionary activities overseas. Under Alfred's provision alms were sent to Christians in the Far East. For the first time in the history of the English Church it is recorded that communication with Christian Churches in India was made in the year 883.[6] During the last year of Aethelred's spiritual rule of Canterbury contact was made with the Church in Jerusalem. In recording this, Asser wrote 'we have seen and read letters, accompanied with presents, which were sent to the king by Elias the patriarch of Jerusalem.'[7]

Under the guidance of the archbishop initial measures were taken for the revival of monasticism by Alfred, who founded and endowed the monasteries of Aethelney and Shaftesbury. Asser lamented that 'the love of monastic life had utterly decayed from the nation' and that because of the riches of the people they 'looked with contempt on the monastic life.' Confirmatory evidence of this situation was seen when Alfred was unable to find monks for Aethelney. It was probably for this reason that he appointed a foreigner to the office of abbot, the learned John, one of the scholars at his court: at Shaftesbury he made his second daughter Aethelgiva abbess. Abbot John could muster but a small community of priests and deacons. The monks were chiefly drawn from Gaul. But Alfred's venture for the revival of monasticism gained little success and seemed doomed to failure after one of the monks had tried to murder Abbot John. Nothing daunted, however, the king planned the foundation of a new minster near the ruins of the old cathedral church at Winchester to which Grimbald was appointed, but its completion had to await Alfred's successor.

For the renewal of the work and witness of the Church the king recognized the supreme importance of having both bishops and clergy who were learned. To this end he took preliminary measures on the death of Aethelred in 889. In finding a successor to Aethelred for the archbishopric of Canterbury some convincing evidence has been adduced to show that Grimbald was first approached for elevation to the throne of St. Augustine. He resolutely refused and urged Plegmund's election to the archbishopric.[8] The record in the *Anglo-*

Saxon Chronicle stating that 'Plegmund was elected by God and all the people to the archbishopric of Canterbury' may convey the impression that the people did not favour a foreigner being appointed to the archbishopric, and made their views known by demanding that Plegmund should be archbishop. There is little doubt that Grimbald was worthy of episcopal office. This was made clear by Archbishop Fulco of Rheims in a lengthy letter to the king commending Grimbald 'to be most worthy of pontifical honour.' He had no doubt that Alfred would advance Grimbald to the episcopate as a pastor and teacher, who had been 'duly consecrated according to ecclesiastical custom.' [9] Writing to Plegmund shortly after his election, Fulco congratulated the new archbishop on his initial reforms of the Church.[10] Previously to this letter Fulco had written to the king in patronizing terms thanking him that 'he had appointed a man so good and devout and suitable according to the rules of the Church as bishop in the city called Canterbury.' [11] Of Plegmund's consecration no record is to be found in the Chronicles. This may be because neither the aged Wulfhere, archbishop of York, nor Plegmund's comprovincials were able to consecrate him owing to the unsettled conditions prevailing at the time. It seems most probable that since Plegmund intended to visit Rome to receive the *pallium* he delayed his consecration until Pope Formosus was able to consecrate him, after which the pope bestowed upon him the *pallium*.[12] While in Rome Plegmund informed the pope of the state of the Church in England, and how paganism had spread amongst the people through the settlements of the pagan Danes. Formosus, a zealous missionary during his earlier ministry, wrote a letter between 893 and 896 which he addressed 'To his brothers and sons in Christ, all the bishops of England.' In no uncertain language he rebuked the bishops for the ineffectiveness of their Christian witness about which Plegmund had told him. But the archbishop had also told him of the change now progressing by the revival of the Church. Formosus, therefore, gave the bishops much encouragement and wrote: 'We send the blessing of Almighty God and of the blessed Peter, Prince of the Apostles, praying that you may persevere in what has been well begun.' Finally, he enjoined, 'do not . . . suffer the Christian Faith to be violated, the flock of God to wander and be scattered and dispersed for lack of pastors,' and urged that on the death of a bishop a successor should be appointed without delay.[13] Both the archbishop of Rheims and Formosus had praised Plegmund on his reforms of the Church from Canterbury, and in all these he had the encouragement and full support of a godly king. The king's practical support of the administrative work of the archbishopric was shown in his own personal labours by the translation of 'The Pastoral Care,' a copy of which he had sent to all the

M

bishops of the province. In addition, personally or with the assistance of the scholars at his court Alfred translated 'The Soliloquies' of St. Augustine of Hippo, a part of Bede's *Ecclesiastical History*, 'The Consolation' of Boethius and 'The History of the World' by Orosius in order to advance the revival of learning in the Church and among the people. His scheme of education for the training of youths and children, from whom the next generation of teachers would be drawn, depended for its success on the diligence of the bishops in finding and training likely candidates. Those whom the bishops wished to prepare for holy orders were to be taught Latin after they could read well in English. This scheme placed an additional responsibility upon the episcopate which had been considerably strengthened by learned bishops of whom Alfred wrote 'they are almost everywhere.' Educational work of this character of necessity extended the pastoral work of the episcopate which had its own problems caused by the existing conditions of the country. Alfred was aware of these problems and probably for this reason delayed appointment to vacant sees until a learned priest could be found. This would account, no doubt, at the time of his death in 901, for the uncertainty in the succession in some of the bishoprics, and the continuing vacancies in others which had been overrun by the Danes. During the last thirty years of the ninth century the years of the consecrations to the see of Winchester are not known. Similarly, records of the succession, about the same period, to the sees of Dunwich, Elmham, Hereford, Lichfield, London, Rochester and Selsey are uncertain, and it would appear that from *c.* 896 to 909 Dorchester was vacant. While this situation resulted from the intensity and widespread raids of the Danes, it also shows how restricted and ineffective had become the pastoral care of the Church in the southern province. Nevertheless, Plegmund resolutely grappled with the problems with remarkable success, but there still remained the need of episcopal oversight in many parts of his province. On his return from Rome, carrying with him the outward symbol of his authority of metropolitan archbishop, the *pallium,* he proceeded to the consecration of Heahstan to the bishopric of London in 892, and in the same year consecrated Alfred's biographer, Asser, who recorded concerning himself that the king 'unexpectedly gave me Exeter, with all the diocese which belonged to him in Saxony (Wessex) and in Cornwall.' [14] He was well qualified to have the pastoral oversight of these parts where the people were known as the West Welsh.

There emerged, however, another factor of considerable importance which could not fail to influence the appointment of bishops in the province of Canterbury. On the death of Pope Formosus in 896 his successor Stephen VII in synod annulled all the acts of Formosus. Although this was rescinded by Theodore II and confirmed by Pope

John IX, when Sergius III ascended the papal chair he confirmed the annulment after fierce controversy in 904.[15] Since Plegmund had been consecrated by and had received the *pallium* from Formosus, the annulment consequentially invalidated his own consecration and his acts of consecration. Of this Plegmund would have been only too conscious in his office of metropolitan archbishop from the date of the annulment in 896. This would doubtless account for the difficulty in assigning definite dates for the consecration of his suffragans during the intervening period until 909. The uncertainty of this situation placed the archbishopric of Canterbury and Plegmund, in the administration of his province, in a position of extraordinary perplexity which hindered the work of the Church. Plegmund finally arranged with King Edward the Elder, who had succeeded his father Alfred in 901, to carry the royal alms and those of the people to Rome, thus providing an opportunity for the archbishop to have an audience with Pope Sergius III.[16] Before his departure Plegmund and Edward had approved a plan, accepted by the synod of Winchester, for the division of the West Saxon bishoprics and the creation of more sees. But the major problem, before giving effect to this plan, was the question of the validity of the consecration of bishops to serve the vacant sees and the proposed new sees if they were consecrated by Plegmund. That the archbishop of Canterbury himself should be the bearer of alms to the Apostolic See was no small compliment to Pope Sergius III. And to inform him of plans for the extention of the Church's activities in the southern province of England was a submissive gesture which could not fail to engender papal goodwill. What actually transpired when Plegmund met the pope can only be deduced from the exercise of his archiepiscopal functions on his return to his archbishopric. By his subsequent acts it is evident that his consecration and reception of the *pallium* had in some way been regularized or confirmed by Pope Sergius III. Without further delay he consecrated seven bishops on the same day at Canterbury.[17] Bishop Asser, who had been translated to Sherborne, and Denewulf, bishop of Winchester, had both died. To Sherborne, Waerstan and to Winchester, Frithestan were consecrated after three new dioceses had been separated from the two existing dioceses. The three new sees were co-extensive with three shires over which Alfred had appointed each to have an ealdorman. To Wiltshire was consecrated Aethelstan with his seat at Ramsbury; to Somerset Aethelhelm with his seat at Wells and to Devonshire was consecrated Eadulf with his seat at Crediton. With the bishops for these five West Saxon sees Plegmund also consecrated Cenwulf for the Mercian see of Dorchester and Beornege for the South Saxon see of Selsey.[18] Never before in the history of the English Church had an archbishop consecrated so many bishops in the same day. An event of such significance, combined with the injunction given by Pope Formosus in his letter to Plegmund not to delay consecration of successors to vacant sees, did not escape the embellishments of fertile imagination which to this day have remained inexplicable. Not until 1107 did a similar occasion arise when Archbishop Anselm of Canterbury consecrated five bishops in his cathedral church on the same day.[19] In recording this unique event Florence of Worcester in his Chronicle made special reference to 'the reign of Edward the Elder when Archbishop Plegmund ordained seven bishops to seven churches in one day.'[20] This Chronicle confirms the account of Plegmund's consecrations at that time although it is not recorded in the *Anglo-Saxon Chronicle* to which Plegmund, the last to survive of Alfred's group of scholars, may have been a contributor.

A letter dated 905, purporting to have been sent by Pope Formosus, in which he threatened to excommunicate King Edward and his people because the West Saxons had been for seven years without a bishop, was the subject for a synod over which Plegmund presided. Formosus had died in 896 so the attribution of the letter being sent by him in 905 is the first of many anachronisms contained in the full text of the letter. Many efforts have been made to give validity to the letter, the chief of which has been the substitution of the name of Pope Sergius III for that of Formosus, since Sergius was the pope at that time. But this by no means rectifies other unauthentic details which it contains. While it records factual particulars concerning Plegmund's visit to Rome and, after his return, the consecration of seven bishops on the same day, and their dioceses, the remainder is of doubtful validity, and must be regarded as spurious.[21]

During Alfred's reign, despite the unsettled state of the country, relations between the archbishoprics of Canterbury and York were maintained. Archbishop Aethelbald of York, about whom little is known, in 895 subscribed to a charter, after Plegmund, by which Alfred made a grant of land in Suffolk to Burric, bishop of Rochester.[22] Since Aethelbald subscribed as archbishop of York in the year that he succeeded Wulfhere, the appearance of his subscription to this charter makes it seem highly probable that he had visited Canterbury to receive consecration from Plegmund.[23] In the same year, Plegmund, himself, endowed his cathedral of Christ Church with land in Kent.[24] By this benefaction Plegmund initiated measures for strengthening the communal life of his *familia* at Christ Church, which had suffered grievously from the Danish raids on the city of Canterbury and from Alfred's hostile action against the archbishopric during Aethelred's archiepiscopate. Three years later at the council of Chelsea in 898 Alfred made some reparation for his earlier aggression against the archbishopric by a grant of land in London to

Christ Church. In the charter of conveyance he signified that he made the grant 'to Archbishop Plegmund of Canterbury and his successors for the work of the monks of Christ Church.' [25] Although there were no monks at Christ Church at this time it is evident that the *familia* had survived and that at least some of its members lived communally. The king's endowment, therefore, for the *opus monachorum* was for those of the archbishop's *familia* who lived under the semi-monastic discipline which Wulfred, during his reforms earlier in the century, had made obligatory. At the same council Alfred made a similar grant of land to Bishop Waerferth for 'the church of St. Mary, Worcester.' [26] These benefactions were the last of his many gifts to the Church of which any record is to be found. But after his death, as the terms of his will became effective, his benefactions continued not only to the Church but also personally to the archbishop and three of his suffragan bishops who received one hundred mancuses each. [27] He further bequeathed 'fifty to *masse prestys* throughout my kingdom, fifty to poor servants of God, fifty to poor men in need and fifty to the church in which I shall be buried.' During the same period that Alfred made his will his namesake, Alfred, the ealdorman, probably of Surrey, also made his will, of which the king was aware since the opening sentence of the will directed that it should be made known to the king. [28] Among the important features of this document not least are the bequests to Christ Church, Canterbury, including one hundred swine and a payment of one hundred pence from a kinsman and his successors 'as long as the Christian Faith last and the money can be raised from that land.' [29] At a later date the same clause was included in a charter by which the ealdorman Alfred and his wife Waerburh donated the 'Golden Gospels' to Christ Church 'for the use of the community which daily raises praise to God in Christ Church,' and they were to remain in the possession of Christ Church 'as long as the Christian Faith endure.' [30] These benefactions of king and ealdorman show that, during the archiepiscopates of Aethelred and Plegmund, the community at the centre of the archbishopric, in the face of immense difficulties and at times of great danger, had not only survived but had continued its daily offices.

Alfred, some time before his death in 901, had made provision for Grimbald to have the charge of New Minster at Winchester. Although the king did not live to see the building erected, such rapid progress was made that *c.* 903 the church was dedicated by Plegmund when the two great scholars of Alfred's court, the archbishop and Grimbald met for the last time, for within a few months Grimbald died. Five years later Plegmund dedicated a lofty tower to St. Mary at New Minster, which had already received benefactions from Alfred's successor King Edward, and after the removal of Alfred's body from the old Minster and its re-interment in New Minster, his generous benefactions continued as shown by the numerous charters which have survived. The most notable of these is the Golden Charter, so-called because it was written in letters of gold, the charter of foundation to which King Edward and his brother with Plegmund and eight of his suffragans subscribed.[31]

Early in his reign Edward renewed the agreement which his father had made with the Danish king Guthrum. By this renewal of peace and friendship with Guthrum II certain penalties were laid upon English and Danes alike if they did not conform to ecclesiastical discipline with a just regard to the authority of the bishops. Fines were demanded of anyone following heathen practices, withholding tithes, light-scot, plough-alms, Rome-fee or St. Peter's pence. Trading on a Sunday, violation of a solemn-feast by a freeman, oaths and ordeals on feast and fast days were all forbidden.[32] That the two kings considered it necessary to re-enact these laws reflects how tenuous was the hold of the Church upon the people in those parts over which Guthrum ruled. Behind these measures may be discerned the wise counsel of Plegmund whose pastoral care of his province of Canterbury was of paramount concern to him. To both Alfred and his son Edward, Plegmund had given the fullest support. Alfred's efforts in conjunction with the archbishop to revive the work and witness and learning of the Church had in general been successful. The revival of monasticism initiated by Alfred, however, had not been successful and even Plegmund's efforts in the *familia* of his archbishopric had failed.[33] A similar situation existed in other dioceses. At Winchester, where Alfred's influence on ecclesiastical affairs may have been the strongest, no monk was to be found in the bishop's *familia*. Before granting to King Edward a lease of land belonging to the *familia* the bishop obtained the agreement of the community to the lease and to a charter of 909, to which Edward, his brother, Plegmund and the bishop of Winchester with others subscribed : no less than eight priests, one deacon and twenty-three other clergy of the *familia* also subscribed.[34] There was no change in Bishop Waerferth's *familia* at Worcester. As one of the eminent scholars summoned to Alfred's court he would have supported the king's efforts to revive monasticism in his kingdom, but it was not until 969 during the episcopate of Oswald that the *familia* became monastic.[35]

Although the revival of monasticism had not been realized, progress had been made in other spheres of the Church's life. Despite the unsettled conditions in the country, the province of Canterbury possessed a learned episcopate fully instructed in its pastoral ministrations and authority, and a more instructed clergy. These attainments were chiefly attributable to Plegmund's understanding of Alfred's desire for the revival of learning and reform of the Church. But there is little doubt that this royal desire was the outcome of the scholarly instruction which the king had received from Plegmund. As chief counsellor to Alfred, Plegmund's reforms and efficient administration of his province considerably increased the influence of the archbishopric of Canterbury in ecclesiastical and political affairs. Nor was this influence diminished during the reign of Alfred's successor, Edward the Elder, whom he had 'crowned with the royal crown,' as the Chronicler records.[36] Although not as learned as his father he was religiously minded and continued his father's policy in Church and State. His provision for the creation of new bishoprics in Wessex under Plegmund gave to the province of Canterbury an increase in its learned episcopate numerically in accord with the Gregorian plan. The efficient administration of his province amidst adverse conditions was one of the greatest achievements of Plegmund's archiepiscopate. While there were recognizable limitations to this in the Danelaw there was no hindrance to the development of the Church and its institutions in Wessex. And it was from this part of Edward's kingdom when Plegmund died in 914 that his successor Aethelhelm, bishop of Winchester, who had been translated from Wells, came.

While Plegmund ruled the archbishopric of Canterbury the king had laboured closely with him for the well-being of the Church, but after the archbishop's death Edward's chief concern was the expansion of his kingdom until he claimed to be 'King of Britain.' This period of military activity coincided with the archiepiscopate of Aethelhelm who had received his *pallium* from Pope John X.[37] Of his ecclesiastical administration of the archbishopric and province nothing is known beyond his consecration of bishops when sees became vacant, and even the date of some of these consecrations remain a matter of conjecture [38] : nor is there any record to be found of his influence in the political affairs within his province. When Aethelhelm died in 923, Bishop Wulfhelm, whom he had consecrated to succeed him in the see of Wells, became his successor upon whom Pope John X later conferred the *pallium*.[39] A year after his translation to Canterbury King Edward died at Farndon in Northamptonshire and was borne to Winchester where he was interred in New Minster. His eldest son, Aethelstan, was elected king of Wessex and shortly after was recognized by the Mercians as their king. On ascending the throne he delayed his coronation until September 925, when, with much pomp and ceremony, he was consecrated king by Archbishop Wulfhelm at Kingston near London.[40]

PRECURSORS OF CHURCH REFORM

The coronation of King Aethelstan was of momentous importance for both Church and State. It was the beginning of the unification of Britain under one ruler; the initiation of co-ordination, as never before, between the ecclesiastical province of Canterbury and York; and the precursor of a deeper relationship between Church and State. Aethelstan was thirty and Archbishop Wulfhelm little more than forty years of age, and each was new to his office; factors which would inevitably draw them more closely together. In Wulfhelm the king found a sagacious counsellor still young enough to understand his aspirations; while in Aethelstan the archbishop had a king who was a powerful ruler and upholder of the Church and the Faith which it taught. Having been brought up in Mercia at the court of his aunt Aethelflaeda, Aethelstan had received a training which fitted him for his kingly obligations.

After having established a peaceful relationship with the Danes in Northumbria he convoked a witenagemot in or about 926 at Grately in Hampshire at which his first laws were made, which dealt with various problems arising from the social conditions of his times. Of special importance, however, was Aethelstan's ecclesiastical legislation. Owing to the invasions and settlement of the Danes, successive archbishops of Canterbury had been unable to convene the traditional synods and in consequence ecclesiastical legislation had not kept pace with the requirements of the changing conditions in the province. His ecclesiastical laws reflect the extensive influence of the archbishopric of Canterbury upon the king. Acknowledgement of this is made by the king in the opening words of his laws: 'I, Athelstan, king, by the counsel of Wulfhelm my archbishop, and other my bishops, command all my reeves.' This corpus of laws concludes with further reference to the archbishop, recording that the laws were decreed at 'the great synod of Grately, where was Wulfhelm the archbishop, with all the noble and wise men that King Aethelstan had called together.'[1] For the first time there was established by law one coinage for the kingdom over which Aethelstan ruled. All coins would now carry the effigy of the king. This effectively removed the effigy of the archbishop of Canterbury from the coins which he minted. Archbishop Jaenberht was the first of the archbishops of Canterbury of whom any record is to be found who minted his own coins.[2] By law, however, the archbishop was authorized to have two mints and the bishop of Rochester one. Although other see cities were mentioned only these two sees were given the minting privilege. Wulfhelm, who was the king's chief adviser, evidently concurred with the decree 'that there shall be one coinage throughout the king's dominions' and 'in Canterbury there shall be seven minters; four of them the king's; two, the archbishop's; one, the abbot's. In Rochester, three; two of them the king's, and one, the bishop's.' The Church was still recovering from the impoverishment caused by the invasions of the Danes and now under these laws the king made provision for its support. Precise directions were given to his reeves concerning the payments of tithes from which neither the king himself nor the bishops were exempt. In the operation of many of the laws, especially those relating to trial by ordeal, both bishops and clergy had certain functions to discharge which indicate how closely integrated was the life of the Church with the State. Further laws were enacted at the council of Exeter in 928 which affected the duties of bishops. There can be little doubt that Wulfhelm, in his endeavours to raise the standard of diocesan administration, had sought the assistance of the king. Of bishops it was decreed 'It does of right concern the bishop to promote every observance, both divine and secular. In the first place he ought to instruct him that is ordained what is right to be done by him . . . bishops ought to be present with secular judges in their judicatures.' They are also advised 'to interpose in diverse matters, that he may know his flock which he received at the hand of God.' Throughout his diocese the bishop was to be involved in something which affected every part of the community for, it was decreed, all measuring rods should be 'adjusted to the bishop's measure, and made even throughout his diocese, and let every weight be the same according to his word.' Laws were also made concerning the pastoral ministry of the clergy; priests in the diocese where they served were directed 'diligently to help everyone as to what was right, and not to suffer, if they can, one Christian to hurt another.' [3]

After his successful invasion of Scotland in 927 Aethelstan was accepted as overlord; peace was made and, indicative of the king's allegiance to the Christian Faith, in the pledges and oaths given the subdued rulers 'renounced all idolatry.' [4] Marching southwards Aethelstan occupied York. While there the archbishopric became vacant, or it became so a few months later, to which he nominated Hrothweard, who was probably consecrated by the archbishop of Canterbury. Since Northumbria was now a part of his kingdom Aethelstan gave immediate representation to the province of York in the councils of state. This was to be seen by the attendance of the archbishop of York with his four suffragans at the witenagemot at Exeter early in 928 at which they subscribed to two documents together with the king and the archbishop of Canterbury with his suffragan bishops. [5] A year later both archbishops with their suffragans subscribed to a charter by which the king granted land to the cathedral church of Worcester.[6] Aethelstan, who subscribed as *Rex Anglorum,* was followed by Wulfhelm, who took precedence as archbishop of the primal see, after whom the archbishop of York subscribed. Hrothweard of York subscribed for the last time to a charter by which the king at the council of Lulling Minster granted land to Beornege, bishop of Selsey.[7] It is evident that at these witenagemot the ecclesiastical provinces of Canterbury and York were regarded as constituting one Church of the whole kingdom over which Aethelstan ruled, as the legal transactions testify. Both archbishops were brought together as counsellors giving advice to the king in matters of ecclesiastical and political concern. Out of this association in common service of advising the king there began to emerge an endeavour on the part of the two archbishops to co-ordinate the work and witness of the whole Church in England. There was no lack of support for the Church by the king. Without delay in 930 or early in 931 when the see of York fell vacant he nominated Wulstan to the archbishopric of York.[8] In the latter year, after his consecration by Archbishop Wulfhelm of Canterbury, he was in attendance at three witenagemot and duly subscribed to the documents issued by these councils.[9]

Aethelstan extended his supremacy in the west of England and compelled the Britons of Cornwall to accept for their boundary the river Tamar. Farther south, however, beyond the Tamar the authority of the archbishopric of Canterbury had been extended before 931 when the king founded a bishopric at St. Germans to which Wulfhelm had consecrated a bishop with the British name of Conan. Bishop Conan as early as March 931 attended the witenagemot at Colchester and subscribed as a suffragan of the archbishop of Canterbury.[10] Recognition of Aethelstan's overlordship was threatened in 934 by the king of the Scots, and for the second time he had to march northwards with his forces. The route which he took allowed him to visit the churches of Beverley, Ripon and the shrine of St. Cuthbert at Chester-le-Street, leaving at each place his royal gifts. Three years later in 937 with his brother Edmund he met the opposing armies of the king of the Scots with those of Olaf of Dublin. Bishop Oda, having returned from a successful mission to France for Aethelstan, journeyed north with Theodred, bishop of London, to join the king's forces. A decisive victory was gained at an unidentified place named Brunanburh by Aethelstan's forces, after which he used the title *Rex totius Britanniae* in documents and on coins.[11]

At this period there was greater recognition of England on the Continent as a west European power. Friendly relations had already been established with the Church on the Continent by King Alfred, and his son, Edward the Elder, strengthened the kingdom's relationship by giving one of his daughters in marriage to Charles the Simple, king of the West Franks. Later, the visit of Bishop Cynewold of Worcester to the monasteries of Pfäfers, Reichenau and St. Gall contributed further to friendship with Britain. At each monastery gifts were made from Aethelstan, Wulfhelm, bishops, abbots and other eminent people whose names were recorded by the monks in the Book of the Confraternity.[12] While Cynewold's mission may have been for the purpose of collecting relics there can be little doubt that his visit was sponsored by Aethelstan so that he could negotiate the marriage of two of the king's sisters. For Edith married Otto, who became the king of the Romans, and Eadhild married Hugh the Great, Duke of the French. These relationships with the courts and churches of Europe influenced the Church in England especially in later measures for the reform of the monasteries. Books and manuscripts were purchased for Aethelstan and when brought to England were given by him to various churches. Prior Radbod of St. Samson's monastery, Doll, wrote to Aethelstan in fulsome terms thanking him for his munificence and sending with his letter relics of saints, which the king gave to monasteries in his kingdom.[13] Throughout his reign Aethelstan made numerous benefactions to the Church, and on Wulstan entering his archbishopric at York he made him a grant of land of Amounderness for his cathedral church of St. Peter, York.[14] Most of the king's benefactions were part of the business transacted at a witenagemot which had evolved during his reign into a larger representative assembly. Illustrative of this is the large number and variety of persons who subscribed to a document issued from the council of Middleton in 932. Those who subscribed after King Aethelstan were the archbishops of Canterbury and York, seventeen suffragan bishops, four abbots, fifteen ealdormen and forty-seven thanes.[15] Of the seventeen bishops fifteen were suffragans of Archbishop Wulfhelm, including Conan, bishop of Cornwall and Cynsige, bishop of Berkshire. Acting with the king's approval, Wulfhelm, for the better pastoral care of the people, had separated Berkshire from the Wiltshire diocese thus creating a new see or had appointed Cynesige as an assistant bishop to Bishop Oda of Wiltshire who had his seat at Ramsbury. This seems the more probable since no successor to Cynsige is to be found after he ceased to subscribe to documents in 934.[16] Provision was made by Wulfhelm for the devastated area of East Anglia where the sees of Dunwich and Elmham were in abeyance. Bishop Theodred of London had the episcopal care of Suffolk and placed his seat in the minster at Hoxne.[17]

Acting independently of the archbishopric of Canterbury a peace-guild was formed of 'the bishops and reeves who belong to London,' who gave their pledges to the archbishop to maintain the king's peace. Influenced by Theodred the king had enacted that no person younger than fifteen committing an offence should receive the penalty of death. Knowledge of this law Aethelstan requested to be conveyed to the archbishop by Theodred.[18]

Many gifts were made by Aethelstan to monasteries and nunneries but there is no evidence to show that throughout the province of Canterbury Wulfhelm adopted any measures for the reform of the monasteries. In the archbishopric itself the *familia* of Christ Church was active and received many notable benefactions, some of which were expressly 'for the work of the monks.' One gift to Wulfhelm for Christ Church was 'for the sustenance of the monks serving God in the same church.' [19] But it would be unwise on the basis of this document alone to assume that Wulfhelm had been able to change his *familia* into a regular monastic community. Wulfhelm's subscription to this same charter emphasizes the extent of his authority for he is 'archbishop of the whole of Britain,' and subscribes himself in this way.[20] There can be little doubt that Wulfhelm encouraged monastic reform and in this had the full support of Aethelstan. Whatever measures were taken by both king and archbishop may only be regarded as indicative of the desire to reform the monasteries which in itself helped to prepare for later reforms. At the king's national assemblies abbots were invariably present and in 932 at Amesbury six abbots attended and a year earlier five were present at Luton.[21] Since Aethelstan brought abbots into his national councils it would appear that certain regular monasteries actually existed and were now of sufficient importance in national affairs for the king to summon the abbots to attend. Initial steps for monastic reform had to wait until after the death of Wulfhelm, when he was succeeded in 942 by Bishop Oda of Ramsbury.[22] When he entered the archbishopric of Canterbury he carried with him lofty ideals and purposeful plans for the revival of monasticism within the province over which he now ruled. He was not a monk and there was no monastery in the country, it would appear, where the Benedictine Rule was strictly observed. Desiring to become a monk, he declared that none but a monk should occupy the chair of St. Augustine. When on an embassy in France Oda had visited the abbey of Fleury-on-the-Loire where reform measures had established the observance of the Benedictine Rule. A friendly relationship had long existed between the abbey and the kingdom of Wessex, and it was now to Fleury that he turned to receive the monastic habit. It would appear that the abbot visited Canterbury and invested Oda, although it is also recorded that he visited the abbey and received cucullation there.[23] But, having become a monk, he was enthroned at Christ Church and duly received the *pallium* from Pope Agapetus.[24]

After the death of Aethelstan, King Olaf of Dublin occupied York and, marching south with his forces, invaded the Midlands. He was repulsed at Northampton and then stormed Tamworth laying waste the country-side. Marching northwards with his army, the young King Edmund, accompanied by Archbishop Oda, met Olaf's forces at Leicester, with whom was Archbishop Wulstan of York. Having frequently attended national councils the two archbishops had often worked together and now jointly they took the initiative to make peace between the two kings in order to prevent further bloodshed. Their mediation was successful and peace was arranged so that Olaf received all the territory north of Watling Street and south of that line the territory remained a part of Edmund's kingdom.[25] Further unrest broke out in 944 and again Edmund led his army north and re-occupied the city of York.

The meeting of the archbishops of Canterbury and York on the battlefield at Leicester had proved politically effective in making peace. But the occasion marked the beginning of a closer relationship between the two archbishoprics which was destined to affect the whole of the Church in England.

On entering his archbishopric Oda had found his cathedral and adjoining church buildings in a dilapidated condition. This situation in no way prevented him from turning his attention to the wider problem of the administration of his extensive province. A Dane by birth and soldier by profession who had served on embassies to France, he now carried the disciplines of his earlier career into reform measures for the Church. Although metropolitans were required by canon law to convoke each year two provincial synods, this requirement had fallen into abeyance owing to the unsettled conditions in the country. Ecclesiastical affairs, however, had not been neglected for they formed a part of the business transacted at the national councils convened by the king. But this urgent pre-occupation with the defence of his kingdom delayed him in convening a national council. Matters concerning the Church in the province of Canterbury were of such importance that attention to them could not be delayed. Without convoking a provincial synod Oda, in the exercise of his archiepiscopal authority, independently initiated measures for Church reform. These began sometime after 943 when he addressed a pastoral letter to all the bishops of his province. This letter was of an original character and did not follow the traditional pattern of a pastoral. It was composed of ten archiepiscopal injunctions framed in the language and form of synodal canons. In the introduction he admits they have been formulated from sources *documenta* of importance but makes no reference to any corpus of canons. With all humility he states that as archbishop, honoured with the *pallium,* he issues his injunctions for the encouragement of Edmund and his subjects so that by hearing them and meditating upon them they may find expression in good works.[26] The Church, he enjoins, should not be subjected to any violence and no taxes should be imposed upon it. And all property wrongly taken from the Church should be restored to it. The king and princes and all in authority are admonished with great humility to be obedient to the archbishops and all other bishops, because the keys of the kingdom of heaven are given to them, and they have the power of binding and loosing. Bishops are enjoined to give attention to their pastoral office and to visit their dioceses, *parochias,* every year. And priests by their good example are to teach the people, and impart to them sacred doctrine, and be dressed in accordance with the dignity of the priesthood. Clergy are to live canonically, and monks are to perform their vows in the churches where they first made them. Marriages with near of kin, nuns and all unlawful unions are forbidden. Concord between bishops, princes and all Christian people and unity and peace in the churches should be maintained. Fasting with alms, Sundays and festivals are to be observed. Finally, Oda charged 'take care to pay tithe of all that you possess' because it specially belongs to the Lord God, and alms should be given from the nine parts which remain. These injunctions possess no originality but show evidence of having been chosen by Oda to meet the conditions and necessary reforms of the Church in his province at that period. His directive concerning kings, princes and all in authority being obedient to their bishops is substantially one of the legatine canons of the council of Chelsea in 786.[27] And his injunction that bishops should annually visit their dioceses was a necessary reform because such visitations in many parts of the province since the Danish invasions began had been impossible. But this was not a new problem. Bede mentioned it, with its attendant problems in large dioceses, when he wrote to Bishop Egbert in 734, and Archbishop Cuthbert's synod at Clofeshoh in 746 issued a canon on the same problem.[28] It is evident that the reform relating to the dress of the clergy required by Pope John VIII in his letter to Archbishop Aethelred and others (873–5) had not been wholly effective, and in consequence Oda found it necessary to enjoin his priests to wear their distinctive dress. Once again as in 786 it was necessary to direct that the clergy should live canonically since a certain slackness of life had affected the seculars.[29] And the problem of monks leaving the monastery of their cucullation and going from monastery to monastery still needed attention as in the days of Archbishop Theodore.[30] Oda's injunctions on Church order and discipline, chiefly relating to the laity, including the peace of the Church, marriage, fasts, alms, festivals and tithes had been invariably matters upon which the synods of the English Church had expressed judgments in similar terms. Here, however, was the authoritative voice of the metropolitan archbishop issuing canons which carried no synodal mandate. From the prefatory passages of his pastoral letter it would appear that Oda's original intention was to have read his injunctions at a synod, since he speaks of them being heard when read aloud. In this manner they would have probably been approved and issued as synodal decrees. Such may have been the position at the time but for some unrecorded cause he was unable to convoke a provincial synod, and for this reason ventured on a course of action never before taken by an archbishop of Canterbury by issuing his own canons for the well-being of the Church. The bishops of his province in due course would have received them but to what extent they implemented them is unrecorded.

It is evident that Oda's injunction relating to monks was intended to be his first step towards monastic reform. By receiving the monastic habit before his enthronement there could be no doubt of his desire for such reform. The reforms in France had reached the monastery of Fleury-on-the-Loire, but at the monastery of St. Bertin in Flanders some of the brethren refused to accept the Benedictine Rule, left the monastery and came to England. Since the monk Grimbald left St. Bertin to join King Alfred's scholars at his court, England had continued its friendship with the monastery which was further strengthened when the monks gave burial to Edwin, the brother of King Aethelstan. This friendship was continued by King Edmund who installed the expelled monks of St. Bertin in Bath Abbey where the Benedictine Rule was not observed.[31] Edmund's action was indicative of the attitude of many eminent laymen in England who showed their dislike for monastic reform by their support of the secular clergy. This climate of opinion effectively delayed any reforms contemplated by the archbishop. But Edmund was a zealous supporter of the Church and his co-operation with the archbishops of Canterbury and York for the well-being of the Church reached its highest expression when he convoked an assembly c. 944 in London. In convoking this council, doubtless on the advice of the archbishops, Edmund took the initiative for the well-being of his whole kingdom which embraced the two provinces of Canterbury and York. The preamble to the laws which were enacted recorded that 'Edmund the king convoked a great assembly at London on the holy feast of Easter, both of ecclesiastical and lay persons. There were Oda and Wulstan, archbishops and many other bishops, consulting for the good of their own souls, and of those who were subject to them.'[32] The first of the six laws directed ecclesiastical persons to instruct God's people by an exemplary life. As if to give emphasis to this the penalties for not so doing, laid down by canon law, were added, namely loss of worldly possessions and being buried on death in unconsecrated ground unless satisfaction were made. All Christian men were enjoined to pay tithes, church-scot and plough-alms. Those who failed to do so were to be excommunicated. If a king's servant or tenant kills a Christian he is forbidden to enter the king's presence until he has served his penance as required by the bishop or confessor. The punishment for an adulterer and the seducer of a nun was the same as for a manslayer unless due penance was made. The fifth law made specific reference to the obligation of a bishop to repair his cathedral church, and the necessity to remind the king that for all God's churches provision should be made. Edmund's ecclesiastical laws conclude with the penalty of 'being cast out from every portion of God' for those found guilty of perjury or sorcery unless they repent and render due penance. Together the archbishops had attended national councils, but never before had they both been called to an assembly by the king so that with lay assistance ecclesiastical laws should be considered and promulgated for the whole kingdom. Elements which needed reform were common to both provinces. The manner of life of the clergy, monks and nuns was considered not to be of a sufficiently high standard to commend their religion to 'the people of God.' To practise Christianity by setting an example was required as well as precept, and by this means instruction should be given. But special mention is made of men and women (nuns) maintaining their orders' requirement of chastity. This applied particularly to the secular clergy, some of whom were married or living unmarried with a woman regardless of canon law which demanded celibacy. Tithing no longer remained as in Theodore's day or at the time of the legatine council of 786 at Chelsea an act of praiseworthy piety. Nor did it remain together with the payment of church-scot and plough-alms a matter of a fine for non-payment as in the laws of Alfred and Guthrum. For there was now the added penalty, for non-payment, of excommunication. These laws marked a distinctive advance in the relationship of Church and State, for they now possessed the authority of the king and his council which extended to the spiritual, moral and material well-being of the Church. The parallels between these laws and the pastoral canons of Oda indicate how far-reaching was the influence of the archbishopric of Canterbury affecting the life of the people throughout the kingdom over which Edmund ruled. Further laws were added later by a similar assembly for extinguishing feuds which often resulted in murder. In such cases it was decreed that satisfaction should be made to God as 'the bishop of the diocese directs.' [33]

In the preamble to the code of laws known as II Edmund the king recorded that he had consulted the wisest of the ecclesiastics and laymen concerning the best way to advance the Christian Faith. During his reign, all too short for he was slain in 946, he had appointed Dunstan to be abbot of Glastonbury and was much influenced by him.

At the time of Edmund's death his two young sons were not old enough to succeed him and the kingdom passed to his brother Eadred, who was consecrated king in the same year at Kingston by Oda.[34] After his recognition as king by the Northumbrians and Scots he conferred upon Archbishop Wulstan of York authority to exercise magisterial powers in the city.[35] But later Eadred found it necessary to march northwards with his forces and, at Tadcaster in Yorkshire, Wulstan and the magnates of Northumbria swore fealty to him and gave security for their obedience. This is the first recorded occasion of an English archbishop swearing allegiance to his king, and there can be little doubt that Oda, archbishop of Canterbury, administered the oath since he was with Eadred's forces. The leaders of Northumbria later broke their oath, with the exception of Wulstan, and revolted.[36] Eadred therefore invaded Northumbria and on reaching Ripon destroyed the monastery which Bishop Wilfrid I had founded. It was at this time that Oda translated the remains of Wilfrid and re-interred them in his cathedral at Canterbury. But it was eventually shown that by mistake the remains of Wilfrid II of York had been removed.[37]

Oda's reforms within his own *familia* had met with little success. His frequent absences from his archbishopric accompanying Edmund and Eadred on their warlike expeditions prevented him from developing any continuous measures of reform. His reputed severity had the effect of compelling the secular canons more scrupulously to observe their canonical rule of life, but it failed to make them receive the monastic habit. Unlike Edmund, Eadred showed his sympathy and support for monastic reform and the revival of monasticism. While this was attributable to the influence of Oda it is probable that in larger measure it was due to the close friendship which existed between Eadred and Dunstan, the abbot of Glastonbury. Eadred's support expressed itself in practical terms. When visiting the ruined abbey of Crowland his chancellor, Turketyl, retired from his office and was invested with the monastic habit in the presence of the king who then presented him with a pastoral staff, after which Ceolwulf, bishop of Dorchester, gave the newly made abbot the blessing. Having verbally granted Turketyl the abbey, Eadred early in 948 convened a council in London, at which by charter he confirmed his benefaction to Turketyl and his monks, and their successors 'serving God there under the rule and order of St. Benedict.'[38] Similarly the king's practical support was shown in the revival of monasticism when he dissuaded Aethelwold, a monk trained by Dunstan at Glastonbury, from going to Fleury, and appointed him to the abbey of Abingdon which was in ruins, and assisted him in its rebuilding.[39]

To Oda's efforts of reform within his archbishopric Eadred gave his support by restoring extensive lands to Christ Church.[40] This action was in full accord with the first of Oda's pastoral canons that any property taken or granted away from Christians should be returned to them as theirs of ancient right.

Although Eadred favoured and openly supported the revival of monasticism he was compelled to exercise much restraint because of the vested interests of many of his powerful ealdormen and others who supported the secular communities. But when he died in 955, and the provisions of his will became known, further and final evidence of his zeal for the monastic revival was to be seen in his bequests to the Old, New and Nuns' minsters at Winchester and the nunneries of Shalbourne, Wilton and Shaftesbury.[41] To the archbishop of Canterbury he bequeathed £400 for the relief of the people of Kent, Surrey, Sussex and Berkshire. And provision was made, had the archbishop died, for the money to remain at Christ Church. Similar bequests were also made to three of his suffragans, Aelfsige, Wulfhelm and Oskytel, and to Abbot Dunstan. Generous bequests were made to individual ecclesiastics, who included the archbishop and 'my' bishops : to the archbishop 200 mancuses and to each bishop 120 mancuses of gold for their special prayers. Each of his chaplains who had charge of relics was to receive 50 gold mancuses and £5 in pence ; and to every priest, who had been attached to the court since he became king, 30 mancuses of gold. He also made provision for twelve almsmen which was 'to continue as long as Christianity shall last, for the praise of God and the redemption of my soul.'[42]

DUNSTAN AND THE MONASTIC REVIVAL

Although the secular canons remained deeply entrenched and possessed the sympathy and support of many powerful laymen, at the time of King Eadred's death at Frome in 955, incipient signs were discernible of the revival of monasticism. In consequence this situation raised political as well as ecclesiastical problems as Eadwig, a boy of fifteen years, ascended the throne. He was the elder of Eadred's two nephews, and in the same year was consecrated king at Kingston by Archbishop Oda. The day of coronation which opened so auspiciously with the dignified ceremonial of crowning closed in dismay and anger through the king's inconsiderate action and caused a breach between Eadwig and Dunstan who had been the close friend and counsellor of Eadred. Early in 946 Eadwig demanded of Dunstan an account of the treasure and documents which his uncle Eadred had entrusted to his care. Rather than betray his trust Dunstan fled the country and was received at the monastery of St. Peter, Ghent, where he was able to live under and to observe the Benedictine Rule. The young king's hostility to Dunstan, the recognized leader of the revival of monasticism, provided a situation in which Eadwig could be easily influenced by the powerful ealdormen who strongly supported the secular canons. Eadwig still had for his chief counsellor Archbishop Oda, who, though growing old, was fully alive to the situation as it affected the work and witness of the Church in his province. But for his sagacious counsel it would appear that the hostility against monasticism would have reached unrestrained excesses. Nevertheless, as Dunstan left England for Blandinium in Flanders his abbey and all his possessions were confiscated. The rebuilding at Abingdon by Abbot Aethelwold was delayed and at this juncture no progress could be made in the life of the monastery.[1] Glastonbury and Abingdon, in all probability, were the only monasteries in the province of Canterbury where any semblance of the Benedictine Rule was observed. For Turketyl of Crowland by that time had accomplished little more than the preparatory stages for the rebuilding of his abbey. William of Malmesbury records that 'all members of the monastic order throughout England were first despoiled of their property, and then driven into exile.'[2] While this may be regarded as an exaggeration when compared with the more restrained record of Eadmer, the authentic note of truth can be heard in William of Malmesbury's lament for his own monastery of Malmesbury which he describes as being 'made a stable for secular canons.'[3]

Throughout Oda's archiepiscopate so far, there had been always present the problem of re-establishing effective episcopal administration in those parts of his province where the work and witness of the Church had been disorganized by the invasions or settlement of the Danes. A vast expanse of the country had been affected in the east of England, stretching southwards from Lindsey to south East Anglia, and because of this episcopal succession in the sees of Dunwich, Elmham and Lindsey had been broken or become obscure. The names of some bishops have survived but it is not known whether they had their seat at Dunwich or Lindsey, and uncertainty remains concerning succession in the see of Elmham from 838 onwards. At some time before 956 Oda arranged for Bishop Theodored of London to have the episcopal care of Suffolk. In extending his pastoral charge Theodored set his seat in the minster of Hoxne where there were twelve canons. It is doubtful, however, whether this could be regarded as a separate see being held *in commendam* by Theodored, but his episcopal oversight was attended with such success that it became possible for the see of Elmham to be revived. Suffolk and Norfolk now constituted the newly formed diocese to which Oda consecrated Eadwulf, from whom before his consecration he received a profession of canonical obedience.[4] Further active measures were adopted by Oda to bring the eastern part of England south of the Humber once again under the pastoral care and administration of a bishop. By the year 953 Leofwine had already been consecrated bishop and was ruling the revived see of Lindsey which had been without a bishop since *c.* 869. On the translation of Oskytel from Dorchester to the archbishopric of York in 958, Leofwine moved his seat to Dorchester-on-Thames and from there ruled his diocese which comprised almost the whole of the eastern midlands inclusive of Lindsey. This large diocese was episcopally administered from Dorchester down to the Norman Conquest except for one brief period beginning towards the end of the tenth century when once again the revival of Lindsey as a separate see was attempted but failed.

Oda's prolonged efforts and final success in giving those parts of his province, which had suffered loss and devastation, an ecclesiastical administration under the direct control and leadership of his suffragan bishops brought to the archbishopric of Canterbury a period of high achievement destined still further to advance the Church during the tenth century.

Although chief counsellor to the young King Eadwig, Oda was unable to restrain him from actions which were divisive. Eadwig's grants of land to gain support alienated wiser and older supporters. And it is probable that the archbishop's action in separating him from his wife Aelfgifu, because of their near kinship to each other further discredited him in the eyes of many who had accepted him as king.[5] A climax was reached in 957 when the Mercians and Northumbrians renounced Eadwig as king and gave their allegiance to his brother Edgar, the Thames being made the boundary between the two kingdoms.[6] As soon as Edgar had established himself as ruler of his part of the country, he summoned his friend Abbot Dunstan to return to England, but he could not return to Glastonbury which was in Eadwig's territory. Soon after his arrival in England Bishop Cenwald of Worcester died and to this see Edgar appointed Dunstan, who was consecrated by Oda. During the following year the bishopric of London fell vacant through death and to this Dunstan was appointed to hold the see *in commendam* with Worcester.[7]

Before Oda died in 958 the archbishopric of Canterbury was in a stronger position ecclesiastically and politically than it had been since the time of Plegmund during the reign of Alfred. The peaceful conditions which now existed in the province assisted the archbishop's full complement of his fifteen suffragan bishops in the efficient administration of their dioceses. Edgar, a year after Oda's death or soon after, promulgated at Andover, certain laws known as Codes II & III Edgar, the first part of which dealt with ecclesiastical affairs. Elements of the first part cover in more detail parts of Oda's pastoral canons, and it is probable that these laws were drawn up in consultation with the king and Bishop Dunstan in order to give legal effect to the relevant parts of Oda's canons. But they awaited promulgation until Edgar was not only ruler of the territory north of the Thames but *Rex Anglorum*, which he became on the death of Eadwig in 959. The importance of the ecclesiastical code in making provision by law for the Church and its maintenance was of the highest significance. It laid down as a first principle that 'God's churches are to be entitled to their rights.'[8] Details for the payment of tithes to the old minster, a church, with or without a graveyard, erected by a thegn on his bookland (land held by written title deed) and to the priest officiating at a burial, are given with the penalty of the seizure, for non-payment, of one's possessions to whom was finally returned only two-fifths of the original possessions. For a person who successively refused on three occasions to pay the hearth-penny on St. Peter's Day the penalty was that 'he is to forfeit all that he owns.' It was enjoined that Sunday, being a festival, and all other festivals and fasts shall be observed. Soul-scot shall be paid to the priest and the right of sanctuary shall be maintained to its past highest standard.

The heavy penalties now exacted by laws for the non-payment of tithes and Church dues indicate that there had been widespread default in payment. Such default in those parts of the country which had been overrun by the Danes is understandable. And no doubt Oda,

in re-establishing bishoprics in those parts, had been confronted with
the problem of maintaining the Church among the people who once
again had come within episcopal pastoral care and administration.
In the code known as III Edgar, laws relating to secular affairs were
promulgated. The shire court was to meet twice a year at which the
shire (diocesan) bishop with the ealdormen was to be present to
expound both the ecclesiastical and secular law. A number of
ecclesiastical regulations known as the 'Canons of Edgar,' formerly
believed to have been decreed by Edgar under Dunstan's influence,
have been shown to be the work of Archbishop Wulstan II of York,
probably before his elevation to the episcopate.[9]

In the prologue to the code known as IV Edgar it is recorded that
King Edgar had inquired concerning a remedy for the pestilence
which had oppressed and reduced his people. Under the year 962 the
A-S Chronicle records a plague, and it was to this, no doubt, that
the king referred. The king and his counsellors concluded that the
pestilence was a punishment for contempt of God's commands and
the failure to pay tithes.[10] Because of this Edgar said 'I and the
archbishop command you not to anger God by withholding God's
dues, but to render tithes to God with gladness and with all willingness.' Reference was made to the decrees issued at Andover which were
now confirmed at 'Wihtbordesstan.' Special provisions were made for
the Danes who were enjoined to preserve secular rights 'according to
as good laws as they best can decide on.' The archbishop to whom
Edgar referred was Dunstan, who by that time had succeeded to the
archbishopric of Canterbury.

Although Edgar ruled over the territory north of the Thames,
Eadwig was the crowned king of Wessex, and on Oda's death he
nominated Bishop Aelfsige of Winchester to succeed him. On journeying to Rome for his *pallium* Aelfsige died when crossing the Alps.
Beorhthelm, bishop of Wells, was elected to succeed him but within a
few months of his translation Eadwig died and Edgar became king
of the reunited kingdom. His chief counsellor was his gifted friend
Bishop Dunstan whom he now desired to occupy the highest office
in the Church. It was generally accepted that Beorhthelm lacked the
necessary qualities of leadership for such high dignity and, doubtless
under political pressure, he returned to his former see of Wells.
Thereupon, as Florence of Worcester records, 'St. Dunstan was by
divine grace and advice of the council chosen to be primate and
patriarch of the metropolis of England.'[11] Within a year of his
translation Pope John XII sent the *pallium* to Dunstan who, on his
first visit to his cathedral, paid tribute to his predecessor by describing
him as 'Oda the Good.'[12] At the time of Oda's death his nephew
Oswald, a monk of Fleury, had returned to England, and was staying

with his kinsman Oskytel, archbishop of York, when he came to the notice of Dunstan. On his commendation to Edgar, Oswald was appointed to the bishopric of Worcester for which he was consecrated by Dunstan. Two years later in 963 Dunstan consecrated Abbot Aethelwold, bishop of Winchester.

From the charters by which Eadwig had made grants to monasteries it is evident that he was not hostile to the revival of monasticism in his kingdom, but political pressure was sufficiently strong to restrain him from giving it active support. When Edgar became the ruler of the reunited kingdom, having for his chief counsellor Dunstan, the movement for the revival of monasticism received a fresh impetus. The three wealthiest sees, Canterbury, Winchester and Worcester, were now held by monks who had shown their deep devotion to the monastic ideal. This triumvirate with the full co-operation of Edgar brought about one of the greatest religious revivals in the English Church. While Dunstan was bishop of London the king had shown the closest co-operation with the bishop in jointly granting privileges to St. Peter's, Westminster, of which Wulfsinus had been made abbot.[13]

Dunstan's basic ecclesiastical policy was the revival of monasticism by which he planned to revive the work and witness of the Church. He inspired Edgar by his religious zeal and thus assured the success of his policy during the sixteen peaceful years of Edgar's reign. Abbot Aethelwold appeared to be the leader in the monastic revival ably supported by Oswald, but the power behind both was without doubt Dunstan who had first pioneered reform measures as abbot of Glastonbury under King Edmund. In order to be informed of the customs of the Benedictine Rule, Aethelwold sent Osgar, one of his monks, from Abingdon to Fleury, and also brought monks from Corbie in France to teach his monks methods of ceremonial and chanting. When he became bishop of Winchester he found clerks in his cathedral and at New Minster; a situation he could not tolerate. Early in 964 the seculars who would not receive the monastic habit were ejected and monks from Abingdon were installed. A year later the seculars were expelled from New Minster and their places taken by monks. These expulsions were effected by King Edgar, but the initiative and inspiration came from Aethelwold.[14] Further reform measures were taken by the bishop at Peterborough, Crowland, Ely, Thorney and probably at Chertsey, St. Albans and St. Neots. Bishop Oswald of Worcester was no less active for, on his arrival in his bishopric, he founded the monastery of Westbury-on-Trym, and later Ramsey, Pershore and Winchcombe. In his own cathedral, however, which was not monastic, he took conciliatory measures to attain his objective of installing monks.[15] To these probably should be added the monasteries of Evesham and Deerhurst thus making the seven which his biographer attributes to him in Mercia.[16] Some time before 970 Dunstan re-installed monks at Malmesbury and Bath, and probably about the same time monks from Glastonbury were established at Milton and Exeter. Of St. Augustine's, Canterbury little is known but it would appear that there was a monastic community there to which Dunstan appointed Sigeric to be abbot. The archbishop's name, however, is not associated with the introduction of monks at his own cathedral of Christ Church, although it is thought that some monks were there during his archiepiscopate,[17] and nowhere in his own diocese did he install monks under the *Regularis Concordia*.

With the revival of monasticism and the consequent increase in the number of communities it became evident that they possessed no common rule of observance. So diverse were their observances that on the advice of Dunstan and others Edgar convened at Winchester *c*. 970 a synodal council to which he sent a letter exhorting 'all to come to an agreement in one common use . . . strictly observing the precepts of the Rule.' [18] There were present with Bishop Aethelwold, bishops, abbots, abbesses and also monks from the Benedictine monasteries of Fleury and Ghent. From this synod a unanimously agreed customary was issued known as *Regularis Concordia Anglicae Nationis Monachorum Sanctimonialiumque*—'The Agreement concerning the Rule of the monks and nuns of the English nation.' King Edgar did not attend and the way in which reference is made to Dunstan makes it seem probable that he was not present. But the whole work of the synod was evidently submitted to him for his scrutiny and confirmation. 'Moreover, Dunstan, the illustrious archbishop of this country in confirming the work of the synod, added a caution as to the dealings of monks with convents of women.' [19] While Bishop Aethelwold doubtless compiled the document it is generally considered that throughout it can be discerned the inspiring mind of Dunstan. It was he who perceived that the new Rule caused difficulties in certain monasteries which had been influenced by contact with the observance of the Benedictine Rule in communities like Fleury, Ghent and Corbie. Rivalries might arise where monasteries might wish to continue the Benedictine Rule and not accept the English *Regularis Concordia*. In this situation the statesmanlike sagacity of the archbishop exercised a moderating influence which restrained those whose zeal would outrun their wisdom.

In general there was little difference between the *Concordia* and other customaries in use on the Continent. Recognition is given, however, to the intimate relationship which existed between Church and State in England. Dunstan's mind may be discerned in the place given to Edgar and his queen by which they were regarded as protectors of all the monastic communities in the kingdom. Special prayers for the king and queen were to be said at every part of the Office, with the exception of Prime, and at the Matin Mass.[20] By this means no day could pass for the monks and nuns without a reminder that although they were members of a separate ecclesiastical community they were still a part of the nation over which the king for whom they prayed bore rule. Another feature peculiarly English was the regulation that the monastic community of a cathedral church shall elect the bishop, if possible from its own body, who shall live according to the monastic rule. In this again may be seen the influence of Dunstan, doubtless, supported by his two episcopal colleagues, by which those who were to be elected to the episcopate should be monks, and to this Edgar was a willing party.[21] The *Concordia* ruled that the community was to have the privilege not only of electing its superior, subject to the royal prerogative, but if possible from among themselves the bishop of the diocese. By this rule the independence of the monastery was assured and a continuing relationship with the bishop who would continue to live with the community. Dunstan's farsightedness in this was destined to affect for many years to come the life and development of the English Church. A new situation was therefore created by which the monastic community of the cathedral church had real contact with the episcopal leader of pastoral and ecclesiastical administration of the diocese. This in itself removed much of the suspicion which formerly existed and placed monastic communities in a living relationship as never before with the Church and nation.[22] In future centuries difficulties inevitably arose when laxity of discipline crept into the monasteries, but in the years preceding the Norman Conquest this rule was conducive to good relationships. For many years after the archiepiscopate of Dunstan the majority of bishops were monks having their place with abbots in the national councils where they exercised a powerful influence. In the primatial see the succession of monk archbishops was unbroken until 1052 when Stigand, a priest, occupied the archbishopric at the time of the Norman invasion. During Dunstan's archiepiscopate, and of his immediate successors, when provincial synods were not convened, the monastic allegiance common to the archbishop and his suffragans contributed much to the unity of purpose in the revival of religion and the administrative efficiency of the Church for which Dunstan unremittingly laboured. While Dunstan ruled at Canterbury the effect of the monastic revival extended far beyond the monasteries themselves. They became centres of culture where learning, caligraphy, music, illumination of manuscripts, craftwork and other pursuits exercised a regenerating and strengthening influence on a national scale both in Church and State. He taught craftwork when abbot of

Glastonbury and on becoming archbishop he continued to practise his own skills in making bells and organs and in composing chants.

The generous assistance given to the Church by King Edgar has not escaped question concerning the motives which prompted it. During the early years of his reign the archbishop greatly influenced him as a counsellor of many years' experience, but the situation was never reached which one writer described when 'Edgar reigned; but Dunstan ruled.' It has been asserted that in his youth the king had a predilection towards a monastic vocation but was unable to attain it because of his royal obligations. For this reason he was willing to follow the advice of Dunstan in religious affairs and became not only the protector and supporter but also *pastor pastorum* of the monastic flocks.[23] On the other hand he has been portrayed as a licentious ruler who took by force a nun from the convent at Wilton to be his mistress. Rebuked by Dunstan the king submitted to the penance which he imposed upon him. At that period the penitential canons had substitutionary provisions by which a wealthy man of standing could evade the exactions of his penance. The king adopted this expedient, but in order to give the widest publicity to the penance Edgar agreed not to wear his crown for seven years.[24] The completion of this penance may have caused the delay in Edgar going to his crowning. For it was not until he had reached his thirtieth year that, in the city of Bath on Whit Sunday in 973, before a vast congregation gathered from all parts of England, he was crowned by Dunstan. Using a form of service drawn up by Dunstan, England had for the first time a 'Coronation Service, properly to be so-called.' There were many notable features in this service one of which will be mentioned here, namely, the threefold oath which the king had to declare before the congregation. At the archbishop's bidding King Edgar declared: 'These three things to the Christian people subject unto me do I promise in the name of Christ: First, that the Church of God and all Christian people under my dominion in all time shall keep true peace; Second, that acts of greed, violence and all iniquities in all ranks and classes I will forbid; Third, that in all my judgments I will declare justice and mercy; so to me and to you may God, gracious and merciful, yield His mercy, Who liveth and reigneth for ever and ever.' To this oath the congregation cried 'Amen.'[25] Dunstan, like many ecclesiastics on the Continent, probably discerned a parallel between the king's anointing and the ordination of a priest, and for this reason may have counselled Edgar to delay until he had reached the age below which no candidate for the priesthood could be canonically ordained. This service in which the king and the metropolitan archbishop of England were the dominant figures was expressive of the harmony and understanding which had been established between the English and the Danes for which the king and archbishop had laboured together to achieve : and, at the same time, it also expressed a deepening recognition, on the part of a united people, of the office of king as the fount of all law both in Church and State. So widespread and acceptable was Edgar's rule that in the same year of his coronation eight tributary kings of their own accord swore fealty to him.[26]

If penance of such an evasive and vicarious character had been allowed for Edgar by Dunstan, it would seem that he had been actuated by political expediency when his action is compared with the rigorous and unrelenting penance which he imposed upon a powerful earl who had contracted a marriage contrary to Church law.[27] On behalf of the earl the king approached Dunstan to grant absolution but without success. Not heeding Dunstan's repeated admonitions he finally excommunicated the earl who, in anger, journeyed to Rome and presented his case at the papal court. Finally, he obtained from the pope a written directive to Dunstan that he should allow the marriage to remain. As immovable as stone, Dunstan was true to his name, so wrote Adelard ; he set aside the papal missive, and would not allow even the pope to interfere with his archiepiscopal authority. He refused to grant the earl absolution until his judgment was obeyed.[28] Such disparity of judgment meted out to king and earl seem contrary to Dunstan's character, and it would make it appear that he was responsible for the delay of Edgar's coronation. Indeed, it would seem that the king's confidence in his chief adviser was stronger than ever since he gave him greater political authority by appointing him to the ealdormanry of Kent, which had lapsed, uniting with it Surrey and Sussex over which the archbishop now ruled.

Never before had any archbishop of Canterbury exercised such extensive secular authority delegated to him by a king. Before receiving this secular authority Dunstan, who had possessed the confidence of Kings Edmund and Eadred, gave counsel which was well received by the youthful King Edgar. Both agreed on the necessity for the unification of the kingdom, and laboured together to make the Danes of eastern England an integral part of the kingdom. So successful were their efforts that later the Danish shires were known collectively as the Danelaw. Oda, Oskytel and Oswald, all of Danish blood, became archbishops and in their time assisted in welding together the Danes and the English into one people. But it must not be assumed that because of the close friendship and common objective of king and archbishop that Dunstan's will was predominant in secular affairs. 'Edgar the Peaceable,' as he became known from the peaceful conditions prevailing during his reign, was able to give attention to ecclesiastical reforms so much desired by Dunstan. It would be a mistake to interpret Dunstan's statesmanlike manner in handling ecclesiastical affairs as the exercise of political influence. Nevertheless, the authority of the archbishopric of Canterbury and unity of Church and State reached their highest expression when the archbishop of York and all the bishops of the kingdom had a part in the ceremony in which Archbishop Dunstan consecrated and anointed Edgar king.

Edgar's sudden death in July 975 let loose political and ecclesiastical rivalries which eventually destroyed much of what he had accomplished. He had contracted two marriages from the first of which he had a son Edward who was in his youth. His second wife was Aelfthryth, daughter of the ealdorman of Devon. Of this marriage there was a son Aethelred, who was hardly ten years of age when his father died. With the support of some of the nobles Aelfthryth attempted to have her son made king but without success. Under the leadership of Dunstan, Oswald, archbishop of York, all the bishops, many abbots and ealdormen met in council and elected Edward, who was consecrated and anointed king by Dunstan in the same year, 975.[29] Edward's coronation did not bring to an end the partisanship which had arisen and gathering strength brought the kingdom almost to the brink of civil war. The political rivalry arising out of the succession dispute immediately affected the Church by a movement led by Aelfhere, ealdorman of Mercia, against the monasteries. He was accused of destroying monasteries; and thegns who possessed an hereditary title to monastic lands asserted their claims; while the dispossessed seculars with their wives returned to monasteries from which the monks had been expelled. Similar action seemed imminent in East Anglia when Aethelwine, supported by his brother Aelfwold and Brithnoth, the East Saxon ealdorman, gathered an army together and prepared to defend the East Anglian monasteries. Armed conflict was averted and a 'great council' was held at Kirtlington in 977 which proved inconclusive probably because during the wordy conflict Sideman, bishop of Crediton, collapsed and died.[30] In the same year or early in 978 another council over which Dunstan presided was held at Calne, the king being absent on account of his age. Assembling in an upper room and attended by 'all the senators of England' the meeting has been described as a great conflict and controversy in which 'weapons of harsh reproach were hurled against Archbishop Dunstan, the most powerful bulwark of the Church.' [31] While the acrimonious debate between the representatives of the monks and seculars was at its height the floor collapsed precipitating those present into the room below. Many were killed, others seriously injured, Dunstan alone escaping uninjured because he was standing on the only beam which did not fall. This was regarded as a miraculous intervention because nothing had been determined, and in consequence the position of the monks remained unchanged. The people generally supported Dunstan's position in defending the monasteries.[32] A third council was held later at Amesbury.

In March 978 the young Edward was murdered at Corfe. His untimely death shocked the nation to such an extent that his youth and innocence gathered to itself a sainthood which gave him a place in the Church's calendar. Even the Chronicler pauses to honour him by the words 'Man murdered him, but God honoured him. In life he was an earthly king; he is now after death a heavenly saint.' [33] Within a month of Edward's murder Aethelred was consecrated king by Dunstan in the presence of the archbishop of York, ten bishops and many counsellors. At this crowning ceremony Dunstan was unable to restrain himself from foretelling the evils which would befall the nation. His short discourse and the removal of Aethelred's mother, Aelfthryth, to the obscurity of a convent may have contributed to the failure to establish a friendly and understanding relationship between Dunstan and Aethelred the Unready (without rede or counsel). As a result, it would appear, the archbishop's influence at court ceased, and he withdrew from the political scene. His departure from the court marked the meridian of the influence exercised by the archbishopric of Canterbury on the political and ecclesiastical life of the nation. Not until after the Norman Conquest did the archbishopric again attain such powerful influence. Dunstan was now in his seventieth year, but his great gifts remained unimpaired and his spiritual zeal undiminished. Although Church and State were closely integrated it meant that no longer could the Church look to the throne for the same measure of encouragement and support which it had received during the years in which Dunstan had been the friend and counsellor of the five preceding kings.

The first three years of Aethelred's reign seemed to be prophetic fulfilment of the words spoken by Dunstan at his coronation. Raiding parties of Danes sacked Southampton and ravaged Thanet and parts of Cheshire. In 981 they sacked the monastery of St. Petroc, Cornwall, and pillaged the coasts of Cornwall and Devon. and a year later the coast of Dorset. When St. Petroc's monastery was sacked it was not the seat of the bishopric of Cornwall, as is shown by Dunstan's letter to Aethelred in which reference is made to St. Germans as the place of the 'bishop's-stool.' By this letter the archbishop sought to resolve a dispute concerning lands at one time held by the bishop of Crediton which he now advised should be surrendered to the bishop of Cornwall. Basing his advice on the evidence of events from Egbert's subjugation of Cornwall down to Edgar's command to consecrate Wulfsige, bishop of Cornwall, Dunstan now requested the king's confirmation of the estates to the bishop of Cornwall 'if God

and our lord grant them.' [34] Dunstan also mentioned the division of
the two bishoprics of Wessex during Edward's reign when Plegmund
consecrated 'five bishops where there were two before.' To another
western part of his extensive province he had consecrated Gucan to
the see of Llandaff and in 980 Aethelgar, abbot of New Minster,
Winchester, one of his former pupils at Glastonbury, to the see of
Selsey. Aethelgar followed a more moderate policy towards the seculars
and did not expel them from Selsey. This policy was followed by all
the bishops, with the exception of Aelfric, who was consecrated by
Dunstan during Aethelred's reign. Dunstan's attitude towards the
seculars grew more liberal during the last decade of his archiepiscopate
although it must be recognized that he never pursued a rigorous policy
against them similar to that of Bishop Aethelwold of Winchester.

Aethelwold had translated the remains of one of his predecessors
St. Swithun in 970 and the consequent liberality of pilgrims enabled
him to complete the major part of his cathedral. Its dedication in 980
was an event of national importance by the presence of Aethelred
and nearly all the lay nobles who went from a witenagemot at
Andover to Winchester. Ecclesiastically it was a significant occasion
for it was probably the last time in the western part of the province
that the authority of the archbishopric of Canterbury was to be seen
during Dunstan's archiepiscopate when he dedicated the church,
accompanied by Bishop Aethelwold and eight other bishops. In this
centre where perhaps monasticism was the strongest, Dunstan's
biographer observes there were among the lay nobles many who were
supporters of the seculars but at this time they became 'sheep instead
of wolves.'

Returning to his archbishopric Dunstan gave much attention to his
familia at Christ Church, but did not make any changes in its constitution. The administration of his extensive province necessitated
the consecration of bishops as sees fell vacant, and despite his absence
from court he exercised his influence in the choice of his suffragans,
as was to be seen when his counsel was followed in the election of
Aelfheah, abbot of Bath, to succeed to the see of Winchester on
Aethelwold's death in 984. Winchester and Abingdon by this time
had become the most distinguished centres of learning in the province,
and Dunstan in the manifold administrative duties of his archbishopric
used his teaching gifts in an endeavour to make Canterbury once
again a seat of learning. These endeavours were interrupted in 986
when Aethelred in a quarrel with Bishop Aelfstan of Rochester appro-
priated some lands belonging to his see. Meeting resistance, Aethelred
laid seige to the city but failing to take it he ravaged the lands of the
bishopric. Swift to defend the Church and the see of which he was
patron, Dunstan rebuked the king and threatened him with the anger

of St. Andrew in whose honour the cathedral had been dedicated.[35] Contemptuous of any threats he continued to ravage the bishopric and not until Dunstan offered him £100, which he accepted, did he withdraw his forces.

Archbishop Dunstan had distinguished himself in many important offices and a wide variety of subjects. He was monk and archbishop of the country (*archiepiscopus patriae*); statesman and counsellor of kings; ecclesiastical administrator and spiritual leader; philosopher and teacher; writer and reformer; redactor and illuminator of manuscripts; musician and composer; skilled in craftwork as the maker of bells and organs. All his gifts were dedicated to the service of God, a service which illumined all his labours and gave to his character a saintliness of life perceived by all. Under his guiding hand the lamp of learning again burned brightly in the archbishopric of Canterbury and once again its renown as a centre of scholarship and true religion was known throughout the land and on the Continent. Not only did he impart knowledge to his students but he also inspired them to serve God and their fellow-men in the Church. This was noted by his earliest biographer writing *c.* 1000, when he remarked on the number of Dunstan's pupils from Glastonbury Abbey who had attained episcopal orders. This was no exaggeration for twelve years after Dunstan's death in 988, two of his pupils had succeeded to the archbishopric of Canterbury and seven others at least had been or were bishops in the province of Canterbury.[36] His mortal remains were laid to rest near the altar of his cathedral church on the Sunday after Ascension Day in 988, but so great and so widely known was his sanctity of life that before the tenth century had ended he had found a place in the Church calendar.[37] His illustrious tenure of the chair of St. Augustine gave to the archbishopric of Canterbury greater distinction and authority than it had possessed for nearly three hundred years. And the reason for this, in the words of his first biographer, was because 'The whole of England is enlightened with his holy teaching.'

HOMILIES AND LEGISLATION: HOSTILITIES AND MARTYRDOM

The archbishopric of Canterbury under the guidance of Dunstan possessed unsurpassed influence in Church and State, and by his death one of the most illustrious chapters in the history of the archbishopric came to an end. During the remaining years of Aethelred's reign there was a gradual decline in the archbishopric's influence largely due to the unsettled conditions in the country caused by the invasions and hostilities of the Danes and, to a lesser extent, due to successive archbishops, although men of sanctity, lacking qualities of leadership and political judgment.

Aethelgar, a former pupil of Dunstan at Glastonbury whom he consecrated to the bishopric of Selsey, was translated to Canterbury. Fifteen months later he died, but during his short archiepiscopate he went to Rome for his *pallium*. Another of Dunstan's pupils named Sigeric, abbot of St. Augustine's, Canterbury, whom he later consecrated bishop of Ramsbury, was now translated to the vacant archbishopric.[1] Sigeric journeyed to Rome and received the *pallium* from Pope John XV, who had sent his legate, Bishop Leo of Treves, to arrange peace between Aethelred and Duke Richard I of Normandy.[2] Later in the same year, 991, in which Sigeric returned to England, further inroads were made by the invaders in Kent, Wessex and Hampshire. Archbishop Sigeric's counsel was immediately sought, but it differed much from the counsel which Dunstan had given during his archiepiscopate. Dunstan's pacific counsel was always based upon constant strength and preparedness to repel the invader. Sigeric, however, counselled a policy of buying peace from the foe. On this basis a treaty was arranged by the archbishop, the ealdormen Aelfric and Aethelweard by which the Danes undertook to keep the peace on payment by the English of £10,000. The Chronicler tersely records 'Archbishop Sigeric first advised that course.'[3]

The archbishop's gifts of scholarship enabled him to continue the labours of Dunstan who had established the archbishopric once again as a centre of learning. Sigeric's work at the school in Canterbury doubtless inspired Aelfric, abbot of Cerne, to dedicate his two series of homilies to him. In the preface he wrote: 'In the name of the Lord, I, Aelfric, a scholar of the benevolent and venerable prelate Aethelwold, send greeting to our master and lord, Archbishop Sigeric.' He tells the archbishop that his book contains expositions of the Gospels and also lives of the saints composed of forty discourses sufficient for the faithful throughout the year 'if they be read to them in the church by God's ministers.' Aelfric concludes his preface by entreating Sigeric to correct any doctrinal errors which he may find in the work and that 'this little work may be hence ascribed to your authority, and not placed to the credit of our insignificance.' [4] Sigeric's acceptance of Aelfric's homilies was shown by his request that they should be read in all the churches of his province. There can be little doubt that this encouragement given by the archbishop to the scholarly abbot inspired him to continue his literary labours to which reference is made later. Aelfric the homilist has been confused with three other Aelfrics, all of whom held high office in the Church.[5] Sigeric's patronage of the homilist, who became the first abbot of Eynsham in 1005, was not, as it has been thought, the Aelfric whom Sigeric probably consecrated in 990 bishop of Ramsbury. It was this Bishop Aelfric who succeeded to the archbishopric of Canterbury in 995 after Sigeric's death. In his efforts to maintain efficient episcopal administration and pastoral oversight in his province Aelfric did not let the lack of the *pallium* prevent him from consecrating bishops to the sees of Elmham, Llandaff, London, Rochester and probably Wells as they fell vacant. Not until 997, even though parts of his province in Cornwall, Devon and Wales were under invasion from the Danes, did he find it opportune to visit Rome for the *pallium*. Further raids were made the following year, and in 999 the archbishopric itself seemed threatened when the Danish fleets sailed up the Thames and Medway laying seige to Rochester and ravaging West Kent. The situation became so desperate for Aethelred's forces after Sussex, Devon and Somerset and the city of Exeter had been under attack that in 1002 a truce was made by the payment of £24,000 tribute money to the Danes. In the same year Aethelred married his second wife Emma, sister of Richard II, duke of Normandy. This event was destined to have unforeseen effects on both the political and ecclesiastical history of England.

One of the most remarkable features in the activities of the archbishopric of Canterbury and, indeed, the Church in England as a whole, under Sigeric and Aelfric was its astonishing resilience amidst all the stresses and disorganization caused by the Danish invasions. This in itself indicates to some extent the depth of the new life which had been imparted to the Church by the monastic revival. Nor had this revival ceased, for Aelfric was able to achieve what some of his predecessors had failed to do by removing the secular clergy from his cathedral of Christ Church and replacing them with monks in obedience to papal command.[6] Whether the community at this time became wholly monastic is open to some doubt in view of the uncertainty of the documentary evidence and the condition of the

community during the archiepiscopate of Aelfric's successor.[7] Whatever measures of reform Aelfric adopted were not oppressive, and it is
probable that the encouragement which he gave to Aelfric the homilist
induced Wulfsige, bishop of Sherborne, to seek his aid in his reforms
among his clergy. Knowing the literary gifts of the homolist, Wulfsige
requested him to write for him a pastoral letter which he could send
to all the clergy of his diocese. Addressing the bishop, Aelfric wrote
in his preface: 'Aelfric, an humble brother, to the venerable Bishop
Wulfsige, health in the Lord. We have readily obeyed your command; but have not presumed to write anything concerning the
episcopal office; because it is your part to know how to be an
example to all by excellent behaviour, and by your continual admonitions to persuade your subjects to be saved: which things I speak in
Christ Jesus because ye ought often to confer with your clergy, and
to reprove their negligence.' He then told the bishop that he had
written the pastoral letter or charge in English 'in such a manner
as if you yourself dictated it with your own mouth, and said to your
subjects of the clergy.' [8]

With almost startling abruptness the letter opens with the words:
'I tell you, priests, that I will not bear your neglects of your ministry.
And I tell you in good sooth how the matter stands with priests;
Christ established Christianity and chastity.' Of the first seven clauses
into which the charge is divided insistence is placed upon the celibacy
of the clergy, and the two following clauses deal with the question
of divorce. He then enumerates the seven orders in the Church and
their respective duties. Describing the functions of the presbyter or
mass-priest he says: 'He halloweth God's housel as our Saviour commanded: he ought by preaching to instruct the people in their belief,
and to give an example to Christians by the purity of his manners.'
He then points out that there is no difference between a bishop and a
priest, except a difference of function, for both have the same order
but the bishop's is more honourable. Mass-priests on Sundays and
mass-days were directed to explain the Gospel, the Lord's Prayer and
the Creed to the people in English so that they would know and
understand their faith. And the priest was reminded of his obligations
as a teacher. He must possess book-learning otherwise he would mislead
the laity through his ignorance. Tithes were now to be received in
church the priest then dividing them into three parts for the repair of
the church, the poor and for God's servants who attend the church.
A priest must remain for his life in the minster to which he was
ordained and must not move for gain to another. The whole of the
priest's life comes under review and directions are given concerning
his ministrations and manner of life. The canons open with reference
to priests' neglect of their ministry, and they draw to a close with

but little hope of the canons being observed because 'you priests love worldly conversation, choosing the office of reeves and abandoning your churches and even these decrees.' Earlier canons relating to the dress of the clergy had not been observed and once again priests are directed how they should dress. They should neither wear the habit of a monk nor dress like a layman but only wear the attire of their order.[9] Wulstan of York, who held the see of Worcester *in commendam,* although distinguished by his literary gifts requested Aelfric the homilist to provide him with a pastoral letter similar to that which he had supplied to Bishop Wulfsige. Since such measures were necessary in the dioceses of Sherborne and Worcester and in the northern archbishopric it would appear that the monastic revival had never been wholly effective in dioceses which did not possess monasteries from which their reforms spread and influenced the life of the ordinary clergy. Wulstan later found that in his own province further measures were required and in order to meet this situation he issued his 'Laws of the Northumbrian Priests.'[10]

Archbishop Aelfric of Canterbury and Wulstan of York in friendly co-operation laboured assiduously together to encourgae learning among the clergy and a more conscientious discharge of their ministerial functions among the people and in their churches. In the archbishopric itself Aelfric had already taken initial steps to remove the secular canons from his cathedral church and to install monks. This transformation and the maintenance of the fraternity was an expensive undertaking which the king regarded with such satisfaction that he granted privileges to Aelfric and confirmed to Christ Church its lands scattered over six counties.[11] Although Aethelred's reign was not peaceful, at one period being compelled to flee the country for his own safety, he was ever considerate of the needs of the Church. No less than sixty documents have survived which record his generous benefactions to ecclesiastics, churches and monasteries. Most of these royal gifts were to monastic foundations and indicate how fully he endeavoured to strengthen the reforms made before he came to the throne.[12] A conflict which arose between the king and the see of Rochester ended when Bishop Aelfstan died, and royal reparation was made by a benefaction to the see on Bishop Godwin's succession. This was no doubt due to Aelfric's influence who, later with the thanes of east and west Kent, gave favourable judgment in a case remitted to them by the king concerning Godwin's claim to land in Canterbury.[13] The monastic reform of his own cathedral of Christ Church could not immediately affect the problems concerning the clergy in the diocese. Similar problems existed in other dioceses of Aelfric's province but they were made more acute in his own diocese by the ravages of the Danes in west Kent. During Aelfric's rule at Canterbury his counsel to the king was such that out of the twelve bishops at least whom he consecrated only four were monks. Aelfgar, whom he consecrated to the see of Elmham in 1001, is particularly described as 'a priest of Canterbury.' [14] Aelfric's consecration of eight bishops drawn from the clergy during the ten years of his archiepiscopate indicates that his influence on the king's nominations was directed to meet an immediate need of an episcopate composed of men who possessed practical experience of the contemporary situation and conditions in which the clergy exercised their ministry, rather than an episcopate more acquainted with the internal disciplines of monastic life.

The contemporary conditions in England c. 1001 are vividly portrayed in Aelfric's will, which shows how widely the archbishopric was involved in the political affairs of the kingdom in addition to those which were his concern in matters relating to the Church. To King Aethelred he bequeathed his best ship, sixty helmets and sixty coats of mail. To the two counties of Kent and Wiltshire he gave each a ship [15]; and to the counties of Kent, Surrey and Middlesex to whom he had lent money, probably to meet tribute demanded of them by the Danes, he cancelled their debt. To the Church he was no less generous in his bequests. He bequeathed three estates to his cathedral of Christ Church. Successively he had served as a monk at Abingdon and abbot of St. Albans, and to each he left estates; to St. Albans where his brother Leofric was abbot, he left all his books and his (travelling) tent. Family bequests were made by him, and his executors were Abbot Leofric and Archbishop Wulstan who 'should act as seemed best to them.' Expressive of the friendship which existed between the two archbishops was Aelfric's bequest to Wulstan of a pectoral cross, ring and psalter, and to Aelfheah a crucifix.[16] The bequests made to the king and the shires by the archbishop show that during his lifetime he met not only his lawful obligations as a citizen but assisted others to do the same in the defence of the kingdom against the Danes.

While maintaining his archbishopric as a centre of learning his administration throughout the province of Canterbury was chiefly directed to the consolidation and expansion of the monasteries. In this the king evidently followed Aelfric's counsel and considerably strengthened monasticism by his many generous benefactions. This progress was jeopardized or destroyed by the Danes in 1006 when they occupied Sandwich and ravaged the south-east later raiding Hampshire and parts of Berkshire. On receiving tribute of £36,000 the Danes departed for a time.

After Aelfric's death, his friend Aelfheah, bishop of Winchester, a man of noble birth and an ardent advocate of Benedictine reform was translated to the archbishopric of Canterbury, and proceeded to Rome for the *pallium*. During a temporary lull from the invaders the new archbishop in collaboration with Wulstan, archbishop of York, formulated a series of laws relating to Church and State. They were promulgated in 1008 and are known as code (V Aethelred) [17] and in the same year another code was issued at Enham known as (VI Aethelred). Both of these codes are characterized by the distinctive literary style of Wulstan, and cover much the same ground although there are some differences of fact between them. The most acceptable explanation of the differences is that Wulstan was authorized to make any alterations to the code which he considered to be needful to meet the particular requirements of his northern province.[18] It would seem therefore that the code known as (V Aethelred) may be regarded here as being applicable to the province of Canterbury. The short prologue states 'This is the ordinance which the king of the English and both ecclesiastical and lay counsellors have approved and decreed.' One of the most remarkable features of these laws is that they were issued when conditions in the country were such that the code concludes with 'Let us loyally support our royal lord, and all together defend our lives and our land, as well as ever we can, and pray Almighty God from our inmost heart for His help.' Many of the people, because of the atrocities perpetrated by the invaders, were shaken in their adherence to the Christian Faith while others had adopted the heathen practices of the Danes. For this reason the first law enjoins that 'all shall love and honour one God and zealously hold one Christian faith, and entirely cast off heathen practices.' All present at the council had pledged themselves to hold 'one Christian faith under the rule of one king.' The laws relating to ecclesiastical matters reveal the extent to which they were shaped by Aelfheah. His insistence on the need for monastic reform had already been shown at his own cathedral, and this same zeal for the reform of the whole Church becomes a legal requirement that God's servants—bishops, abbots, monks, nuns, priests and women devoted to God—are to live according to their rule. Canons secular are required to live communally in refectory and dormitory, where the property made it possible, and in chastity; failure to do so carried the penalty of ejection from the property. Celibacy was also required of priests.

The protection of churches is the obligation of all Christians for the churches are under the protection of God, the king and all Christian people. Churches were no longer treated as other buildings such as mills and bartered for sale ; and no longer could a priest be expelled from his church without the bishop's consent.[19] Support of the Church came under review : not only were God's dues to be paid readily each year but they were to be advanced zealously as is needful. Christians are enjoined to confess and to atone for their sins ; to prepare regularly to partake of the Holy Eucharist; and carefully to keep oath and pledge. All these ecclesiastical laws are set in the context of a country at war or preparing for defence against the invader. Details for the maintenance of peace and other obligations are given for 'in future God's law is to be eagerly loved by word and deed; then God will at once become gracious to this nation.' The code concludes as it began, 'We must all love and honour one God and entirely cast out every heathen practice.'

Although this code reiterates much contained in earlier laws, it is specifically stated that this code is for the improvement of 'the country in religious and secular concerns.' [20]

Certain elements in the country were ready to forswear their Christian faith and to adopt heathen practices in order to obtain the relief which peace with the Danes would bring. With little persuasion others would willingly renounce their allegiance to Aethelred because of his weakness and misgovernment. Amidst these conditions the archbishopric of Canterbury still exercised great authority and was a stabilizing influence both to king and people. Aelfheah was a resolute character and practised the same ascetic manner of life as in the days when he was abbot of Bath. He set a splendid example by his allegiance to his Church and his loyalty to his king, and his way of life showed how piety and patriotism should go together hand in hand.

The year 1008 may be said to have been one of law making and ship building. By 1009 the nation possessed a great fleet which was at anchorage at Sandwich awaiting conflict with the Danes. Treachery and tempest weakened the English fleet to such an extent that it was unable to engage the enemy and sailed for the harbour of London, the Danes entering Sandwich and landing a great army which marched towards Canterbury. Perceiving the immediate threat to the city its citizens with the people of east Kent obtained peace from the Danes at a cost of £3,000. Later the Danes ravaged the counties of Sussex, Hampshire and Berkshire, and so grave had the situation become throughout England in 1009 that probably in August of that year an edict or code of laws known as (VII Aethelred) was decreed 'when the great army came to the country.' [21] The Latin version of the edict, as distinct from the Old English version, says the edict was decreed by Aethelred and his counsellors at Bath. It may have been written by Wulstan of York since two of his homilies make use of the code.[22] But the substance of the code undoubtedly follows the counsel given by Aelfheah to the king and his council, which was received and authorized. All the clauses of the code are firmly set in the context of a threat of national disaster in which the whole nation would be subjugated by the invader. In consequence the code is an authoritative call to national repentance giving precise instructions how the response to the call should be made, for 'all in common, ecclesiastics and laymen, are to turn eagerly to God and to deserve His mercy.' For three days a penitential fast was to be observed, presbyters and people going barefoot to church, there 'to call on Christ eagerly from their inmost hearts.' Slaves were to be made free for the three days so that they could go to church; and all members of a household were to bring their offerings to church. Every priest was to say a mass for the king and people; and in each minster every day another mass was to be said with special reference to the nation's urgent need 'until things become better.' [23] God's dues were to be paid correctly every year 'to the end that Almighty God may have mercy on us and grant that we may overcome our enemies. God help us. Amen.' The poignant cry 'God help us' was no empty cry. Within less than eighteen months after landing at Sandwich in 1009, as the Chronicler records, the Danes had overrun the whole or part of fifteen counties. In mid-September of 1011 Canterbury was besieged and by the treachery of Aelfmaer was betrayed.[24] Archbishop Aelfheah, Bishop Godwin of Rochester, monks and canons, Abbess Leofrun, the king's reeve and many others were taken captive, but Aelfmaer, abbot of St. Augustine's was allowed to go free.[25] When the archbishop refused to purchase his freedom for £3,000, Christ Church was plundered and destroyed by fire while crowded with people. Forbidding the people to pay the ransom by using the treasure of the churches, Aelfheah was fettered and dragged wounded to the Danish ships, and remained in prison seven months at Greenwich. The Chronicler's comment on this situation shows how deep-rooted in the minds of the people was the authoritative influence of the archbishopric of Canterbury during such calamitous days. Referring to Aelfheah he wrote, 'He was then a captive who had been head of the English people and of Christendom.' [26] To such good effect did Aelfheah use the months of his imprisonment that some of his captors were converted to the Christian Faith and were baptized by him. As the festival of Easter drew near in 1012 renewed demands were made for the payment of the ransom to preserve the archbishop's life. At this time the Danes were feasting and many were inebriated by the liberal supply of southern wines. Infuriated when the ransom was not forthcoming they pelted Aelfheah with ox-bones from the feast, mortally wounding him. A Dane nearby, supposed to have been one of Aelfheah's converts, struck him with his axe to put an end to the agony of his sufferings.[27] The Danish leaders on sober reflection, though thwarted in exacting the ransom, did not prevent the body of the archbishop being carried to London where it was received by Bishop Aelfhun of London, Bishop Eadnoth of Dorchester and the citizens, and interred in St. Paul's Cathedral.[28]

The people already staggering under the burden of raising tribute of £48,000 for the Danes to leave the country, which they had denuded of its wealth by their destructive ravages, were further demoralized by the murder of Alfheah whom they esteemed so highly that they regarded him as the head of the nation and of Christendom. His murder also reacted on the Danes themselves, for one of their prominent leaders named Thorkell the Tall, who it is said offered all his possessions excepting his own ship for the life of the arch-bishop, was so distressed by the barbaric murder perpetrated by his own countrymen that when they sailed from England he remained and with his fleet of forty-five ships joined the forces of Aethelred.[29] Thorkell's defection provided sufficient grounds for Swein of Denmark to launch an expedition against England which was so successful that Aethelred fled the kingdom for the court of his brother-in-law, Richard II of Normandy, to whom he had sent his wife Emma and their two sons accompanied by the bishop of London and the abbot of Peterborough. The throne now being unoccupied and Swein having military possession of the country 'all the nation regarded him as full king.'[30]

Throughout the years from 842 onwards Canterbury, the see city of the archbishopric, had repeatedly been subject to attacks from the Danes, and on no less than three occasions had been sacked.[31] Although Canterbury was accessible from the south-east coast and was the chief city of Kent it was not for these reasons alone that the Danes marched against it and stormed its walls. London was also accessible but probably more difficult to attack but its occupation militarily would have achieved more. But from the outset of their invasions the Danes had perceived the importance of the seat of the archbishopric because the occupant was the chief counsellor of the king and exercised an authority and influence over the nation which became more powerful when England was ruled by a weak king. So weak and uncertain had become the rule of King Aethelred and correspondingly so influential had the archbishopric of Canterbury become that when Archbishop Aelfheah was murdered by the Danes in 1012 he was regarded by the nation as its leader.

King Swein ruled only a few months and on his death early in 1014 his son, Cnut, was elected king by the Danes. Meanwhile the ecclesiastical and lay counsellors of the English assembled and sent messengers to Aethelred saying 'that no lord was dearer to them than their natural lord, if he would govern them more justly than he did before.'[32] Prior to Aethelred's leaving the country Lyfing, bishop of Wells, had been translated to the archbishopric of Canterbury which had remained vacant for nearly a year after Aelfheah's murder. Unable to enter his archbishopric he had accompanied the king to

Normandy, but on their return in 1014, with the advice of his counsellors, Aethelred issued an ordinance known as code (VIII Aethelred)
relating to matters concerning the Church. This code speaks of taking
for an example the decrees of Kings Aethelstan, Edmund and Edgar.
It would seem that Aethelred was not unmindful of the qualified
invitation which he had received from the people to return: for
emphasis is placed on the loyal support to be given to 'one royal
lord.' [33] Here, however, is to be seen how far the Christian conception
of kingship had developed in England. 'A Christian king is Christ's
deputy in a Christian people, and he must avenge very zealously
offences against Christ.' [34] It is upon this clause that the whole structure of the code is built, and there is little doubt that the guiding
hand throughout was that of Archbishop Lyfing, the king's chief counsellor. The identification of the Christian king as Christ's deputy
among Christian people doubtless accounts for the exhortatory character of the major part of the code. Regulations are given concerning
the right of sanctuary given by churches, their protection and compensation. Injunctions relating to the obligation of the payment of
tithes and other dues are made. One clause, which is without precedent, makes the celebration of a mass the criterion by which an
accused priest may vindicate himself: 'If a priest, who lives according
to a rule, is charged with a simple accusation, he is to say mass, if he
dares, and alone clear himself on the Host itself.' [35] The challenge
to the priest 'if he dares' reveals the discerning wisdom of the archbishop, without doubt, who would be aware that every priest would
know the implications of the Pauline dictum, 'Anyone who eats the
bread or drinks the cup of the Lord unworthily will be guilty of
desecrating the body and blood of the Lord.' [36] An attempt to halt
the decline in monastic discipline was made by desiring 'abbots and
monks to live more in accordance with the rule than they have been
in the habit of doing up till now.' [37] All people are urged to honour
the true Christian religion and utterly to despise all heathen practices.
This was the objective of Aethelred's rule, despite his weakness, after
he had regained his throne.

CANTERBURY AND CNUT'S ECCLESIASTICAL POLICY

The high hopes of the English people on King Aethelred's return never matured despite the ideals expressed in his ecclesiastical laws. By the ravages of the Danes and the devastation of the country-side the organization of the Church had been destroyed in some places and in others disrupted or impeded. Of the churches which had escaped destruction there were too few clergy to serve them. Though the monasteries were not unscathed they remained the most stable feature in the life of the Church. A bishop's pastoral care of his diocese had become a perilous undertaking for there was little respect for 'God's sevants.' Many people had abandoned the Christian Faith and sunk into heathenism, and even monks and priests had been known to forsake the Faith.[1]

By the destruction of Canterbury cathedral and the ecclesiastical buildings of the archbishopric and the murder of Aelfheah the Church in the province and the whole of the country was dealt such a blow from which it hardly recovered before the Norman Conquest. The lapse of over a year before Lyfing succeeded Aelfheah, his imprisonment for seven months by the Danes and then his absence from his archbishopric with the king in Normandy militated against the recovery of his archbishopric and the Church in the province.[2] During the archbishop's absence in Normandy Aelfwig was elected to the vacant see of London, his election probably being confirmed, in the absence of the king, by the council which invited Aethelred to return to his throne. Aelfwig did not await the return of Archbishop Lyfing but journeyed to York and there received consecration at the hands of Wulstan. On his return to England Lyfing, because of the uncertainty of the political situation and the needs of the Church in his province did not journey to Rome for the *pallium.* Consequently he exercised all his functions of metropolitan archbishop without the *pallium,* and during his archiepiscopate consecrated at least seven bishops for his province of Canterbury. Lyfing was a wise counsellor both in Church and State and is described as 'very wise both for God and the world.' Confronted by the departure of the monks and clergy who had survived in the sacked city of Canterbury, he was unable to do little more than re-roof his cathedral, restore the sanctuary and prepare plans for the rebuilding of accommodation in which monks and seculars were later to be housed. Christ Church, however, had lost its exclusive monastic character, which it possessed for a short time, by the Danes' latest occupation and destruction of the city. The warlike conditions which still prevailed in England on his return prevented Lyfing from any pastoral visitation of his province. Nevertheless, from the continuing benefactions of the king it is evident that the archbishop kept the king fully informed of the Church's needs and activities. Aethelred was not unmindful of the loyalty of the city of London and that the remains of the murdered Aelfheah rested in St. Paul's minster. Doubtless, following the counsel of Lyfing the king issued what was probably the last writ of his reign by which he declared that 'his priests in St. Paul's minster are to have their sake and soke within borough and without, and as good laws as ever they had in the days of any king or any bishop.' [3]

Although little is known of Lyfing's archiepiscopate there can be no doubt that it was the archbishop's counsel which he followed when Aethelred issued his laws in 1014. But they were powerless to arrest the decline of the Church and the moral decay of the nation. The pious exhortations of the laws are interspersed with laments that the standards both in Church and State which prevailed in Edgar's reign no longer existed. '. . . since the days of Edgar, Christ's laws have waned and the king's laws dwindled; and then was separated what had been common to Christ and the king in secular penalties, and ever things grew worse in Church and State; may they now improve, if it is God's will.' [4] These laws give in outline a picture of England at that time, but the completed picture is to be seen in 'The Sermon to the English' preached by Wulstan, archbishop of York, in 1014 or between the year of the king's flight to Normandy in 1013 and his death in 1016. [5] The reason why 'things go from bad to worse,' says Wulstan, is 'because of the sins of the people.' A general neglect of the Christian religion was to be seen in the way the bishops, abbots, priests and monks had been deprived of protection and respect—men in holy orders being injured. Churches had been violated and despoiled of their ancient privileges, and Christians had been sold into slavery overseas. So irreligious had the nation become that 'God's laws are hated and His precepts despised.' There was also great disloyalty in matters relating both to Church and Throne; and successive defeats over a long period, expressive it was said of God's anger, had greatly disheartened the people. Wulstan of York in his historic sermon compared the country's condition with that of the Britons about whom Gildas wrote: 'We know worse deeds among the English than we have heard of anywhere among the Britons.' Wulstan pleaded 'let us love God and follow God's laws and perform very eagerly what we promised when we received baptism.' [6] Archbishop Lyfing was a spiritually minded man and had faithfully discharged the demanding responsibilities of his high office and had proved himself a wise counsellor to Aethelred. Nevertheless, during this period of national degeneracy and the prevailing warlike conditions the influence of the archbishopric of Canterbury reached a very low ebb.

King Swein's son Cnut left the country only to return in the summer of 1015, later occupying Essex. During his preparations to besiege London Aethelred died and Edmund, surnamed Ironside, was chosen king by the citizens. He fiercely defended his throne but finally was decisively defeated at Ashingdon in Essex when Bishop Eadnoth of Dorchester and Abbot Wulfsige of Ramsey, who were present to pray for Edmund's victory, were slain with almost all the English nobility. Peace was made on the basis of a partition of the country, Edmund and Cnut each ruling over a part. On Edmund's death in 1016 Wessex, over which he had ruled, accepted Cnut as king and he was crowned by Lyfing.[7] In this last recorded national act of the archbishop was shown the pre-eminent position of the primatial archbishopric of Canterbury and its recognition by Cnut. The new king had been baptized into the Christian Church long before he set foot on English soil,[8] but this did not restrain him from putting to death without trial four leading Englishmen who had fought against him. From the outset of his reign Cnut showed a friendly interest in the Church, a respect for its spiritual authority and increasing devotion to its teaching. The intimate relationship which existed between him and the archbishop of Canterbury enabled Lyfing to tell him that his cathedral of Christ Church no longer possessed the privileges which it formerly had. Cnut authorized Lyfing to compile a new list of the privileges which he then approved. Afterwards, visiting the restored sanctuary of Christ Church, the king, in the presence of witnesses, placed upon the altar a deed by which he confirmed to Christ Church all the privileges it had formerly possessed.[9] At the same time he regarded the Church as an integral part of his realm over which he exercised authority : and in confirming a grant of land to Burhwold, bishop of Cornwall, in 1018, he refers to him as 'a most faithful bishop of mine.'[10] His kingly authority over the Church was further shown when, without consultation with chapter or the witan, he issued his mandate to Wulstan, archbishop of York, directing him to consecrate Aethelnoth, archbishop of Canterbury, in succession to Lyfing who had died. Aethelnoth was of noble birth and is described by William of Malmesbury as first among the great and learned men of his day, and the seventh monk of Glastonbury to become archbishop of Canterbury. When Cnut appointed him he was 'monk and dean of Christ Church,' and senior chaplain to the king.[11] Archbishop Wulstan of York consecrated Aethelnoth at Canterbury in November 1020, and afterwards informed King Cnut in a letter which is of extraordinary interest since it was written by one who for many years had considerably influenced affairs of Church and State, and was probably the foremost in his contribution to the literature of his times. Addressing the king, he wrote 'Archbishop Wulstan greets humbly King Cnut his lord and lady Aelfgifu. And I inform you both, beloved, that we have acted concerning Bishop Aethelnoth according as notice came from you : that we have now consecrated him. Now I pray for the love of God and for all God's saints that you may show that respect to God and to the holy order that he may be entitled to all those things which the others before him were, Dunstan who was good, and many another ; that this man also may be entitled to rights and dignities. That will be profitable for you both in religious concerns and also becoming in secular concerns.' [12] In response to this letter the king issued a writ in which he informed 'in friendship all my bishops and all my earls and my reeves in every shire in which Archbishop Aethelnoth and the community at Christ Church hold land' that he had granted the temporalities of the archbishopric to Aethelnoth, and that any violation of this grant would be 'on pain of forfeiting my friendship.' [13] Three years later he granted the haven of Sandwich to Christ Church with all the 'landing and dues of both sides of the stream' for the subsistence of the monks, having first of all laid his 'kingly crown' upon Christ's altar in Canterbury for the benefit of the monastery.[14] Aethelnoth continued the restoration of the buildings within his immediate archbishopric initiated by his predecessor but did not re-establish an exclusive monastic community, and secular canons living under their rule again found a place at Christ Church. But his labours for the revival of the Church extended throughout his province.

Before Aethelnoth's appointment to the archbishopric, Wulstan, archbishop of York, accompanied by several bishops, had consecrated a stone minster at Ashingdon which Cnut had erected in thanksgiving for the decisive victory he had gained there. This evidently set the pattern, followed in the early years of Aethelnoth's archiepiscopate, by which he gave encouragement to the king's determination to restore monasteries and churches which had been partly destroyed during the military operations of himself or his father. In every place where he had fought a battle Cnut founded a church and placed a priest in charge of it. Under the archbishop's guidance and by the king's practical measures for the well-being of the Church, the monasteries were strengthened and the ministry of the clergy at minsters and churches again effectively influenced the life of the nation. All these activities are evidences that the ancient Church of the English with its age-long and venerable traditions had awakened in Cnut a sense of his responsibilities to the Church which he strove conscientiously to fulfil.

After the religious life of the nation had been given this new impetus Aethelnoth journeyed to Rome in 1022 where he was received with great honour by Pope Benedict VIII, who bestowed upon him the *pallium*. The archbishop was accompanied to Rome by Leofwine, abbot of Ely, who had been wrongfully driven from his abbey. His case was heard by the papal court which cleared the abbot of the accusations made against him.[15]

While in Rome it would appear that reference was made to the martyrdom of Aelfheah, for on Aethelnoth's return he obtained permission from Cnut to remove the remains of the martyr from St. Paul's, London, for re-interment in the cathedral Church of Christ, Canterbury. It is recorded by the Chronicler that in June 1023, 'The illustrious king and the archbishop, and the diocesan bishops, and the earls, and very many ecclesiastics and also lay-folk conveyed his (Aelfheah's) holy body on a ship across the Thames to Southwark, and there entrusted the holy martyr to the archbishop and his companions.' With due ceremonial the remains were re-interred at the north side of the altar in Christ Church by Aethelnoth and the bishops of Winchester and Wells.

At this time Cnut's policy, in which he was fully supported by Aethelnoth, for the unification of the English and the Danes in England into one people, a policy which had been initiated by Edgar assisted by Dunstan in the tenth century, now led to other activities concerning Denmark over which Cnut had ruled since 1019. It was Cnut's other kingdom which now provided the English Church with an opportunity for missionary expansion under the aegis of the archbishopric of Canterbury.

English missionaries had been evangelizing in Scandinavia in the tenth century, and a missionary bishop, named John, had baptized Olaf Tryggvason before his invasion of England. While in England Olaf received further instruction in the Christian Faith from Aelfheah, and on his return to Norway in 995 he took with him bishops and priests from England to evangelize his kingdom.[16] King Cnut, however, devised a plan for his kingdom of Denmark by which the Church would be episcopally administered under the archbishopric of Canterbury as a part of its province. He sent many bishops from England to Denmark among whom were three priests bearing German names whom he sent to Aethelnoth for consecration. The three bishops, Bernard, Gerbrand and Reinhart were for the dioceses respectively of Scania, Roskilde and Fionia.[17] These three dioceses were within the metropolitical jurisdiction of Unwan, archbishop of Bremen, and he showed his displeasure in no uncertain terms when he learned that at Cnut's request Aethelnoth had consecrated three bishops to serve within his province. Before Gerbrand arrived in the diocese of Roskilde Archbishop Unwan demanded from him a profession of canonical obedience before he would allow him to exercise his episcopal functions within the diocese. Shortly afterwards Unwan sent legates carrying his gifts and congratulations to Cnut on his government of England and a rebuke for his presumption in sending bishops from England into his province. Cnut replied graciously and agreed that in future he would observe Unwan's metropolitical rights. This missionary activity of the English Church accorded well with the traditions established by Boniface, Willibald and Willibrord. There can be little doubt that the missionary enterprises of the English Church towards the end of the tenth century and the early decades of the eleventh received their initial impetus from the monastic revival.[18] Despite the ravages of the Danes and their calamitous effects on the Church the missionary activities of Cnut's reign show that true religion had not perished among the people. Once again the archbishopric of Canterbury, under the discerning leadership of Aethelnoth, ably supported by Cnut, had guided the Church in England into a resurgence of life which found expression in the expansion of the Church beyond its own shores.

Cnut's sense of royal obligation to the Church sprang from deep religious devotion rather than a desire to attain political power. But it is evident that his pilgrimage to Rome in 1027 was inspired by both of these. While in Rome he was present at the coronation of the Emperor Conrad with whom he negotiated privileges for merchants and pilgrims passing through his territories which bordered Cnut's own frontier. Aethelnoth, before Cnut set out on his pilgrimage, had fully informed the king of the burdensome amount of money, demanded by custom from archbishops when they visited Rome to obtain the *pallium*. In this Aethelnoth had been supported by Aelfric, archbishop of York, who received the *pallium* in 1026 at Rome from Pope John XIX. During the pontificate of Gregory the Great the council of Rome in 595 abolished all fees at the bestowal of the *pallium*.[19] A voluntary gift remained permissible but within sixty years the payment of fees had again become the accepted practice, until they had reached such intolerable proportions that Cnut obtained from the pope a decree which stated that no longer would archbishops petitioning for the bestowal of the *pallium* be required to pay such large fees. Having obtained this concession from the pope, Cnut while still in Rome sent a special messenger, Abbot Lyfing, bearing a letter conveying the information to 'Aethelnoth, metropolitan, and Aelfric, archbishop of York, and to all the bishops and prelates, and to the whole nation of the English, both the nobles and the commons.'[20] The benefits of this reform were eroded by the permissible voluntary offerings which gradually increased since no metropolitan suppliant would wish to appear ungenerous when petitioning for this papal dignity. This was not the first time that problems had arisen in the Church in

England concerning the *pallium*.[21] But this was not peculiar to
England, for the Church on the Continent had its own problems
after the significance of the *pallium* had been revived by Boniface.[22]

Cnut's letter was not solely concerned with this matter of the
pallium. After informing the recipients of the letter that he had made
peace with the surrounding nations he directs them to their obligations to God, himself and the Church. 'I now command you,' he
wrote, 'and adjure all my bishops and governors of my kingdom, by
the duty they owe to God and myself, to take care that before I come
to England all dues belonging to God, according to the old laws, be
fully discharged.' Details of these dues are given and special mention
is made of the first-fruits of grain payable 'to every one's parish
church' (ciric-sceat). This letter with all the ecclesiastical details had
been written probably by Lyfing, abbot of Tavistock, who had accompanied the king to Rome as his chaplain. Mention of laws in his
letter referred to the codes known as (I & II, King Cnut) which were
issued, no doubt, before the death of Archbishop Wulstan of York in
1023 whose style they carry. No less than a quarter of Cnut's extensive
laws is entirely concerned with ecclesiastical matters. They cover
much the same ground as earlier laws by Aethelred and Edgar, and
are exhortatory in character enjoining upon clergy and laity alike
obedience to the laws of God, the king and the Church.[23] Upon the
Christian laity was laid the obligation of knowing the *Pater Noster*
and the *Credo* so that 'with the one the Christian could pray to God
and with the other declare his right faith.' A learned episcopate able
to teach and interpret the faith was desired by the king, who reminded
bishops that they were preachers or heralds *praecones* and interpreters
of God's laws; and that both bishops and mass-priests should protect
the flock of God by their wise instruction.[24]

Cnut's liberal benefactions to the Church were to the benefit of both
monks and secular clergy. On occasion it would appear that he
regarded monks as living on a higher spiritual level than the secular
clergy. On the other hand, however, he surrounded himself at court
with secular clergy who were his royal chaplains. His ecclesiastical
policy was largely influenced by the counsel which came from the
archbishopric of Canterbury during the archiepiscopates of Lyfing and
Aethelnoth. It was no new departure for Cnut to have chaplains at
his court. Many Anglo-Saxon kings had had their own chaplains, and
during King Alfred's reign owing to the movement of his court from
place to place a chaplain at court became a necessity. The most
notable of Alfred's chaplains was Asser who became his biographer
and bishop of Sherborne. These royal mass-priests were the guardians
of the king's *halidom,* relics, and did the writing which was required
at court. King Edgar had two distinct bodies of chaplains, and in his

will be made bequests to his chaplains who had the charge of his relics and smaller bequests to the priests of his household. It appears, however, that Cnut constituted a 'royal chapel' of chaplains of a similar character to those which existed at the court of Conrad and other European rulers with whom he had become friendly on his visit to Rome. This would probably account for his 'royal chapel' including not only English priests but also Lotharingians. These clerks were available for preparing the royal writs which Cnut increasingly issued without waiting for the confirmation of the witenagemot or national council.

To the office of royal chaplain came greater importance when the former chaplain Eadsige was elevated to the highest ecclesiastical office in the kingdom. Prior to this another royal chaplain Duduc, a Lotharingian, had been appointed bishop of Wells, while Wythmann, a German, received the abbacy of Ramsey. Both Harold and Hardacnut in turn were very much dependent upon their secular chaplains in ecclesiastical and secular affairs, and for their services to the king were rewarded by ecclesiastical preferment although they were more acquainted with political matters than the spiritual concerns of the Church. It also made the royal chaplains so desirous of preferment that some degraded their office by resorting to simony. From among his chaplains Cnut found suitable men for high preferment and later a similar practice was expanded by King Edward the Confessor. It was one of his chaplains, Eadsige, whom Cnut appointed in 1035 to be bishop in the diocese of Canterbury with his seat in the city at St. Martin's Church and made provision for his maintenance.[25] Eadsige was a priest whom it would appear the king intended to nominate to the archbishopric whenever it became vacant, since he required Eadsige to be made a monk at the monastery of Folkestone.[26] Having been cucullated this precluded any possibility of objection to his elevation, on the grounds that he was not a monk, by the community of Christ Church and the monastery of St. Augustine. In his office as chaplain he would have been known to Aethelnoth and probably of some assistance to him as chief adviser to the king, and it is most likely that Eadsige's appointment was made at the archbishop's request or was in full accord with his wishes. Eadsige's consecration by Aethelnoth to the see of St. Martin's Church as a suffragan bishop or *chorepiscopus* within the diocese of Canterbury would have given him authority to exercise episcopal functions including ordinations, confirmations, the consecration of churches and in the archbishop's absence to exercise his authority in the city and diocese. Cnut's appointment of Eadsige and Eadsige's consecration of a Canterbury suffragan after becoming archbishop raises the much debated question concerning the existence of *chorepiscopi* in the

P

English Church. Over what period and how often the see of
St. Martin's was occupied is uncertain. But evidence of its suppression
during the archiepiscopate of Lanfranc is to be found in a fragment
of a document which records that he suppressed the office of
chorepiscopus at Canterbury, which had been established by Archbishop Theodore with the authority of Pope Vitalian.[27]

In the same year, 1035, of Bishop Eadsige's consecration Aethelnoth
was summoned to Shaftesbury where Cnut lay dying. The king was
much concerned about his successor to the English throne. His marriage to Aelfgifu had never been recognized by the Church, and when
he married King Aethelred's widow, Emma, she was received as his
lawful wife. At their marriage Cnut gave some kind of undertaking
concerning the succession of the sons of their union. Before Cnut had
made his throne secure and the nation had been united under his
kingship he had perceived that the archbishopric of Canterbury was
the symbol of stability, unity and continuity. At his bedside was
Aethelnoth the representative of the stability, unity and continuity of
the Church in England and to him Cnut now turned for the assurance
that when he died his undertaking to Queen Emma would be fulfilled.
After Cnut's death and his burial in Old Minster, Winchester, the
nation was divided on the question of succession to the throne. Harold,
and Hardacnut, about whom there was some doubt, were claimed to
be sons of Cnut's alliance with Aelfgifu and rightful claimants to the
throne. The situation caused by Hardacnut's delay in Denmark was
resolved by a council at Oxford when Harold was made regent, but on
Hardacnut's continued absence from the country Harold was chosen
king by his followers and presented himself before Aethelnoth,
probably at Winchester, for coronation. Aethelnoth carried the crown
with him from Christ Church, Canterbury, where Cnut had placed
it upon the altar in 1023. Having arrived at the place where Harold
desired to be crowned, the archbishop placed the crown and sceptre
on the altar in seeming preparation for the ceremony. Harold commanded and prayed Aethelnoth to consecrate him, to crown him and
to give him the sceptre and 'that he should be led by the archbishop,
since it was not legal that this should be done by another, to the lofty
throne of the kingdom.'[28] Archbishop Aethelnoth, in a scene full of
drama, addressed him 'I lay the sceptre and crown upon the holy
altar, and to you I neither refuse nor give them; but by my apostolic
authority, I forbid all bishops that any one of them should remove
these things, or give them to you or consecrate you.' [29] In this way
Aethelnoth uncompromisingly fulfilled his solemn undertaking to his
late king. Not only was Aethelnoth the custodian of the crown and
sceptre, entrusted to him by Cnut, but the occasion revealed most
clearly the primatial authority of the archbishopric of Canterbury in

a situation involving a grave constitutional issue. All the bishops, including the archbishop of York, of the Church in England, some of whom may have had political sympathies differing from those of Aethelnoth, gave unswerving loyalty in their recognition and preservation of the prerogatives of the archbishopric.

At this period the influence of the archbishopric of Canterbury in the affairs of state was without doubt the chief stabilizing power in the kingdom. Archbishop Aelfric of York, whom Aethelnoth had consecrated, continued the close co-operation which had been established between the two archbishoprics during Wulstan's archiepiscopate, so that both provinces laboured together for the common good of the Church, and of the whole country even when it was divided between the two rulers Harold and Hardacnut. Loyally supported by King Cnut, Aethelnoth had led the Church into a resurgence of life which had found expression in missionary activities in Scandinavia and the maintenance of ecclesiastical relationships with other European countries. He had consecrated more men of other races probably than any of his predecessors. In addition to three bishops, apparently of German origin, he also consecrated Duduc, one of Cnut's clerks, to the bishopric of Wells, and Joseph and Bleduc respectively to the sees of Llandaff and St. Davids.[30] And when Aethelnoth died in 1038 a great epoch in the history of the archbishopric of Canterbury came to an end. Already there were indications of ecclesiastical changes in the province which would adversely affect the authority and influence of the archbishopric, and the country was divided in its political allegiance. There was no delay in King Harold's appointment of Bishop Eadsige of St. Martin's, Canterbury to the vacant chair of St. Augustine. Eadsige was well qualified to adjust the archbishopric to the new situation which was emerging in Church and State and in their relationship to each other. Having served as chaplain to the king he knew the demands of secular affairs as they impinged on the ecclesiastical; and having become a monk he was conscious of the need for spiritual disciplines within the Church; and having served as suffragan bishop within the city and diocese of Canterbury he had gained from Aethelnoth a knowledge of purposeful administration for the well-being of the Church and kingdom.

At the outset of his archiepiscopate he was confronted with the political rivalries and dissensions of Harold's reign which had an adverse effect on the administration of the Church. Through the influence of Godwin, the powerful earl of Wessex, Lyfing, bishop of Crediton and Cornwall, obtained in addition to his own bishopric the see of Worcester. Stigand, the king's chaplain, and Grymketel with scheming and bribery tried to obtain bishoprics but were thwarted at this juncture in their efforts probably by Archbishop Eadsige, who in such circumstances felt the lack of spiritual authority which possession of the *pallium* might have given. But it was not until 1040 after Harold's death and the succession of Hardacnut that he found it opportune to visit Rome for the *pallium*. During his absence strife broke out in the diocese of Worcester after the deprivation of Lyfing of his see and its occupation by Archbishop Aelfric of York because Lyfing and earl Godwin were suspected by the king of being chiefly responsible for the death of Alfred the elder son of King Aethelred. Within a short time both were restored to favour and Lyfing was reinstated in his bishopric. Hardacnut only reigned two years and before his burial at Winchester in 1042 the citizens of London led by Archbishop Eadsige, earl Godwin and Bishop Lyfing with acclamation received Edward the younger son of Aethelred as king of England. On Easter Day in 1043 Edward was anointed king by Eadsige assisted by the archbishop of York and nearly all the bishops of the land.

Whatever political issues may have delayed Edward's coronation the intervening months had given the archbishop opportunity to discern what might be the new king's emerging qualities of kingship. The king's upbringing in Normandy of necessity had shaped his character and religious outlook, and on coming to England Robert, abbot of Jumièges, had accompanied him or followed him soon after. Between Edward and Robert there existed a deep friendship the bonds of which had been made stronger by some service Robert had rendered Edward while in Normandy. At Edward's court Abbot Robert was without doubt the prime mover in transforming and expanding the royal chapel.[31] Lotharingians who had served under Cnut were replaced by Normans among whom were the priests William and Ulf. This chancery or chapel soon began to exercise a wider influence in governmental affairs to such an extent that it diminished the influence which the archbishopric of Canterbury over many centuries had traditionally exercised.

Edward's training in Normandy coupled with his religious disposition had given him a deep respect for ecclesiastics, and there was no lack of high regard for Eadsige, primate of all England, whose influence in political as well as ecclesiastical affairs he had observed when he was acclaimed king. But now the royal chapel dominated by Abbot Robert was increasing in power and Edward was more and more following its counsel. Being fully aware of this, Eadsige therefore made the coronation an occasion for giving the new king admonitory instruction in the sacred obligations of kingship.[32] Nevertheless, the influence of Robert of Jumièges increased and was still further strengthened when in 1044 the king appointed him to the bishopric of London. He encouraged the king to appoint Normans to high office in the country and high preferment in the Church. All these changes which affected Eadsige and the Church in general made the demands of the administration of the archbishopric more exacting. In consequence Eadsige made known his need for episcopal assistance to the king, and privately to earl Godwin, and was given authority to consecrate Siward, abbot of Abingdon, as his suffragan in the city and diocese of Canterbury with the title of bishop of Upsala.[33] At his consecration Siward was given the assurance that he would succeed to the archbishopric. His appointment was unable to prevent Eadsige from a nervous breakdown which made him incapable of administering the archbishopric and of performing his archiepiscopal functions. The close friendship which existed at this time, after Godwin had given the king his daughter in marriage, between Edward and the earl, led the king to consult the earl about the archbishopric, which he placed in sequestration and authorised Siward to assume the oversight of the archiepiscopal see. Siward was so ill-natured towards the sick archbishop that he scarcely allowed him the bare necessities of life. While the archbishopric was in sequestration, Eadsige being still alive, Siward subscribed to documents describing himself as archbishop.[34] However, Eadsige recovered his health and entered fully into the responsibilities of the archbishopric again. Shortly after, Siward fell ill and died in 1048, being outlived by Eadsige.

At this period King Edward initiated measures which affected the Church and nation. Having petitioned the pope for his consent, he transferred the see of Crediton to Exeter, and from earlier codes compiled a corpus of ecclesiastical law attributed to him.[35]

In his appointment of bishops and abbots Edward continued to regard such preferments as rewards for the secular service at court of his chaplains, who were proficient in political affairs but generally devoid of knowledge in spiritual matters. On his return to his see Eadsige found that the king had nominated no less than four of his chaplains to bishoprics during the period that Bishop Siward had the oversight of the archbishopric.[36] Stigand, a former king's chaplain, having relinquished Elmham, on securing for himself the see of Winchester from the king, succeeded in having his brother Aethelmaer consecrated bishop of Elmham. It was probably through the influence of Bishop Robert that the king appointed Ulf, one of his Norman chaplains, to the see of Dorchester and invested him with a pastoral staff. Since Eadsige was too ill to consecrate him, Ulf, in his eagerness to receive consecration, crossed the Channel to Vercelli, where the pope had convoked an ecclesiastical council, and sought consecration from some of the bishops attending the council. On examining Ulf they found him well-informed concerning secular affairs but having little knowledge of ecclesiastical matters and imperfect in the divine office. Having been refused consecration, Ulf produced a large sum of money and after some bartering he received consecration. This was no doubt the most discreditable appointment made by Edward, who, despite his religious scruples, continued to regard high preferment for his chaplains as a reward for their successful discharge of secular business at his court. This appointment was doubtless made on the advice of Robert of Jumièges, who, as bishop of London, was in a stronger position to influence the king although his influence was often countered by the powerful earl Godwin who still possessed the confidence of the king.

ARCHBISHOPRIC, PAPACY AND THRONE

When Archbishop Eadsige died in 1050 the question of ecclesiastical appointments became a grave issue in which the archbishopric of Canterbury was involved. English sees and abbeys when they became vacant were filled by the witenagemot electing persons whom the king had nominated. A bishopric was 'given' by the king's writ and seal, he himself placing in the hand of the bishop-elect a pastoral staff. In general the community of the cathedral church of the diocese with the king's consent proceeded to the election of their bishop, but in some instances the community elected to the bishopric and then petitioned the king for his confirmation of their choice. This latter procedure was now adopted at Christ Church. They elected Aelfric, a monk of their own community with exceptional gifts and eminently suitable.[1] The monks of St. Augustine's fully agreed with his election and pressed Aelfric's claims upon his kinsman, earl Godwin. It was at this juncture that the appointment to the archbishopric began to assume political implications.

Although the authority and influence of the archbishopric had declined since Edward became king the primacy still possessed its inherent rights and potentialities as the highest office close to the throne. Godwin already virtually possessed political dominance of the kingdom and if his kinsman, Aelfric, became archbishop of Canterbury he would have been in a position still further to extend his power in the country. The archbishop of Canterbury alone possessed the right of receiving from the people their acceptance of the king to rule over them. He alone required the king to swear on oath that he would rightly govern his people. It was for the archbishop of Canterbury alone lawfully to take the king by the hand and to lead him to the throne.[2] He alone could anoint, consecrate, place the crown upon the head of the king and the sceptre in his hand. With Aelfric duly installed in the archbishopric Godwin would have brought himself effectively within the shadow of the throne and before long would have tried to grasp the substance of it.

Whether King Edward discerned this or not, there is little doubt that Bishop Robert and the Normans at court regarded Godwin's presentation of the petition for Aelfric's appointment as another attempt to gain further power for the English party of which he was the leader. Godwin's success in this would have been a defeat for Robert of Jumièges and a drastic curtailment of the influence of the Norman tradition which Edward had supported since he became king.

It would appear that Godwin's political ascendancy in the country had led him to under-estimate the strength of the bonds of friendship which bound Edward and Robert together, and the powerful influence which Robert exercised over the king. Although eminent in ecclesiastical affairs Robert was continually involved in political intrigue, and his influence over the king was not good. But so complete was Edward's confidence in Robert that a Chronicler observed 'if the bishop said a black crow was white the king would have believed the bishop more than his own eyes.' [3]

In a similar context another writer considered the bishop exercised a bad influence over the king and quoted the Pauline dictum 'Bad company is the ruin of a good character.' [4] The king rejected Godwin's petition for the appointment of Aelfric and at his Lenten council in 1051 nominated Bishop Robert to the archbishopric much to the disapproval of the community of Christ Church and the Church in general. This setback to Godwin and his party was to some extent alleviated by Edward's nomination of Spearhafoc, abbot of Abingdon, and a supporter of Godwin, to the bishopric of London now vacated by Robert.

Now that Robert was archbishop his greater power only served to reinforce his hostility against Godwin and his party. But without delay he set out for Rome to obtain his *pallium* from Pope Leo IX, who already had some knowledge of conditions in England from the bishop of Wells and the two abbots who in 1047 had attended the council of Rheims, and from bishops Ealdred and Herman who had visited Rome on the king's behalf. From the pope they had obtained a dispensation releasing Edward from his vow to make a pilgrimage to Rome. In granting the dispensation Leo had commanded the king to build or restore a monastery : this command he obeyed and erected Westminster Abbey.[5] While in Rome Robert informed the pope of Edward's nomination of Spearhafoc to succeed him in the see of London. It was known that Spearhafoc, a skilled craftsman in gold, had made a crown and had presented it to the king.[6] Knowing Leo's zeal for Church reform, Robert, in his opposition to Godwin's party, may have hinted at an element of simony in the gift which the king had received from the abbot. Whatever may have transpired between the pope and the archbishop the outcome of the meeting became evident on Robert's return to England when Abbot Spearhafoc, seeking consecration from Robert, presented the king's writ of appointment to the see of London. The archbishop informed Spearhafoc that he had been forbidden by the pope to consecrate him. Neither the exhibition of the royal writ which Spearhafoc had received from the king nor his defiant possession of the temporalities of the see proved of any avail. Confronted by this unique situation by which his royal writ was set aside by the pope and in consequence rejected by his friend Archbishop Robert, Edward bowed to the inevitable, and issued another writ nominating William, a Norman, one of his chaplains, to the bishopric of London, whom the archbishop duly consecrated. While the significance of the constitutional and ecclesiastical issues raised by the pope's action which involved both the archbishopric and the throne should not be unduly stressed it proved itself to be, in the light of future events, the beginning of the Apostolic See exercising a greater influence in Church and State in England.

Encouraged by his successes, in using the full weight of the authority which the archbishopric now gave him, in thwarting Godwin's influence in two of the most important ecclesiastical appointments, Robert aroused still further antagonism when he claimed that land occupied by Godwin adjoining Church lands really belonged to his archbishopric. This was bitterly disputed and compelled Godwin to complain to the king about the archbishop's intrigues, which also became evident at court where, in the king's presence, Robert repeatedly accused Godwin of the murder of Alfred, the king's elder brother. These accusations and an armed encounter by Godwin with Edward's brother-in-law, Eustace of Boulogne, when visiting England, roused the anger of the king and almost precipitated civil war which was only averted through the intervention of earl Leofric. Godwin's banishment was imminent and in a last effort to secure a reconciliation Bishop Stigand, who enjoyed Godwin's patronage, intervened but without success. Finally, at a council in London in 1051 Godwin and his family were outlawed. Prior to this, the archbishop had taken most irregular action in trying to persuade the king to separate from his wife contrary to the law of the Church, thus dishonouring his high office and discrediting the religious influence of the archbishopric in order to accomplish his political designs.[7] King Edward was obdurate in his refusal to separate from his wife, Edith, although she was the daughter of Godwin, but sent her for safety to the nunnery at Wilton where she had been educated. His confidence in Robert appears to have remained unshaken for soon after he sent him on an embassy to William of Normandy, whom Edward wished to be regarded as his heir to the throne. For the first time during Edward's reign his court was free from contending parties which had been led by Robert of Jumièges and Godwin. In this freedom from contention, Godwin being in exile, there was an immediate resurgence of the ecclesiastical and political influence of the archbishopric of Canterbury while Robert was the chief adviser of the king. But this resurgence was to be short lived. A Norman himself, the archbishop's activities were chiefly in favour of strengthening Norman influence in the country regardless of the ill-effects on the English people. Edward willingly advanced the archbishop's policy by bestowing his patronage on the Normans to such an extent that the English hated the foreigners, especially those in positions of authority 'who instituted bad laws and judged unrighteous judgment, and brought bad counsels to the land.' [8]

The situation in the country grew worse, and the knowledge that the king wished the Duke of Normandy to succeed him added still more to the people's discontent and hostility. Learning of these conditions Godwin arrived with a fleet at Southwark and was assured by the citizens of London of their support. When conflict seemed imminent, Godwin having the initiative the king was willing to discuss peace terms. Bishop Stigand of Winchester who accompanied Godwin persuasively mediated between the king and Godwin, both sides agreeing to exchange hostages while discussions took place. On learning of this arrangement Robert realized that inevitably there would be a reconciliation between the king and Godwin and the consequent restoration of Godwin's influence with the king. Robert did not await the outcome of the peace talks but in fear of his life fled from London to the Continent with Bishop William of London, Bishop Ulf of Dorchester and many of the Norman nobles.[9] Although his Norman supporters were no longer with him, the king held a witenagemot in London which was attended by Godwin and his followers. In open council Godwin proved his innocence of the crimes with which he had been charged and for which he had been outlawed. Full restoration to Godwin and his family was made by the king and at the same council Robert and his companions were proclaimed outlawed 'because they chiefly made the discord between earl Godwin and the king.' [10] After his restoration it is recorded that Godwin exercised a good influence in the land. Godwin's influence, the goodness of which is not without question in church affairs, was exercised with the king so that Bishop Stigand, who had taken a leading part in bringing about the reconciliation between Godwin and the king, was allowed to occupy the archbishopric of Canterbury. This new situtation immediately raised the question whether Robert, having been proclaimed an outlaw, had thereby been deprived of his archbishopric. For his own safety Robert had fled from his archbishopric. This was not without precedent for Archbishop Aethelheard towards the close of the eighth century fled for his own safety to the Continent from his archbishopric, but returned later in response to the pleadings of Alcuin.[11] Robert in his flight from his archbishopric had not vacated it, and was still metropolitan archbishop of Canterbury according to the canon law of the Church. The sentence of outlaw passed upon Robert by the witenagemot meant banishment from the country which included his province and his archbishopric of Canterbury. More than two centuries earlier in 821 King Cenwulf had threatened to deprive

Archbishop Wulfred of Canterbury of his archbishopric and of all his possessions and to banish him from the kingdom unless he obeyed his commands. Wulfred had received the support of Pope Leo III in resisting Cenwulf's demands but the king, casting aside papal authority, compelled the archbishop to submit under threat of exile.[12] Wulfred finally submitted to the king's commands and consequently retained his see. Like Wulfred, Archbishop Robert visited Rome, and stated his case to Pope Leo IX who gave him letters of reinstatement to his archbishopric. But he never regained his see and, journeying homewards, died at the abbey of Jumièges.[13]

From the time of Constantine onwards rulers in Christendom had established bishoprics and nominated to them their own candidates. Charlemagne created archbishoprics and appointed his own candidates and also removed them when he considered it necessary. His secular authority in the Church was so far-reaching that Pope Hadrian I had heard rumours that the emperor was making plans to remove him from the Apostolic See. In England King Offa created an archbishopric and appointed his own candidate to occupy it. And now King Edward with his council had banished Robert and thereby made it impossible for him to occupy his archbishopric and, regarding the see as vacant, exercised his secular power and permitted Bishop Stigand to hold the archiepiscopal see in addition to the bishopric of Winchester. But such secular action could not abrogate canon law. Canonically Robert was still archbishop of Canterbury until he died despite the fact that Stigand now occupied the archbishopric. Here then were the elements of a conflict between the secular and the ecclesiastical; the king and the pope. King Edward's high regard for the papacy and ecclesiastical authority, and any desire to reinstate Robert, had to be set aside because of the political pressures which had arisen in his kingdom. Stigand's simony and avarice must have been well known; nevertheless, he possessed qualities, particularly as a mediator, which enabled him after the death of his patron, Godwin, to retain the confidence of the king who gave him further patronage. But royal patronage was insufficient to convince churchmen in England that Stigand's occupancy of the archbishopric of Canterbury was not irregular and contrary to the law of the Church.

Two traditions in England had been increasingly observed: first, that the archbishop-elect must visit Rome in order to receive his *pallium* personally from the pope; and, secondly, that the distinctive functions attaching to the dignity of an archbishop should not be performed until the *pallium* had been received. In his flight from the country Robert had left his *pallium* behind, and Stigand was well aware that he could not obtain the *pallium* because of his uncanonical position which had been made patently clear by the pope's letters requiring Robert's reinstatement. The significance of the *pallium* did not escape the Chronicler, who recorded that Robert set sail 'leaving his *pallium* and all Christendom here on land, as God ordained, because he had obtained an honour which God disclaimed.'[14] The same Chronicler a year later in 1053 observed 'This year there was no archbishop in this land; but Bishop Stigand held the see of Canterbury at Christ Church, and Cynesige that of York.' At that time Cynesige had left the country to obtain his *pallium* from the pope by whom he was consecrated. Nevertheless, in the same year Stigand subscribed himself as *archiepiscopus*.[15] But further evidence that he did not possess the spiritual authority of the archbishopric was to be seen after Edward nominated Wulfsige and Leofwin respectively to the sees of Dorchester and Lichfield. Both went overseas for consecration. Their action in not seeking consecration from Stigand emphasizes not only his uncanonical position but also the increased recognition of papal authority in the Church in England. Since the archiepiscopate of Lyfing in the second decade of the century when, without a *pallium,* he consecrated his own suffragan bishops, the bestowal of the *pallium* by the pope had become of such importance that an archbishop not having it was considered not to possess the *plenitudinem officii pontificalis,* which Pope Innocent III later claimed the recipient possessed.[16] But there was also a graver reason why bishops-elect sought consecration elsewhere: Stigand was under papal interdict, and remained so under Popes Leo IX, Victor II, Stephen IX, Nicholas II and Alexander II. The archbishopric of Canterbury received yet another setback when in 1056 Herewald, bishop-elect of Llandaff, within the province of Canterbury, was consecrated by Archbishop Cynesige of York.[17] Stigand finally received a *pallium* which earl Harold, when on a pilgrimage to Rome in 1058, obtained from the anti-pope Benedict X, who the following year was deposed from the papal throne. Immediately after receiving the *pallium* Stigand proceeded to the consecration of Aethelric and Siward respectively to the bishoprics of Selsey and Rochester.[18] Stigand's reception of a *pallium* from a pope who was a usurper adversely affected the archbishopric of Canterbury not only ecclesiastically but also politically. Earl Harold manifestly was Stigand's patron and exercised extensive political power in England. Knowledge of this situation widened the breach with Rome when Nicholas II became pope, and within a few years probably inclined the papacy to support William of Normandy's invasion of England.

However much King Edward may have desired a reconciliation with Rome by the removal of Stigand from the archbishopric, he was unable to take any action, even if he had wished to do so, because of earl Harold's support of Stigand and political influence in the country. Although Stigand was under excommunication and was therefore incapable of exercising any of his priestly and episcopal functions, his attestation of documents bearing the king's subscription show that he still retained the king's confidence and was accepted at court and in the council. Nevertheless the people became increasingly aware that Stigand possessed no spiritual authority and that he was archbishop of Canterbury in name only. Earl Harold in 1060 was now well aware of Stigand's position and brought Cynesige, archbishop of York, into the province of Canterbury to consecrate Waltham Abbey which he had founded. Further grievous blows were dealt against the archbishopric of Canterbury as its age-long prerogatives were exercised by others and its provincial authority set aside.

Bishop Ealdred of Worcester, who had distinguished himself by ambassadorial missions to the Continent for the king, after holding the see of Hereford *in commendam* surrendered it on being elected to the archbishopric of York. To the vacant see the king nominated the queen's chaplain, Walter, and to Wells his chaplain, Giso, who both came from Lorraine. Once again the situation arose when there was not an archbishop in the English Church and, perceiving this position, the king directed the two bishops-elect to go to Rome for consecration by Pope Nicholas II.[19] Giso and Walter were joined by Ealdred, archbishop-elect of York, who was journeying to Rome to obtain his *pallium,* and they were accompanied by Tostig, earl of Northumbria, a brother of earl Harold. Knowing the state of the Church in England with the excommunicated Stigand occupying the archbishopric of Canterbury, the see of Winchester and monastic preferments, and the existence of simony, Pope Nicholas II, on the arrival of Giso, Walter and Ealdred convoked a synod at which to consider the petitions of the three supplicants. Having examined Giso and Walter as to their fitness for the episcopate the synod investigated whether there was any evidence of simony. No evidence was found of simony either in the case of Giso or Walter who then received consecration. Bishop Ealdred on his own confession was found guilty of simony and was deprived by the pope of his see of Worcester and refused the *pallium.* On leaving Rome, Ealdred and Tostig were attacked by robbers and lost everything except the scantiest clothing. Returning to Rome they appeared before the pope and told him of their misfortunes. Earl Tostig, angered by the loss of their belongings and the harsh punishment meted out to Ealdred, blamed the pope for the robbery as being caused by his ill-rule. He also demanded compensation for their losses. Finally, Tostig added 'No doubt the king of England on hearing of their misfortunes would repair their loss by deducting the amount from the tribute of St. Peter.'[20] On hearing this threat and probably moved by their misfortunes, Nicholas made compensation and conferred the *pallium* upon Ealdred on condition that on his return to England he would seek out a suitable person for the bishopric of Worcester. In order to see that this provision was duly fulfilled and for other ecclesiastical matters two papal legates, one of whom was Ermenfrid, bishop of Sion, were sent to England. With the exception of the visit of the bishop of Treves in 991 to arrange peace between King Aethelred and Duke Richard I of Normandy no papal legates had been sent to Britain on ecclesiastical business since the archiepiscopate of Jaenberht in the eighth century. Although Jaenberht was at that time in conflict with King Offa, the legates George and Theophylact rightly first visited the archbishop of Canterbury. But on this occasion in 1062 no visit was made to Canterbury because Stigand, who occupied the archbishopric, was under excommunication. Since the archbishopric of Canterbury was ignored, the privilege of receiving the legates was taken by the archbishop of York who accompanied them on their journey through England, thus traversing through parts of the province of Canterbury.

On reaching the bishopric of Worcester, of which he had been deprived by the pope, Ealdred, before journeying to York to take possession of his archbishopric, arranged for Wulstan, the prior of Worcester, to give hospitality to the legates at the monastery. Observing his manner of life, his rule of the monastery and his erudition they decided that Wulstan was eminently suitable to become bishop of Worcester. When Archbishop Ealdred returned to accompany them to the court of Edward, they gained his support to their commendation of Wulstan to the king for nomination to the vacant bishopric. It had been reported that Wulstan had been elected by monks, clergy and people of Worcester, and in consequence he was unanimously approved for the see by Edward and his council. Stigand, who was at court, was fully aware of his own position since bishops-elect for the province had received consecration on the Continent, with the exception of the two bishops whom he had consecrated while possessing a *pallium* from the anti-pope, and Herewald whom Cynesige of York had consecrated for the see of Llandaff. But now preparations for the consecration of Wulstan, whose diocese was in the province of Canterbury, were being made by Ealdred of York who stood in a special relationship to the bishop-elect, the prior of Worcester. The archbishopric of Canterbury possessed no ecclesiastical authority because of Stigand's excommunication, and he was powerless to prevent Ealdred from consecrating Wulstan.

At this juncture Stigand perceived the irreparable injury which the archbishopric of Canterbury would suffer if, before consecrating Wulstan, Ealdred should demand from the bishop-elect a profession of canonical obedience. The situation was further complicated because as prior of Worcester Wulstan had been subject to Ealdred when he occupied the bishopric. Stigand for the first time during his occupancy of the archbishopric now took definite action to preserve one of the prerogatives of the archbishopric of Canterbury. And in order to make it quite clear that Ealdred's consecration of Wulstan would not set a precedent, Ealdred 'was ordered to declare before the king and the great men of the realm, that he would not thereafter claim any submission, either in ecclesiastical or temporal affairs, in right of having consecrated him (Wulstan), or of his having been his monk, before he was consecrated.' [21] This made the significance of Stigand's excommunication more widely realized throughout the country because he was unable to consecrate one of his own suffragans. Despite this further blow to Stigand and the archbishopric of Canterbury, King Edward did not yield to any pressures which may have been made by the papal legates for Stigand's removal, but was content to leave Stigand in possession of the archbishopric.

The other ecclesiastical affairs for which the legates came to England doubtless included the delivery of a new decree of excommunication upon Stigand from Pope Alexander II,[22] and an inquiry into the extent of simony in the Church, and the problem of the pluralism of bishoprics. At Dunstan's request in 972, Oswald, on becoming archbishop of York, continued to hold the see of Worcester *in commendam,* and all his successors, with the exception of Ealdred's immediate predecessor, Cynesige, held the see *in commendam* at some period during their archiepiscopate. Ealdred did not relinquish hope of treating Wulstan as his *chorepiscopus* so that his impoverished archbishopric would benefit from the emoluments of his former diocese. Bishop Wulstan, however, finally succeeded in establishing the complete independence of his see which was confirmed by a writ of the king.[23] Later, Wulstan made a profession of canonical obedience to Archbishop Lanfranc in which he asserted that neither to Ealdred nor to Stigand had he made any profession.[24]

Having failed to bring the diocese of Worcester within his jurisdiction, Ealdred turned his attention to the bishopric of Dorchester held by the ageing Wulfsige. Taking advantage of the lack of administrative oversight in the province of Canterbury over which Stigand could not exercise ecclesiastical authority, Ealdred laid claim to ecclesiastical jurisdiction over Lindsey which was a part of the diocese of Dorchester. Paulinus, when Bishop of York, had brought the Gospel to the people of Lindsey, and Theodore consecrated Eadhed, bishop of Lindsey, while it was a part of the Northumbrian kingdom before being conquered by the Mercians. Bishop Wulfsige could not appeal for support from the powerless Stigand so he made his appeal direct to Pope Nicholas II, who issued a judgment in his favour thus frustrating Ealdred's designs.[25] When King Edward the Confessor, as he was later called, assembled his council at Westminster for the 'crown-wearing' on Christmas Day, 1066, his health was rapidly failing. But on this occasion, to the Christmas festivities was added the ceremony of the hallowing of the church of St. Peter, Westminster, which he had erected. On the 28th December the rites of hallowing, performed by Archbishop Ealdred of York, assisted by other bishops were completed. Stigand, still under excommunication, had taken no part in the ceremonies although he was in attendance on the king, and subscribed to the charters, the third of which contained Edward's petition to Pope Nicholas II on behalf of the abbey and the pope's bull granting the privileges which he had sought. Stigand's subscription appears in a form not previously used by him, as follows: 'I, Stigand, bishop of the holy church of the city of Canterbury, have subscribed.' [26] After his subscription appear those of Archbishop Ealdred, ten bishops, six abbots and others.

Within twelve days the abbey church was the scene of more solemn rites when King Edward was interred within its sanctuary. No sooner had the burial rites ended than Harold was elected king and crowned by Ealdred in the same church.[27] Stigand's deprivation of all spiritual authority made it impossible for him to exercise the prerogatives and privileges which by tradition and right belonged to the archbishopric of Canterbury. The extent to which Stigand had degraded his high office and impaired the archbishopric was exhibited to the nation when those prerogatives and privileges of Canterbury were exercised by the archbishop of York in his performance of the crowning ceremony.

Harold repealed unjust laws and initiated legislation of an equitable character. To the churches and monasteries he became their patron and protector; to the bishops, abbots, monks and clergy he paid due reverence and cared for their interests; and showed goodwill to the people, but would not tolerate evildoers.[28] His reign of such early promise was soon thrown into disorder as he became militarily involved in the defence of his kingdom. Having defeated the forces of Harold Hardrada at Stamford Bridge he learned that William of Normandy's fleet had anchored in Pevensey Bay. Harold marched his forces south with all haste and the armies of William and Harold met in battle at Hastings when William gained a decisive victory and Harold with the flower of English manhood perished in the fight.

After having rested his army, William marched through Romney along the coast to Dover, and then northwards to Canterbury where he remained in the city or its vicinity for about a month. Stigand was not at Canterbury, but there is little doubt that William was aware that Pope Alexander II who had given his blessing upon his invasion of England had also excommunicated Stigand. He would also have learned that Stigand, who was the leader of the party supporting Edgar the Aetheling, had gone to London to gather support. Marching towards London, William's forces, having partly encircled the city, then crossed Surrey, the northern part of Hampshire, Berkshire and finally reached Wallingford. While there, Stigand, who had deserted the Aetheling's party in London, came to William and swore fealty to him. Ravaging the countryside, William's forces came to Berkhamsted, where he met representatives of the English people. They were led by Archbishop Ealdred of York, the saintly Bishop Wulstan of Worcester, Bishop Walter of Hereford, Edgar, Edwin, Morcar and leading citizens of London. In their submission to William they made oaths of allegiance and gave hostages while he in turn promised to be a faithful lord to them.[29] Nevertheless, his army continued to ravage the country-side as he marched towards London, which he entered without opposition from the inhabitants.

Preparations were made without delay for William's coronation in Westminster Abbey on Christmas Day, 1066. Knowing that Stigand was excommunicated, and that Harold II had been crowned by Archbishop Ealdred, William requested Ealdred to perform the ceremony of coronation. This the archbishop agreed to do, once again exercising the prerogatives and privileges belonging to Canterbury. Before proceeding to the actual 'crowning' he required William to make oath upon the Gospels that he would protect the churches of God and their leaders and that like the kings before him he would rule justly if the people were faithful to him. As the ceremony was in progress an unprecedented element was introduced. William had claimed the throne by kinship with King Edward and by conquest but the nation had not chosen or elected him to be their king. It was, therefore, considered necessary to give an opportunity for the people of the vast congregation to express their acceptance of him as their king. To give effect to this the question was first put in English by Archbishop Ealdred and then in French by Geoffrey, bishop of Coutances, whether they acknowledged William as their lord and king. The vociferous reply of the congregation on being heard by the guards outside the abbey made them think that the congregation had risen in rejection of William, and the guards, in their panic, set fire to the buildings surrounding the Abbey. Archbishop Ealdred, however, continued the ceremony in which he hallowed, crowned and enthroned William, king of England.[30]

Having assured himself that his throne was secure, King William returned to Normandy two months after his coronation, leaving as governors of England his brother Bishop Odo of Bayeux and William Fitz-Osborne, whom he had created earl of Hereford. He took with him the chief of the political leaders who had opposed him, among whom were Stigand, Edgar the Aetheling and earls Edwin and Morcar. Although Stigand had sworn allegiance to him, the king perceived the immense political influence which Stigand wielded among those who had opposed him, and would not give any opportunity for him to lead a rebellion.

From the time of Stigand's first appearance as the king's priest of the church of Ashingdon erected by Cnut, he became a political figure, and when he aspired to a bishopric he became a discredited ecclesiastic because of his simony. Having for his patron the powerful earl Godwin, he exploited any political advantage and secured the see of Winchester. Stigand was sufficiently astute to escape King Edward's wrath when Archbishop Robert's party succeeded in the overthrow of Godwin, who was then banished by the king. On Robert's flight to the Continent, Godwin's return from exile and his reinstatement by Edward, Stigand's political position was of such a character that with the concurrence of Edward or by his gift he took possession of the archbishopric of Canterbury although by ecclesiastical law it had not been vacated by Robert's departure from England.[31] A contemporary record of Stigand's action in occupying the archbishopric is to be found in Bishop Wulstan's profession of canonical obedience to Lanfranc, in which he wrote 'Stigand had for some time usurped the Holy Church at Canterbury . . . and by violence and cunning had driven the metropolitan from his seat.' [32] When Stigand was deposed from the archbishopric and the see of Winchester by a council held in that city in 1070, three canonical grounds for his deposition were adduced: his pluralism of sees; his invasion of the archbishopric while Robert of Jumièges was still alive and wearing his *pallium* while celebrating mass; and receiving a *pallium* from Pope Benedict X who had usurped the papal see and was later deposed.[33] This was the position of the archbishopric of Canterbury when William became king except that Robert was no longer alive. For one brief year Stigand had possessed the ecclesiastical authority of the archbishopric while he held the *pallium* from Benedict, but at the end of that time, when Benedict was deposed, all Stigand's ecclesiastical actions, chiefly the consecration of two bishops, were invalidated by his further excommunication. Nevertheless, possessing no authority to discharge the ecclesiastical privileges and prerogatives of the archbishopric he clung to the husk of office from which he derived emoluments, political influence and secular power. In doing this he witnessed the historic and traditional prerogatives of the archbishopric of Canterbury pass to the archbishopric of York at two coronations in Westminster Abbey, and only once did he set himself to defend the archbishopric of Canterbury when, before King Edward and his council, Ealdred, archbishop of York, was required to declare that by his consecration of Wulstan he would not claim from him submission in either ecclesiastical or secular affairs. A successor for the see of Worcester had been the subject of a directive which Ealdred had received from the pope when visiting Rome, and it was in order to have assurance of the implementation of the directive that the pope sent two of his legates to England. While their visit may escape being described as papal interference with the internal affairs of the English Church, no such situation would have arisen had it not been for Stigand's excommunication. Before this, however, during Edward's reign the insularity of the Church in England had been gradually broken down by an increasing recognition of papal authority in sending representatives to the councils of Rheims and Vercelli; by Edward's petition for the pope's permission to remove the see of Crediton to Exeter; and by the pope's refusal to allow Archbishop Robert to consecrate Spearhafoc for the see of London. In some of these matters the king had taken the initiative to bring the Church in England closer to Rome, but on the other hand he showed a total disregard for papal authority by permitting Stigand under excommunication to occupy the archbishopric of Canterbury. This situation reveals the weakness of Edward and his dependence upon Stigand, especially after the death of earl Godwin, for his counsel in political affairs and matters of State—a dependence which grew during the ill-health of the ageing king. Edward was not unaware of the true character of Stigand who was a gifted politician and well-versed in affairs of State. And when explaining one of his visions he described him as 'the simoniacal traitor, Stigand, prelate of Canterbury.' [34] But Stigand's rapacious and avaricious character was widely known among the people and undoubtedly caused them to ignore the teaching of the Church since he was an archbishop in name only and possessed no spiritual authority in his province and the country. Towards the close of his life Edward said of the Church, 'Bishops, prelates and priests no longer seek to be good pastors : They seek not to feed the sheepfolds.' [35] These words were spoken by the king in Stigand's presence and, turning aside to others, he mockingly attributed them to the king's dotage. Although King Edward the Confessor was a religiously-minded man, his religion, except at that time, appeared to have little depth, otherwise he would not have regarded ecclesiastical preferments as rewards for secular service at his court and churches as beneficial assets to be given to ecclesiastics and monasteries. In none of these things was there any element of saintliness later attributed to him by monastic writers chiefly because he did not consummate his marriage.

At Canterbury the community of Christ Church ignored its rule of discipline and lived luxuriously and expensively and was given to hawking and riding.[36] From this it would appear that the community had been able to keep its considerable wealth out of the predatory hands of Stigand. To what extent the declension of the Church, during the immediate Pre-Conquest period, was attributable to Stigand is difficult to assess, but any corruption attaching to the highest ecclesiastical office in the land could not fail to affect clergy, monks and people. At that time most of the bishops were illiterate, except for some notable bishops, like Wulstan of Worcester, who were known throughout the country for their piety, wisdom and learning. Only a few monasteries remained where the Rule was observed and were centres of holy living and learning. In general, however, the decline in true religion had spread with paralysing effect in the monasteries. Among the clergy the situation was even worse. Their lack of learning made them incompetent to discharge their priestly functions and their manner of life did not commend the religion they professed to teach. The description of the conditions in the Church re-echo King Alfred's words in his Prologue to his translation of 'The Pastoral Care,' in which he described the conditions in the Church when he ascended the throne in 871. There were, however, bishops, clergy and monks who were faithful to their vocation who, with unremitting zeal, attended to the pastoral needs of the people and thus maintained the work and witness of the Church, so that those who adhered faithfully to the Church desired to see the restoration of true religion in the land.[37]

King William perceived the conditions which prevailed in the Church in England and its need of reform, but he did nothing until four years after becoming king to remove Stigand from the archbishopric of Canterbury. From 1052 onwards Stigand had occupied the archbishopric and, having been excommunicated by five popes, was an archbishop only in name. But the pre-eminence and spiritual authority of the archbishopric of Canterbury could not be destroyed by an excommunicated and unworthy occupant, although its privileges and prerogatives were temporarily exercised by the archbishopric of York. The Church in England looked hopefully forward to the time when the archbishopric of Canterbury would be held by a spiritual leader who would shepherd the Church along the path of reform. And that time was not far distant when, under Lanfranc, the archbishopric regained the ancient rights, prerogatives and privileges appertaining to the office of primate and metropolitan archbishop of all England which enabled him to lead the Church and nation into a resurgence of true religion.

A MAP SHOWING THE PROVINCE OF CANTERBURY WITH THE DIOCESES
SEPARATED FROM IT IN THE EIGHTH CENTURY AND RESTORED TO IT IN
THE NINTH CENTURY

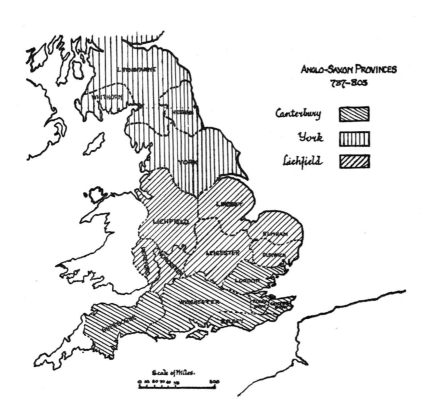

ARCHBISHOPS OF CANTERBURY

Augustine, 597
Laurentius, 604–609?
Mellitus, 619
Justus, 624
Honorius, 627
Deusdedit, 655
*Theodore, 668
†Berhtwald, 693
Tatwine, 731
Nothelm, 735
Cuthbert, 740
Bregowine, 761

Jaenberht, 765
Aethelheard, 793
Wulfred, 805
Feologild, 832
Ceolnoth, 833
Aethelred, 870
Plegmund, 890
Aethelhelm, 914
Wulfhelm, 923
Oda, 942
Aelfsige, 959
Beorhthelm, 959

Dunstan, 960
Aethelgar, 988
Sigeric, 990
Aelfric, 995
Aelfheah, 1005
Lyfing, 1013
Aethelnoth, 1020
Eadsige, 1038
Robert of Jumièges,
1051
Stigand, 1052

* First to be designated 'archbishop.'   † First to be designated 'primate.'

245

ABBREVIATIONS

ASC.   *Anglo-Saxon Chronicle:* Everyman's Library, No. 624 ed. J. Ingram:
        Text–*Two of the Saxon Chronicles, parallel;* C. Plummer; 2 vols;
        1965 ed.
BCS.   W. de G. Birch, *Cartularium Saxonicum,* 4 vols., 1885–89.
CD.   J. M. Kemble, *Codex Diplomaticus Anglo-Saxonicus,* 6 vols., 1839–48.
EHD.   *English Historical Documents,* c. 500–1042, ed. D. Whitelock, 1955.
FW.   *Florentii Wigornensis, Chronicon ex Chronicis,* ed. G. Howard; London,
        1592.
HE.   *Historia Ecclesiastica Gentis Anglorum; Venerabilis Baedae Opera His-
        torica,* ed. C. Plummer, 2 vols., 1896; for English translation, Everyman's
        Library, No. 479.
HS.   A. W. Haddan and W. Stubbs, *Councils and Ecclesiastical Documents
        relating to Great Britain and Ireland;* 3 vols., 1869–78.

NOTES

CHAPTER I

[1] *Historia vero testis temporum, lux veritatis; Cicero, De Oratore,* III, 9.

[2] *Venerabilis Baedae Opera Historica;* ed. C. Plummer; 2 vols., Oxford 1896. This contains Bede's *Historia Ecclesiastica Gentis Anglorum,* a good translation in English is in the Everyman Series, No. 479. A later translation of the major parts are to be found in *English Historical Documents,* c. 500–1042; ed. D. Whitelock, London 1955. HE., II, 1.

[3] *Gregorii I. Papae Registrum Epistolarum,* VI, 10; *Monumenta Germaniae Historica;* ed. P. Ewald and L. M. Hartmann, Berlin 1887–99.

[4] C. Hole, *A Manual of English Church History,* p. 1, London 1910.

[5] *Sacrorum Conciliorum Nova at Amplissima Collectio,* II, 476; ed. J. A. Mansi, II, 696 and 702. *Sulpicii Servi Historia Sacra,* II, 41; P.G., 152B.

[6] *Leonis Magni et Aliorum Opera;* E. XCV; ed. J. Ulimmerius, Paris 1623.

[7] HE., I, 13; I, 17–21; III, 4. *The Celtic Church in Britain and Ireland,* pp. 7–39; H. Zimmer, 1902. *Christianity in Celtic Lands,* pp. 26–31; L. Gougaud, trans. by M. Joynt, London, 1932.

[8] HE., I, 22. Gildas, *Badonicus de Excidio Britanniae:* a translation is to be found in W. E. Wade-Evans' *The Emergence of England and Wales.*

[9] *Gregorii Turonensis Opera; Historia Francorum;* IV, 26 and IX, 26; *Scriptores Germaniae Merovingicarum;* ed. W. Arndt and B. Krusch, Hanover 1884.

[10] *Greg. Epp.,* XI, 35.

[11] *Ibid.,* VI, 37.

[12] *Ibid.,* VI, 49.

[13] HE., I, 23.

[14] *Greg. Epp.,* VI, 50a.

[15] *Ibid.,* VI, 49–57.

[16] *Ibid.,* V, 58. In this letter and his letter to King Childebert Gregory denounced in strong terms simony, and the ordination of laymen to the episcopate, which were prevalent in the Gallican Church (V, 59).

[17] HE., I, 25. Thorn later identifies the place and regards Richborough as a part of Thanet. (*Historiae Anglicanae Scriptores Decem;* Col. 1759. London 1652.) Thanet at that time was completely separate from the mainland. See also Dean Stanley's *Historical Memorials of Canterbury,* p. 20.

[18] HE., I, 25.

[19] *Ibid.*

[20] *Ibid.*

[21] Thorn, op. cit., 1759. See also *Historia Monasterii S. Augustini Cantuariensis* by Thomas Elmham; (R.S.) ed. C. Harwick, p. 91.

[22] This is based on Daniel 9:16 and forms an antiphon in the observance of Rogation Days.

[23] HE., I, 26.

[24] *Ibid.* R. P. C. Hanson, *St. Patrick: his Origins and Career,* 1968, p. 151, note 2.

CHAPTER II

[1] HE., I, 25.

[2] *Qui data a me licentia a Germaniarum episcopis episcopus factus. Greg. Epp.,* VIII, 29.

[3] HE., I, 27. Bede is in error when he states that Aetherius was bishop of Arles. This was copied by Thorn (1760) and Elmham (91). Aetherius at that time was bishop of Lyons. Wharton (*Anglia Sacra,* I, 89) says that Augustine was consecrated on his first journey through Gaul, while on his way to Britain, and bases his argument on Gregory's letter to Queen Brunchilda in which he refers to Augustine as 'our brother' and 'fellow bishop.' J. Lingard in his *History and Antiquities of the Anglo-Saxon Church,* I, 368, effectively dismisses Wharton's statement by showing that the letter in question was written after Augustine had established the work in Kent.

⁴ The exceptions were the metropolitans of Achaia, Cagliari, Dalmatia, Ravenna and Thessalonica. *Vide Greg. Epp.*, I, 26; I, 60, 62 and 81; II, 47; III, 8; IX, 196. Gregory addressed some as patriarchs as for instance Eulogius, patriarch of Alexandria, X, 21.

⁵ *Greg. Epp.*, VIII, 29.

⁶ *Greg. Epp.*, XI, 37.

⁷ HE., I, 26.

⁸ *Ibid.*, I, 33.

⁹ *Greg. Epp.*, XI, 39.

¹⁰ Council of Chalcedon, 451; canon 17. *Vide Notes on the Canons of the First Four General Councils;* W. Bright, Oxford 1882. *L'Organisation Ecclesiastique par Jacques Zeiller; Histoire de l'Église; A. Fliché et V. Martin;* II, 401.

¹¹ R. G. Collingwood and J. N. L. Myres, *Roman Britain and the Empire Settlements*, p. 172. See also Wade-Evans, op. cit., p. 121.

¹² *Notitia Dignitatum,* ed. O. Seeck, p. 171, 1962 edition.

¹³ HE., II, 3.

¹⁴ Canon 17.

¹⁵ 'The Canterbury Edition of the Answers of Pope Gregory I to St. Augustine' by Margaret Deanesly and Paul Grosjean, contained in *The Journal of Ecclesiastical History*, Vol. X, No. 1, p. 43. This scholarly and critical study of the *Responsiones* is vital to the true understanding of Augustine's metropolitanate.

¹⁶ *Greg. Epp.*, XI, 56a. HE., I, 27.

¹⁷ *Ibid.*

¹⁸ M. Deanesly, *The Pre-Conquest Church in England*, p. 194.

¹⁹ *Greg. Epp.*, XI, 56a. HE., I, 27. See a valuable essay entitled 'The Familia at Christ Church, Canterbury, 597–832,' by Margaret Deanesly, to be found in *Essays in Mediaeval History*, presented to Thomas Frederick Tout; ed. by A. G. Little and F. M. Powicke, Manchester 1925.

²⁰ *Leonis Magni et Aliorum Opera;* ed. *J. Ulimmerius*, Paris 1623. *Epp. CXVIII et CXIX. Greg. Epp.,* VIII, 9; X, 9.

²¹ L. Gougaud, *Christianity in Celtic Lands*, pp. 217ff. G. G. Coulton, *Scottish Abbeys and Social Life*, pp. 17ff.

²² Council of Nicea, Canon 4; Mansi, IV, 407.

²³ HE., II, 8 and 16.

²⁴ *Greg. Epp.*, V, 58 and 59.

²⁵ *Ibid.*, XI, 45.

²⁶ HE., I, 17 and 18. *Sanctuarium seu Vitae Sanctorum,* ed. W. Levison; *Monumenta Germaniae Historica; Scriptores Rerum Merovingicarum,* VII (i; 1919), pp. 225–83.

²⁷ *Greg. Epp.*, XI, 56a. HE., I, 27.

CHAPTER III

¹ M. Deanesly and P. Grosjean, op. cit., pp. 43–3.

² *Greg. Epp.*, XI, 39. HE., I, 29.

³ *Greg. Epp.*, XI, 56a. HE., I, 27.

⁴ *Greg. Epp.*, XI, 37. HE., II, 2.

⁵ HE., II, 2.

⁶ *Fasti Eboracensis,* ed. W. H. Dixon and J. Raine, p. 96. N. K. Chadwick, op. cit., IV, pp. 201–42. The writer concludes 'There's was in Arthur's day no archbishop of Canterbury; the primate and legate of the time had his see in Wales; Samson was an archbishop, but archbishop of York, not of St. Davids. David was also an archbishop, but he too was not archbishop of St. Davids,' p. 210.
  A. W. Haddan and W. Stubbs, *Councils and Ecclesiastical Documents relating to Great Britain and Ireland*, Vol. I, pp. 142–51, also Vol. III, p. 41, note c. *Greg. Epp.*, XI, 56a. The document recording that Dinoot claimed to be the 'overseer' of the British bishops is in the opinion of A. Plummer spurious. See Plummer's notes in HE., II, 75.

⁷ St. Matthew 11:29.

⁸ G. Fritz, *Pâques les Controverses Pascales; Dictionnaire de Théologie Catholique;* ed. A. Vacant, E. Mangenot et E. Amann, XI, part ii, 1932; Cols. 1948–70. See also Plummer, op. cit., II, 348, Excursus on the Paschal Controversy.

⁹ *Greg. Epp.*, I, 41.

¹⁰ *Ibid.*, IV, 9. *Innocentii Epistolae,* I, 3; Mansi, III, 1028ff.

¹¹ *Greg. Epp.*, I, 41.

¹² St. Mark 16:15.

[13] HS., I, 154. See also Plummer's HE., Vol. II, 75–7. *Christianity in Britain, 300–700*, ed. M. W. Barley and R. P. C. Hanson, 1970, p. 94.

[14] HE., I, 22. Here Bede quotes Gildas.

[15] *Ibid.*, III, 26; V, 21 and 22.

[16] *Greg. Epp.*, XI, 56a. HE., I, 27.

[17] HS., I, 102, 112, 113, 140, 141, 154, 155. Greg. Epp., XI, 56a.

[18] 1 Corinthians 15:14.

[19] HE., II, 2. Bede's use of the title 'archbishop' is an anachronism. He takes the familiar usage of his own day and reads it back into the events which he records. Not until the time of Theodore was a metropolitan bishop of Canterbury designated 'archbishop.'

[20] N. K. Chadwick, op. cit., p. 13.

[21] ASC., 605; ed. C. Plummer and J. Earle, 2 vols. In recording this battle Bede does not give the date, but it must have been between 613 and 616. See F. M. Stenton, *Anglo-Saxon England*, p. 77. HE., II, 2.

[22] M. Dillon and N. K. Chadwick, *The Celtic Realms*, p. 186, London 1967.

[23] *Annales Cambriae*, p.14; ed. ed. J. W. A. Ithel, R.S., 1860. HS., I, 287 and 674.

CHAPTER IV

[1] HS., I, 142–51; III, 41.

[2] *Ibid.*, III, 40, note a. Plummer, op. cit., II, xii.

[3] W. Bright, op. cit., p. 59.

[4] Klaus Gamber, *Wege zum Urgregorianum*, Beuron 1956, p. 20. Mr. Gamber is doubtful whether Augustine carried with him to England the Gregorian Sacramentary. But Dom H. Ashworth in an article in *Ephermerides Liturgicae*, lxxii, 39–43, 1958, considers the question 'Did St. Augustine bring the *Gregorianum* to England?' answers it by saying that Augustine would hardly leave for Britain without taking with him whatever parts of the *Urgregorianum* were available, and that it was possible that when other parts were ready they were sent to him.

[5] *Dialogus Ecclesiasticae Institutionis a Domino Egberto*, 2 and 3; D. Wilkins, *Concilia Magnae Britanniae et Hiberniae*, I, 82, London 1737.

[6] HE., I, 27. Greg. Epp., XI, 56a.

[7] L. Duchesne, *Origines du culte Chrétien*, ed. 1898, p. 99. A *Dictionary of Christian Antiquities*, II, 1035 and 1830. M. Deanesly, op. cit., pp. 154–9 and 187–90.

[8] M. Deanesly and P. Grosjean, op. cit., pp. 5ff.

[9] *Ibid.*, p. 27. *S. Bonifatti et Lulli Epistolae*, ed. M. Tangl, No. 33 and compare No. 63; *Monumenta Germaniae Historica*, Vol. I, Berlin 1955.

[10] M. Deanesly and P. Grosjean, op. cit., p. 43. Plummer, op. cit., II, 47ff. III, 32, note b.

[11] HE., I, 27. Greg. Epp., XI, 56a.

[12] *Ibid.* HS., III, 42.

[13] The *Jus Antiquum*, Chap. II of *The Canon Law of the Church of England*, p. 9, London 1947.

[14] This is particularly discernible in Nos. 3, 4, 5, 7, 8 and 9. Greg. Epp., XI, 56a. HE., I, 27.

[15] HS., III, 118. Dr. W. Hunt in *A History of the English Church 597–1066*, p. 137, writes 'He (Theodore) produced a collection of canons compiled by Dionysius Exiguus.'

[16] HE., II, 5, *cum consilio sapientium*. This is undoubtedly the first recorded instance of an Anglo-Saxon king taking legislative measures 'with the counsel of prudent men,' later known as the 'witan' or 'witenagemot.'

[17] *Ibid.*, I, 32. Greg. Epp., XI, 37.

[18] *Ibid.*, I, 30. *Ibid.*, XI, 56. During the episcopate of Paulinus at York, before the conversion of King Edwin of Northumbria, the idols and pagan temple were destroyed by Coifi at Goodmanham (HE., II, 14) in 627.

[19] Elmham, op. cit., pp. 79–81. A. P. Stanley, *Memorials of Canterbury*, p. 37.

[20] HE., I, 33.

[21] *Ibid.* Elmham, op. cit., pp. 81 and 92.

[22] Gregory of Tours, op. cit., IV, 26 and IX, 26. He gives the date of Bertha's marriage to Aethelbert as 560.

[23] HE., II, 3.

[24] *Ibid.*

²⁵ Council of Nicea, c. 4; Mansi, IV, 407. HE., II, 4. Gregory of Tours, V, 43 and VI, 15, has some comments to make on a bishop nominating and consecrating his own successor.

²⁶ Stenton, op. cit., p. 109. Plummer, op. cit., II, 79. J. M. Kemble, *The Saxons in England,* I, pp. 148 and 149. Kemble gives instances in which there was a divided sovereignty in Kent. These were later and because of this it may be unwise to conclude that similar instances existed at this period.

²⁷ HE., V, 24. In his recapitulation of his History Bede gives the date of the conversion of Saberht as 604. See also II, 5.

²⁸ Wilkins, *Concilia,* I, 32. In his letter to Justus, Pope Boniface V confirmed Canterbury as the see city of the metropolitan bishop. III, 73 gives the date of this letter as 624 or 625. Pope Leo III in 798 wrote to King Cenwulf confirming Canterbury as the see city of the metropolitan. *Vide Cartularium Saxonicum,* I, 208 and 214; W. de G. Birch. For a discussion on this see J. W. Lamb, *The Archbishopric of Lichfield,* pp. 31–5.

CHAPTER V

¹ Illustrative of this relationship see HE., I, 32 and *Greg. Epp.,* XI, 37.

² HS., III, 42.

³ HE., II, 4.

⁴ *Ibid.* Columban was the founder of Luxeuil and later of Bobbio where he died in 615. He founded a monastic rule which bears his name. See Plummer, op. cit., II, 83.

⁵ HE., II, 4. Mansi, X, 504. HS., III, 62–5.

⁶ Elmham, op. cit., pp. 127–31.

⁷ HE., II, 4. P. Jaffé, *Regesta Pontificum Romanorum,* p. 155. Jaffé appears to question the authority of this council because he knows of no evidence for it but Bede's.

⁸ HS., III, 65. Bede says that Pope Boniface IV sent a letter by Mellitus to the king (II, 4), but in note a, p. 65, Haddan and Stubbs are doubtful about its genuineness.

⁹ The letter to Aethelbert is the first of a series of letters given by William of Malmesbury in his *Gesta Pontificum Anglorum,* Rolls Series, pp. 46ff. It was produced for the first time by Archbishop Lanfranc of Canterbury in 1072, together with other letters, claiming to show the supremacy of Canterbury over York.

¹⁰ Queen Bertha, it would appear, had died so this would be Eadbald's second wife. After the dissolution of his incestuous marriage he married a daughter of the king of the Franks, BCD., I, 20. HS., III, 70.

¹¹ Florence of Worcester; *Monumenta Historica Britannica,* I, 250 and 262, speaks only of two sons and gives their names as Sexred and Saeward. In his text, however (I, 13), he follows Bede and gives three without names.

¹² HE., II, 5. Wilkins following Spelman who dignifies this meeting by describing it as a Council of Kent in 617. Wilkins, *Concilia,* I, 30.

¹³ HE., II, 7.

¹⁴ Plummer, II, 92 suggests that the letter is composite and advances two probabilities: 1, that the first part was addressed to Justus and Romanus and 2, that it was addressed to Mellitus and Justus. But none of these three bishops was instrumental in the conversion of King Eadbald (HE., II, 8; Wilkins, I, 31) but only Laurentius.

¹⁴ *Ibid.*

¹⁵ HE., II, 9.

¹⁶ *Greg. Epp.,* XI, 39.

¹⁷ Mansi, II, 476. J. W. Lamb, *The Archbishopric of York,* p. 17.

¹⁸ St. Berin; F. E. Field, p. 33.

¹⁹ Honorius is described by HE., V, 19 '*unus ex discipulis beati papae Gregorii, vir rebus ecclesiasticus sublimiter institutus servabat.*' This description and Bede's statement '. . . *electus est archiepiscopus cathedrae Doruuernensis sextus Deusdedit de gente Occidentalium Saxonum . . .*' (HE., III, 20); and Elmham's mention pp. 192–3 that Deusdedit was the first native archbishop sufficiently meet the suggestion that Honorius was English (M. Deanesly, *Augustine of Canterbury,* p. 112).

²⁰ HE., II, 16.

²¹ *Ibid.,* III, 18.

²² *Ibid.,* II, 20. Both Bede and the *Anglo-Saxon Chronicle* give the date as 633 for the death of Edwin, but Stenton, op. cit., argues that it was in 632.

[23] *Ibid.*, II, 20. The archbishop of Canterbury possessed the right until 1148 to appoint to the see of Rochester.

CHAPTER VI

[1] *Ibid.*, II, 17.
[2] *Ibid.*, I, 27 and II, 20.
[3] *Ibid.*, II, 8. Lamb, op. cit., p. 57.
[4] Theodore divided the diocese in 673, creating Elmham in the northern part, Dunwich remaining in the south. Dunwich became extinct in the ninth century owing to the ravages of the Danes. It was revived as a suffragan bishopric in 1934.
[5] *Greg. Epp.*, IV, 26.
[6] HE., III, 7. ASC., 635. Bede wrongly speaks of Asterius as bishop of Genoa. Asterius resided at Genoa but was metropolitan of Milan. See Plummer, op. cit., II, p. 142.
[7] *Ibid.* This is Dorchester near Oxford.
[8] J. W. Lamb, op. cit., p. 29. HE., III, 25.
[9] HE., III, 25.
[10] *Ythancaestir* has now been identified with St. Peter's Chapel, Bradwell-on-Sea, where remains of Cedd's church are still to be seen. It was, during the Roman occupation, the station of Othona.
[11] W. H. Jones, *Diocesan History of Salisbury*, p. 24. See also HE., II, 17 and HS., III, 83–5.
[12] HE., II, 5. Wilkins, I, 30.
[13] *Ibid.*, III, 8.
[14] *Ibid.*, ASC., 640.
[15] *Ibid.*, II, 13. Before the conversion of King Edwin of Northumbria his chief priest, Coifi, destroyed the idols and set fire to the pagan temple at Goodmanham in Yorkshire. King Eorcenberht enforced by law the destruction of idols in the home. King Wihtred in 696 enacted laws against those who sacrificed to idols. HS., III, 235. Wilkins, I, 60 and 61.
[16] The masters and teachers who went from Canterbury to assist Felix in the schools in East Anglia (HE., III, 18) evidently went from well established centres of learning. Sigeberht's interest in the founding of the school in East Anglia has been claimed as the origin of Cambridge University. William of Malmesbury, *Gesta Pontificum*, II, 74 elaborates Bede's statement: '*Scolas quoque litterarum oportunis locis instituens, barbariem gentis sensim comitate Latina informabat.*'
[17] HE., III, 20. ASC., 655. This is yet another instance of a consecration solely by one bishop. Bishop Berctgils of Dunwich was not present. As in previous cases mentioned—Augustine's consecration of Laurentius; Romanus by Justus; Justus Romanus, the consecration of Honorius by Paulinus; and now Ithamar by Deusdedit. All these consecrations were irregular but valid.
[18] *Ibid.* Deusdedit was the second native to adopt another name on consecration. Berctgils adopted the name Boniface in 652 when consecrated by Bishop Honorius to the bishopric of Dunwich (HE., III, 20).
[19] HE., III, 25. '*Haec dicente rege, faverunt adsidentes quique sive adstantes mairoes una cum mediocribus, et abdicata minus perfecta institutione, ad ea, quae meliora cognoverant, sese transferre festinabant.*'
[20] HE., III, 28. '*Non enim erat tunc ullus, excepto illo Wini, in tota Brittania cononice ordinatus episcopus.*' Bede is evidently astray here. Berctgils, bishop of Dunwich, was still alive and had been consecrated by the metropolitan bishop Honorius in 652. Bede, himself, records that Berctgils or Boniface held his see for seventeen years (IV, 5) so that gives the date 669, five years after Chad's consecration. There is a little uncertainty about the date of Damian's death, bishop of Rochester, but he was probably still alive when Chad journeyed to Canterbury (IV, 2). Not until Theodore was archbishop of Canterbury did he consecrate Putta to the see of Rochester in 669.

CHAPTER VII

[1] ASC. (E), 655. HE., IV, 6. The Chronicle refers to Wini as bishop of London. He did not become bishop of London until 666, and he was still bishop of Winchester in 664 (HE., III, 28). Although the Chronicle gives an earlier date the middle of the year 664 seems the most probable for at that time Deusdedit was still alive, Tuda a bishop and Wilfrid still a priest. (HS., III, 99 and 100 note b).
[2] *Historia Abbatum auctore Baeda*, p. 3; Plummer, op. cit., I, 366.

³ HE., III, 29. Wilkins, I, 40. *'Domino excellenti filio Osuio Regi Saxonum, Vitalianus Episcopus, Servus servorum Dei.'*

⁴ M. Deanesly, *A History of Early Medieval Europe, 476–911*, p. 219. Stenton, op. cit., p. 130.

⁵ HE., III, 29. Bede in his *'Historia Abbatum'* mentions that all those who accompanied him also died of the plague. This made the position such that Vitalian was able to act with freedom. *'Qui videlicet Uicghardus Romam veniens, cum cunctis qui secum venere comitibus, antequam gradum pontificatus perciperet, morbo ingruente defunctus est'* (p. 3).

⁶ The Monothelite heresy held that there was only one will in the God-man. It was still raging in the Eastern Church in the seventh century and was more political than religious and was really designed to bring back the heretical Monophysites (who held that in the Person of the Incarnate Christ there was but a single Divine Nature as against the orthodox faith of a double Nature Divine and Human after the Incarnation) to orthodoxy. The Monothelite heresy was finally settled at the synod of Rome in 679 and confirmed by the Council of Constantinople in 680.

⁷ HE., IV, 1. ASC., 668.

⁸ *Ibid.*, IV, 1.

⁹ *Ibid.*, IV, 2. Eddius, c. 14.

¹⁰ HE., IV, 5. *'Ego quidem Theodorus, quamvis indignus, ab apostolica sede destinatus Doruuernensis ecclesiae episcopus.'* Theodore did not claim vicarial authority but he appears to emphasise unduly his appointment by the Apostolic See.

¹¹ HE., III, 7.

¹² *Ibid.*, IV, 2. Elmham, 6.

¹³ *Ibid.* *'Isque primus erat in archiepiscopis, cui omnis Anglorum ecclesia manus dare consentiret.'*

¹⁴ *Gesta Pontificum Anglorum*, p. 51 (R.S.).

¹⁵ *Thorni Willielmi Chronica, Historiae Anglicanae Scriptores X*; ed. R. Twysden, chapter, 1769. *'Anno Dominicae Incarnationis DCLXX sexto Kal Junii beatus Theodorus missus a Vitaliano Papa ad regimen Cantuariensis ecclesiae, acceperat enim legationis potestatem a praefato apostolico super Angliam, Scotiam et Hiberniam.'*

¹⁶ Council of Nicea, c. 8. Council of Ephesus, c. 8.

¹⁷ *Eddio Vita Wilfridi Episcopi; Historians of the Church of York and its Archbishops*, Vol. I, ed. J. Raine. (Rolls Series), c. XV. See also *The Life of Bishop Wilfrid by Eddius Stephanus*, Text, Translation and Notes by B. Colgrave, c. 15.

¹⁸ HE., III, 7. *'Consecratus in ipsa civitate, multis annis episcopatum Geuissorum ex synodica sanctione solus sedulo moderamine gessit.'*

¹⁹ The date of the synod of Hertford according to Bede was in the third year of Ecgfrith, the king of Northumbria, which would make the date 672. The record of the synod written by Titillus, Theodore's notary, which Bede later copied, states that the synod was held in 673, the year in which King Egbert of Kent died (IV, 5).

²⁰ HE., IV, 5.

²¹ Although the names of bishops usually followed the order of seniority of consecration no great importance should be attached to the order given here. Wilfrid was, doubtless, consecrated before Bisi but his name was not placed first because he was not personally present but only represented by his legates. It is probable that Bisi was the first bishop to be consecrated by Theodore and for that reason he gave him precedence since Wilfrid himself was not present in person.

²² HE., IV, 5. *'Theodorus cogit concilium episcoporum, una cum eis, qui canonica patrum statuta et diligerent, et nossent, magistris ecclesiae pluribus.'*

²³ *Ibid.* See also Additional Note D in Bright's *Early English Church History*, 2nd edition, pp. 454–5.

²⁴ Clofeshoh still escapes identification. Because of the similarity of the name, Cliff at Hoo was at first suggested. Later it was thought to be Abingdon because of the sound of its old name Sheovesham. Other suggestions have been made, and it is significant that Theodore did not follow the *capitulum* of Hertford but held his next synod at Hatfield. HS., III, p. 122 makes reference to the use of the expression by Boniface in 742 *'synodus Londinensis,'* and suggests that in all probability Clofeshoh is London.

²⁵ HE., II, 5. Spelman in his *Concilia*, p. 131 refers to *Concilium Cantianum tempore Eadbaldi Regis Cantii.* and gives the date 617. Wilkins follows Spelman and describes it as the Council of Kent. I, 30.

[26] Bright, op. cit., p. 258. See also Green's *History of the English People*, p. 30 and his *Making of England*, pp. 333 and 382.

[27] HE., IV, 5. '*VIIII capitulum in commune tractatum est: "Ut plures episcopi crescente numero fidelium augerentur"; sed de hac re ad praesens siluimus.*'

[28] *Ibid.*

[29] *Ibid.*, IV, 6. *Offensus a Wynfrido Merciorum episcopo per meritum cuiusdam inobedientiae, Theodorus archiepiscopus, eum de episcopatu.* William of Malmesbury in his *Gesta Pontificum*, III, 100; p. 221 says King Aethelred expelled him '*quia Egfridi partium fuerat.*' This would put the date of his deposition to 679, whereas Saxwulf became bishop of Mercia in 675.

[30] Canon 74.

[31] Canon 35.

[32] J. Bingham, *The Antiquities of the Church*, 10 vols.; Oxford 1855, vol. II, xvi, 16.

[33] *Ibid.* Hilary of Arles deprived Celedonius of his bishopric of Besancon or Vesontium, but on Celedonius appealing to Rome Hilary's judgment was quashed. See *Ep. LXXXIX; Leonis Magni et Aliorum Opera*, ed. J. Ulimmerius, Paris 1623. Bishop Rothad was also deposed by Archbishop Hincmar of Rheims; *Hincmari Epistolae*, II, XVII, XXIV and XXVI, Paris 1645.

[34] The council of Antioch in 379 decreed that 'all bishops observe that the bishop of the metropolis has the care of the whole province, because all men that have business or controversies to be decided resort from all parts to the metropolis' (Canon 9). At the council of Turin 398, the principle of ecclesiastical government by metropolitans was definitely formulated (Canon 2).

[35] *Novellae*, vi, c. 8. *Justiniani, Authenticae seu Novellae Constitutiones*, ed. J. Holander, Antwerp 1575.

[36] Bede nowhere identifies the former bishop of Rochester as the bishop of Hereford. William of Malmesbury (*G.P.*, IV, 163, p. 298) gives the name of Putta first in his list of the bishops of Hereford. Florence of Worcester records the death of Putta, bishop of Hereford, under the year 688. There can be little doubt that it is the same Bishop Putta, who, after relinquishing the see of Rochester, was sent by Bishop Saxwulf of Mercia to the remote and difficult of access part of his diocese, south of the river Severn, occupied by people known as the *Magonsaetan*.

[37] HE., IV, 12. Bede's description of the political situation in Wessex differs from that of the *Anglo-Saxon Chronicle* which records that King Cenwalh was succeeded by his queen, Saxburh, who reigned for a year, being followed by Aescwine. He was succeeded by Centwine who is described by Eddi, XL, as 'king of the West Saxons.'

[38] *Ibid.*, IV, 12 and V, 18. At the end of his 'Penitential' Theodore describes in verse, beginning with the words 'Te nunc sancte speculator,' and pays high tribute to Haeddi's character and sanctity of life. See HS., III, 203, note 21.

[39] Spelman, I, 168. BCS., 52.

CHAPTER VIII

[1] Eddius, XXIV.

[2] *Ibid.*

[3] *Ibid. Nullam criminis culpam in aliquo nocendi tibi ascribimus, sed tamen statuta de te iudicia non mutamus.*

[4] Mansi, III, 23. *Baronii Annales Ecclesiastici sub anno 445;* Antwerp 1599–1603.

[5] Eddius, XXIV. *Cum concilio coepiscoporum suorum iudicium apostolicae sedis magis elegit.*

[6] Spelman, I, 170. *Sperebamus deinde (inquit) de Britannia Theodorum confamulum atque coepiscoporum nostrum, magnae insulae Britanniae Archiepiscopum et Philosophum, cum aliis, qui ibidem hactenus demorantur, exinde ad humilitatem nostram conjungere, et hac de causa hucusque; concilium distulimus.*

[7] *Ibid.*, I, 158.

[8] *Ibid.*, I, 158. Although neither Eddius nor Bede makes any reference to this council, its authenticity appears to be unquestionable in view of the fact that the Abbot John carried its decrees to Britain and delivered them to Theodore. Acting upon the papal instructions contained in the decrees Theodore convoked the council at Hatfield in 680 at which decrees were passed in accordance with the requirements outlined at the council in Rome. It should not be suspect as suggested by HS., III, 135, because it appears to support the controversy between Canterbury and York in the 11th and 12th centuries.

[9] *Ibid.*, I, 171ff.

10 Mansi, XI, 23. Spelman, I, 191.

11 HE., IV, 17 and 18.

12 *Ibid. Praesidente Theodoro, gratia Dei archiepiscopo Britanniae insulae et civitatis Doruuernis; una cum eo sedentibus caeteris episcopis Brittaniae insulae viris venerabilibus, praepositis sacrasanctis evangeliis . . . fidem rectam et orthodoxam exposuimus.* Similarly in recording the subscriptions at the end of the document *Et nos omnes subscribimus, qui cum Theodoro archiepiscopo fidem catholicam exposuimus.*

13 HE., IV, 18.

14 Under the year 675 a spurious passage of the *Peterborough Chronicle* makes the Witan meet at Hatfield to receive a privilege of Pope Agatho for the abbey of Medeshamstede which Wilfrid delivered to King Aethelred at the Witan. See BCS., 48.

15 Eddius, XXXII.

16 Spelman, I, 161–2.

17 Eddius, XXXIV.

18 HE., III, 28. *Hrypensis ecclesiae praesul factus est.* It is probable that Eadhed's diocese of Lindsey had already been taken by King Aethelred of Mercia from the kingdom of Northumbria before Saxwulf had been consecrated to serve the Mercian bishopric. In consequence Lindsey ceased to be a part of the diocese of York and became as formerly a part of the diocese of Mercia. See HE., IV, 12 and FW., 680. As late as 685 Eadhed's subscription is to be found as bishop of Lindsey to a deed of a grant of land by King Ecgfrith to Cuthbert (BCS., 66). See also HE., IV, 12. *Eadhaedum de Lindissi reversum, eo quod Aedilred provinciam recepisset, Hyrpensis ecclesiae praefecit.*

19 HE., IV, 12 and 24.

20 Canterbury, London, Winchester, Dunwich, Elmham, Hereford, Worcester, Lindsey, Lichfield, Leicester, York, Lindisfarne, Hexham, Ripon, Rochester and Abercorn.

21 BCS., 25, 28, 35, 36, 38, 42–5, 49, 52, 57, 59, 66 and 67.

22 CD., XXVI.

23 *Historia Abbatum auctore Baeda,* c. 6; Plummer, I.; HE., IV, 18.

24 HE., IV, 28. *Vita Cuthberti,* XXIV; HS., III, 165.

25 Eddius, XLIII.

26 *Ibid.*

27 HE., V, 19 . . . *sedem suam et episcopatum ipso rege invitante recepit.*

28 *Ibid.,* IV, 29. See also *Registrum Sacrum Anglicanum,* p. 7, under John of Beverley.

29 *Poenitentiale Theodori,* II, vi, 8. HS., III, 195.

30 *Regesta Pontificum Romanorum,* 1548, ed. P. Jaffé, Berlin 1851. BCS., 11 gives the date as 611.

31 BCS., 48 and 49; 55 and 56; *Hist. Abbatum,* op. cit., c. 4, I, 369.

32 *Hist. Abbatum,* op. cit., c. 3, I, 389.

33 *Ibid.*

34 HE., I, 27.

35 HS., III, 42.

36 HS., III, 215.

37 BCS., 25–9, 32–7, 39–45, 47, 50, 51, 54, 57–67, 69–74.

38 *Bonifatti et Lullii Epistolae, Tomus I, Monumenta Germaniae Historica,* ed. M. Tangl, p. 168, no. 78. *'Lac et lanas ovium Christi oblationibus cotidianis ac decimis fidelium suscipiunt et curam gregis Domini deponunt.'*

39 HS, III, 215.

40 *Ibid.,* III, 191. *Poenitentiale Theodori,* II, ii, 8. *'Presbitero decimas dare non cogitur.'* II, xiv, 9 and 10. *'Tributum ecclesiae sit, sicut consuetudo proviniciae, id est, ne tantum pauperes inde in decimis aut in aliquibus rebus vim patientur.'* *'Decimas non est legitimum dare nisi pauperibus et peregrinis, sive laici suas ad ecclesias.'*

41 Stenton, op. cit., p. 154. King Edgar's Code at Andover(?) (II and III Edgar, 959–63); A. Ecclesiastical, i, 1; iii, 1; EHD., 395.

42 Eddius, XLV.

43 *Epistola Baedae ad Ecgbertum Episcopum;* Plummer, I, 411–12; pp. 8 and 9.

44 HE., III, 23.

45 *Poenitentiale Theodori,* I, ix, 7. *'Presbiter in propria provincia . . . ,'* II, i, 1. *'Ecclesiam licet ponere in alium, si necesse sit . . . ,'* II, ii, 7. *'Presbitero licet missas facere et populum benedicere in Parasceue . . . .'* HS., III, 185, 190 and 191.

[46] Eddius, XXII, speaks of Wilfrid's activities in the diocese of York, c. 673. *'In omnibus locis presbiteros et diacones sibi adjuvantes abumdantur ordinavit.'*

[47] *Epis.*, op. cit., para. 5.

[48] In Professor M. Deanesly's *The Pre-Conquest Church in England*, Chapter IX, entitled 'Minster and Parish' is considered the origin and use of these two terms in the Anglo-Saxon Church. See also Dean Addleshaw's *The Beginnings of the Parochial System* in St. Anthony's Hall Publications, No. 5, York.

[49] Elmham, *Titulus*, VIII, 151.

[50] ASC., 669. HE., V, 8. Deanesly, op. cit., p. 210.

[51] HE., V, 4 and 5. *Historians of the Church of York*, ed. J. Raine (R.S.), I, 249.

CHAPTER IX

[1] Eddius, XLIII. Genesis 27:4.

[2] ASC., 694.

[3] HE., V, 8. *'Ut enim breviter dicam, tantum profectus spiritalis tempore praesulatus illius Anglorum ecclesiae quantum numquam antea potuere ceperunt.'*

[4] *Ibid.* ASC., 692.

[5] *Ibid.*

[6] HE., V, 8.

[7] *Gesta Pontificum Romanorum*, edited by T. Mommsen, Berlin 1898, p. 216.

[8] *Eadmeri Historia Novorum in Anglia*, ed. M. Rule (R.S.), p. 266. William of Malmesbury, op. cit., p. 52.

[9] *Ibid.* *'Et vos igitur, dilectissimi ac Christianissimi filii, ejus vobis auctoritate collatum antistitem Bertwaldum, Cantiae sedis praesulem totiusque Britanniae primum pontificem, alacri pectore, menteque devota suscipite.'*

[10] William of Malmesbury, op. cit., p. 54; Eadmer, op. cit., p. 268. *'Die Falschungen Erzbischof Lanfranks von Canterbury,'* H. Boehmer; *'Studien zur Geschichete der Theologie und der Kirche,'* G. N. Bonwetsch and R. Seeberg, Leipzig 1902, p. 91. Boehmer argues that since so little is known of the chancellery of Pope Sergius I it could not be asserted that the letter is a forgery. And expresses the opinion that a true document relating to the *pallium* lies behind it. Both letters are accepted as authentic by P. Jaffé (to the kings and bishops). *Vide Regesta Pontificum Romanorum*, pp. 171 and 172.

[11] Boehmer, op. cit., pp. 89–91. Eddius, LIII, speaks *'sancti archiepiscopi Berhtwaldi Cantuariorum ecclesiae et totius Brittanniae,'* and again in LX he refers to *'Berhtwaldus Cantuariorum ecclesiae et paene totius Brittanniae archiepiscopus.'* Bishop Waldhere speaks of him as *'Totius Britanniae gubernacula regens,'* BCS., 115.

[12] HE., V, 8. ASC., 693.

[13] Mansi, XI, 23. Spelman, I, 191.

[14] Eddius XLV. HE., IV, 23.

[15] HE, IV, 23 and V, 11. Headda subscribed to a charter date c. 692, so it would appear that Wilfrid consecrated him while he was acting bishop of the Middle Angles. See BCS., 76.

[16] Eddius, XLVI and XLVII.

[17] *Ibid.*, LIII.

[18] *Ibid.* '. . . *Wilfrithus episcopus judicia sancti archiepiscopi Berhtwaldi Cantuariorum ecclesiae et totius Brittanniae, ab hac apostolica sedi emissi, statuta coram synodo contumaciter renuens contempsit.'*

[19] *Ibid.*, LVIII.

[20] *Ibid.*, LX. HE, V, 19. Aldfrith's death is given as 14th December 705. Eadulf who succeeded him was deposed after two months and succeeded by Osred who was at the Nidd synod. This would make its date 706.

[22] Tangl, op. cit., No. 73.

[23] *Epistola Bedae Ecgbertum Episcopum;* Plummer, I, 405. Date, 5th November 734.

[24] HS., III, 214.

[25] *Ibid.*

[26] Spelman's *Concilia*, I, 127.

[27] BCS., 36, 44 and 45.

[23] *Epistola Baedae Ecgbertum Episcopum;* Plummer, I, 405. Date, 5th November version gives *Birhtwald Bretone heah-biscop.*

[29] *Ibid.*

[30] HS, III, 238.

[31] *Ibid.*, III, 241, note b. Deanesly, op. cit., 210 and 216.

³² HE., V, 18. HS., III, 267–8.

³³ *Ibid.*, IV, 12 and 23. *Ibid.*, III, 130, note e.

³⁴ *Anglia Sacra,* ed. H. Wharton, Vol. I, p. 193. See *Historia Major Wintoniensis Thomae Rudborne.*

³⁵ HS., III, 267 and 275.

³⁶ HE., V, 18. Wm. of Malmesbury, *G.P.,* V, 223, p. 375. HS., III, 275.

³⁷ Wm. of Malmesbury, op. cit., V, 225, p. 380. BCS., 114. The place may have been Adderbourne on the banks of the river Nodder.

³⁸ Wm. of Malmesbury, op. cit., V, 223 and 224, p. 376.

³⁹ HE., IV, 16.

⁴⁰ BCS., 115. This letter was written before Bishop Haeddi's death on 7th July 705, and after King Cenred had ascended the throne of Mercia in 704. The two bishops concerned, therefore, were Waldhere of London and Haeddi of Winchester.

⁴¹ *Ibid.* 'Si non aliorum inventione me prius miscuissem quid plura elego quae elegeris rennuo quae rennueris et id ipsum in omnibus tecum sapiam.'

⁴² BCS., 128. Professor Whitelock draws attention to the fact that the ransom offered was the 'wergild' of a person of the highest rank in Kent. EHD., 166, p. 731. Tangl, op. cit., prints this letter (No. 7) and gives the date as 709–12.

⁴³ *Vita Sancti Bonifatii Willibaldo,* c. IV.; *Monumenta Moguntina,* ed. P. Jaffé; *Bibliotheca Rerum Germanicarum,* ed. P. Jaffé, Berlin 1866. A translation of this life is to be found in *The Anglo-Saxon Missionaries in Germany* by C. H. Talbot, London 1954.

⁴⁴ HE., V, 18. Elmham, p. 266 records that Eadberht was consecrated to serve the new diocese of Selsey. This must have been after 709 in which Forthere had been consecrated. The *Anglo-Saxon Chronicle* says Ine was at war with Geraint, king of the Britons in 710, so it would appear that the first synodal council summoned by Ine was in 709 or early in 710. Boniface was ordained to the priesthood in 710 after which he was the chief representative chosen by the king and council to lead the embassy to Canterbury. This also seems to confirm the date of the council as 710.

⁴⁵ *Ibid.,* V, 18 and 19. Eddius, LX.

⁴⁶ BCS., 126, p. 186. HS., III, 283.

⁴⁷ *HE.,* V, 18. HS., III, 268.

⁴⁸ *Ibid.,* IV, 5.

⁴⁹ BCS., 115. '. . . si non tuum judicium in ordinatione episcoporum implere festinarent, quod adhuc neglectum habentes non perficiebant.'

⁵⁰ *Vita Sancti Bonifatii,* c. IV.

⁵¹ *Ibid.* Tangl, No. 7ff.

⁵² BCS., 76, 111 and 113. The bishopric of Leicester was separated in 737 and continued until Ceolred who was consecrated in 840.

⁵³ HE., V, 18.

⁵⁴ *Ibid.,* III, 28 and IV, 12. The bishopric of Ripon was revived in 1836.

⁵⁵ *Ibid.,* V, 20. ASC., gives the date as 710.

⁵⁶ BCS., 91, 124 and 127.

⁵⁷ FW., 721. HE., V, 6 and 23.

⁵⁸ HE., III, 4 and V, 23.

CHAPTER X

¹ HE., V, 23. Stenton, op. cit., pp. 84 and 201ff.

² BCS, No. 154.

³ *Simeonis Dunelmensis, Historia de Gestis Regum Anglorum,* ed. T. Arnold (R.S.) II, 30–1. The seventh in the Malmesbury Series of Letters, purporting to have been sent by Pope Gregory III to the English bishops, states that Tatwine visited Rome, presented his petition and received the *pallium* from the Pope. This letter is considered to be spurious. Haddan and Stubbs, III, 311. Wm. of Malmesbury, *Gesta Pontificum,* p. 55.

⁴ ASC., gives 734. See J. W. Lamb, *The Archbishopric of York,* pp. 48ff, and Part iv, Notes, 4.

⁵ *Epistola Baedae ad Ecgbertum Episcopum;* Plummer, I, 405.

⁶ *Thorni Willielmi Chronica,* col. 1772; *Historiae Anglicanae Scriptores,* X, R. Twysden, London 1652.

⁷ The researches of Nothelm in the papal archives receive full examination in *The Canterbury Edition of the Answers of Pope Gregory I to Augustine* by M. Deanesly and P. Grosjean, pp. 2, 12 and 36.

⁸ HE., *Prefatio ad regum Ceoluufum.*

[9] *Ibid.*, I, 29. *Greg. Epp.*, XI, 39.

[10] BCS., 156. HS., III, 337.

[11] *Ibid.*

[12] Simeon of Durham, 737. The subscriptions of Torthelm and Hwitta are to be found to a charter (BCS., 165) and they were present at a synod in 747 at Clofeshoh (BCS., 174).

[13] BCS., 159.

[14] Tangl, 33. M. Deanesly and P. Grosjean, op. cit., p. 9. These two scholars conclude that 'Responsio V cannot have been written by Gregory I.' 'Responsio V' and the problem which it raised is fully discussed in reaching this conclusion.

[15] *Ibid.*

[16] *Ibid.*, 54. His letter to Gemmulus is dated 742–3.

[17] See his letters to Bishops Daniel, Pechthelm and Torthelm; Tangl, 23, 39, 63, 64; 47; 32, also to Abbess Eadburg; 10, 30, 35, 65 and 70, and to others.

[18] The *Abbreviationes Chronicorum Radulphi de Diceto*, I, 87; *Historiae Anglicanae Scriptores X*, ed. R. Twysden, London 1652, record that he received the *pallium* from Pope Gregory III, which must have been before November 741 the date of Gregory's death. A similar statement is made by Gervase; *Actus Pontificum Cantuariensium*, cc. 1640–1; *Historiae Anglicanae Scriptores X*. Boniface refers to Cuthbert's *pallium* in his letter to him (Tangl, 78) '*Major enim nobis sollicitudo ecclesiarum et cura populorum propter pallium credita et recepta quam ceteris episcopis, quia proprias tantum procurant parrochias incumbit.*'

[19] For surviving records of Aethebald's benefactions during this period, see BCS., 134–9; 153–7; 163–5, 171 and 177.

[20] *Vita Sancti Bonifatti Willibaldo*, c. VII.

[21] Tangl, No. 51.

[22] *Ibid.*, Nos. 75 and 51.

[23] *Ibid.*, No. 73. Of the seven fellow-bishops of Boniface three were Anglo-Saxons. They were Abel of Rheims, Burgheard of Würzbury, Hwitta of Buraburg, Wera of Utrecht, Willibald of Eichstatt. The sees of the other two, Leofwine and Werberht, cannot be identified, and the names of Hwitta and Leofwine are found only in the *Life of St. Ecgwine* (p. 751). Spelman, I, 232 only gives the names of five co-bishops of Boniface.

[24] *Ibid.*, 73.

[25] See the Prologue to the synod, BCS., 174. *Regesta Pontificum*, P. Jaffé, *Anglorum populum per duo scripta admonet, ut disciplinam corrigant, anathematis poena eos terrens*, No. 2279.

[26] William of Malmesbury in his *Gesta Pontificum*, lib. I, p. 9 wrongly says that the synod was convoked at the instigation of Boniface and Aethebald, whereas it was assembled under the directive of Pope Zacharias as the Prologue indicates. The suffragans of Cuthbert who were present were Ecgwulf of London, Dunn of Rochester, Hunfrith of Winchester, Podda of Hereford, Hwitta of Lichfield, Mildred of Worcester, Torhthelm of Leicester, Alwig of Lindsey, Eardulf of Dunwich, Sigga of Selsey, Herewald of Sherborne. Of his twelve suffragans the only absentee was Aethelfrith of Elmham.

[27] HE., III, 23. Eddius, XXII. *Poenitentiale Theodori*, I, ix, 7; II, i, 1; II, ii, 7. *Epistoal Baedae*; Plummer, I, 411.

[28] The three monasteries Coxwold, Stonegrave and Donaemuthe were the objects of an appeal made by Abbot Forthred to Pope Paul I. See BCS., 184 and Haddan and Stubbs, III, 394–6, also Mansi, XII, 651.

[29] Tangl, 78. Spelman, Wilkins and others have argued that this letter from Boniface to Cuthbert caused Cuthbert to convoke the synod. But both had exchanged details of reform measures in their respective Churches before the date of this letter in which reference to these exchanges is made. In his letter Boniface makes reference to a letter from Pope Zacharias the date of which is 1st May 748, after the synod of Clofeshoh. It is also to be noted (as HS., III, 383 point out) that Wm. of Malmesbury, *G.P.*, lib. I, p. 11, states that Cyneberht, the deacon of Cuthbert, carried the findings of the synod of Clofeshoh to Boniface, who refers to Cyneberht's visit to him with presents and a letter and to the conversations which he had with Cyneberht. It is generally accepted that the letter to Cuthbert was after the synod of 746 over which he presided.

[30] Tangl, 75 and 91.

[31] *De Vita Contemplativa, Julianus Pomerius; Patrologia Latina*, LIX, c. 413.

[32] BCS., 177.

[33] BCS., 178.

R

³⁴ *Poenitentiale Theodori,* II, ix, 7; II, i, 1; II, ii, 7.

³⁵ *'Ut presbiteri per loca et regiones laicorum, quae sibi ab episcopis provinciae insinuata et injuncta sunt, evangelicae atque apostolicae praedicationis officium in baptizando, et docendo, ac visitando sub legitimo ritu ac diligenti cura studeant explere . . .'* HS., III, 365.

³⁶ Tangl, 112.

³⁷ Tangl, 111. There is some uncertainty about the date of his martyrdom, and this accounts for the difference in the year of observance. The Germans observe the martyrdom as having been in 754 whereas the English consider it to have been in 755.

³⁸ ASC., 757.

³⁹ Spelman, I, 289. Thorn's *'Abb. S. Augustini,'* in Twysden's *Scriptores X,* cols. 1772–3 records the details of the change made by Cuthbert in the place of burial. This was not the only instance of Cuthbert's influence in a place of burial. In the cathedral church of Hereford, the see of which he was bishop before his translation to Canterbury, he erected over the tomb of some of his predecessors a memorial on which was inscribed one of his commemorative verses. He also gave a magnificent cross to the cathedral inscribed with another of his short poems (Wm. of Malmesbury, *G.P.,* p. 299). See also Elmham, p. 317 and W. Dugdale, *Monasticon Anglicanum,* 82, 128.

⁴⁰ Eadmer gives a description of the cathedral church before its destruction by fire in 1067 and it would appear that the church had apses at both east and west. W. Stubbs, *Vita Dunstani* (R.S.), p. 271.

⁴¹ 'The Early Community at Christ Church, Canterbury,' by J. Armitage Robinson in *Journal of Theological Studies,* xxvii (1926), pp. 225–40.

CHAPTER XI

¹ Henry of Huntingdon's *Historia Anglorum,* ed. T. Arnold (R.S.), p. 121.

² BCS., 183.

³ Tangl, No. 117.

⁴ Mansi, XIII, 321–6. *Grégoire le Grand les États Barbares et la Conquête Arabe (590–757) par L. Brehier et R. Aigrain; Fliche et Martine,* V, 366; *Histoire de l'Église,* 8 vols., Paris 1947.

⁵ Mansi, XIII, 844.

⁶ Tangl, No. 78.

⁷ Simeon of Durham—764—Eadberht to Leicester; 765—Cuthfrith to Lichfield. Bishop Osa of Selsey subscribed to a charter dated 765 (BCS., 198).

⁸ BCS., 291. HS., III, 399.

⁹ *Ibid.* Ibid., III, 512.

¹⁰ Tangl, No. 122.

¹¹ BCS., 193, 194 and 196. Offa's grant, BCS., 195.

¹² Elmham, pp. 328–30. HS., III, 397, note a, discusses the date of Bregowine's death and shows that Osbern's *Vita Bregwini,* A.S. II, 76 confirms the date given by Simeon of Durham, the Chronicle of Melrose, and Roger Hoveden. The year 765 is also confirmed by the charters of the period.

¹³ *Registrum Sacrum Anglicanum,* p. 22. BCS., 196. In this charter Jaenberht subscribes himself *Ego Jaenberhtus gratia Dei archiepiscopus consensi et subscripsi.* The charter granting land by King Egbert of Kent to Eardulf, bishop of Rochester, is dated 765, so it would appear that Jaenberht, as archbishop-'elect' subscribed although it is not given in his subscription.

¹⁴ P. Jaffé, *Regesta Pontificum Romanorum,* p. 198. Elmham, p. 330.

¹⁵ BCS., 221. *Cum consensu meorum episcoporum omniumque principum.*

¹⁶ Simeon of Durham, 767. Aluberht was consecrated at the same time as Albert, Ceolwulf and Ealhmund; Aluberht being consecrated at York. See *Registrum Sacrum Anglicanum* which gives *Vita S. Liudgeri;* Pertz, I, 407. Liudger was a fellow scholar with Aluberht in Archbishop Egbert's school at York.

¹⁷ *Ibid.,* 201.

¹⁸ *Ibid.,* 207. 'Rector' head, leader or ruler. (*Ego Iambertus archiepiscopus et rector catholicae ecclesiae consensi et subscripsi.*)

¹⁹ *Ibid.,* 208.

²⁰ BCS., 213–15.

²¹ *Ibid.,* 214. *Offa rex totius Anglorum patriae.*

²² *Ibid.,* 209.

²³ *Ibid.* During the archiepiscopate of Bregowine a grant of land was made to Eardulf, bishop of Rochester, by King Sigered who is referred to in the

charter as *Ego Sigeredus rex dimidiae partis provinciae Cantuariorum.*
²⁴ *Ibid.*, 227 (778) and 228 (779). In the year 784 a charter (BCS., 243) is to be found by which a certain King Ealmund of Kent made a grant to the monastery of Reculver. He displaced Egbert's successor in 782. The ASC. under 852 says the people of Kent were wrongly forced away from Egbert's kinsmen.

²⁵ G. C. Brooke, *English Coins*, p. 19 and Plate III, pp. 14–18.

²⁶ BCS., 227.

²⁷ BCS., 234–6.

²⁸ *Ibid.*, 241. Aethelbald's charter granting the land was issued in 736 (BCS., 154). During the archiepiscopate of Theodore King Osric of the Hwicce granted land in 676 to Abbess Bertana at Bath where she had a nunnery (BSC., 43).

²⁹ BCS., 241. The land to which Offa relinquished his claim was situated in his territories at Stratford, Stour, Bredon, Hampton and Stour in Ismere. Professor Whitelock in *English Historical Documents*, p. 466 suggests that Offa had a political interest in obtaining the adjacent land of thirty hides for the purpose of strengthening the southern boundary of his kingdom. Jaenberht's suffragans, all of whom subscribed, were Diora of Rochester, Aethelwulf of Elmham, Heardred of Dunwich, Eadberht of Leicester, Hygeberht of Lichfield, Aethelmod of Sherborne, Cyneberht of Winchester, Ceolwulf of Lindsey, Heathored of Worcester, Gislhere of Selsey, Eadberht of Hereford and Ealdberht of London.

³⁰ BCS., 247 and 248.

³¹ *Ibid.*, 245.

³² *Vita Offae*, Wilkins, *Concilia*, I, 152.

³³ *Monumenta Alcuiniana*, Ep. 85 ; Vol. VI, *Bibliotheca Rerum Germanicarum*, ed. by Wattenbach and Duemmler ; ed. P. Jaffé.

³⁴ *Vita Offae*, Wilkins, I, 152.

³⁵ See *Notker Balbulus ; Gesta Caroli Magni*, ed. P. Jaffé ; *Monumenta Carolina ; Bibliotheca Rerum Germanicarum*, vol. IV, c. 25. Cf. Paul the Deacon, Charlemagne's preface to his collection of Sermons ; Migne, *Patrologia Latina*, vol. 95, pp. 1159–60.

³⁶ *Monumenta Carolina*, op. cit., IV, 279.

³⁷ *Vita Offae ;* op. cit., I, 152.

³⁸ Spelman, I, 294. HS., III, 450, c. 4.

³⁹ BCS., 250.

⁴⁰ *Ibid.*, 288. This letter of Leo III to Cenwulf, king of the Mercians, indicates that the division of the province of Canterbury and the creation of the archbishopric of Lichfield was considered at the synod of Chelsea in 787. It was at this synod that Offa made his vow. The mancus was the equivalent of thirty silver pennies. This payment was probably the origin of 'Peter's Pence,' but how far Offa could pledge his successors to continue its payment raises many questions. In 855 King Aethelwulf made a gift of three hundred mancuses : 100 for the Pope, and 100 each to burn lights in honour of St. Peter and St. Paul. (See also Wharton's *Anglia Sacra*, I, 461.)

⁴¹ *Ibid.*

⁴² The ASC. says : 'Hygeberht was chosen by King Offa.' Hygebeht was already at that time bishop of Lichfield, and this refers to the king's choice of him to be archbishop.

⁴³ Bishop Totta of Selsey and Bishop Aethelmod of Sherborne were present at the synod and subscribed (BCS., 250).

⁴⁴ Wm. of Malmesbury, *G.P.*, p. 16.

⁴⁵ *Einhardi Vita Karoli Imperatoris*, c. 33 ; *Monumenta Germaniae Historica*, vol. II, ed. G. H. Pertz, Hanover 1829.

⁴⁶ BCS., 253.

⁴⁷ BCS., 254–7.

⁴⁸ *Ibid.*, 256. '. . . factum est conciliabulum in loco famosa qui dicitur Celchyth praesidentibus duobus archiepiscopis Jamberhto scillcet et Hygberhto. . . .'

⁴⁹ ASC., 788.

⁵⁰ BCS., 291.

⁵¹ EHD., 779.

⁵² *Anglia Sacra*, I, 462.

⁵³ FW., 793.

⁵⁴ BCS., 265. The subscriptions to this charter are probably spurious.

⁵⁵ *Ibid.*, 272.

⁵⁶ *Ibid.*, 280 and 281.

⁵⁷ *Ibid.*, 279.

[58] *Caroli Magni Regis Epistola;* Labbe, *Concilia,* VII, 1049. *Mon. Alcuin,* Ep. 130. See Mansi, XIII, 909 for the canons of this council.
[59] *Monumenta Carolina,* Ep. 8, ed. P. Jaffé, Berlin 1867.
[60] *Alcuini Opera,* I, Epp. 42 and 43, ed. S. Froben, 2 vols., Ratisbon 1777.
[61] *Monumenta Carolina,* Ep. 11. Pope Hadrian I died in December 795.
[62] *Baedae Continuatio,* Plummer, I, 361. Bede records that King Ceolwulf of Northumbria was forcibly tonsured and incarcerated in a monastery.
[63] BCS., 288.
[64] *Monumenta Alcuiniana,* Ep. 28, ed. W. Wattenbach and E. Duemmler; *Bibliotheca Rerum Germanicarum,* ed. P. Jaffé, Berlin 1873. See also *Alcuini,* Epp. 48 and 51, ed. S. Froben.
[65] *Ibid.,* Ep. 60. See EHD., 789.
[66] *Ibid.,* Ep. 59.

CHAPTER XII

[1] BCS., 277 and 279.
[2] *Textus Roffensis,* 248, ed. T. Hearne, Oxford 1720. This profession opens with the words *'Domino meo vere amantissimo Ethelhardo archiepiscopo Eadulfus Eboracensis humilis episcopus.'* No bishop of the name of Eadulf or Aldulf occupied the see until 922 *(Reg. Sacr. Angl.,* 31). The word *Eboracensis* evidently was substituted for the word *Lindisfarorum* or some other variant for 'Lindsey' by another hand at a later period when the controversy was raging between the archiepiscopal sees of Canterbury and York.
[3] Tangl, 28.
[4] *Ibid.,* 161.
[5] *Ad Episcopos de jure Metropolitanorum; Hincmari Opuscula,* II, xliv, Paris 1645. See also Mansi, XVI, 562.
[6] *Textus Roffensis,* 254.
[7] *Ibid.,* 251, 253 and 256.
[8] BCS., 301, where his subscription is found.
[9] Ibid., 294. '. . . *Venerabili archiepiscopo Aethelardo et primato tocius Britanniae. . . .'* See also No. 94.
[10] *Ibid.,* 287. EHD., 791.
[11] *Ibid.,* 288. *Ibid.,* 793.
[12] *Monumenta Alcuiniana,* Epp. 172 and 173.
[13] *Ibid.,* Ep. 171.
[14] The sobriquet which Alcuin used for Charlemagne was 'David.' Alcuin was appointed abbot of St. Martin's, Tours, by the emperor in 796.
[15] Wm. of Malmesbury, *G.P.,* I, 37, p. 57. BCS., 305 and in HS., III, 536. See translation, EHD., 798.
[16] *Monumenta Alcuiniana,* Epp. 171 and 190.
[17] *Ibid.,* Ep. 190.
[18] With his letter to the pope in 798 (BCS., 287) Cenwulf sent a gift of 120 mancuses (a mancus was worth thirty silver pennies) to the pope who only acknowledged it by a reference to Offa's vow to give 365 mancuses annually (Wharton's *Anglia Sacra,* I, 461). Cenwulf did not consider himself bound by Offa's vow, but with his letter in 801 or 802, which Leo III acknowledged (BCS., 306) in 802, he sent another gift of 120 mancuses. See BCS., 306 and HS., III, 538.
[19] BCS., 310. See Johnson's *English Canons,* I, p. 296 and EHD., 799.
[20] *Ibid. Wulfred Archidiaconus.* These subscriptions are to be found in documents 'B' and 'C.' The earliest use of the title 'archdeacon' is to be found in the treatise of Bishop Optatus against the Donatists, in which he refers to Archdeacon Caecilian. *Sancti Optati Episcopi de Schismate Donatistarum,* I, xvi.; Migne's *Patrologia Latina,* XI, 916.
[21] BCS., 310 and 312.
[22] *Ibid.* Bishop John of York consecrated Wilfrid II and then withdrew to the cloister (HE, V, 6), and it is probable that Wilfrid did the same after consecrating Egbert. J. W. Lamb, *The Archbishopric of York,* p. 47.
[23] Tidferth made his profession to Aethelheard alone. *Textus Roffensis,* 256.
[24] Before his consecration by Pope Gregory II Boniface was interrogated by him concerning the Christian Faith and the traditions of the Church. At his own request Boniface submitted a written confession of faith and was afterwards consecrated. *Vita Sancti Willibaldo,* c. VI. Tangl, No. 16.
[25] HS., III, 545.
[26] BCS., 309.

27 *Ibid.*, 317.

28 *Textus Roffensis*, p. 258. Beornmod's subscription is first in 805. BCS., 319.

29 BCS, 214. Offa's gift to Jaenberht is described as follows: '*Ego Offa rex totius Anglorum patriae dabo et concedo Jaenberhto archiepiscopo ad ecclesiasm Christi aliquam partem trium aratrorum. . . .*' Similarly in his gift to the familia Offa's gift was *ad opus familiae Christi id est monachorum qui in ecclesia Christi . . .* (BCS., 215).

CHAPTER XIII

1 BCS., 312. At the council of Toledo in 633, over which Isidore of Seville presided, a metropolitan archdeacon exercised his office. This included bidding the members to stand up and to pray and, if a layman desired to make an appeal to the council he could only do it through the metropolitan archdeacon who had authority to raise the matter in full council (Canons 3 and 4; Mansi, X, 617).

2 BCS., 321 and 322.

3 *Anglia Sacra*, I, 462.

4 ASC., 806. FW., 804.

5 G. C. Brooke, *English Coins*, 3rd ed. 1950, pp. 18 and 19.

6 *Leonis III*, Ep. 2; *Monumenta Carolina*, 311.

7 *Registrum Sacrum Anglicanum*, 17 and 18.

8 BCS., 328.

9 BCS, 339.

10 *Ibid.*, 335.

11 *Ibid.*, 332.

12 HS., III, 450, c. 4.

13 BCS., 214.

14 'The Familia at Christ Church, Canterbury, 597–832' by Margaret Deanesly, p. 10. This valuable essay is contained in *Essays in Mediaeval History* presented to Thomas Frederick Tout, ed. by A. G. Little and F. M. Powicke, Manchester 1925. *Regula Chrodegangi*, cc. 3, 8, 21 and 25; Labbe, VII, 1447–54.

15 Deanesly, op. cit., pp. 10 and 11.

16 HS., III, 509.

17 BCS., 380.

18 HS., III, 579ff. BCS., 358.

19 *Ibid.* Canons 4, 7 and 8.

20 Labbe, *Concilia*, VII, 1281, c. 43.

21 HS., III, 581, c. 5.

22 *Ibid.*, III, 583, c. 9.

23 *Ibid.*, III, 584, c. 11. See also III, 119, c. 2.

24 *Ibid.*, III, 584, c. 11. '*Quia caput est suarum episcoporum.*' This phrase repeats the language of *The Apostolical Constitutions* (edited by J. Donaldson; *Ante-Nicene Christian Library*, vol. XVII, ed. A. Roberts and J. Donaldson, Edinburgh, 1870). See vol. XVII, p. 261 where reference is made that the bishops should know who is chief among them and should esteem him as 'the head,' and should not do anything of importance without his consent. This ruling was in the late fourth century. When Anselm's authority was challenged in his province he sought the advice of Bishop Wulstan of Worcester; Migne, P.L.; CLIX, cols 44 and 202.

25 ASC., 814.

26 BCS., 384.

27 *Ibid.*, 366 and 367.

28 Bede records the excommunication of an individual (HE., III, 22). For interdicts pronounced by a bishop of Bayeux; by Bishop Francon of Aix on King Sigeberht; by Bishop Leo of Agde on Count Gomachaire see *Histoire du Christianisme par l'Abbe Fleury*, II, XXXIV, LIII; Paris 1836. Bishop Hincmar of Laon pronounced an interdict in the ninth century (*Cathedra Petri*, VII, 3, 279). Thorpe, p. 73.

29 Mansi, XII, 807a.

30 The Epistle of Ignatius to the Smyrnaeans, A-N.C.L., 250. *Cathedra Petri*, VI, 202. Fabian was pope from 236–50.

31 *Cathedra Petri*, II, 354. *Greg. Epp.*, II, 18 and 20

32 BCS., 384.

33 *Ibid.*, 366, 367 and 368.

34 BCS., 370 and 371. Details of Kenelm's murder and burial are in Elmham, p. 343. BCS., 373 and 374. ASC., 823.

[35] BCS., 378 and 379. EHD., 476.
[36] *Ibid.,* 384. HS., III, 601, note b.
[37] BCS., 389–93 and 398; 395, 411, 413 and 418.
[38] *Ibid.,* 380 and 381.
[39] *Ibid.,* 402. See also Margaret Deanesly's essay in *Essays in Mediaeval History,* op. cit., p. 12.
[40] BCS., 333, 334, 354, 355, 369, 375, 376, 388, 397 and 399.
[41] *Ibid.,* 312, 318, 319, 321, 322, 332, 373 and 384.
[42] ASC., 834.
[43] *Actus Pontificum Cantuariensis Gervasio,* cols. 1643 and 1650; *Historiae Anglicanae Scriptores X,* ed. R. Twysden, London 1652. Haddan and Stubbs, III, 611, note a, observe that in the use of the title 'dean' Gervase confused Ceolnoth with Ethelnoth who carried that title two centuries later.

CHAPTER XIV

[1] BCS., 396, 404 and 406.
[2] M. Deanesly, 'The Archdeacons of Canterbury under Archbishop Ceolnoth,' *The English Historical Review,* vol. XLII, pp. 1ff.
[3] *Hincmari Capitula;* Mansi, XV, 497.
[4] *Ibid. Capitula Walterii Episcopi Auralianensis,* I and II; P.L., CXIX, 725–9. Diocesan Organisation in the Middle Ages; H. A. Thompson, *Proceedings of the British Academy,* vol. XXIX, p. 159, note 2.
[5] BCS., 562.
[6] FW., 1101. Reference is made to Aelfmar the abbot and to Aelfmar the archdeacon. It is probable they were one and the same person.
[7] Spelman, I, 496, 6 and 7. For a translation of these Laws see EHD., 435.
[8] *Fragmentum de Institutione Archidiaconatus Cantuariensis; Anglia Sacra,* I, 150ff.
[9] Labbe, *Concilia,* VII, 1169 and 1617.
[10] BCS., 516. '. . . *dabo et concedo meo fideli amico Wighelme presbytero unam sedem in loco dicitur sancti Martini ecclesia.*'
[11] *The English Historical Review,* vol. XLII, p. 9. HS., III, 685a.
[12] BCS., 516. CD., CCXXVIII.
[13] F. E. Harmer, *Select English Historical Documents,* 1914, p. 86.
[14] BCS., 611, 620, 623–8. W. Stubbs suggests that this Wighelm may have been a bishop of Selsey. See *Registrum Sacrum Anglicanum,* p. 23.
[15] Gervasio, *Actus Pontificum Cantuariensis,* col. 1650.
[16] *Anglia Sacra,* I, 150. After the pope's decretal 'chorepiscopi' continued to use the title. Ratbold subscribed to an edict of the Emperor Lothair as *Ratoldus presbyter vocatus episcopus.* Labbe, *Concilia,* VII, 1771.
[17] Bishop Kentsec had his seat in the monastery of Dinnurrin, Cornwall. See BCS., 527.
[18] *Ibid.,* 416.
[19] *Ibid.,* 421.
[20] 421–3. See HS., III, 617 and 625, note a, in reference to a council at Wilton.
[21] BCS., 503.
[22] *Ibid.,* 507.
[23] *Ibid.,* 516.
[24] *Ibid.,* 406.
[25] *Willelmi Malmesbiriensis De Gestis Regum Anglorum,* II, c. 3; ed. W. Stubbs (Rolls Series).
[26] *Annals of the Reign of Alfred the Great* by Asser, p. 70; *Six Old English Chronicles,* ed. J. A. Giles, London 1900.
[27] BCS., vols. I and II.
[28] *Annales Bertinani sub anno 839; Monumenta Germaniae Historica,* ed. G. H. Pertz, vol. I, p. 433. In BCS., the date is given as c. 850. See No. 456.
[29] M. Deanesly, *A History of Early Medieval Europe 476–911,* p. 296.
[30] BCS., 424.
[31] BCS., 521.
[32] *Ibid.,* 519; 535 which is a confirmation of the charter by which King Aethelred in 671 founded the monastery at Gloucester. See No. 60.
[33] ASC. and FW. give the same date—870.
[34] *Actus Pontificum Cantuariensium auctore Gervasio; Hist. Angl. Script, X,* col. 1643.
[35] BCS., 529, 531, 536, 538 and 539.

[36] EHD., 221. In HS., III, 264 and BCS., 119 the document gives no names in the address, and in consequence was wrongly attributed to John VI or VII.

[37] ASC., 874.

[38] Mansi, XVII, cols. 54ff. For a translation of this see EHD., 220.

[39] W. H. Stevenson, *Chronicon Fani Sancti Neoti; Asserius de rebus Gestis Aelfredi*, pp. 136–7, Oxford 1904.

[40] Mansi, XVII, cols. 54ff.

[41] ASC., 878. The chrysom-loosing ceremony was the removal, eight days after baptism, of the white fillet or cloth bound round the head after anointment.

[42] Spelman, I, 390.

[43] BCS., 553. EHD., 492.

[44] EHD., 373, 49, 8. Spelman, I, 303.

[45] *Ibid.*, I, 366, 3; 368, 9; 370, 16. Also EHD., 374, 3; 376, 15; 379, 40.

[46] *Ibid.*, I, 370, 18. EHD., 380, 43.

[47] Asser, p. 72. *Annales Cambriae*, ed. J. W. A. Ithel (R.S.), p. 14 record that Novis died in 873.

[48] *Aethelredus Dorobernensis archiepiscopus, hic Chevelliauc episcopum Landaviae, et post Libau episcopum Landaviae, et post Lunverd episcopum Sancti David, Cantuariae consecravit. Abbrevationes Chronicorum auctore Radulfo de Diceto; Hist. Angl. Scrip.* X, col. 451. The consecration of Libau at this time seems doubtful since his consecration is dated as taking place thirty-eight years later, after Aethelred's death (HS., I, 209, notes a and h). See *Registrum Sacrum Anglicanum*, pp. 37, 217 and 219.

CHAPTER XV

[1] EHD., 818.

[2] *Ibid.*, p. 819, note 1. The book-marker 'aestel,' a little spear or a thin piece of wood, was some kind of a pointer to assist the eyes of the reader along the line he was reading. This book-marker was very valuable, being worth fifty mancuses, which at that time would be the value of three hundred sheep or fifty oxen. A book-marker of this type would be wrought in precious metal and set with jewels. Wm. of Malmesbury in his *G.R.*, I, 133, says the 'aestal' was of the value of one mancus.

[3] In the opening line of address a space was left for the insertion of the bishop's name to whom it was addressed. The copy sent to the bishop of London has survived and in it is the bishop's name 'Heahstan.'

[4] *Ibid.*, p. 819.

[5] Asser, op. cit., p. 65. ASC., 885.

[6] *Ibid.*, 883.

[7] Asser, op. cit., p. 78. Asser wrongly gives the name of the patriarch as 'Abel.' This visit to Jerusalem by Alfred's embassy must have been in 888 or the following year.

[8] From the *Vita Grimbaldi* and other sources P. Grierson in *English Historical Review*, No. LX (October 1940), pp. 529–61, discusses Grimbald's life and activities in England.

[9] EHD., No. 225.

[10] *Ibid.*, p. 813, No. 224.

[11] *Ibid.*, p. 813, No. 223.

[12] *Actus Pontificum Cantuariensis Ecclesiae auctore Gervasio*, cols. 1643–4, *Historiae Anglicanae Scriptores X*, R. Twysden, London 1652. Of Plegmund it is recorded *Hic Romam profectus a Formoso papa sacratus est, palliumque suscepit et metropolitani plenitudinem potestatis.*

[13] BCS., 573 and Wm. of Malmesbury, *Gesta Pontificum* (R.S.), pp. 59–61. EHD., No. 227. This letter becomes suspect because of the last part of it in which the claims of the primacy of Canterbury as against York are stated, reminiscent of the controversy between the two archbishoprics in the eleventh century. It is evident that this part is spurious, but it does not invalidate the earlier part of the letter which bears its own evidence of authenticity.

[14] Asser, op. cit., p. 73.

[15] See the preface in vol. II, p. lvi, to Wm. of Malmesbury's *G.R.*

[16] Aethelweard's Chronicle 908. Spelman, I, 387.

[17] Spelman, I, 387. Malmesbury's *G.R.* (R.S.), I, 141.

[18] *Ibid. Registrum Sacrum Anglicanum*, pp. 23 and 24 points out that the names of the bishops are to some extent conjectural. They are quoted as authentic by Archbishop Dunstan in his letter to King Aethelred (980–8). See No. 7 in *The*

Crawford Collection of Early Charters, ed. A. S. Napier and W. H. Stevenson, Oxford 1895.

[19] FW., 1107.

[20] *Ibid.*

[21] Wm. of Malmesbury, *G.P.* (R.S.), p. 177, note 6; also his *G.R.* (R.S.), vol. I, p. 140, note 3. A full discussion of the document is found in the preface to vol. II of the *G.R.,* by W. Stubbs, pp. liv–lx. See also BCS., 614 and Spelman, I, 387.

[22] BCS., 571. The evidence of this charter appears more acceptable than the record of Simeon of Durham, who gives the date of Aethelbald's consecration as 900. It is most improbable that the archbishopric of York was vacant after the death of Wulfhere in 893 or 895. See *The Archbishopric of York: The Early Years* by J. W. Lamb, 1967.

[23] BCS., 571.

[24] *Ibid.,* 572.

[25] *Ibid.,* 577 and 578.

[26] *Ibid.*

[27] *Ibid.,* 553. See EHD., No. 96. In a prefatory note Professor Whitelock points out that Alfred's will, which is in Old English, is the earliest surviving will of an English king. 'And to the Erchebyschop, I give an hunderyd mark; and Esne, byschop, and Werferthe; and to hym of Schyrburn.'

[28] BCS., 558.

[29] *Ibid.,* 272. In a charter by which King Offa granted land to Worcester Cathedral (791–796). '. . . . *Quamdiu fides Christiana apud Anglos in Bryttannia maneat.*' There can be little doubt, since this occurs infrequently, that the clause was included because of the uncertainty already mentioned.

[30] BCS., 558 (871–889). This eighth century illuminated manuscript in Old English is in the Royal Library of Stockholm. It has been regarded as coming from Canterbury but recently it has been suggested that it may be assigned to Lichfield. How it reached Stockholm is not known, but it may have been loot carried there by the Danes after their raids in England.

[31] *Ibid.,* 602 and 603.

[32] Spelman, I, 390ff. Johnson, op. cit., pp. 332–5.

[33] BCS., 558.

[34] *Ibid.,* 618 and 622.

[35] FW., 969.

[36] Aethelweard's Chronicle, 901.

[37] *Actus Pontificum Cantuariensis Gervasio,* col. 1644.

[38] *Registrum Sacrum Anglicanum,* pp. 24–5.

[39] *Actus Pont. Cantuar.,* col. 1644.

[40] Neither the *Anglo-Saxon Chronicle* nor Florence of Worcester speak of Aethelstan's 'coronation' but of his 'consecration.' Florence wrongly attributes the consecration to Archbishop Aethelhelm who had died a year before the event. Wm. of Malmesbury in *G.R.* (R.S.), vol. I, p. 141 records *'apud regiam villam quae Kingestune coronatus est'* but not by whom. Ethelweard in his Chronicle records that 'Aethelstan gained the crown of the kingdom.'

CHAPTER XVI

[1] Spelman, I, 396ff. Johnson, I, 339ff.

[2] G. C. Brooke, *English Coins,* p. 19 and Plate III, 14–18.

[3] Spelman, I, 405, c. 11. Johnson, I, 349.

[4] ASC., 927.

[5] BCS., 663 and 664.

[6] *Ibid.,* 665.

[7] *Ibid.,* 669.

[8] Simeon of Durham's *Epistola de Archiepiscopis Eboraci,* col. 79; T. Stubbs, *Actus Pontificum Eboracensium,* 1698.

[9] BCS., 675, 676 and 677.

[10] Conan subscribed as Cunan, Cuman and Cayman. HS., I, 676.

[11] BCS., 682, 694ff., 707, 714, 728. EHD., 96.

[12] J. Armitage Robinson, *The Saxon Bishops of Wells,* pp. 60ff.

[13] BCS., 643 and 693. J. Armitage Robinson, *The Times of St. Dunstan,* pp. 51–71.

[14] J. W. Lamb, *The Archbishopric of York,* p. 119. BCS., 703.

[15] BCS., 689.

[16] Cynsige's subscription first appears at the witenagemot of Colchester in 931.

BCS., 674. The last deed in which his subscription is to be found is dated 16th December 934. BCS., 705.

[17] BCS., 1008. EHD., No. 106, pp. 509ff.

[18] EHD., No. 37. VI Aethelstan, Prologue; II, X, XII, 1–3, pp. 387–91.

[19] BCS., 747.

[20] *Ibid., Ego Wlhelmus archisacerdos totius Britanniae confirmo.*

[21] *Ibid.,* 677 and 692.

[22] Wm. of Malmesbury, *G.P.* (R.S.), p. 20.

[23] *Vita Odonis Archiepiscopi Cantuariensis; Anglia Sacra,* II, 82. Wm. of Malmesbury in his *G.P.* (R.S.), p. 22, clearly states Oda visited Fleury to receive the habit.

[24] *Actus Pontificum Cantuariensis Ecclesiae Gervasio;* op. cit., col. 1644.

[25] *De Arch. Ebor.,* op. cit., col. 134.

[26] Spelman, I, 415ff. Johnson, op. cit., 358–65.

[27] Plummer, op. cit., I, 411, c. 8.

[28] Spelman, I, 246, c. 3. Johnson, op. cit., I, 244.

[29] *Ibid.,* I, 294, c. 4. Johnson, op. cit., I, 268.

[30] C. of Hertford, c. 4. Spelman, I, 153, c. 4.

[31] EHD. (Acts of the Abbots of St. Bertin), No. 26, p. 318.

[32] Spelman, I, 419. The Anglo-Saxon text gives the word 'synoth' and the Latin version 'coetus' to describe this council. Alms-fee = plough-alms.

[33] *Ibid.,* I, 422. Johnson, op. cit., I, 368, translates 'diocesis' as 'shire.'

[34] FW., 946. ASC., 946.

[35] J. W. Lamb, *The Archbishopric of York,* pp. 125–7; BCS., 818.

[36] J. W. Lamb, op. cit., pp. 125ff. ASC., 947.

[37] Malmesbury's *G.P.* (R.S.), pp. 22 and 245.

[38] Spelman, I, 418. *The History of Ingulph; The Church Historians of England,* ed. J. Stevenson, vol. II, part II, pp. 610ff.

[39] J. Stevenson, *Chronicon Monasterii de Abingdon* (R.S.), vol. II, pp. 257ff.

[40] BCS., 811.

[41] *Ibid.,* 912. EHD., 511.

[42] BCS., 912–14.

CHAPTER XVII

[1] F. M. Stenton, *The Early History of the Abbey of Abingdon,* p. 49.

[2] Malmesbury's *G.R.* (R.S.), vol. I, p. 163.

[3] *Ibid.*

[4] BCS., 918.

[5] ASC., gives 957 in C(B). FW., gives 958. Osbern's *Vita Dunstani* gives 956, but 957 falls rightly into place with other events of the time.

[6] FW., 957.

[7] *Ibid.*

[8] EHD., 395. Johnson, op. cit., I, 409.

[9] EHD., 46. Spelman, I, 447ff. K. Jost, Anglia, LVI, pp. 288–301.

[10] EHD., 398.

[11] FW., gives 959, but not until 960 does Dunstan subscribe to charters. The ASC. gives 961.

[12] Malmesbury's *G.P.,* p. 30. BCS., 1069. FW. wrongly asserts he went to Rome.

[13] *Ibid.,* p. 178. BCS., 1048 and 1050.

[14] Stenton, op. cit., p. 127.

[15] Knowles, op. cit., p. 34.

[16] *Vita S. Oswaldi; Historians of York,* I, 439.

[17] Knowles, op. cit., Appendix III, p. 696. E. S. Duckett, *St. Dunstan of Canterbury,* p. 89.

[18] BCS., 1168. Preface to the *'Concordia';* W. Dugdale, *Monasticon Anglicanum,* I, xxxviiff.

[19] *Ibid.* Robinson, op. cit., p. 146. See also *Regularis Concorda,* ed. and trans. by Dom Thomas Symons, 1953.

[20] *Ibid.* Knowles, op. cit., p. 45.

[21] *Ibid.*

[22] H. Bohmer, *Kirche und Staat in England und in der Normandie,* 1899, p. 56.

[23] Robinson, op. cit., p. 166.

[24] *Anglia Sacra,* II, 111. Wilkins, *Concilia,* I, 249. Malmesbury, *G.P.* (R.S.), p. 191.

[25] ASC., and FW., 973. P. E. Schramm, *A History of the English Coronation,* pp. 19–22.

[26] W. J. Stevenson in *English Historical Review,* XIII, 505ff.
[27] W. F. Hook, *The Lives of the Archbishop of Canterbury,* I, 408.
[28] *Anglia Sacra,* II, 111. Malmesbury's *G.P.,* p. 191. Stubbs, *Memorials,* pp. 60 and 200ff.
[29] ASC., 975. FW., 975.
[30] *Ibid.,* 977. Spelman, I, 493.
[31] Spelman, I, 494. ASC. gives the date as 978.
[32] Malmesbury's *G.R.* (R.S.), vol. I, p. 183.
[33] ASC., 978.
[34] *The Crawford Collection of Early Charters and Documents,* VII, p. 18, ed. A. S. Napier and W. H. Stevenson, Oxon 1895.
[35] FW., 986. Malmesbury's *G.R.,* vol. I, p. 171. The archbishop possessed the right of appointment to the see of Rochester down to 1148. Honorius appointed Paulinus (HE., II, 20). Augustine appointed Justus in 604 (HE., II, 3).
[36] *Vita auct. B. Mem. of St. Dunstan,* 26. Knowles, op. cit., p. 65 and note 3.
[37] *Anglia Sacra,* II, 116–19; 229–31. Robinson, op. cit., p. 99.

CHAPTER XVIII

[1] Stubbs, *Memorials of St. Dunstan,* p. 388, note 3. FW., 990.
[2] EHD., No. 230. Malmesbury's *G.R.,* vol. I, p. 191.
[3] ASC., 991.
[4] B. Thorpe, *The Homilies of the Anglo-Saxon Church,* vol. II, p. 1. (Cf. I, 1.)
[5] The contemporaries of this name were: Aelfric, archbishop of Canterbury; Aelfric, abbot of Eynsham, the Homilist; Aelfric-Puttoc, archbishop of York; Aelfric, abbot of Malmesbury.
[6] Malmesbury in his *G.P.,* p. 32 is unreliable here and even reverses the order of Aelfric's succession with that of Sigeric. A paragraph of some detail contained in the ASC. is now regarded as spurious. See EHD., 214, note 3.
[7] Knowles, op. cit., Appendix III, p. 696.
[8] Johnson, op. cit., I, 388ff. Spelman, I, 572ff.
[9] *Ibid.* B. Thorpe, *Ancient Laws and Institutes,* II, pp. 342–93.
[10] EHD., No. 53. Spelman, I, 495.
[11] Spelman, I, 504.
[12] P. H. Sawyer, *Anglo-Saxon Charters,* pp. 262–85.
[13] J. M. Kemble, *Codex Diplomaticus Aevi Saxonici,* 700; 1848.
[14] Dunstan, *Memorials,* 64.
[15] Evidently to assist the ship-levy of the shires. See ASC., 1008.
[16] CD., 716. EHD., 126.
[17] Spelman, I, 510ff.
[18] *Ibid.,* EHD., 44. See the prefatory notes where this is discussed.
[19] EHD., 44, 10, 2. Spelman, I, 517. . . . *nec ministrum ecclesiae ejiciat, inconsulto episcopo.'*
[20] EHD., 44, 33, 1.
[21] EHD., 45.
[22] *Ibid.,* p. 45, note 4, also see the prefatory note on p. 409.
[23] *Ibid.,* p. 410, note 1. The Latin version adds 'Every priest is to sing 30 masses and every deacon and cleric 30 psalms'; and the special mass is entitled 'against the heathen' (note 7).
[24] FW., 1011 gives Archdeacon Aelfmaer as the betrayer of the city.
[25] ASC., 1011. Abbot Aelfmar of St. Augustine's, Canterbury, was allowed to leave the city by the Danes. For this reason it has been thought that probably he was the betrayer. But this is negatived by the fact that later he became bishop of Sherborne.
[26] ASC., 1011.
[27] *Ibid.,* 1012.
[28] *Ibid.* See also the Chronicle of Thietmar of Merseburg, Book VIII, 42 and 43; EHD., 27.
[29] ASC., 1012. FW., 1012.
[30] *Ibid.,* 1013.
[31] See ASC. and FW., under the years 842, 851, 864, 870, 1009 and 1012.
[32] *Ibid.,* 1014.
[33] EHD., 46, 44, 1.
[34] *Ibid.,* 46, 2, 1.
[35] *Ibid.,* 46, 22.

36 New English Bible ; 1 Cor. 11 : 27.
37 EHD., 46, 31, 1.

CHAPTER XIX

1 EHD., 46, 41.
2 F. Godwin, *De Praesulibus Angliae Commentarius*, pp. 77, 28, London 1616.
3 P. H. Sawyer, *Anglo-Saxon Charters*, pp. 285, 945. The right of holding a court which tenants are required to attend.
4 EHD., 46, 37, 38.
5 'The Sermon of the Wolf to the English' ; EHD., 240. See the prefatory note.
6 *Ibid.* D. Whitelock, *Sermo Lupi ad Anglos*, 3rd edition.
7 Ingulph, p. 649.
8 *Adami Historica Ecclesiastica*, p. 64 ; *scholia*, note 32 ; Lyons 1595.
9 Thorpe, pp. 304–5 and 308–9.
10 EHD., 131. CD., 728.
11 ASC., 1020.
12 CD., 1314. This translation is given in EHD., 133. See also Thorpe, p. 313.
13 EHD., 134.
14 Thorpe, p. 316. See also *The Crawford Charters*, p. 24.
15 ASC., 1022.
16 Adam of Bremen, *Historica Ecclesiastica*, p. 57.
17 Adam of Bremen, *Historia Archiepiscoporum Bremensium*, p. 18, Lyons 1595.
'. . . *Quo etiam tempore multos in Daniam ab Anglia adduxit episcopos. De quibus, Bernardum posuit in Sconiam, Gerbrandum in Selandiam, Reinherum in Firne.*'
See also CD., 734 in which Gerbrand subscribes to a charter of 1022 issued by Cnut to Ely.
18 Knowles, op. cit., p. 68 shows that among the missionaries there were monks.
19 *Decreta Gregorii;* Mansi, X, 435.
20 FW. gives 1031 ; but ASC. gives 1027 which is the date of Conrad's coronation.
21 J. W. Lamb, *The Archbishopric of Lichfield*, Appendix, p. 58.
22 *Ibid.*, p. 55.
23 EHD., 50. See prefatory note.
24 Spelman, I, 538ff. Johnson, op. cit., I, 501ff.
25 Godwin, op. cit., p. 78 confuses him with Aelfwin of Winchester. Thorpe, pp. 324 and 328. A-S Charters, 974. CD., 1325 and 1327.
26 CD., 1327. Thorpe, p. 324.
27 *Fragmentum de Institutione Archidiaconatus Cantuariensis; Anglia Sacra,* I, 150ff. *Supra,* pp. 163 and 164.
28 *Encomium Emmae Reginae*, ed. A. Campbell, pp. 38–41, Royal Historical Society, 1949. '. . . *et se duci ab eodem, quia ab alio non fas fuerat, in sublimi regni solum.*'
29 *Ibid.*
30 *Reg. Sacrum Angl.*, pp. 33 and 37.
31 An account of the king's chapel is to be found in *The Conquest of England* by J. R. Green, vol. I, pp. 267ff. See also Deanesly, op. cit., p. 257 and my article 'Chapalin' in *The Encyclopaedia Britannica*.
32 Malmesbury, *G.P.*, p. 34.
33 *Anglia Sacra.*, I, 106. Both Malmesbury, *G.P.*, p. 34 and Godwin, op. cit., confuse him with Siward, bishop of Rochester, who was consecrated in 1058.
34 Kemble, 1335.
35 Ordnance Survey Facsimiles of Anglo-Saxon Manuscripts, II, Exeter, xiii.
36 Stigand to Elmham ; Herman to Wiltshire (Ramsbury) ; Leofric to Crediton and Heca to Selsey. Ordnance Survey Facsimiles of Anglo-Saxon Manuscripts, ed. W. B. Sanders, Part II ; Exeter xii ; Southampton 1874–84.

CHAPTER XX

1 *Vita S. Edwardi Confessoris Regis Angliae* (R.S.), ed. H. R. Luard, p. 399.
2 *Encomium Emmae*, op. cit., pp. 40–1.
3 *Anglia Sacra*, I, 291. *Annales Monastici* II, 21 (R.S.), ed. H. R. Luard.
4 *Vita S. Edwardi*, op. cit., p. 399. 1 Cor. 15 : 33, N.E.B. translation.
5 *Ibid.*, pp. 174 and 224–7.
6 *Hist. Abingdon*, op. cit., I, 461.

[7] *William of Poitiers*, p. 85; *Gesta Willelmi*, ed. J. A. Giles. This is discussed in *The Norman Conquest*, III, 682, by E. A. Freeman.

[8] ASC., 1052.

[9] Bishop William of London returned and occupied his see until he died in 1075 (Malmesbury, *G.P.*, p. 66, note 1).

[10] ASC., 1052.

[11] J. W. Lamb, *The Archbishopric of Lichfield*, p. 28.

[12] Wilkins, *Concilia*, I, 173.

[13] Malmesbury, *G.P.*, p. 35. *Annales Monastici*, op. cit., II, 25.

[14] ASC., 1052.

[15] CD., 799. Thorpe, pp. 371 and 373.

[16] *Innocentii Pontificis Maximi Opera*, p. 334; Cologne 1575.

[17] *Reg. Sacra Angl.*, p. 36.

[18] ASC., 1058.

[19] *Ecclesiastical Documents*, ed. J. Hunter, 1840, p. 16.

[20] Malmesbury, *G.P.*, pp. 251–2.

[21] ASC., 1062. See also J. W. Lamb, *St. Wulstan*, pp. 49–51.

[22] Spelman, I, 617.

[23] Additional Charters, 19, 802 in the British Museum.

[24] *St. Wulstan*, op. cit., p. 110

[25] Lincoln Charters, *Registrum Antiquissimum*, I, 186–8, ed. C. W. Foster. Thomas appealed to Alexander II against the judgment of Nicholas but in vain. Malmesbury, *G.R.*, II, 351. Archbishop Thomas, Ealdred's successor, claimed three dioceses in the province of Canterbury—Worcester, Dorchester and Lichfield—but totally failed in his claim. See also *G.P.*, p. 41.

[26] Spelman, I, 631–6. Thorpe, op. cit., pp. 406ff.

[27] ASC., 1065. FW., 1065. *Vita S. Ed.*, p. 174.

[28] ASC., 1066. FW., 1066.

[29] *Ibid.*

[30] *Ibid.* Stenton, op. cit., pp. 589ff.

[31] It is doubtful whether Edward issued a writ of appointment. Most references speak of Stigand 'invading' the archbishopric as he did the see of Winchester (*G.P.*, p. 35). Bishop Wulstan in his letter to Archbishop Anselm (Wilkins, *Concilia*, I, 373 and *Patro. Lat.*, Migne, CLXIX, col. 202) says that Stigand held the archbishopric 'by gift of secular authority.'

[32] MS. Cleo.E.I., p. 9242, Brit. Mus.

[33] FW., 1070.

[34] *Vita S. Ed.*, p. 283.

[35] *Ibid.*, pp. 284–6.

[36] Eadmer, *Vita S. Dunstani* (*Mem. S. Dunst.*), p. 236. *G.P.*, p. 36.

[37] *G.R.*, II, 304–5. Cf. EHD., 818.

INDEX